Hayner Public Library District-Alton
O9-BSA-065
No Longer the Property of
Hayner Public Library District
REFERENCE
BRANCH

North America in Colonial Times

An Encyclopedia for Students

Editors

JACOB ERNEST COOKE
John Henry MacCracken Professor of History Emeritus
Lafayette College
Lafayette, Pennsylvania

MILTON M. KLEIN
Alumni Distinguished Service Professor Emeritus
University of Tennessee
Knoxville, Tennessee

Consultants

BEVERLEY ACKERT
Teacher of Government, retired
Mount Vernon High School
Mount Vernon, New York

ELEANOR J. BROWN
Library Media Specialist and Head, Information Center
Mount Vernon High School
Mount Vernon, New York

NEAL SALISBURY
Professor of History
Smith College
Northampton, Massachusetts

North America in Colonial Times

An Encyclopedia for Students

Jacob Ernest Cooke and Milton M. Klein, *Editors*

Volume 2

CHARLES SCRIBNER'S SONS
Macmillan Library Reference USA
Simon & Schuster Macmillan
New York

SIMON & SCHUSTER AND PRENTICE HALL INTERNATIONAL
London Mexico City New Delhi Singapore Sydney Toronto

Developed for Scribners by Visual Education Corporation, Princeton, N.J.

Library of Congress Cataloging-in-Publication Data

North America in colonial times : an encyclopedia for students / Jacob Ernest Cooke and Milton M. Klein, editors.

p. cm.

Adaptation and revision of Encyclopedia of the North American colonies for young readers.

Includes bibliographical references and index.

Summary: An encyclopedia of the history of the American colonies and Canada, including Native Americans, Spanish missions, English and Dutch exploration, the slave trade, and the French and Indian War.

ISBN 0-684-80538-3 (set : alk. paper).— ISBN 0-684-80534-0 (v.1 : alk. paper).— ISBN 0-684-80535-9 (v.2 : alk. paper).— ISBN 0-684-80536-7 (v.3 : alk. paper).— ISBN 0-684-80537-5 (v.4: alk. paper)

1. Europe—Colonies—America—History—Encyclopedias, Juvenile. 2. North America—History—Encyclopedias, Juvenile. [1. North America—History—Colonial period, ca. 1600–1775—Encyclopedias.] I. Cooke, Jacob Ernest, 1924– . II. Klein, Milton M. (Milton Martin), 1917– . III. Encyclopedia of the North American colonies.

E45.N65 1998

970.02—dc21

98-29862

CIP

AC

1 2 3 4 5 6 7 8 9 10

PRINTED IN THE UNITED STATES OF AMERICA

Time Line of North America in Colonial Times

ca. 20,000 B.C. *The first human inhabitants of the Americas cross from Siberia into Alaska.*

A.D. 985 *Erik the Red establishes a Norse colony in Greenland.*

ca. 1000 *Leif Eriksson lands on the coast of North America.*

ca. 1420 *Prince Henry of Portugal establishes a school of navigation at Sagres, from which seamen set out and discover the Canary, Madeira, and Azores islands.*

1492 *Christopher Columbus, attempting to sail west to Asia, finds the "New World."*

1494 *The Treaty of Tordesillas divides the world between the Spanish and Portuguese empires.*

ca. 1500 *The French begin fishing off the coast of Newfoundland.*

The Mohawk, Oneida, Onondaga, Cayuga, and Seneca peoples unite to form the Iroquois Confederacy.

1507 *Martin Waldseemüller calls the land explored by Columbus "America" in honor of Amerigo Vespucci, an Italian navigator who was the first to use the term "New World."*

1513 *Juan Ponce de León claims Florida for Spain.*

1518 *African slaves are brought to Hispaniola (Haiti and Dominican Republic) to work in gold mines.*

1518–1521 *Hernando Cortés conquers the Aztecs in Mexico.*

1519–1522 *Ships under the command of Ferdinand Magellan sail around the world.*

1524 *Giovanni da Verrazano explores the North American coast.*

1534–1536 *Jacques Cartier explores the Gulf of St. Lawrence and the St. Lawrence River as far as Montreal.*

1539–1543 *Hernando de Soto explores North America from Florida to the Mississippi River.*

1540–1542 *Francisco Vásquez de Coronado explores the Southwest as far as the Grand Canyon.*

1562–1568 *John Hawkins makes slave-trading voyages from Africa to the West Indies.*

1564 *France establishes Fort Caroline in Florida but quickly loses it to the Spanish.*

1565 *Pedro Menéndez de Avilés founds St. Augustine in Florida.*

1565–1574 *Spain sets up missions and forts between Florida and Virginia.*

1572 *Chief Powhatan unites Algonquian-speaking tribes in the Chesapeake region to form the Powhatan Confederacy.*

1578 *Francis Drake sails around South America and lands in present-day California.*

1583 *Sir Humphrey Gilbert leads an expedition to Newfoundland.*

1585–1590 *The English attempt twice to establish a colony at Roanoke Island. The second settlement mysteriously disappears.*

1598 *Juan de Oñate founds the colony of New Mexico.*

1602 *Bartholomew Gosnold explores the Atlantic coast from southern Maine to Narragansett Bay and transmits smallpox to his Indian trading partners.*

1604 *Samuel de Champlain and Pierre du Gua de Monts establish a French settlement at Port Royal in Acadia (present-day Nova Scotia).*

1606 *James I of England grants charters to the Virginia Company and the Plymouth Company to colonize the Atlantic coast of North America.*

1606–1608 *The Plymouth Company establishes Saghadoc, an unsuccessful colony in present-day Maine.*

1607 *Colonists found Jamestown, the first permanent English settlement, in Virginia.*
Massasoit becomes chief of the powerful Wampanoag of New England.

1608 *Samuel de Champlain establishes a French settlement at Quebec.*

1609 *Henry Hudson explores the Hudson River as far north as present-day Albany.*
Santa Fe is founded in New Mexico.

1612 *New varieties of tobacco are planted in Virginia, launching a tobacco boom in the Chesapeake region.*

1613 *English forces destroy the Acadian town of Port Royal.*

1614 *Captain John Smith explores the New England coast.*
New Netherland Company gains a monopoly on trade in the Dutch colony.

1616 *Africans arrive in Bermuda, the first slaves in the English colonies.*

1619 *The Dutch bring the first blacks to Virginia.*

1620 *The Pilgrims establish Plymouth colony.*

1622 *Powhatan Indians fight the English in Virginia.*

1624 *Thirty families arrive in the Dutch colony of New Netherland.*

1625 *Jesuits arrive in Quebec.*

1626 *Peter Minuit becomes director general of New Netherland and buys Manhattan Island from the Indians.*

1628 *The English take over Acadia and Quebec, which are returned to France in 1632.*

1630 *The Massachusetts Bay Company establishes a new colony at Boston.*

1630–1642 *The Great Migration brings 16,000 settlers from England to the Massachusetts Bay colony.*

1632 *George Calvert, Lord Baltimore, receives a grant to found the colony of Maryland.*

1633 *French Jesuits establish Quebec College.*

1633–1638 *English colonists begin settling along the Connecticut River.*

1636 *Roger Williams founds the colony of Rhode Island.*
Harvard College is established at Cambridge, Massachusetts.

1636–1637 *In the Pequot War, English colonists in Connecticut destroy most of the Pequot tribe.*

1636–1638 *Anne Hutchinson challenges the authority of religious leaders in Massachusetts, is exiled, and settles in Rhode Island.*

1638 *Peter Minuit founds New Sweden on the Delaware River.*

1639 *North America's first hospital, the Hôtel-Dieu, is established in Quebec.*

1641 The Bay Psalm Book, *the first book printed in the English colonies, appears in Boston.*

1642 *French fur traders establish a base at Montreal.*

1642–1649 *The English Civil War pits supporters of the monarch against Parliamentarians (mostly Puritans). King Charles I is executed in 1649, and England becomes a commonwealth.*

1643 *Massachusetts Bay, Plymouth, Connecticut, and New Haven colonies form the New England Confederation.*

1646–1665 *Iroquois Indians raid the Algonquin, Huron, and other neighboring tribes, driving refugees into Quebec and the Great Lakes region.*

1647 *Peter Stuyvesant becomes director general of New Netherland.*

1649 *Maryland passes the Act of Toleration establishing religious freedom for Christians; the act is repealed in 1654.*

1650 *Poems by Anne Bradstreet, the first published American poet, are printed in London.*

1652–1654 *First war between English and Dutch colonists.*

1653–1660 *England is ruled by Oliver Cromwell, Lord Protector of the Commonwealth.*

1654 *The first Jews arrive in New Amsterdam.*

1655 *Peter Stuyvesant conquers New Sweden, ending Swedish colonization in North America.*

1660 *The first Navigation Act requires all goods going into or out of the English colonies to be carried on English ships. The English monarchy is restored under Charles II.*

1663 *Louis XIV of France declares New France a royal province. Charles II of England gives eight proprietors a grant for the colony of Carolina.*

1664 *English naval forces capture New Netherland, which is renamed New York.*

1665–1667 *Second war between the English and the Dutch.*

1666–1667 *French colonial forces attack the Iroquois Confederacy and force it to accept French terms for peace.*

1668 *The English establish Charles Fort at the mouth of the Rupert River in present-day Canada.*

1669 *John Locke draws up the Fundamental Constitutions, a proposed plan of government for the Carolinas.*

1670 *The Hudson's Bay Company gains control of the fur trade in the Hudson Bay region.*

1672 *Royal African Company gains a monopoly on the English slave trade to America and the West Indies.*

1672–1674 *In the third war between the English and the Dutch, the Dutch temporarily regain control of New York.*

1673 *Louis Jolliet and Father Jacques Marquette explore the Mississippi River.*

1675–1676 *King Philip's War: Wampanoag leader Metacom, called King Philip, leads Indians of southern New England in an unsuccessful uprising against the English.*

1676 *Bacon's Rebellion: Virginia settlers, led by Nathaniel Bacon, seize control of the colony.*

1680 *Pueblo Revolt: Pueblo Indians drive Spanish from New Mexico.*

1681 *William Penn receives a charter to establish Pennsylvania from King Charles II of England.*

1682 *English colonists attack Quebec.*

René-Robert Cavelier, Sieur de La Salle, claims Mississippi River valley for France, calling it Louisiana.

1686–1689 *King James II of England creates the Dominion of New England, which includes the colonies of New Hampshire, Massachusetts, Rhode Island, Connecticut, New York, and New Jersey. Sir Edmund Andros is renamed governor of the new province.*

1687 *Father Eusebio Francisco Kino establishes mission settlements in Pimería Alta (modern Arizona).*

1688 *Protestant monarchs William II and Mary ascend the throne in England in what is called the Glorious Revolution.*

1689–1691 *Glorious Revolution in America: Colonists revolt against the Dominion of New England and receive new charters from William and Mary.*
Leisler's Rebellion: Jacob Leisler seizes control in New York and is executed in 1691.

1689–1697 *King William's War brings French and English colonies and their Indian allies into conflict.*

1692–1693 *Salem witchcraft trials: Nineteen people are hanged as witches in Massachusetts.*

1693 *The College of William and Mary is founded in Virginia.*

1696 *Carolina adopts the first slave laws in the British mainland colonies.*
Spain reconquers New Mexico from the Pueblo Indians.

1699 *Pierre Le Moyne d'Iberville founds the first French settlement in Louisiana.*

1701 *Anglicans create the Society for the Propagation of the Gospel (SPG) to convert Indians and Africans.*
Yale College is established in New Haven.
Antoine de la Mothe Cadillac founds Detroit.

1702–1713 *Queen Anne's War brings new conflict between French and English colonists and their Indian allies.*

1707 *The Act of Union unites England and Scotland into the United Kingdom of Great Britain.*

1709 *African and Indian slavery is legalized in New France.*

1710 *British forces conquer Port Royal in Acadia and rename it Annapolis Royal.*

1711–1713 *Tuscarora War: Carolina colonists join the Yamassee to defeat the Tuscarora Indians.*

1713 *Treaty of Utrecht: France gives up Acadia, Newfoundland, and Hudson Bay to Great Britain.*

1715–1728 *Yamassee War: Yamassee attack South Carolina towns and plantations and are defeated by British and Cherokee forces.*

1718 *Jean Baptiste Le Moyne de Bienville founds New Orleans.*

1729 *North and South Carolina become separate royal colonies.*

1729–1731 *Natchez Revolt in Louisiana.*

1730 *The Great Wagon Road is begun. It eventually stretches from Philadelphia to Georgia.*

1731 *Benjamin Franklin establishes a circulating library in Philadelphia.*

1732 *Franklin publishes* Poor Richard's Almanack.

1733 *James Oglethorpe founds Georgia as a refuge for British debtors.*
British Parliament passes the Molasses Act, taxing sugar and molasses from the French West Indies.

1734–1735 *Clergyman Jonathan Edwards leads a religious revival in Massachusetts.*

1735 *The trial of publisher John Peter Zenger in New York promotes the principle of freedom of the press.*

1737 *"Walking Purchase": Delaware Indians sell the colony of Pennsylvania the entire Lehigh Valley.*

1738–1745 *Great Awakening: English preacher George Whitefield sparks religious revivals throughout the British colonies.*

1739 *Stono Rebellion: Slaves in South Carolina revolt and are stopped by the militia.*

1740s *Eliza Pinckney begins indigo cultivation in South Carolina.*

1741 *Rumors of plots by slaves to revolt lead to arrests and executions in New York.*

Russian explorer Vitus Bering lands in Alaska.

1743 *Benjamin Franklin establishes the American Philosophical Society in Philadelphia.*

1744–1748 *King George's War: European war between Britain, France, and Spain spreads to North America.*

1746 *College of New Jersey (later Princeton University) is founded.*

1754 *French and Indian War begins when Virginia sends its militia, led by George Washington, to challenge the French in the Ohio Valley. France and Britain officially declare war in 1756.*

1755 *Britain expels French colonists from Acadia. Many Acadians migrate to Louisiana.*

1759–1760 *British forces under General James Wolfe capture Quebec. A year later, the French surrender at Montreal.*

1762 *Spain declares war on Great Britain.*

1763 *Treaty of Paris: Great Britain wins Florida from Spain and Canada and Cape Breton from France. Spain gains Louisiana. Britain issues proclamation forbidding colonists to settle west of the Appalachian Mountains.*

Touro Synagogue opens in Newport, Rhode Island.

1763–1766 *Chief Pontiac of the Ottawa leads an alliance of Indians against the British in the Great Lakes region.*

1764 *The Sugar Act imposes high import taxes on non-British sugar, leading to colonial protests.*

1765 *The Stamp Act provokes outrage and widespread protest in the colonies and is repealed.*

1766 *British Parliament passes the Declaratory Act to emphasize its "full power and authority" over the colonies.*

1767 *Jesuits are expelled from Spanish territories. Franciscans take over the western missions.*

In the British colonies, the Townshend Acts impose new taxes on certain imported items.

1769 *Junipero Serra founds the first Spanish mission in California at San Diego.*

1770 *Boston Massacre: British troops fire into a crowd, killing five colonists.*

1773 *Boston Tea Party: Colonists protest the tea tax by dumping a shipload of tea into Boston harbor.*

Publication of Poems on Various Subjects, Religious and Moral *by Phillis Wheatley, a slave in Boston.*

1774 *Parliament passes the Intolerable Acts to strengthen British authority in Massachusetts.*

In the Quebec Act, Parliament extends the borders of Quebec province southward and grants religious freedom to Catholics, angering American colonists.

The First Continental Congress meets in Philadelphia.

1775 *Battles are fought at Lexington and Concord.*

The Second Continental Congress assembles in Philadelphia.

George Washington takes command of the Continental Army.

1776 *Thomas Paine's* Common Sense *is published in Philadelphia.*

American colonists issue the Declaration of Independence to explain their separation from Great Britain.

1777 *Under military pressure, Cherokee Indians yield their lands to North and South Carolina.*

Vermont declares its independence from New York and New Hampshire.

1778 *Captain James Cook explores the northern Pacific coast.*

1779 *Spain declares war on Britain and enters the American War of Independence.*

1781 *American troops under George Washington and French forces under General Rochambeau defeat British troops led by General Charles Cornwallis at Yorktown, Virginia, winning independence for the United States.*

1783 *Treaty of Versailles: Great Britain recognizes the independence of the United States of America. Florida is returned to Spain.*

1784 *New Brunswick province is established in Canada as a refuge for American Loyalists.*

1789–1793 *Alexander Mackenzie reaches the Pacific coast by traveling overland across Canada.*

1791 *Constitution Act: Britain divides the province of Quebec into Lower Canada (Quebec) and Upper Canada (Ontario).*

1792 *Captain George Vancouver explores the west coast of Canada.*

1794 *Slavery is abolished in French colonies.*

1799 *The Russian-American Company is chartered and given a monopoly to conduct trade in Alaska.*

1800 *Spain returns Louisiana to France.*

1803 *Louisiana Purchase: France sells Louisiana to the United States for $15 million.*

1812–1841 *The Russian-American Company maintains a base at Fort Ross, in northern California.*

1819 *The United States acquires Florida from Spain.*

1821 *Mexico declares independence from Spain.*

1825–1832 *Stephen F. Austin brings American colonists to Texas.*

1833 *Great Britain declares an end to slavery in all its possessions, beginning in 1834.*

1840 *The Act of Union reunites Upper and Lower Canada and grants them self-rule.*

1867 *The British North America Act establishes the Dominion of Canada.*

Russia sells Alaska to the United States.

Education

Education in the North American colonies took a variety of forms. Overall, its purpose was to bring European culture and values to the "New World" and to pass them on to future generations. Colonists believed that education should also develop basic skills, a strong sense of morality, and good citizenship. They thought that the role of higher education was to train leaders and prepare young people for professional careers.

Colonists generally placed a high value on learning and devised ways to provide basic instruction in reading, writing, and arithmetic to most children—at least, to the boys. In many places, children learned these skills from their parents or perhaps as a part of APPRENTICESHIP training. Wealthy families, particularly in the southern colonies, might hire private tutors or send children to Europe for an education or for professional training.

Educational opportunities were by no means equal. Middle- and upper-class children usually received a better education than poor children. Women generally had less schooling than men. Though some girls learned to read and write, most of their instruction focused on such skills as sewing, cooking, music, and drawing. African Americans rarely received any education at all. Few people in North America had the chance for any advanced education. By the end of the colonial period, only the British colonies and NEW FRANCE had established COLLEGES.

Churches played a leading role in education in colonial America. In New France and the Spanish Borderlands*, schooling took place within the framework of the ROMAN CATHOLIC CHURCH. SCHOOLS and MISSIONS provided instruction in Catholic beliefs along with basic skills such as reading and writing. The Dutch Reformed Church played a similar role in the Dutch colony of NEW NETHERLAND, while the PURITANS, QUAKERS, Anglicans, and other Protestant groups influenced education in the British colonies.

* ***Spanish Borderlands*** northern part of New Spain, area now occupied by Florida, Texas, New Mexico, Arizona, and California

The British Colonies

The British colonies developed the most extensive educational system in North America. Children received instruction at home, through apprenticeships, in various types of public and private schools, and also from private tutors. The British colonies also had the largest number of colleges.

Basic Education. In 1647 Massachusetts Bay became the first English colony to require each town to support a school. Other New England colonies soon adopted this system, creating the best-organized public educational system in the English colonies. New England's elementary schools provided instruction in reading, writing, and other basic skills, reflecting the Puritans' belief that people should be able to read the BIBLE and that education helps build a strong community. Some New England towns also established Latin grammar schools for advanced students. The first of these, Boston Latin School, was founded in 1635.

A unified educational system did not develop in New York, New Jersey, or Pennsylvania, colonies with many different religious and ethnic groups. The various groups wanted schools that supported their particular language, heritage, and beliefs. The Quakers of Pennsylvania, for example, placed a great value on education and were strong believers in equality. For

The New England Primer

The most popular and widely used textbook in the British colonies was *The New England Primer.* Based on a book that had been used for centuries in England, the primer was first published in Boston in 1690. It combined basic learning in reading and spelling with religious instruction. The book was said to have "taught millions to read and not one to sin." *The New England Primer* remained the leading schoolbook in that region until the 1840s.

* ***philosophy*** study related to ideas, the laws of nature, and the pursuit of truth

that reason, they provided opportunities for girls, African Americans, and Indians to receive instruction.

Formal systems of education were less developed in the southern colonies because of their rural character and scattered population. With no organized system of schools, education was essentially the responsibility of individual families. As a result, the children of poor families had very limited educational opportunities. Wealthy families relied on tutors or sent their children to one of the colonies' rare private schools or to Europe for an education.

Advanced Education. Very few young people had a chance to continue their schooling beyond the basics. The most common opportunity for advanced training was an apprenticeship, where adolescents—mostly boys—could learn the skills of a particular trade. Wealthy parents might send their children to a private academy held in the home of an educated adult, to college in Europe, or perhaps to a college in the colonies. Attending college was very expensive, as was studying at a private academy or with tutors.

Harvard, the first college in the British colonies, was founded in 1636. By the time of the American Revolution, eight more colleges had been established. These institutions provided instruction in such subjects as Latin, Greek, religious history, science, mathematics, and philosophy*. They hoped to pass on the values and ideals of Western culture, prepare students for adult occupations, and develop good citizens. The underlying goal of college education was to prepare leaders for the colonies.

The Dutch, French, and Spanish Colonies

The Dutch, French, and Spanish colonies developed somewhat different forms of education. Moreover, children in these colonies generally had fewer educational opportunities than young people in the British colonies.

Basic Education. The leaders of New Netherland made sure that the colony's children received instruction in basic skills. The public elementary schools, sponsored by the Dutch Reformed Church, taught reading, writing, religion, and arithmetic. Most of the students were boys. Girls generally stayed home to learn reading and writing, as well as homemaking skills, such as sewing and cooking. Parents who wanted their children to receive additional or better instruction had to hire tutors or send their children to schools in New England or in Europe.

In New France, education was designed to teach Roman Catholicism and prepare young people for church membership. Because Catholics did not consider reading the Bible to be an essential part of religious faith, teaching children to read and write was not given as much emphasis as in the Protestant colonies. Instead, the focus was on moral education. Nevertheless, most church districts tried to establish schools that would provide a basic education. Wealthy parents often sent their children to private schools in the cities, which offered a more complete education. In rural areas, girls tended to receive more formal instruction than boys because boys often had to work on family farms. In LOUISIANA, neither the government nor the church became

involved in education. Even children of wealthy families had little schooling, and what they received came primarily from their parents.

Education had a strong religious element in the Spanish Borderlands. Parents were expected to teach their children the principles of the Catholic faith. Middle- and upper-class children might receive some instruction from private tutors. The only organized educational institutions were the missions, which were aimed primarily at converting Native Americans to Christianity and teaching them Spanish customs and values.

Advanced Education. Opportunities for a college education were extremely limited in the Dutch, French, and Spanish colonies. No colleges existed in either New Netherland or the Spanish Borderlands. Wealthy families in those regions had to send their children to Europe or, in the case of the Spanish Borderlands, to colleges in Mexico or other parts of NEW SPAIN. New France had a college in Quebec. Founded in 1635 by the JESUITS, a Catholic religious order, it was said to provide an advanced education as good as that of any Jesuit school in Europe. (*See also* **Literacy.**)

Edwards, Jonathan

1703–1758
Puritan minister and religious thinker

Jonathan Edwards was a controversial figure—admired by some for his powerful sermons, opposed by others for his strict interpretation of Puritan beliefs. This engraving of Edwards is based on a portrait painted by Charles Willson Peale.

Jonathan Edwards was one of the most important theologians, or religious thinkers, in the British colonies. By challenging some of the PURITANS' practices, he played an important role in launching a religious revival known as the GREAT AWAKENING.

Born in East Windsor, Connecticut, Edwards was the son of a minister and the grandson of Solomon Stoddard, one of the most famous and powerful Puritan preachers in New England. Edwards entered Yale College when he was not quite 13 years old. After receiving his bachelor's and master's degrees, he had a deeply religious experience that prompted him to follow in the footsteps of his father and grandfather and become a minister.

Edwards served briefly as a pastor in New York City, then returned to Yale as a tutor. In 1726 he left to become his grandfather's assistant at a church in Northampton, Massachusetts, the most important Puritan church outside of Boston. When Solomon Stoddard died two years later, Edwards took over his ministry. In 1731, at the invitation of Puritan officials in Boston, the young minister delivered a forceful public sermon, which earned him almost immediate recognition as a commanding speaker and religious thinker.

Edwards's emotional preaching helped bring about a brief but intense religious revival in the Connecticut River valley in the mid-1730s. Hundreds of colonists renewed their faith and restored their bonds to their churches. This revival, known as the "Little Awakening," was the first stage of the Great Awakening, a religious movement that swept through the British colonies in the early 1740s. Though not alone in launching this religious renewal, Edwards's fiery preaching contributed to its early success. In 1741 he delivered a sermon in Connecticut called "Sinners in the Hands of an Angry God"—perhaps the most famous sermon in American history. In it, Edwards used frightful images of fire and floods to emphasize the idea that sinners can be saved only through the grace of God's will, not by their own good deeds.

After the Great Awakening calmed down somewhat, Edwards continued to encourage highly emotional religious experiences. At the same time, he was a stern minister who demanded rigid orthodoxy* of his followers. His relationship with his own congregation became strained, primarily because of his unyielding views on church membership. Edwards was opposed to allowing anyone who wanted salvation to join the church. He insisted that only the genuinely faithful, those chosen for salvation, could participate in Communion* and other religious rituals*. This view created great controversy in his congregation and led to his dismissal in 1750.

* ***orthodoxy*** strict adherence to established traditions and beliefs

* ***Communion*** taking bread and wine in celebration of Christ's Last Supper

* ***ritual*** ceremony that follows a set pattern

Edwards spent most of the remaining years of his life in western Massachusetts. In 1751 he accepted a position as minister of a frontier church in Stockbridge, Massachusetts, where he directed missionary work among the Indians. Despite the hardships of frontier life and the responsibilities of his ministry, Edwards wrote several important books during this time, including *A Careful and Strict Inquiry into . . . Freedom of Will* (1754). In 1757 Edwards became president of the College of New Jersey (now Princeton University), but he died only a few months after arriving at the college.

Jonathan Edwards had tremendous influence on the religious thinking of colonial America. As the foremost theologian of his time, he combined traditional Puritan beliefs with the ideas of ENLIGHTENMENT writers, who believed that the universe was governed by laws that could be explained by reason. Emphasizing personal religious experience, Edwards focused on such issues as original sin, free will, and the need for grace. (*See also* **Calvinists; Literature; Religious Life in European Colonies; Whitefield, George.**)

British colonists had a limited voice in their governments. The British crown and Parliament had final authority over colonial affairs and appointed most government officials. Nonetheless, colonists who were qualified voters did have an opportunity to choose some local officials as well as representatives to colonial ASSEMBLIES. In New England, male citizens participated in local government through TOWN MEETINGS.

Colonial laws generally restricted VOTING RIGHTS to adult freemen—white, male, property owners—and denied suffrage* to women, blacks, and often Jews and Catholics. Although a great many colonists were excluded from the election process, a very high percentage of white men could qualify as property owners because land was readily available.

* ***suffrage*** right to vote

Although most voters came from the lower and middle classes of colonial society, the majority of the officeholders belonged to the upper class—and all were men. Colonists tended to elect their "betters"—men of high social and economic standing. Members of the upper class dominated elective, as well as appointive, offices in every colony. But voters held all officials—no matter what their social or economic background—accountable for their actions. They never hesitated to turn someone out of office for unsatisfactory service or unpopular policies.

Before 1725 voters took their civic responsibility seriously, and participation in elections was generally high. Campaigns were often hotly contested, rowdy affairs, with candidates making promises in exchange for voter

support. The reelection rate was very low, with as many as 70 or 80 percent of officials voted out of office in each election. As a result, most officials held office for a short time and did not develop skills in governing.

After 1725 the situation changed. Colonial governments became more stable, and the king and Parliament temporarily relaxed their efforts to control the colonies. During this period of calm, fewer voters went to the polls except when important local issues were at stake. Colonial growth also played a role in voter participation. As populations increased, each official had to represent a greater number of colonists, and as new settlements arose far from government centers, voters became more isolated from officeholders. Because this led to more distant relations between voters and elected officials, participation in elections declined.

With governments more stable and predictable, an increasing number of colonial officials were reelected regularly to office. Because elected leaders now spent many years in office, they gradually improved their political skills and became professional politicians. They learned how to make compromises, avoid conflict, and settle issues more calmly. This helped the government run more smoothly. At the same time, however, voters now accepted more readily the authority of their leaders and became less passionately involved in the election process. (*See also* **Colonial Administration; Government, Provincial.**)

Elizabeth I

1533–1603
Queen of England

Intelligent and well-educated, Elizabeth I was one of the most effective rulers England ever had. During her reign, the English began to explore and colonize North America.

When Elizabeth took the throne in 1558, England and Spain were bitter rivals. A Protestant country surrounded by Catholic nations, England had been isolated from European politics for decades and knew little about European activities in the Western Hemisphere. Spain already possessed settlements throughout the Americas, and France had established trading posts in North America.

England's rivalry with Spain carried over into the "New World." In the 1560s, Elizabeth allowed John Hawkins to lead an expedition to the Caribbean, where he had established a profitable SLAVE TRADE. The Spanish objected to the English presence in the Caribbean, which they considered their territory, and attacked Hawkins's vessels. Elizabeth sought revenge by sending Francis DRAKE and other English privateers* to raid Spanish treasure ships.

* ***privateer*** privately owned ship authorized by the government to attack and capture enemy vessels; also the ship's master

* ***nationalism*** patriotic devotion to one's country

Under Elizabeth's powerful leadership, England developed a strong sense of nationalism* and, in turn, an interest in expanding overseas. The success of English raiding ships such as Drake's showed that Spain could be challenged successfully. After consulting with financial advisers, Elizabeth decided that North America offered new opportunities for long-term English prosperity.

In 1577 the queen approved Francis Drake's plan for a voyage to the Pacific coast of the Americas. The explorer sailed around South America and then continued north along the Pacific coast to present-day Washington.

Rather than retracing his route, Drake returned to England by way of the Pacific Ocean, becoming the second person after Ferdinand Magellan to sail around the world. Elizabeth rewarded Drake with a knighthood.

*** charter** written grant from a ruler conferring certain rights and privileges

In 1584 the queen granted Sir Walter RALEIGH a charter* for a colony in North America. The colony was established on ROANOKE ISLAND, and the region was called Virginia in honor of Elizabeth, "the Virgin Queen" who never married. Although the Roanoke settlement failed, later English colonists gave the name Virginia to the land around the Chesapeake Bay. (*See also* **Exploration, Age of.**)

Encomiendas

*** tribute** payment made to a dominant power

The *encomienda* was a grant of land by the Spanish crown to reward valuable service. In Spain the monarchs gave these grants to nobles and knights who aided them in their struggle to drive the Muslims from the country. The *encomienda* included the right to rule and collect tribute* from the people living on the land. In the "New World," many *encomenderos*—individuals who received grants—used their position to build great power and wealth in the colonies.

The Encomienda Policy. The Spanish government changed the system somewhat in the Americas. *Encomenderos* had the right to enjoy revenues from the land, but they did not own the land. Nor did they possess legal power over those who lived on the land—although many assumed that they had such power. Finally, in the Americas, the right to an *encomienda* involved a time limit. It lasted only for the life of the individual and of one heir. In return for these rights, *encomenderos* had certain obligations. They were required to establish a family in the town nearest the land, to protect the Indians, and to convert the Indians to Catholicism.

Spanish monarchs found the system useful in the early years of colonization. With no formal colonial government in place to administer the newly acquired lands, they needed some way of controlling the native population. The *encomienda* system seemed to provide the way.

The System in Practice. Though useful in theory, the system had a number of disadvantages. Harsh treatment of Indians by *encomenderos* on Caribbean islands contributed to the destruction of native populations there. By 1512, just 20 years after Columbus's first voyage, Spain issued a law to restrict the power of the grant recipients. King Charles V tried to prevent the establishment of the *encomienda* system in Central America, but with little success. In 1522 Hernando CORTÉS, who conquered territory in what is now Mexico, made a plea for maintaining the system, arguing that he was forced to give these grants to many of his followers. Cortés failed to mention that he took the largest number of *encomiendas* for himself—some 23,000.

The *encomenderos* gained wealth and power from their grants. They used Indian labor to mine gold and silver, work in the fields, herd animals, and build homes, which they then rented to new settlers arriving from Spain. *Encomenderos* began to dominate colonial society—and even enjoyed some independence from the Spanish government. At the same time, members of the

Dominican religious order, particularly Bartolomé de LAS CASAS, vigorously protested the system.

In 1542 Spain passed the New Laws of the Indies, which attempted to end the *encomienda* system by declaring that each grant would end when the current holder died. The *encomenderos* protested, and the government backed down. Still, Spanish authorities remained determined to limit the power of *encomenderos.* They made grants less frequently during the 1600s and gradually replaced the system with another, called *repartimiento.* Under this new system, grant recipients could claim only a certain amount of Indian labor each year.

Resentment over the *encomienda* system contributed to a revolt of the PUEBLO INDIANS of New Mexico in 1680. When the Spanish regained control of the area, they tried to make some new grants but eventually realized that the local Indians would never accept forced labor. In 1721 Spain formally abolished the *encomienda* system. (*See also* **Pueblo Revolt.**)

England

See ***Great Britain.***

Enlightenment: Influence in North America

The Enlightenment was a European intellectual movement of the 1600s and 1700s that combined many of the values of ancient Greece and Rome with new scientific ideas and principles. People such as John Locke and Francis Bacon emphasized the use of reason and believed that society could be improved through human efforts. Enlightenment principles and ideals greatly influenced the development of colonial North America and laid the groundwork for the political ideals behind the INDEPENDENCE MOVEMENT in the British colonies.

Enlightenment Principles.

The Enlightenment rested on three major intellectual foundations. The first was admiration for the writings of the ancient Greeks and Romans. These works led Enlightenment philosophers* to adopt a critical attitude toward the accepted ideas of the time and also inspired a new respect for the power of the individual.

* ***philosopher*** person who seeks wisdom and truth

The second principle of the Enlightenment was the emerging scientific method, in which scientists made careful observations of natural phenomena*, formed theories to explain them, and tested these theories through careful experiments. Enlightenment thinkers were confident that the scientific method would enable them to discover the "natural laws" that lay behind all physical phenomena in the universe. This approach, they believed, could expand human knowledge. Sir Isaac Newton's mathematical equation for gravity lent support to the view that all occurrences could be explained by simple, rational* laws.

* ***phenomenon*** occurrence or fact that can be detected by the senses

* ***rational*** based on reason

The third principle underlying the ideas of the Enlightenment was a strong faith in the power of human reason. Supporters believed that the universe worked in a rational way, that individuals could discover universal "truths" through reason, and that all institutions should be judged on the basis

One of the most important goals of the Enlightenment was to expand scientific knowledge. Benjamin Franklin made a number of significant contributions in this area, including his famous experiment with a kite, in which he demonstrated that lightning is a form of electricity.

of their reasonableness. They rejected ideas founded on superstition, tradition, or emotion, arguing that human society comes closest to perfection when organized according to rational principles.

The Enlightenment and Science. Many European colonists in North America embraced the principles of the Enlightenment. They contributed to scientific knowledge by making detailed observations of the "New World"—a subject of great fascination for Europeans. In the French colonies, settlers gathered specimens of plants and animals and wrote reports about their findings. The French government supported efforts to learn more about the continent by funding expeditions to explore as far west as the Rocky Mountains.

Spanish rulers and colonial officials also sponsored expeditions to explore the continent and learn about its landforms, plants, and animals. Enlightenment ideas, however, did not have as great an impact in the Spanish colonies as in other colonial areas. Both the Spanish government and the Catholic Church feared that the influence of the Enlightenment might undermine the authority of church and state.

Many British colonists participated enthusiastically in the Enlightenment, and a number of them made notable contributions to the expansion of

scientific knowledge. John WINTHROP of Massachusetts, who gained respect as a colonial scientist, became the first North American member of England's Royal Society, an exclusive organization of scientists. Cadwallader COLDEN of New York studied plants and the ways of Native Americans. Undoubtedly, the best known scientist in the British colonies was Benjamin FRANKLIN, who formed the AMERICAN PHILOSOPHICAL SOCIETY to debate scientific issues and whose experiments with electricity were widely published in Europe.

The Enlightenment and Religion. The Enlightenment's emphasis on reason influenced religious thinking in North America as well, especially in the British colonies. Some clergymen argued that religion should be based on reason. They believed that God had created a rational universe and given humans the power of reason so they could tell right from wrong and free will so they could decide how to act. Not all religious leaders accepted these ideas, however. Some ministers joined the religious movement known as the GREAT AWAKENING, which emphasized the importance of feeling rather than reason in religion.

Perhaps the greatest influence of the Enlightenment on religious thought was in promoting the idea of freedom of worship. The Virginia Declaration of Rights of 1776, for example, proclaimed that laws should not limit an individual's "liberty of conscience." In 1791 the United States government adopted the Bill of Rights, the first ten amendments to the U.S. Constitution. The first of these guarantees religious freedom to all Americans.

The Enlightenment and Government. The Enlightenment greatly affected political thinking and government in North America. In the years before the American Revolution, British colonists initially protested policies they believed denied their rights as British subjects. When their protests failed to bring change, colonial leaders such as Samuel ADAMS and John ADAMS began speaking and writing about "natural laws" and "natural rights," claiming that these took priority over laws of the British government.

Remember: *Words in small capital letters have separate entries, and the index at the end of Volume 4 will guide you to more information on many topics.*

The DECLARATION OF INDEPENDENCE strongly reflected Enlightenment thinking. Thomas JEFFERSON, its author, said his goal was to explain "the common sense" of the American cause to the world by relying on the Enlightenment idea that reason could lead people to understand the truth. Jefferson also wrote that the colonies wished to gain the "separate and equal" status to which they were entitled by "the laws of nature." In arguing that governments derive their powers from "the consent of the governed," Jefferson claimed that governments have authority only because citizens freely agree to obey their laws. His arguments relied heavily on John Locke's theory of the social contract, which stated that the people have the right to withdraw their support and overturn the government if it makes unjust laws and abuses its power.

Enlightenment political thinking reached its fullest expression in the United States Constitution, written in 1787. In creating a government that was led by officials elected by the people, Americans put into practice the Enlightenment ideals of freedom and choice. The Constitution and the principles it contains continue to inspire people around the world. (*See also* **American Revolution; Revolutionary Thought.**)

See *Navigation Acts.*

Environmental Impact of Colonization

Europeans arriving in North America marveled at the continent's resources—its vast FORESTS, abundant animal life, and well-stocked waters—and its great expanses of unclaimed territory. They learned to grow crops that thrived in the local environments and assumed that the soils would remain fertile forever.

Confident in the endless bounty of the "New World," Europeans used its land and resources with no thought for the future. By the end of the colonial period, their actions had brought drastic changes to the North American environment. The impact Europeans had on the environment formed part of a major shift in the course of human life called the Columbian Exchange. For thousands of years, people, animals, and plants in Europe and the Americas had existed in isolation from one another. With the voyages of Christopher COLUMBUS and later explorers, those two worlds came into contact—and both were transformed forever.

Indian Practices. Europeans were not the first people to affect the environment of North America. Native Americans had lived on the continent for thousands of years, and their practices had already brought changes to the land. Eastern Woodlands tribes, for example, periodically burned sections of forest to clear areas for growing crops. After many years of use, the soil became unproductive, and the Indians moved to a new place, clearing more land in the same way. This practice also affected animals. Areas that had been farmed and abandoned provided an ideal environment for deer and certain other animals, and their populations increased significantly.

Eastern Indians also used fire within forests to keep their hunting trails clear, while PLAINS INDIANS ignited stretches of prairie grassland to encourage the growth of new grasses. Indians tried to limit the extent of these fires by burning only in certain seasons and specific areas. Yet flames often raged out of control, causing unintended destruction. Indians in the arid Southwest affected the environment in another way when they built irrigation systems to bring water from streams to their fields. Their construction shifted the populations of animals and fish and the distribution of various plants.

The impact of Native American practices on the environment was slight, however, in comparison with the changes caused by Europeans. Spurred by the desire for wealth, Europeans exploited* natural resources aggressively and carelessly. Some believed they were "improving" the landscape. Others justified their actions with passages from the Bible that, in their view, gave humans power over all plants and animals. In general, Europeans did not respect nature. They believed that nature existed to serve humans, and they took steps to control the environment without considering the long-term effect of their actions.

* ***exploit*** to use for selfish reasons without regard to the consequences

The Loss of Forests. By the time Europeans began colonizing the Americas, the forests of their homelands had largely disappeared as a result

of centuries of cutting trees to obtain farmland, wood, and fuel. Europeans quickly began using North American forests for the same purposes.

As early as the 1630s, sawmills in northern New England were producing lumber. Lumbering quickly spread to other areas, supplying building material for the colonies and for export to Europe. The major use of trees, though, was for fuel. During the 1760s alone, colonists burned about 100 million cords*. Colonial ironworks industry used large quantities of wood as fuel, often consuming all the trees in an area within about 20 years and then moving to another area that had a good supply of wood.

* ***cord*** amount of wood in a stack four feet long, four feet wide, and eight feet high

The loss of the forests caused great damage to the North American environment. Tree roots help absorb water and hold soil in place. When the trees were removed, water runoff increased and carried good topsoil into streams and rivers, leaving the land less fertile. As waterways filled with silt, they became shallower, and some types of fish did not survive the new environment. Although trees often grew back, the character of forests changed dramatically. Certain species*, such as cedar and white pine, did not grow well in once-cleared areas, and trees such as maple and beech took their place. Deforestation* also contributed to the drying up of lakes and streams.

* ***species*** group of plants or animals with similar characteristics

* ***deforestation*** destruction and elimination of forests

* ***pelt*** skin and fur of an animal

Impact of the Fur Trade. Soon after Europeans arrived in North America, they began acquiring animal pelts* for export to Europe. By the 1700s, the FUR TRADE had taken an enormous toll on a variety of animals, particularly beavers. Hunters found it easy to track and kill beavers, which tended to

As colonists converted forested areas to farmland, the dirt that tree roots had held in place began to wash away. Vast fields of grain stripped nutrients from the soil, leaving it less fertile. Animals that had lived in wooded areas moved away as their homeland disappeared.

stay in the same place throughout the year. Furthermore, beaver populations were slow to recover because the animals do not produce many offspring.

The loss of beavers had unexpected effects on the environment. The dams they built on streams contributed to the diversity of plant and animal life in the surrounding area. Animals and birds came to feed on the fish living in ponds behind the dams. In addition, beaver dams tended to raise the water level, which often helped prevent flooding. As the beavers were killed off and their dams disintegrated, the environment changed. The loss of beaver dams and ponds, however, brought some benefits for the colonists. Grasses flourished in the former beaver ponds, providing colonists with ideal pastures for livestock—without their having to cut down trees to clear the land.

In the southern colonies the demand for animal skins focused on deer, which led to a dramatic decline in the deer population. By the mid-1700s, Indian hunters in the Southeast had great difficulty finding enough deer skins to maintain a profitable trade. The fur trade also significantly reduced the number of bears, muskrats, otters, wildcats, and raccoons in the East.

Impact of Colonial Farming. As colonial settlements spread, more and more trees were cut down to clear fields for crops. Colonial farming changed the environment in various ways besides the loss of forests, however. By planting extensive fields of one crop, such as corn or wheat, colonists altered natural balances that had existed for centuries. Besides using up the nutrients in the soil, their farming methods contributed to outbreaks of plant diseases, the growth and spread of weeds, and infestations of insect pests that thrived on certain crops. In some parts of the South, agriculture involving irrigation created large areas of stagnant* water, which became breeding grounds for disease-carrying mosquitoes.

* ***stagnant*** not flowing, stale, and sometimes polluted

Colonial farming also had an impact on the animal life of North America. The Indian practice of clearing the land and then moving on had created "edge" environments in which forests gradually grew back in once-cleared fields. Animals such as deer, elk, turkey, porcupine, and rabbit all flourished in that type of environment. Colonists, however, created permanent fields. As "edge" environments disappeared, the animals that thrived in them began to decline in number. As early as 1672, settlers in Massachusetts noticed that wild turkeys had become very rare.

Colonial farming endangered animals in other ways as well. Colonists killed wild animals such as foxes that posed a threat to their chickens and other livestock. The animal they feared most was the wolf. In Europe wolves had been hunted almost to extinction. A similar fate threatened wolf populations in North America. By the end of the colonial period, wolves had been wiped out in much of the East, except for the northernmost areas of New England. Farmers also killed squirrels and rabbits that ate their crops. Most of these animals, however, did not face extinction.

The Other Side of the Exchange

The Columbian Exchange worked in both directions. Settlers from Europe brought many new plants and animals to the "New World" and transformed the environment. But the contact between the continents also led to the cultivation of American plants—including corn, beans, potatoes, tomatoes, cocoa, peanuts, tobacco, and rubber—in the "Old World." These new plants developed into important food crops and industries, changing the diet and economy of peoples in Europe, Africa, and Asia.

Introduction of New Animals and Plants. The grazing livestock that Europeans introduced to North America—the horses, cattle, and sheep—had a profound impact on the environment. Aside from the buffalo, no large grazing animals existed on the continent. The new European livestock consumed large quantities of native grasses, which could not grow back

fast enough. But European grasses such as Kentucky bluegrass—introduced accidentally in the form of seeds on the hides of imported livestock—flourished in their place and spread throughout the continent.

Cattle, sheep, and horses had an especially damaging effect on the arid lands of the Southwest. Large herds pounded and packed down the thin soil with their hooves, making it difficult for plants to grow. Their grazing destroyed grasses that had helped hold water in the soil. As a result, water runoff increased dramatically, eroding the landscape and turning some areas into desert. Throughout the continent, herds of livestock that had become wild roamed woods and grasslands, trampling and destroying native vegetation.

By introducing European animals and following European practices, the colonists in North America had tried to re-create a familiar landscape. In doing so, they significantly altered the continent's environment and changed much of its appearance forever. (*See also* **Agriculture; Economic Systems; Industries.**)

Equiano, Olaudah

ca. 1745–ca. 1801

Slave and author

Stories of the lives and sufferings of slaves are part of the rich literature of colonial America. The finest of these slave narratives was written by Olaudah Equiano, a former slave who was also known as Gustavas Vassa.

Equiano was born in Benin in West Africa. When he was 11 years old, he was shipped as a slave to Barbados and then to Virginia. He had several masters and soon learned English. He explained that once he got over the loneliness of being sold away from his shipmates, "I now not only felt myself quite easy with these new countrymen, but relished their society and manners." Equiano educated himself and became a polished writer. He managed to purchase his freedom and moved to England, where he worked to abolish slavery and the SLAVE TRADE. His account of his life was published in 1789.

See color plate 6, vol. 3.

Equiano called his work *The Interesting Narrative of the Life of Olaudah Equiano, or Gustavas Vassa, the African, Written by Himself.* The phrase "written by himself" is an important part of the title. It shows the emphasis that Equiano placed on his ability to read and write and on his power to tell his own story.

Like many of the early slave narratives, Equiano's work contains vivid scenes of brutality. In describing the terrible conditions of his forced voyage to America, he wrote: "The shrieks of the women, and the groans of the dying, rendered the whole a scene of horror." Despite the brutality of the Christian slaveholders, Equiano accepted Christianity and gave credit to God for the good fortune of his life. His narrative enjoyed great success and was reprinted five times in five years. (*See also* **Literature; Slavery.**)

Eriksson, Leif

See ***Norse Settlements.***

Eskimo Peoples (Inuit)

The Eskimo, whose lands stretch from southeastern Alaska across northern Canada to Greenland, were the first native people in North America to meet Europeans. Norse seafarers arrived in Greenland about A.D. 1000. The term *Eskimo* comes from an Algonquian word meaning "eaters of raw meat." However, these people call themselves *Inuit,* which means "the people."

Living in the harsh environment of the far north, the Eskimo learned to make use of every available resource. Along the coasts, they fished and hunted seals and whales, which they fearlessly pursued in their skin-covered boats. Around Hudson Bay, they hunted caribou, a type of reindeer. Most Eskimo lived in tents in the summer and sod houses in the winter. They built igloos, or domed ice houses, as temporary shelters while they were hunting. The Eskimo developed special technology to survive the extreme conditions of the Arctic climate. They used saucer-shaped stone lamps that burned whale or seal oil for heat and light. They wore clothes of sealskin and caribou hide and special footgear to protect against the cold, and they used dogs to pull sleds over snow and ice.

In 1576 English explorer Sir Martin Frobisher landed on what is now called Baffin Island in the Arctic region. In search of the NORTHWEST PASSAGE, a water route across North America, Frobisher and his party traded with the Eskimo and kidnapped one to take back to England. Other European explorers followed. They also came in hope of discovering a water route that would provide a shortcut to Asia. In the early 1700s, Christian missionaries from Greenland and Europe arrived to convert, educate, and trade with the Eskimo. On the other side of the continent, Russians moved onto the mainland of Alaska in the 1760s. Most of their contact was with the ALEUT PEOPLES, but Russian fur traders treated the Alaskan Eskimo harshly.

European diseases killed thousands of native peoples. By the end of the 1700s, the Eskimo population had been reduced to about 30,000, roughly half of what it had been before the arrival of the Europeans. (*See also* **Exploration, Age of; Norse Settlements; Russian Settlements.**)

Estaugh, Elizabeth Haddon

1680–1762
Founder of Haddonfield, New Jersey

Elizabeth Haddon Estaugh, the daughter of English QUAKERS, founded the town of Haddonfield in western New Jersey. Her father had bought 500 acres of land in that colony, hoping to move his family there to escape persecution against Quakers in England. But business and poor health prevented him from carrying out his plan.

When Elizabeth Haddon was just 21 years old, she decided to go to North America and settle on her father's land in order to establish a haven in the wilderness for Quakers. Before leaving England, though, the young woman had met and fallen in love with a young minister named John Estaugh. In 1702 he came to New Jersey to visit her. According to tradition, Elizabeth Haddon asked him to marry her, saying that she had received a call from God to love him. (The American poet Henry Wadsworth Longfellow told this story in his *Tales of a Wayside Inn.*) They were soon married. Years later she wrote that "few, if any, in a married state ever lived in sweeter Harmony than we did."

While her husband traveled for his ministry and on business related to Quaker land investments, Elizabeth Haddon Estaugh managed the family's estate. She welcomed visiting Quakers to her home and cared for the sick in the area. In 1713 she built a new house, Haddon Hall, around which the village of Haddonfield grew up. With no children of her own, she adopted a nephew and in her old age was surrounded by grandnieces and grandnephews. Elizabeth Haddon Estaugh died after a long illness, "as one falling asleep, full of days, like a shock of corn fully ripe," according to local accounts.

Esteban (Estevanico)

died 1539
African servant and guide

* ***Moor*** North African Muslim

See first map in Exploration, Age of (vol. 2).

The first Africans in North America arrived with the Spanish explorers in the early 1500s. Most had already adopted the Spanish language and culture, and they came as slaves, servants, or soldiers. The most famous of them was Esteban, "a black Arab, native of Azamjor" (in North Africa), also known as Estevanico the Moor*.

In 1527 Esteban took part in an expedition to Florida led by the Spanish explorer Pánfilo de Narváez. Storms, disease, and hostile Indians killed off most of the members of the expedition. The only known survivors were Esteban, the Spanish explorer Alvar Núñez CABEZA DE VACA, and two other Spaniards. After ten years among the Indians, these four men began an overland journey to the western coast of what is now Mexico—a distance of more than 6,000 miles. The trip took eight long years. During that time, Esteban's skills as a healer, interpreter, and diplomat helped the Spaniards survive and communicate with the Indian tribes along the way.

When Esteban and the others arrived in Mexico, they brought tales of cities of fabulous wealth somewhere in the interior of North America. These stories—which the Spaniards claimed to have heard from the Indians—inspired the legend of the SEVEN CITIES OF CÍBOLA. In 1539 Father Marcos de Niza mounted a small expedition to find the fabled cities. He hired Esteban to serve as a guide because of the skills, experience, and knowledge the African had gained during his long journey from Florida. However, when the party reached the village of Háwikuh in the territory of the ZUNI INDIANS, Esteban was killed by the Indians. Feeling lost without their guide, the Spaniards returned to Mexico. (*See also* **Exploration, Age of.**)

During the 1400s, economic, political, and religious factors combined to push Europeans to seek new horizons beyond their known world. Spurred by improvements in technology and a thirst for knowledge, they launched the Age of Exploration. Venturing into uncharted territory, Europeans discovered a "New World" on the other side of the Atlantic Ocean—one that seemed to promise great wealth. Soon European powers were competing for empires in the Americas. Over the next few centuries, their rivalries had a major impact on developments in North America—and events in North America affected Europeans as well.

Global Empires

The European contest for empire was a global struggle that raged in many corners of the world. The Portuguese had territory on the coasts of Africa, Arabia, India, and China and controlled the East Indies. The Dutch seized the East Indies in the 1600s and also planted a colony on the southern tip of Africa. Spain held the Philippines, while France and Britain competed for power in India. The British won control of India in the mid-1700s and considered it their most prized possession. The competition for empire continued into the 1800s as European nations carved up Africa and parts of Southeast Asia.

Growth and Development

In 1492 Christopher COLUMBUS sailed west from Spain in search of a new route to Asia. Instead of achieving that goal, he landed in the Americas. Columbus's voyage of "discovery," though it changed the world, was not an isolated event. It resulted from ideas and economic and political trends that had been developing in Europe for many years.

Reasons for Expansion. For centuries Asia had been a symbol of wealth and luxury to Europeans, as well as a source of valuable silks and spices. For centuries, too, Europeans had engaged in conflicts with the Muslims of the Middle East, who lived at the crossroads of Europe and Asia and controlled trade routes between the two continents. Conflict with the Muslims also had religious causes. European Christians resented Muslim control of the Holy Land (ancient Palestine) and feared that Muslims would prevent them from visiting Jerusalem and other sacred sites.

Between 1095 and 1464, thousands of Christians left Europe to fight wars against Muslims in the hope of capturing the Holy Land. These wars, known as the Crusades, led to lasting hostility between Muslims and Christians. When the Crusaders returned home to Europe from their travels in Asian lands, they brought luxurious items that stirred great interest. Europeans' desire for Asian goods increased as trade with Asia developed from the 1200s to the mid-1300s. During that time, European merchants and adventurers such as Marco Polo traveled overland to Asia. The tales they brought back of glorious cities and fabulous wealth further sharpened Europeans' appetite for Asian riches.

Then, in the 1300s, disaster struck. A terrible plague* known as the Black Death killed millions of people in Europe. The loss of population led to a decline in European economies. At the same time, political instability in the Middle East and Central Asia disrupted the trade routes that ran through those regions. By the late 1400s, the European economies had rebounded. Yet Asian trade routes lay firmly in Muslim hands, and outbreaks of hostility between Europe and Asia periodically interrupted trade.

* ***plague*** disease that swept across the medieval world several times

European life changed greatly in the 1400s as a result of the Renaissance—a period of great artistic and intellectual activity inspired by renewed interest in the art and the writings of ancient Greece and Rome. During the Renaissance, Europeans began looking at the world in new ways, and the knowledge they gained spread quickly after the invention of the printing press. Important advances in technology took place in Europe as well, including two navigational devices adopted from the Muslims—the compass and astrolabe*. With these instruments, European sailors could safely venture far out to sea. In addition, improvements in mapmaking led to more accurate charts of land, sea, and ocean currents, while better shipbuilding techniques produced faster ships that could carry more cargo and enter shallow harbors. Europe now stood poised on the brink of the Age of Exploration.

* ***astrolabe*** instrument that allowed navigators to determine their location by the position of the sun and stars

First Ventures. As early as the 800s, adventurers from Scandinavia had sailed west across the Atlantic Ocean. These Vikings, or Norsemen, even

established some settlements in present-day Newfoundland and Labrador in the 1000s. By the 1400s, however, accounts of these Norse voyages and settlements survived only in Scandinavian legend and were unknown to the rest of Europe. Thus, the period of exploration that began in the 1400s was really the beginning of large-scale European colonization.

PORTUGAL and SPAIN were the first European nations to sail far beyond Europe. Their immediate goal was to find an ocean route to Asia that would bypass the Muslims in the Middle East. Both of these seafaring nations with Atlantic coastlines produced skilled sailors and navigators. Both had powerful monarchies that supported exploration. Furthermore, in both nations, strong religious feelings fueled the desire to defeat the Muslims and spread Christianity.

Portugal began first. In the mid-1400s, Portuguese sailors headed south through the Atlantic Ocean, exploring the west coast of Africa and various islands in the Atlantic and establishing outposts* for trade. The Portuguese eventually traveled around the southern tip of Africa and sailed east to India, mapping out an ocean route to Asia.

* ***outpost*** frontier settlement or military base

When Spain began to explore the same regions, a strong rivalry for trade and territorial rights developed between the two nations. In 1479 they signed a treaty, which gave Portugal exclusive right to explore the coastal regions of Africa. As a result, Spain began looking westward. In 1492 the Spanish monarchs supported Christopher Columbus's voyage across the Atlantic in search of a route to Asia. His "discovery" of the Americas began an era when European nations established colonial empires.

Starting New Empires. Spain quickly established a foothold in the Western Hemisphere. Portugal followed soon after, but its claims were limited by the TREATY OF TORDESILLAS, an agreement signed with Spain in 1494. The treaty established an imaginary line through the Atlantic Ocean that divided Spanish and Portuguese realms.

> ***Remember:*** *Words in small capital letters have separate entries, and the index at the end of Volume 4 will guide you to more information on many topics.*

At first the Spanish did not realize they had found a "New World." By the early 1500s, however, it became clear that the Americas included two separate continents. Moreover, it turned out that the Treaty of Tordesillas had given Spain the rights to all of this "New World" except a portion of present-day Brazil in South America.

Spain found great wealth in its American empire. The conquest of the native civilizations in present-day Mexico and Peru yielded vast amounts of gold and silver, and Spanish ships sailed home each year laden with riches. The colony of NEW SPAIN included Mexico, Central America, and most of the WEST INDIES and eventually extended north into present-day Florida and the southwestern part of the United States. Spain's other American colonies—New Granada, Peru, and Río de la Plata—covered the western half of South America.

See map in Spanish Borderlands (vol. 4).

Other European powers envied Spain's growing wealth and wanted to explore opportunities in the Americas. FRANCE was among the first countries to do so. By the 1520s, the Italian mariner Giovanni da Verrazano had claimed parts of the Atlantic coast of North America for France. In the 1530s and 1540s, Jacques CARTIER led expeditions to the area around the ST. LAWRENCE RIVER in present-day Canada and established French claims in the region.

See map in New France (vol. 3).

Finding no gold or other riches, however, the French made little attempt, at first, to create a colonial empire. It was not until the early 1600s—almost a century after they first sailed across the Atlantic—that the French began to settle parts of North America.

England also took a while before launching any serious expeditions to the Americas. In the 1560s, Francis DRAKE and other English sea captains began raiding coastal towns in New Spain and looting treasure ships bound for Europe. The English soon realized, however, that trading posts and colonies would provide greater opportunities for long-term prosperity and power in North America. The earliest attempts to found settlements failed, including the ill-fated community at ROANOKE ISLAND in present-day North Carolina. By the early 1600s, however, the English had established several colonies in North America.

See map in British Colonies (vol. 1).

The Dutch entered the competition for overseas empires as well. In the late 1500s, Dutch merchants began challenging the Portuguese monopoly* on trade with the East Indies in Southeast Asia. Within a few decades, they had driven the Portuguese from the region and created a commercial empire. The Dutch then set their sights on the Western Hemisphere. In 1621 Dutch merchants formed the DUTCH WEST INDIA COMPANY, which was to make money in the Americas for its investors through trade and colonization.

* ***monopoly*** exclusive right to engage in a certain kind of business

The Contest for North America

By the early 1600s, Spain, France, and England had all established footholds in North America, and the NETHERLANDS was preparing to do so. Over the next 150 years, competition among these European powers would shape the settlement of North America. During that time, military and commercial dominance passed from Spain to the Netherlands and then to France and Britain.

Spanish Power in the Americas. For about 60 years after the voyages of Columbus, Spain's powerful position in the Western Hemisphere was unchallenged. The nation claimed exclusive rights to the Americas and sought to maintain control over the great riches to be gained there.

Spain's growing wealth became the envy of other European powers. The French and English presented the first challenge in the 1560s, raiding Spanish settlements and treasure ships in the Americas. During the remainder of the 1500s, France and England viewed North America primarily as a base from which to launch such attacks against the Spanish.

Rivalry between England and Spain erupted in war in 1585. Spain suffered a major loss in 1588, when the English defeated its mighty fleet—the Spanish Armada. Spain recovered quickly, but even so, by the time the war ended in 1603, its power in the Americas had begun to decline. Both England and France established their first permanent settlements in North America during the period of peace that lasted until 1621. These settlements became the foundations of NEW FRANCE and the BRITISH COLONIES.

The Dutch Challenge. The Dutch dealt a more serious blow to Spanish control in the Americas. In 1621 war broke out between the Netherlands and

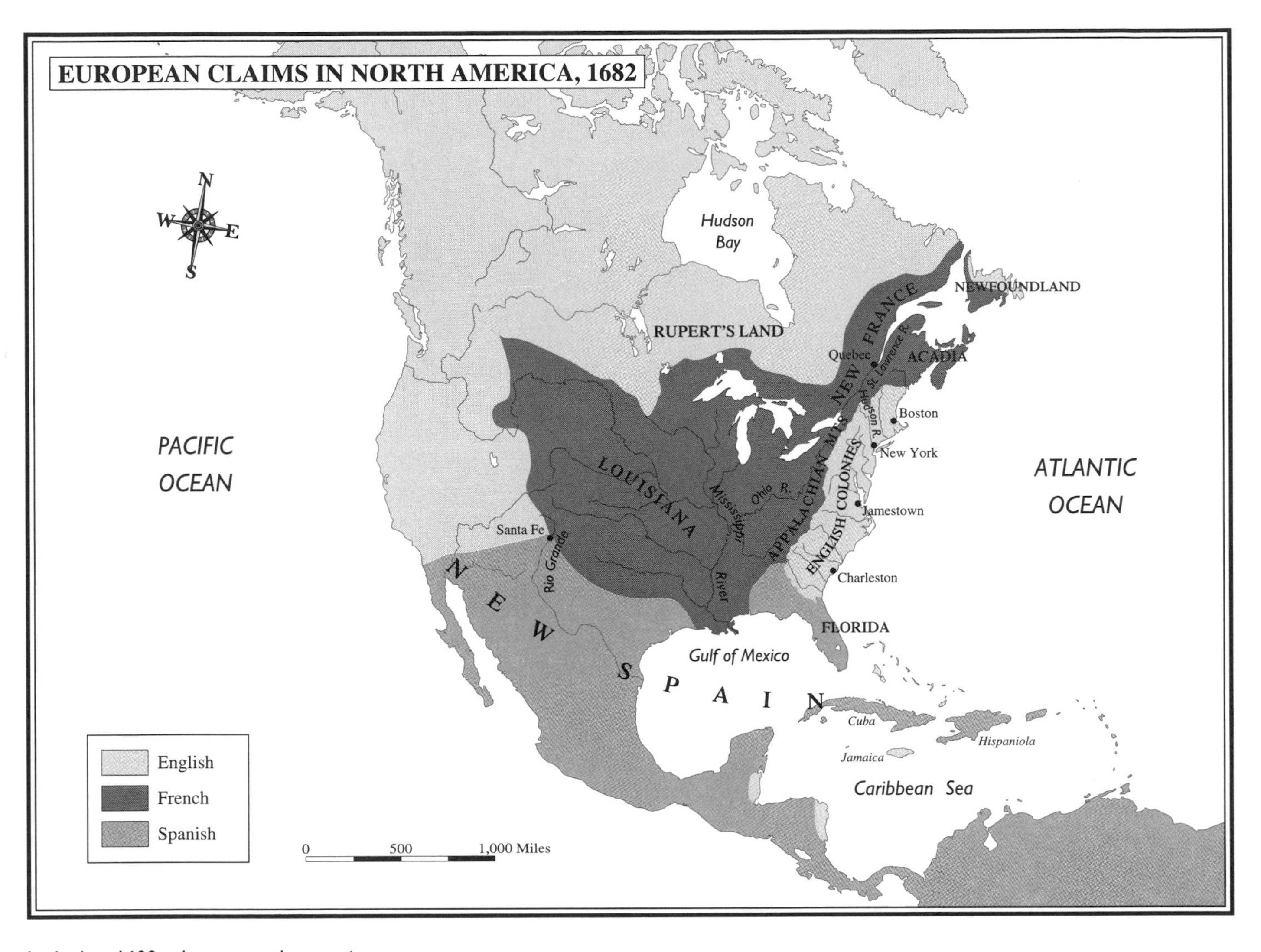

In the late 1600s, there were three major players in the European contest for North America: England, France, and Spain. The Spanish controlled the southern part of the continent, while the English held the extreme north and east. France claimed a large region in the continent's interior but fought continually with the English over its boundaries.

Spain, a continuation of the Dutch struggle to break free of Spanish rule. The Dutch struck at the edge of Spain's American empire by capturing the rich port of San Salvador in Brazil. (Although Brazil belonged to Portugal, Portugal was ruled by Spain at this time.) To regain this crucial port, Spain brought ships and other important resources from the Caribbean, leaving that region unprotected. France and England quickly moved in and seized a number of Caribbean islands.

Spanish power was further weakened in 1628, when the Dutch captured an entire Spanish treasure fleet in the Caribbean. This loss crippled the Spanish treasury and damaged the nation's war effort against the Dutch. Meanwhile, the Dutch raided Spanish settlements in the Caribbean, disrupted Spanish trade, and took over several key islands. In the midst of these developments, the Dutch founded their first settlements in North America, which became the colony of New Netherland.

See map in New Netherland (vol. 3).

The Netherlands built Europe's most efficient trading empire and replaced Spain as the model of successful empire. At the same time, the nation's success provoked economic and military rivalries that affected trade and colonization. Dutch traders introduced sugar production to English and French colonies in the Caribbean, which spurred the growth of the SLAVE TRADE. They offered Native Americans higher prices and better-quality goods in exchange for tobacco and furs, beating out other Europeans in the competition for trade.

Tensions between the Dutch and the English over trade led to war in 1652. The fighting had little immediate effect on the American colonies of either nation. Ten years later, however, the English renewed hostilities and gained control of New Netherland. With the loss of their colony, the Dutch dropped out of the contest for North America.

English and French Conflict. By the late 1600s, only England and France were left in the competition for control of North America. Although Spain had its colonies in the Spanish Borderlands*, it focused on Mexico and other possessions to the south. The rivalry between England and France intensified as their American colonial empires expanded. The nations were rivals in Europe as well. From 1688 to 1763, tensions between the two nations resulted in a series of wars. Though the conflicts usually began in Europe, they spread to French and British colonial possessions.

* ***Spanish Borderlands*** northern part of New Spain, area now occupied by Florida, Texas, New Mexico, Arizona, and California

The fighting in North America involved not only soldiers from Europe but also colonial troops and the Indian allies of each nation. The first of the colonial conflicts, KING WILLIAM'S WAR, lasted from 1688 to 1697. Much of this war involved raids on frontier settlements by one side or the other. In the end, neither side gained a clear victory, and no territory changed hands.

Next came QUEEN ANNE'S WAR (1702–1714). Once again, most of the fighting took place on the frontier. A British attempt to capture QUEBEC failed. But in the TREATY OF UTRECHT of 1713, which ended the war, Britain gained control of the French colony of Acadia. France had lost an important piece of its North American empire.

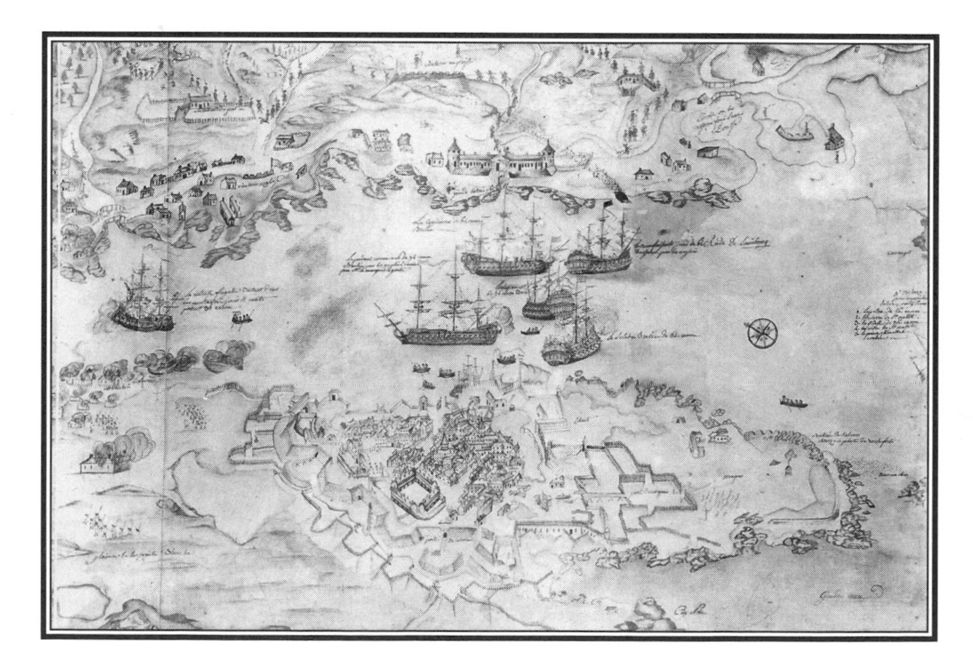

For 13 years, the British tried to capture Louisbourg, the French fort that guarded the entrance to the St. Lawrence River. In 1758 British forces laid siege to the fort, as illustrated in this drawing, and finally forced the French to surrender.

For the next 25 years, there was no open conflict between Britain and France in North America, but the two powers competed in several ways. The French began developing their colony of LOUISIANA. They also launched a major effort to build FORTS throughout North America, particularly in frontier regions claimed by both Britain and France. The British responded by establishing forts of their own.

Fighting erupted again between the two countries in KING GEORGE'S WAR, which lasted from 1744 to 1748. This war, too, took place mostly along the frontier and did not result in any territorial changes. Although the British captured the French port of LOUISBOURG on the Atlantic coast, the peace treaty returned it to France. This time, however, the uneasy truce did not hold. War broke out once more about six years later.

The FRENCH AND INDIAN WAR (1754–1763), described by one historian as "the great war for empire," was the most extensive and decisive conflict between Britain and France. It began over disputed claims to the Ohio Valley. In the late 1740s, British colonists were moving into this frontier region, also claimed by France and various groups of Native Americans. French attempts to block British expansion in the Ohio Valley led to the outbreak of war. For the first time, Britain and France committed large numbers of European soldiers to the fighting instead of relying mainly on colonial militia*. In this conflict, fighting was more widespread, and victories were more significant. Britain won the war decisively. In the TREATY OF PARIS (1763), France gave up almost all of its claims and territory in North America. Britain emerged as the dominant power on the continent.

* ***militia*** army of citizens who may be called into action in a time of emergency

See map in French and Indian War (vol. 2).

The Remains of Empire. British power in North America did not go unchallenged. Britain lost its most prosperous colonies in the AMERICAN REVOLUTION, when it was forced to recognize the independence of the UNITED STATES. But the British did hold on to Canada, which remained under their rule until the mid-1800s.

See map in Canada (vol. 1).

Other European powers still had colonies in North America. In the late 1600 and 1700s, while the British and French were struggling over territory in the eastern part of the continent, Spain had strengthened its control in the Southwest. Settlements in the Spanish Borderlands grew, and Spanish culture became firmly rooted in those regions.

In the mid-1700s, Spain became concerned about developments along the western edge of its North American empire. Russian fur traders, who had maintained trading outposts in what is now Alaska, began moving south along the Pacific coast. This development challenged long-standing Spanish claims to CALIFORNIA, and the Spanish responded with their last major wave of colonization. Beginning in 1769, they established a string of MISSIONS and forts along the California coast and encouraged settlement in the region.

Meanwhile, Spain had obtained Louisiana from France as part of the peace treaty after the French and Indian War. At first Louisiana and the Spanish Borderlands served as a buffer* between the main areas of settlement of New Spain and the British colonies. They soon came to be a buffer between New Spain and the growing power of the United States. By 1821, however, Spain had lost all its North American territory. Louisiana and Florida had become part of the United States, and Mexico had won independence from

* ***buffer*** protective barrier between two rivals

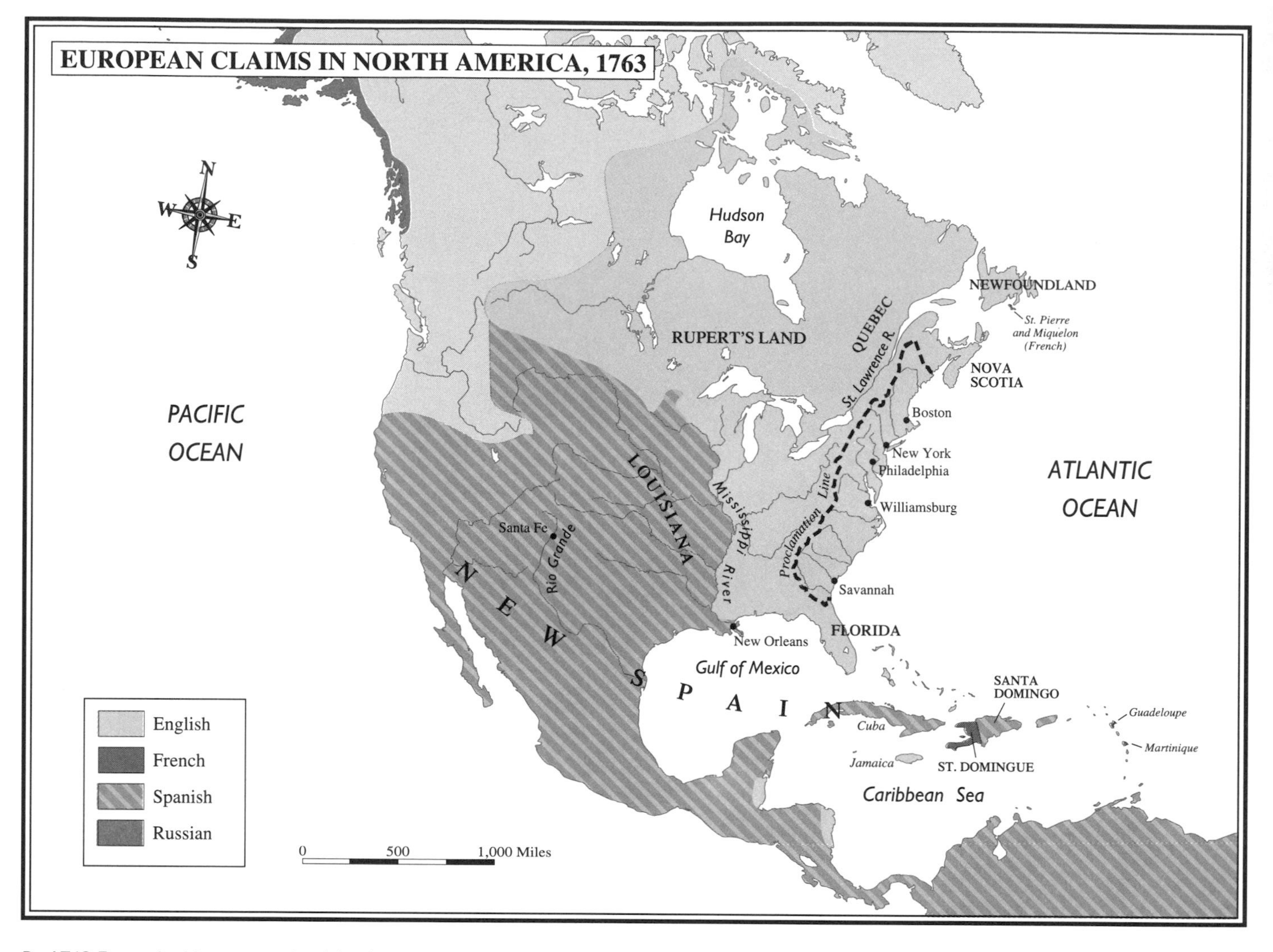

By 1763 France had lost most of its North American territory. England controlled the northeast, and Spain held the area west and south of the Mississippi River. Russia's possessions were mostly bases for fur trading.

Spain and gained control of the Spanish Borderlands. The European contest for empire in North America was over. (*See also* **Acadians; Exploration, Age of; Fur Trade; Great Britain; Norse Settlements; Russian Settlements; Spanish Borderlands; Swedish Settlements.**)

Exploration, Age of

The Age of Exploration began in the 1400s, when Europeans ventured away from their continent on long sea voyages. Explorers sailed south along the coast of Africa, across the Atlantic Ocean, and eventually around the world. The era produced one of history's most decisive events: the European discovery of the Americas. After Christopher COLUMBUS's voyages, the nations of Europe devoted considerable energy to exploring this "New World." Their efforts led to the conquest and settlement of North and South America. Although the Europeans considered themselves the discoverers of the Americas, the first people on the scene were the Asian nomads who came across on the BERING LAND BRIDGE more than 15,000 years ago.

* ***Crusades*** series of wars in the Middle Ages in which European Christians attempted to win the Holy Land from the Muslims

Expanding Horizons. Although the Age of Exploration began in the 1400s, its roots date back several centuries. The Crusades* brought Europeans into contact with the trade centers of the eastern Mediterranean and western Asia, giving them a taste for exotic goods such as spices and silk. In the 1200s, the Venetian merchant Marco Polo traveled across Asia to China, paving the way for other Europeans to explore overland routes to the East.

At the same time, advances in technology allowed Europeans to make longer, safer ocean voyages than ever before. The mariners of Venice and Genoa, Italian city-states that prospered from seafaring trade, pioneered many of these advances. They were among the first to use the magnetic compass as an aid to navigation, and they improved ship design so that vessels could survive rougher seas. Their maps of sailing routes and coastlines were among the most accurate of the day.

* ***exploit*** to use for selfish reasons without regard to the consequences

Motives for Exploration. Commerce provided the main reason for the Age of Exploration. Long-distance trade had become an important part of the economy of Europe, and the governments of many countries, along with their bankers and merchants, were eager to extend their trade over even greater distances. Their chief goal was a sea route to the East so that they could obtain goods directly from India, China, and Southeast Asia without the costly services of the people who transported trade goods overland in caravans. The quest for a sea route to Asia led to Columbus's accidental "discovery" of the Americas. Once Europeans realized that the land Columbus had reached was not the Indies—as Asia was known—but a new continent, they lost no time in searching for and exploiting* its resources, especially GOLD. At the same time, they continued to look for a water route through North America to Asia, which they called the NORTHWEST PASSAGE. The search for the passage lay behind much of the exploration of the continent.

Political motives such as national pride, rivalry with other countries, and the desire to build large empires also played a role in the Age of Exploration. They spurred nations to compete for control of new trade routes, resources, and territories. But religion also played a powerful role in the expansion of Europe. The Age of Exploration was an intensely religious period, and European powers believed they were doing God's work in discovering new lands and converting native peoples to Christianity. Catholic France and Spain sought to spread Catholicism, while the Dutch and the English were determined to extend the reach of Protestantism. Many of the explorers saw themselves as God's agents and often included priests, ministers, and missionaries on their expeditions.

Norse Exploration

The first Europeans to explore North America arrived long before the Age of Exploration. The Vikings—Norse, or Scandinavian, seafarers—crossed the Atlantic almost 500 years before Columbus.

The Vikings were skilled mariners with sturdy ships, who began sailing west from their homes in northern Europe in the late 700s. They raided English and Irish communities and established settlements on the Orkney,

Shetland, and Faeroe Islands in the North Atlantic. Sometime in the mid-800s, Norse sailors bound for the Faeroes were blown off course and sighted an unknown island to the west. They settled that island, which they named Iceland. Sailing westward from Iceland in the 900s, the Vikings discovered a large land mass they called Greenland and established a series of settlements along its west coast. From their Greenland base, they traveled to North America.

The Viking who led that voyage was Leif Eriksson, son of Erik the Red, the founder of the Greenland colony. Around the year 1000, Eriksson sailed west and south from Greenland and made three North American landings. The first was on an island between Greenland and Arctic Canada, now known as Baffin Island. The second was on a large peninsula that juts out from Canada's east coast—present-day Labrador. The last stop was the island of NEWFOUNDLAND, south of Labrador. Eriksson called this place Vinland because of the grapes he found growing there. Eriksson's friends and relatives made several journeys to Vinland and may have sailed south along the North American coast. Although Vikings from Greenland tried to establish a colony on Vinland, they gave up by about 1020, perhaps because of attacks from the local Indians. In the centuries that followed, the Greenlanders made occasional trips to Labrador or Newfoundland to bring back timber, which was in short supply in Greenland. There is no firm evidence of Viking exploration or activity elsewhere in North America.

Remember: *Words in small capital letters have separate entries, and the index at the end of Volume 4 will guide you to more information on many topics.*

The Norse settlements in Greenland disappeared sometime in the 1400s. Generations of people of Iceland and Scandinavia told stories of Leif Eriksson and the land he had discovered in the west. However, these tales were largely unknown to the rest of Europe and had little influence on the efforts of later European explorers.

Portuguese Exploration

In the late 1200s, some Europeans thought that it might be possible to reach Asia by sailing around Africa, but they had no knowledge of the sea around the southern part of the continent or how far south they would have to sail. In 1291 Genoa sent an expedition, led by two brothers named Vivaldi, to test a possible route: west from the Mediterranean Sea into the Atlantic, south along the coast of Africa, then east around Africa and north to the Indies. No one knows how far this expedition got because neither the Vivaldi brothers nor their crew ever returned.

About this time, however, mariners from southern Europe began probing the Atlantic. Some made trading voyages north to England and the Netherlands. Others traveled west and south. By the end of the 1300s, they had found the Madeira Islands, the Azores, and the Canary Islands. The Portuguese took over the Madeira Islands and the Azores, and Spain claimed the Canary Islands. The most western of these islands, the Azores, were more than a thousand miles from Portugal and farther west than Iceland. In the course of exploring and colonizing the islands, European navigators became familiar with the wind and current patterns of the mid-Atlantic. They learned to sail southwest from Europe on trade winds from the northeast and to return on winds from the west. (This knowledge would later help Columbus and other

mariners cross the Atlantic and return.) In addition, the Atlantic island groups were stepping-stones for Portugal's 80-year-long attempt to sail around Africa.

Prince Henry the Navigator. Dom Henrique of Portugal, also known as Prince Henry the Navigator, actively promoted Portuguese exploration for 40 years. In 1419 he returned from a military mission to North Africa, where he had heard about the profitable trade in ivory and gold with the land of Guinea, a region south of the Sahara. Determined to reach Guinea by sea, Henry sent out a series of explorers who ventured south along Africa's west coast. The prince also collected maps, navigational instruments, and geography books and hired the finest shipbuilders available.

Henry launched the first systematic national program of exploration. In the 1440s, his mariners brought back shiploads of African slaves, marking the beginning of the European SLAVE TRADE. In the 1450s, they located the Cape Verde Islands off the African coast. Here Portugal started the earliest experiments in plantation agriculture, using black slaves and Portuguese masters. The twin developments of slave trading and plantation farming would have enormous consequences in the Americas in later centuries.

African Voyages. After Henry's death in 1460, the Portuguese monarchs continued the program of exploration. They wanted to benefit from the resources of Africa, chiefly gold and slaves, and discover a route around Africa to Asia. They claimed huge stretches of the African coast for Portugal and established colonial outposts*, sending navigators farther and farther south. In 1488 Bartolomeu Dias sailed around the southern tip of Africa to the continent's east coast, returning to Portugal to report that he had discovered a sea route to the East. Ten years later Vasco da Gama followed Dias's route around Africa and continued on to India. He and his surviving crew members returned to Portugal in triumph in 1499 as the first Europeans to reach Asia by sea. The stories of these explorations greatly impressed Europeans of the time.

* ***outpost*** frontier settlement or military base

Africa and Asia interested the Portuguese crown far more than the Americas did. In fact, the nation's largest territorial claim in the Western Hemisphere came about by accident. In 1500 Pedro Alvares Cabral set sail from Portugal at the head of a large expedition to India. He knew from Dias and da Gama that he should go far out into the South Atlantic to catch the winds and currents that would carry him east around Africa, but he sailed too far to the west and arrived in South America. He claimed the land, which eventually became the Portuguese colony of Brazil.

North America attracted little attention in Portugal. In 1500 João Fernandes and Pedro Maria de Barcelos, from the Portuguese colony in the Azores, reached Greenland and perhaps Newfoundland. That same year, another Azorean, Gaspar Corte Real, crossed the North Atlantic and sighted "a land that was very cool and with big trees," probably Newfoundland. Corte Real returned to Portugal and prepared three ships for a second, more ambitious expedition. They landed in Newfoundland and captured several Indians to take back to Portugal as a gift for the Portuguese king Manoel. Only two ships returned, however. The third, with Corte Real aboard, had set out

The Land and the Labrador

João Fernandes, one of the Azoreans who sailed to North America for Portugal in 1500, was a *lavrador*—a farmer or minor landholder. Fernandes was the first to sight land. In his honor, his shipmates called the region Tierra del Lavrador, meaning "Land of the Farmer." European mapmakers put the name *Lavrador, Labrador,* or *Larbradore* on their maps. When later geographers realized that Fernandes had sighted Greenland, which already had a name, they simply shifted the name to the large peninsula in eastern Canada that is now known as Labrador—although João Fernandes probably never saw it.

Spain's Mission

Throughout the Age of Exploration, the rulers of Spain had religious reasons for exploring and colonizing unknown lands. In 1486 Pope Innocent VIII had issued the Real Patronato, or Royal Patronage, instructing Ferdinand and Isabella to use their power as rulers to promote Catholicism. In 1493 Isabella sent missionaries along on Columbus's second voyage "to influence, and to attract the people of the Indies in order to convert them to our holy Catholic faith." When the Spanish realized that the lands Columbus had reached were not part of Asia, they continued to send missionaries to the "New World" to spread Catholicism among the local peoples.

to explore the coast south of Newfoundland and disappeared. In 1502 Miguel Corte Real sailed west to look for his missing brother. Neither he nor his ship was ever seen again.

Spanish Exploration

Christopher Columbus set Spain on its path of exploration and exploitation of the Americas. After pioneering the mid-Atlantic sea route from Europe, he founded a settlement in the WEST INDIES, where Spaniards brutalized and killed many Indians while searching for gold—a pattern that would be repeated in later colonies. Focusing on present-day Mexico and Central and South America, Spanish explorers and warriors laid the foundation for a huge colonial empire. The empire's northern borderland stretched from present-day Florida to California.

The Voyages of Columbus. Cristoforo Columbo, known in English as Christopher Columbus, was a Genoese mariner. After a voyage to England and Iceland with a Genoese trading fleet in the 1470s, he settled in Portugal and devoted himself to the study of geography and navigation. Columbus also lived for a time in the Madeira Islands and gained experience sailing the open Atlantic. By about 1484, he had worked out the details of an ambitious expedition to reach Asia by heading west across the Atlantic.

Columbus was not the first to propose that Europeans could reach Asia by sailing west. Like other navigators and educated people of his time, he knew that the world was round. Therefore, a ship that went west would go around the world and eventually reach Japan, which according to Marco Polo's account, was the easternmost part of Asia. The biggest unknown was the distance between Japan and Europe. By juggling figures, Columbus came to believe that earlier estimates of the distance were too high and that Japan was less than 2,300 miles from the Canary Islands. In reality, the distance is more than 9,500 miles. Columbus also assumed incorrectly that no land lay between the Canary Islands and Asia.

Columbus hoped that Portugal would back his project. However, King John II of Portugal was more interested in finding a sea route around Africa and turned Columbus down. Columbus also failed to win support from Spain, England, and France. He tried Spain again, pleading his case to King Ferdinand and Queen Isabella, and in 1492 the queen agreed to support him. In September of that year, Columbus left the Canary Islands with three ships—the *Santa Maria, Niña,* and *Pinta*—and sailed west. On October 12, he reached an island he named San Salvador. Believing he had landed in the Indies, he called the native inhabitants Indians.

After visiting several other islands, including Cuba, and leaving some men to establish a settlement on an island he called HISPANIOLA, Columbus returned to Spain with a little gold he had found. The Spanish king and queen also believed that Columbus had been to Asia, and they outfitted him generously for a second voyage. He set sail in 1493, accompanied by 1,200 settlers for a new colony. Among them were many ruthless, violent, ambitious soldiers who set the tone for Spain's early relations with the Indians.

The second voyage disappointed both Columbus and his royal backers because he failed to locate the rich cities of China and India. In addition, Columbus and his brothers, who had joined him, ran into trouble in Hispaniola. The brothers were poor administrators, and the settlers complained about their rule to the Spanish government. Discouraged, Columbus returned to Spain in 1496.

After Columbus's two voyages, Spain believed it had found a western sea route to Asia. Portugal had just established its own Asian route that went around Africa. The two nations began quarreling over their territorial rights. The pope settled the argument in 1494 with the TREATY OF TORDESILLAS, which drew a line down the middle of the Atlantic. The treaty gave Spain the right to establish colonies west of the line and Portugal the same right east of the line. Accordingly, Africa became Portuguese territory, and the Americas became Spanish territory. The only place in the "New World" that Portugal could claim was Brazil, Cabral's landing place on the eastern coast of South America. The pope changed the treaty in 1533 to include only those lands that had already been discovered, allowing other European nations to participate in the scramble for new territory.

When the two nations signed the Treaty of Tordesillas, however, they still believed the lands Columbus had found were outlying areas of Asia. Hoping to locate the rich cities of the East, Columbus made a third voyage

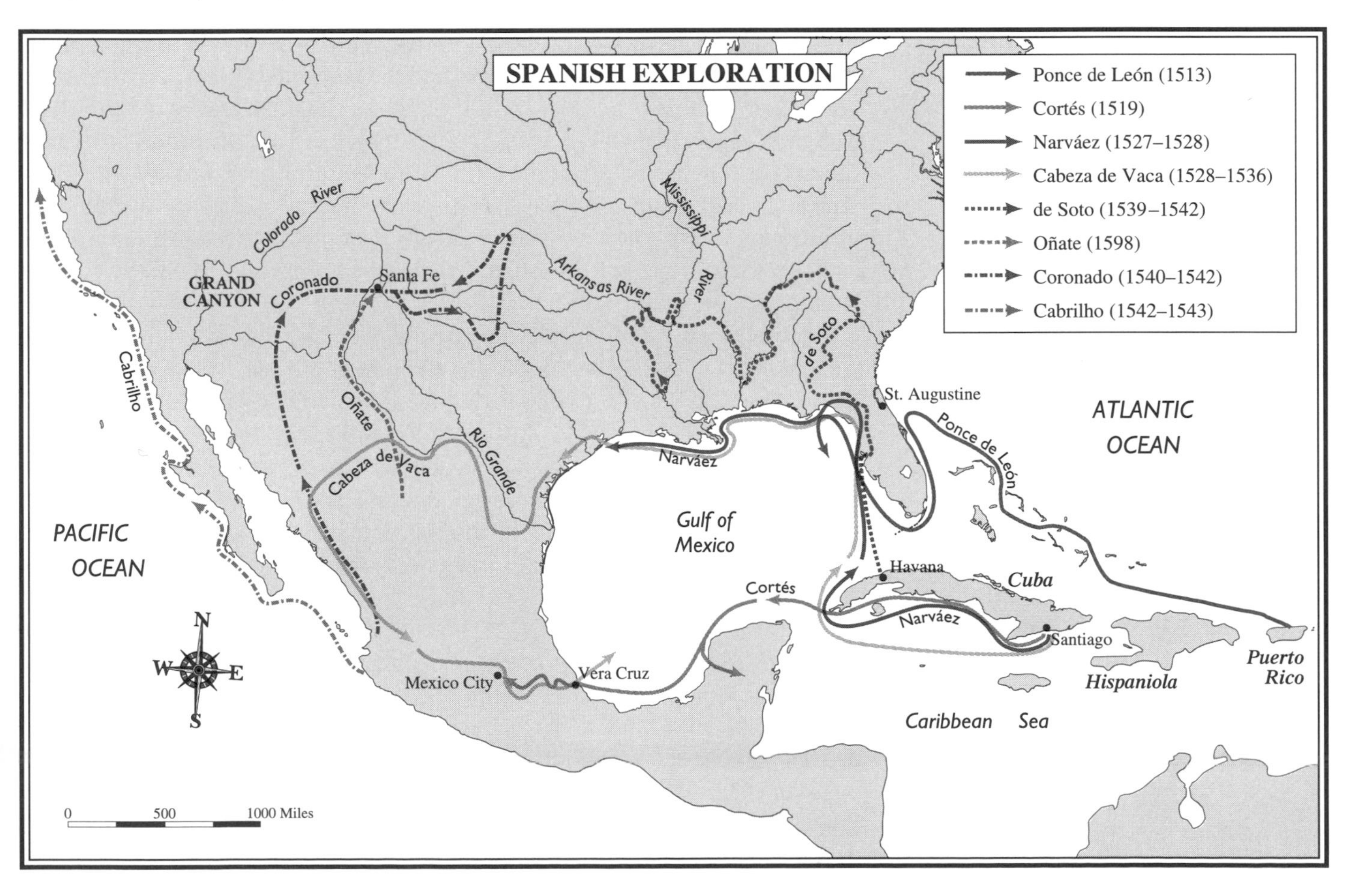

Throughout the 1500s, Spain explored and colonized the southern parts of North America. Sea voyages and overland expeditions paved the way for a Spanish colonial empire that would include Mexico, several Caribbean islands, and most of present-day Florida, Texas, New Mexico, Arizona, and California.

The Spanish explorers in this 1731 engraving were probably part of Hernando de Soto's unsuccessful expedition to colonize Florida. Spain eventually gained control of Florida in 1565.

in 1498. This time he landed on the northern coast of South America. Soon after, an investigator from Spain arrested the Columbus brothers on charges connected with their administration of Hispaniola and shipped them back to Spain. Nevertheless, in 1502 the Spanish crown permitted Columbus to make a fourth voyage. This time he sailed along the coast of Central America, searching for a passage to some part of Asia that was known to Europeans. He found no such passage, and in 1504, describing himself as "completely broken in spirit," Columbus returned to Spain for the last time.

A few people had already suggested that Columbus's "discoveries" were not part of Asia. One of the first to publish this idea was Genoese navigator Amerigo Vespucci, who had twice made voyages to the east coast of South America. He called the lands he and Columbus had explored a *mundus novus,* or new world. The year after Columbus died, German mapmaker Martin Waldseemüller created a map showing two new land masses between Europe and Asia. He named the southern land mass after Amerigo Vespucci. Eventually, these continents became known as North and South America.

Conquistadors and Explorers. Columbus opened the way for the conquistadors, Spanish warriors who flocked to the Caribbean islands and the American mainland in search of treasure, glory, and royal favor. Vasco Núñez de Balboa, one of the conquistadors, extended the boundaries of the known world in 1513. After marching across Central America, he caught sight of the Southern Sea, the European name for the Pacific Ocean. This seemed to confirm the belief that the Americas were not part of Asia and that the Indies lay

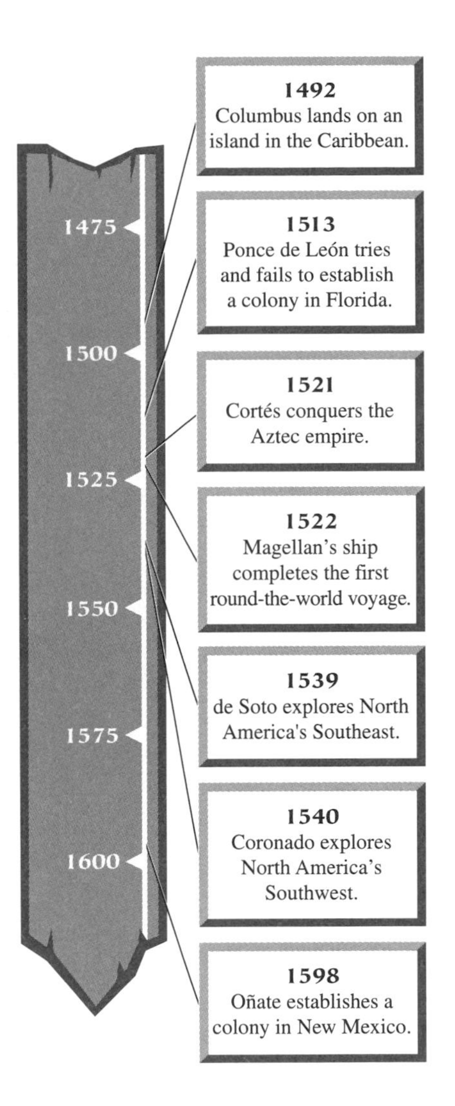

on the far side of the Southern Sea. But to cross the sea and reach the Indies, Europeans had to put ships in that sea.

Ferdinand Magellan, a Portuguese navigator working for Spain, achieved this task a few years later when he sailed around the southern tip of South America through a waterway now called the Strait of Magellan. His expedition then headed west toward Asia. Magellan died in the Philippines, but one of his ships completed the journey, returning to Spain in 1522. This first round-the-world voyage changed Europeans' view of the earth's geography.

Meanwhile, the conquistadors accumulated territory and treasure. In 1521 Hernando CORTÉS defeated the rich Aztec empire of MEXICO, bringing its vast lands under Spanish rule and paving the way for Spanish colonization in North America. A few years later, Cortés led several thousand men south through the jungle into Honduras, the first large-scale European overland exploration in the Americas. In the 1530s, Francisco Pizarro launched the conquest of South America with his victory over the fabulously wealthy Inca in Peru.

Many conquistadors tried their luck in the SPANISH BORDERLANDS, the area stretching from present-day Florida to California. The first was Juan PONCE DE LEÓN, who made an unsuccessful attempt to colonize Florida in 1513. Spanish efforts to establish a colony in what is now South Carolina or Georgia also failed, but expeditions around the Gulf of Mexico did provide information for maps of the coast between Florida and Mexico. In 1527 Pánfilo de Narváez once again tried to start a Spanish settlement in Florida. From Tampa Bay, he led his followers north and then west past the present-day site of New Orleans. Battered by severe storms and divided by conflict among its members, the expedition fell apart. Four men managed to make their way to Spanish territory in Mexico, traveling by foot across present-day Texas and the rugged Southwest. Among them were Alvar Núñez CABEZA DE VACA and a North African named ESTEBAN, the first known black explorer of the Americas.

In 1539 Hernando DE SOTO led an expedition that was supposed to lay the foundation for a Spanish empire in North America. Instead, it became a random, bloody search for gold through the Southeast. The expedition's main contribution to geographic knowledge was finding the MISSISSIPPI RIVER, which would serve later explorers as a waterway into the center of the continent from the north. Spain finally succeeded in establishing a colony in Florida in 1565. Pedro MENÉNDEZ DE AVILÉS founded ST. AUGUSTINE, the oldest European city in what is now the United States.

The West. Spanish authorities also sent expeditions to the Spanish Borderlands to look for the SEVEN CITIES OF CÍBOLA, mythical cities filled with gold and precious gems. In 1536 Cabeza de Vaca and Esteban arrived in Mexico after an eight-year journey across North America. Cabeza de Vaca repeated tales he had heard from Indians about towns of great wealth in the interior of the continent. The Spanish listened eagerly, hoping for treasures such as those found in Mexico and Peru. In 1539 Antonio de Mendoza, the viceroy* of NEW SPAIN, sent Marcos de Niza to explore Indian trails to the north, with Esteban as his guide. After Esteban died at the hands of hostile Indians, Niza returned to New Spain with word that the Seven Cities of Cíbola lay far to the north.

* ***viceroy*** person appointed as a monarch's representative to govern a province or colony

Mendoza then sent Francisco Vásquez de CORONADO with a major military expedition to locate Cíbola. Coronado found that the "cities" were actually poor Indian villages with no gold or treasures. After venturing into the interior as far as present-day Kansas, Coronado returned home empty-handed. Although his journey and that of de Soto had revealed the enormous size of North America and charted some of its geography, they had failed to find riches. Neither did the expeditions lead to large-scale colonization.

In the mid-1500s, the Spanish surveyed the continent's west coast. João Rodrigues Cabrilho, a Portuguese navigator working for Spain, left a port in northwest Mexico in 1542. Like other Europeans who explored the Pacific coast, he hoped to find the western end of a Northwest Passage through the continent. Although Cabrilho discovered San Diego Bay and Catalina Island, he never found the water route he sought. He died during the voyage, but his men continued north along the coast of what is now Oregon before returning to Mexico.

Remember: *Consult the index at the end of Volume 4 to find more information on many topics.*

Sebastián Vizcaíno led one of the most significant coastal voyages in 1602. His mission was to locate harbors where Spanish ships sailing from the Philippines to Mexico could land safely if blown off course. Vizcaíno explored the California coast, discovered Monterey Bay, and produced the first detailed charts of the coastal region.

About the same time, Juan de OÑATE led an expedition east into the Great Plains, west as far as the mouth of the Colorado River, and north as far as what is now Kansas, searching for mythical golden cities. In 1598 Oñate and his followers founded New Mexico's first permanent colony, a remote outpost on the northern frontier of New Spain. After about ten years, the Spaniards moved the capital of their colony south to a new settlement called SANTA FE. Soon after, Spain suspended exploration in North America while it focused on other parts of its empire and wars and politics in Europe. Not until the 1700s did significant numbers of Spanish explorers, soldiers, missionaries, and settlers push north from Mexico. Gaspar de PORTOLÁ and Father Junípero SERRA traveled overland to California, founding San Diego in 1769 and a series of other MISSIONS and forts in the following years.

British Exploration

When the Age of Exploration began, English mariners had already had years of experience sailing and navigating in the stormy North Atlantic Ocean. They were fishing off the coast of Iceland by the late 1300s, and seafaring traders and merchants from England's east and west coasts soon ventured to Iceland as well. Yet England's entry into world exploration was slow and halting. Unlike the Portuguese and Spanish, the English did not see the "New World discoveries" of the 1400s and 1500s as a source of profit and power. They also hesitated to trespass on the territories claimed by their powerful rival—Spain.

Beginning in the late 1500s, the English began to make greater efforts to seek out opportunities in the Americas, partly as a result of Spain's weakening power. At first they focused on finding a Northwest Passage through

North America, but after establishing their first North American colonies, they began exploring the continent's interior.

Early Voyages. English fishing vessels may have reached Newfoundland as early as the 1480s, although there are no records to prove this. England's first known voyage to the Americas was made by an Italian navigator, John Cabot. In 1497 he sailed west across the North Atlantic and landed off the coast of Newfoundland, which he believed to be the eastern shore of China. In a second expedition from England in 1498, Cabot was lost

The earliest British and Dutch expeditions on the northeastern coast of North America. Navigators such as Sebastian Cabot, Henry Hudson, John Davis, and Martin Frobisher explored this area in search of the fabled Northwest Passage, which would provide a long-sought sea route to Asia.

ENGLISH AND DUTCH EXPLORATION OF NORTH AMERICA, 1497–1610

Baffin Bay
GREENLAND
John Davis
Davis Strait
Baffin Island
Sebastian Cabot
Frobisher
Hudson
Frobisher Bay
Hudson Strait
N
E
W
S
John Cabot
Hudson Bay
LABRADOR
NEWFOUNDLAND
Gulf of St. Lawrence
NEW BRUNSWICK
ACADIA
Hudson
St. Lawrence River
Hudson River
Sebastian Cabot
ATLANTIC OCEAN

ENGLISH
John Cabot (1497)
Sebastian Cabot (1508)
Martin Frobisher (1576)
John Davis (1585–1587)
Henry Hudson (1610)
DUTCH
Henry Hudson (1609)

0 250 500 Miles

English explorers landed at Roanoke Island (in present-day North Carolina) in 1584. They had been sent by Sir Walter Raleigh to locate a good site for a colony. The Roanoke colony was founded there the following year.

at sea. England used Cabot's voyages as the basis for its claims to North America. Spain insisted that the lands fell within the territory granted to it by the 1494 Treaty of Tordesillas. The English king Henry VII took another view—that occupation should be the primary factor in determining claims in the Americas.

John Cabot's reports that the waters around Newfoundland were teeming with fish sent English fishermen from Bristol across the Atlantic. In the early 1500s, the boats came back from their American voyages loaded with fish. But Bristol merchants did not support further exploration because they saw little opportunity for profitable trade in the northern lands across the sea.

John Cabot's son Sebastian was the first explorer to seek the Northwest Passage. On a voyage in 1508, he may have sailed as far north as the entrance to Hudson Bay before large chunks of floating ice forced him to turn back. Cabot returned to England in 1509 but failed to convince the king to support another expedition.

Seventy years went by before the English resumed their exploration of North America. Driven by the desire to find a Northwest Passage, Martin Frobisher sailed along the southern coast of Baffin Island in 1576. He returned to the same region two years later. Frobisher was doomed to disappointment—the waterway he thought was the Northwest Passage proved to be only a bay. He also shipped back to England hundreds of tons of rocks he believed contained gold, but the rocks turned out to be worthless. The unlucky Frobisher did, however, see the waterway now called Hudson Strait, which leads into Hudson Bay. Some people thought the Hudson Strait might be the Northwest Passage.

John Davis made several voyages to North America in the late 1580s. Ice prevented him from entering the Hudson Strait, but he explored another, larger waterway between Greenland and Baffin Island. Davis followed this passage until it, too, was blocked by ice. Although he could not prove that this waterway—now called Davis Strait—was the Northwest Passage, he did survey the west coast of Greenland and the east coast of Baffin Island.

The English mariner Henry HUDSON made his first voyage to North America for the Dutch, but in 1610 he set out to explore the Davis Strait for his homeland. He managed to enter the waterway Frobisher had sighted, which led Hudson to the huge bay that now bears his name. After spending a harsh winter on an island in the bay, Hudson planned to continue his explorations to the west, but his men mutinied and left him there to die. They did, however, carry his map of the bay back to Europe. Hudson's voyage established the English claim to the region around Hudson Bay. A few decades later, an English company set up trading posts on the shores of the bay to bargain with Indians for fur pelts*. The HUDSON'S BAY COMPANY was the beginning of English Canada.

* ***pelt*** skin and fur of an animal

During the 1500s, the English had begun to threaten Spanish settlements on the west coast of Central and South America. In the late 1570s, Francis DRAKE sailed around South America and headed north along the Pacific coast, plundering numerous Spanish ports along the way. He searched in vain for the western outlet of a Northwest Passage. Drake did land in present-day California in 1578, claiming the land he called New Albion for England. The English did not follow up this claim, however, and Spain later ignored it.

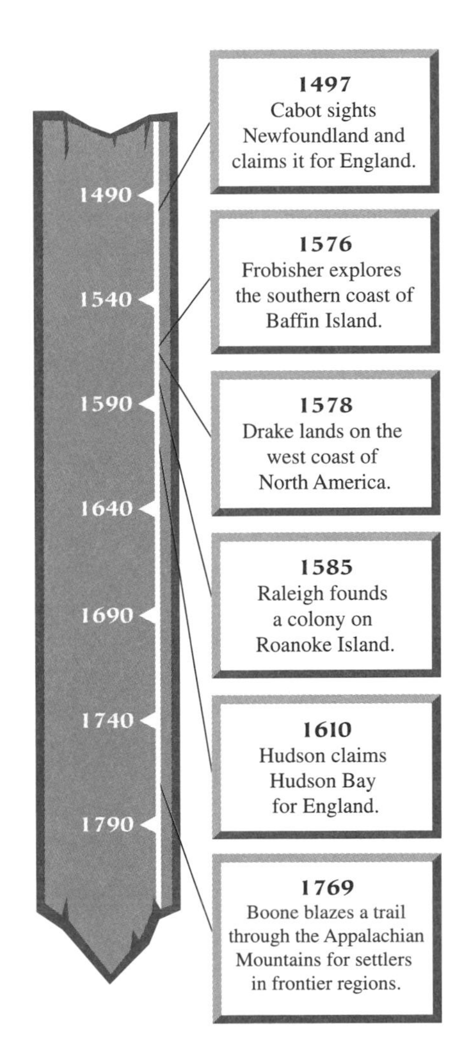

Into the Interior. Meanwhile, the English began to make plans for colonies in North America. In the late 1500s, Humphrey GILBERT set sail for the "New World" to establish a colony. The first time bad weather forced him to turn back. The second time, in 1583, he took possession of Newfoundland but lost his life at sea on the way back to England.

A few years later Gilbert's half-brother, Walter RALEIGH, founded a short-lived settlement at ROANOKE ISLAND that led to English exploration of the region. Two men from the colony, John WHITE and Thomas Harriot, surveyed and mapped the country as far north as Chesapeake Bay. Upon returning to England, Harriot published a booklet about America, and many of White's drawings were engraved and published. Their works gave Europeans some early images of the continent.

In 1607 a more stable colony took root at JAMESTOWN in present-day Virginia. The colony's leader, John SMITH, mapped the Chesapeake Bay and the nearby rivers, including the James, Potomac, and Rappahannock. His maps of the bay region aided colonists and mariners for the next hundred years.

After the first colonies were established along the Atlantic coast, the English began venturing farther west. Unlike previous explorers, they were looking primarily for fertile farmland rather than gold. But the APPALACHIAN MOUNTAINS, which run parallel to the coast, presented an obstacle to both exploration and expansion. Beginning in the 1650s, colonists made repeated attempts to find a route through the mountains. Eventually, several explorers and traders discovered trails that pioneers could follow across the Appalachians to the Ohio River valley.

The westward movement of the colonists gathered speed in the 1700s. Governor Alexander Spotswood of Virginia blazed a trail into the Shenandoah Valley of western Virginia in 1716. In the 1770s, not long before the American colonies declared their independence from Britain, Daniel Boone established a route through the Cumberland Gap of the Appalachians into Kentucky, and he led groups of settlers westward over that route. Several roads to the American heartland now lay open to pioneers from the East.

Far to the north, England was beginning to investigate the vast interior of Canada. During the first century or so of its operation, the Hudson's Bay Company had done little exploration. In the 1690s, Henry Kelsey, a company official, accompanied a group of Indians all the way to the plains of Saskatchewan in western Canada. But his report on opportunities in the west aroused little enthusiasm among leaders of the company, who preferred to let Indians bring their trade goods to the company's eastern posts.

In the 1730s, French Canadian traders moved north and west from the ST. LAWRENCE RIVER and captured some of the FUR TRADE from the Hudson's Bay Company. In an effort to expand its territory, the company sent agents to explore and chart the interior. In 1770 Samuel Hearne, with the help of an Indian guide named Mattonabe, crossed a huge portion of the Canadian interior to reach the coast of the Arctic Ocean. In 1783 some Montreal traders formed the North West Company to compete with Hudson's Bay. North West employees explored the Rocky Mountains and the western lands. The company's most notable explorer, Alexander Mackenzie, became the first European to cross the entire continent. He traveled overland from central Canada to the Pacific Ocean in 1793, more than ten years before American explorers Lewis and Clark reached the Pacific. By that time, the British navigators James Cook and George Vancouver had finished mapping the west coast of North America. Many parts of the interior and the Arctic regions remained to be charted, but the shape and size of the continent were no longer a mystery.

Remember: *Consult the index at the end of Volume 4 to find more information on many topics.*

Dutch Exploration

The Dutch arrived late in the Americas. During the early part of the Age of Exploration, the Netherlands was not a unified nation but a cluster of independent city-states and provinces under the control of Spain. After Portugal opened the sea route around Africa to Asia, many Dutch mariners sailed to the Indies in the service of Portugal. In the late 1500s, the Dutch provinces united and declared their independence, and the merchants of Amsterdam began forming companies to send their own ships to Asia for spices. Out of these enterprises emerged the DUTCH EAST INDIA COMPANY. At the same time, the Dutch sent expeditions to explore the waters beyond Scandinavia, looking for a sea passage eastward to the Indies.

The Dutch began to take an interest in North America in the early 1600s. Dutch trading firms sent ships to Newfoundland and the St. Lawrence River for fish and furs. In 1609 the Dutch East India Company hired the English mariner Henry Hudson to look for the Northeast Passage in northern Europe.

After encountering bitterly cold weather and stormy seas, Hudson's crew convinced him to abandon the original plan. The mariner decided to cross the Atlantic and explore the coast of what is now southern New England. Sailing along the shore, Hudson came to a river that the Italian navigator Giovanni da Verrazano had discovered in 1524. Hudson hoped that this might prove to be the Northwest Passage. He sailed up the river—today known as the Hudson—as far as the site of modern ALBANY, New York, before the water became too shallow to continue. The East India Company established a fur-trading post, Fort Nassau, there in 1613. About ten years later, another Dutch trading company received authorization to establish a colony in this area and founded two settlements—Fort Orange, at the site of Fort Nassau on the Hudson, and NEW AMSTERDAM on Manhattan Island, at the mouth of the river.

Fur Wars

Many French fur traders were also explorers. In 1659–1660 Pierre Esprit Radisson and his brother-in-law, Médard Chouart, Sieur des Groseilliers, traveled deep into the unknown interior—perhaps as far as present-day Minnesota—and returned with a huge load of furs. The French authorities seized the furs because Radisson and Groseilliers did not have official permission to engage in fur trading. Disgusted, the two men offered their services to the English and soon opened a trading post on Hudson Bay. Their enterprise became the Hudson's Bay Company, which competed fiercely with the French fur traders for many years.

French Exploration

During the 1400s, France was more concerned about strengthening its position in the Mediterranean region than in exploring the world. Still, in the early 1500s, French fishermen learned the route to the fishing grounds off the Newfoundland coast. In 1522, after one of Magellan's ships returned to Europe from the first round-the-world voyage, the French king Francis I and his country's silk merchants decided to sponsor a search for a better route to the Indies.

The French hired Giovanni da Verrazano to lead their expedition. In 1524 he sailed to present-day North Carolina and then headed north to Newfoundland, examining the coast as he went for signs of the Northwest Passage. During his journey he sighted New York Bay, Block Island, and the mouth of the Hudson River. Verrazano and his crew made several stops along the coast, trading with local Indians and exploring the continent's natural resources. Verrazano's expedition firmly established France's presence in the "New World."

Along the St. Lawrence. Francis I continued his efforts to claim part of North America's riches for France. In 1535 the king sent Jacques CARTIER to investigate reports of a large waterway that appeared to lead into the interior of the continent, as well as to look for "gold and other things." Cartier became the first European to navigate and map the Gulf of St. Lawrence. During his voyage, he also established relations with the HURON INDIANS, who later became important French allies. After a brief visit to France, Cartier resumed his exploration of the area. This time his Indian allies led him to the St. Lawrence River, which he followed as far as present-day MONTREAL before coming up against impassable rapids. He and his men spent a winter near Montreal, an experience they barely survived, and sailed back to France in 1536.

In 1541 the French king sent Cartier on a third voyage to locate a mythical kingdom of great wealth the Hurons had described and to found a colony on the St. Lawrence. The colony failed, as did Cartier's attempt to find riches. Like the English explorer Martin Frobisher, he carried back a load of worthless rocks, believing that they contained gold and diamonds. But Cartier's explorations were of great value. The St. Lawrence River that he discovered and mapped gave France a major route to the interior of North America.

In the years following Cartier's voyages, France abandoned exploration and colonization along the St. Lawrence, though French traders continued to visit the region for fish and furs. Meanwhile, a group of French Protestants tried to found a settlement far to the south. In the 1560s, these HUGUENOTS explored the southeastern coast of North America, looking for both riches and a refuge where they could be safe from religious persecution. They attempted to establish colonies in South Carolina and in Florida, but the Spanish drove them out of both places. The Huguenots' efforts did

French exploration in North America focused on two areas: eastern Canada and the Mississippi River valley. These two regions developed into the French colonies of New France and Louisiana. France quickly established friendly relations with the Indians, who became important partners in the profitable fur trade.

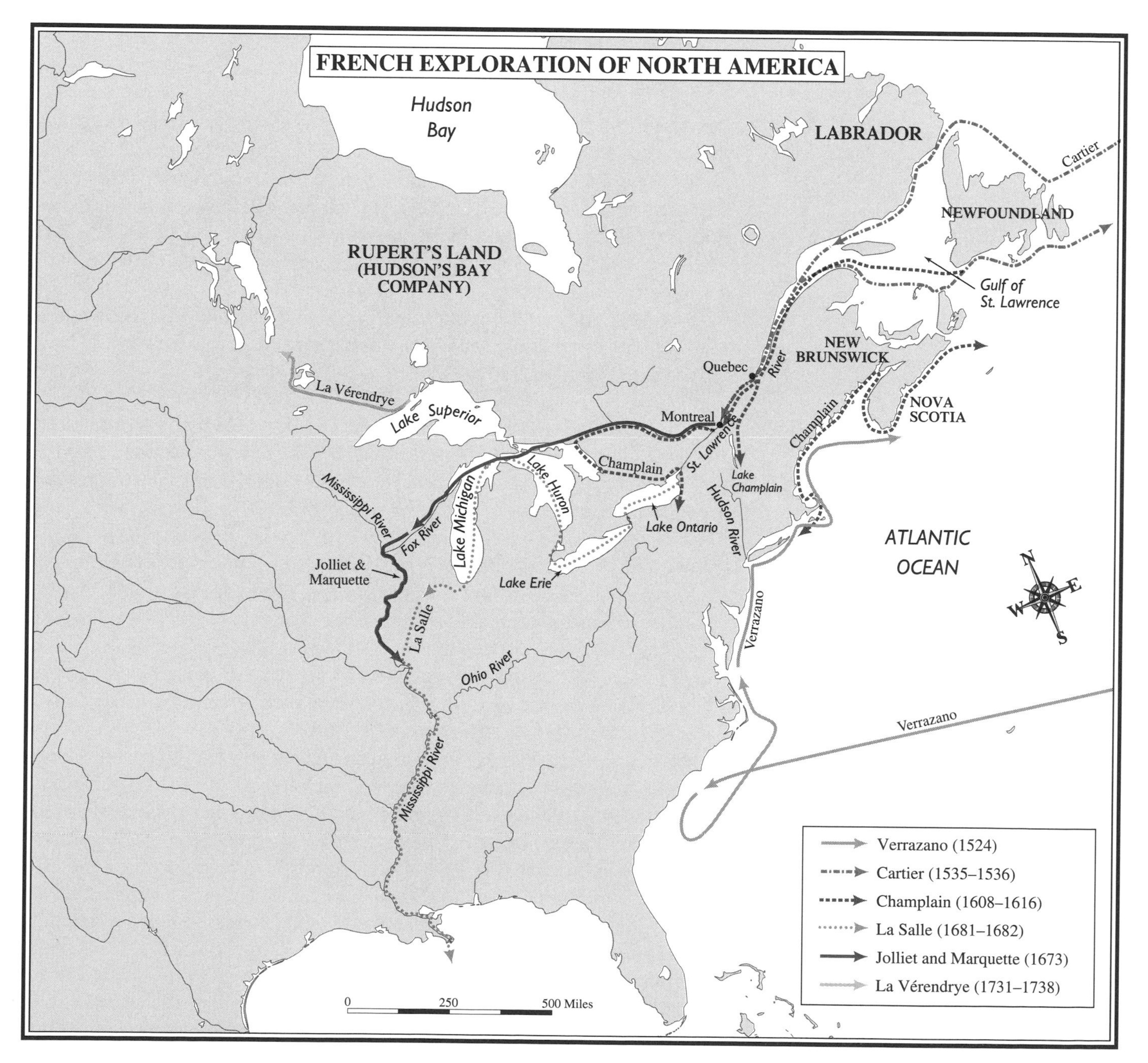

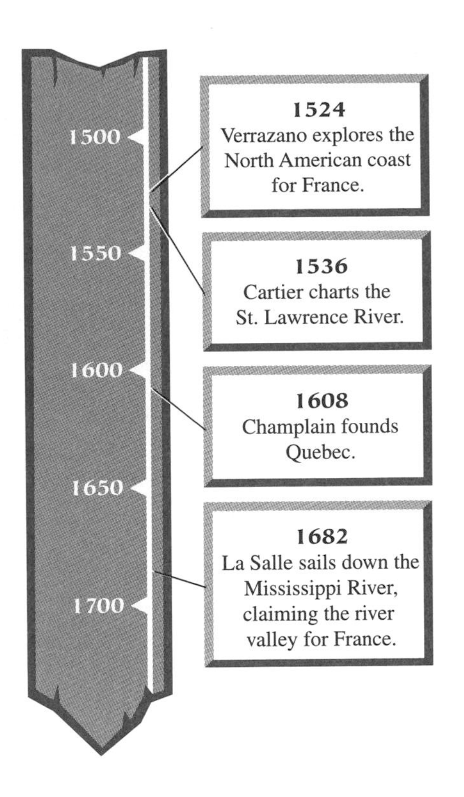

lead to the founding of the Spanish city of St. Augustine as a base from which to attack the French.

French exploration of what is now Canada resumed in the 1600s with Samuel de Champlain. Coming to the St. Lawrence in 1603 as the geographer and chart maker for a trading expedition, Champlain surveyed the river in greater detail than Cartier had done. A year later he and Pierre du Gua, Sieur de Monts—who held an exclusive royal permit to trade in and colonize New France—brought a group of settlers to North America. After establishing a temporary base in Acadia—present-day Nova Scotia—Champlain spent years exploring and mapping the North Atlantic coast as he searched for a permanent location. The colony came to an abrupt end after the French king withdrew Monts's royal permit.

In 1608 Champlain founded another small settlement called Quebec, which he hoped would become the center of a large and prosperous colony built on fur trading. Champlain strongly believed that a network of trails and waterways linking the interior and Quebec was necessary to the success of New France. He devoted years to exploring and mapping the region from the east coast to the Great Lakes, laying the foundation for France's colonial empire in North America. Champlain also formed valuable and long-lasting alliances with the Algonquin and Huron Indians.

In 1618 Champlain still believed that the St. Lawrence River would turn out to be the Northwest Passage. Trying to win the king's support for the colony, Champlain listed all the resources of New France. One of them was "that shortcut to China by way of the St. Lawrence River." The dream of the Northwest Passage remained alive.

Down the Mississippi. In 1634 Champlain sent Jean Nicolet on an expedition that led to Lake Michigan. The Indian guides who had brought Nicolet there told him of a great river nearby that flowed to the sea. Assuming that the river the Indians had described must lead into the Pacific Ocean, the French believed they were finally close to finding a waterway to Asia.

War with the Iroquois Indians—traditional enemies of France's Indian allies, the Algonquin and the Huron—occupied New France for many years. Not until 1673 could the authorities send an expedition to follow the course of the rumored river. The expedition's leaders were Louis Jolliet and Father Jacques Marquette, a missionary. After crossing Lake Michigan to the Fox River on the west side of the lake, they made the portage* to the large river they hoped would lead to the Pacific.

* ***portage*** carrying of goods or boats from one body of water to another

The explorers soon realized that this river was the center of a huge drainage system. They also determined, with considerable disappointment, that they were traveling south—not west. It became clear that this river, the Mississippi, emptied into the Gulf of Mexico rather than the Pacific Ocean. Its southern branches had been known to Europeans since the explorations of Hernando de Soto more than a century earlier. Not wanting to run into any Spanish patrols, Jolliet and Marquette turned back about 400 miles from the mouth of the Mississippi.

Nine years later another French explorer, René-Robert Cavelier de La Salle, traveled all the way down the Mississippi to its mouth. La Salle later died in an unsuccessful attempt to establish a French colony on the Gulf

This engraving bears the title *The Unfortunate Adventures of Sieur de La Salle,* because it shows the French explorer's ill-fated attempt in 1685 to establish a French colony in what is now Texas.

coast. He did, however, claim the entire Mississippi River valley for France, which became the basis of the French colony of LOUISIANA.

As the French completed their exploration of the Great Lakes and the Mississippi, they developed a theory that an inland sea lay west of the Great Lakes. This imaginary body of water appeared on French maps of the time labeled Mer de l'Ouest (Sea of the West). The French believed it was connected on the west to the Pacific Ocean and on the east to the river-and-lake network they were busy charting.

Among the first explorers to search for the Mer de l'Ouest was Pierre Gaultier de Varennes, Sieur de La Vérendrye. He and his four sons pushed the frontiers of the French empire farther west. In 1731 they established fur-trading posts at a place called Lake of the Woods on the Red River in Canada, far to the west of the Great Lakes and the Mississippi. Here they heard stories of people living to the south on the banks of a great river. Thinking that they were on the trail of the western sea, the explorers traveled south into the present-day Dakotas. Eventually they reached the settlements

of the Mandan Indians along the Missouri River, which flows southeast to empty into the Mississippi—not west as they had hoped.

La Vérendrye and his sons made other journeys of exploration to the Saskatchewan River and the Dakota Black Hills. Neither they nor anyone else found a trace of the Mer de l'Ouest, and French hopes of an easy waterway to the Pacific faded. But the fur trade boomed, and by the middle of the 1700s France controlled the trade with the Indians of the North American interior.

France's domination did not last long. By 1763 Britain had defeated its long-term enemy in the FRENCH AND INDIAN WAR and taken possession of French territories in North America. The Age of Exploration had ended, the North American colonial era was drawing to a close, and the only European powers that remained on the continent were Spain and Great Britain. (*See also* **European Empires; Fish and Fishing; Frontier; Maps and Charts; Norse Settlements; Ships and Shipbuilding.**)

Family

Every culture has its own idea of family. Most societies think of it as a group of people who live together and are related to one another by ties of blood or marriage. In some cultures, a family consists only of a man, a woman, and their children—a grouping known as a nuclear family. In others, the definition of family includes grandparents, aunts, uncles, cousins, and others—an extended family.

The roles and responsibilities of individuals within a family also vary, according to the laws, religious beliefs, and customs of each culture. In general, though, most societies expect adults to marry and produce children, parents to care for their children and prepare them for adult life, and children to obey and respect their parents.

The North American colonies were a meeting ground for different types of families. Native Americans defined family in various ways. European settlers brought the family systems of their homelands, sometimes changing old patterns to meet the demands of colonial life. African Americans—free blacks as well as slaves—struggled to preserve some elements of their traditional family structures.

Although these peoples defined family in different ways, each regarded it as the basic building block of society. The family influenced everything from an individual's social position to the organization of entire communities. In frontier regions, where settlers often lived far apart with no close neighbors, a family became an entire society in itself. Members of frontier families did not merely care for one another but relied on the labor and skills of each other for survival.

Native American Families

Each North American Indian group had its own customs regarding the living arrangements for newlyweds. New couples rarely set up independent households apart from the husband's or wife's family. Most often the couple lived with or very near a senior family member—the husband's father or uncle in

This watercolor by John White shows a woman of the Pomeiooc tribe with her young daughter. Native American children were raised by their grandparents, aunts, and uncles, as well as their parents.

some tribes, the wife's mother in others. Sometimes a young couple resided with the wife's family until the birth of their first child and then moved to join the husband's family. Among other Indian groups, the husband and wife divided time between both of their families. All these arrangements reflected the basic idea that a family included not just parents and children but also a large community of relatives.

Grandparents, aunts, and uncles all took a major role in raising children. Native Americans did not punish their children often or harshly, but they did discipline youngsters when they considered it necessary. The task of handing out punishment often fell to a child's uncle rather than the parents. Grandparents shared with parents the responsibility for teaching skills and moral behavior to the young.

Some Indian groups allowed men to have more than one wife at a time. Societies that did not follow this practice generally permitted married couples to divorce, and divorce occurred frequently. As a result, many Native American men and women had more than one spouse in the course of their lives.

In the East, Southwest, and Pacific Northwest, Indians often belonged to clans—groups of related families—as well as to families. The clan was a unit of social organization that created bonds of kinship among people who might or might not be related by blood. Each village or community consisted of members of a number of clans. Most of these were named for animals, such as the Raven clan or the Bear clan. Depending on the particular Indian tribe, a child belonged to either the mother's or the father's clan.

Clans served a variety of purposes. Sometimes they controlled names, so that each child received a personal name that belonged only to his or her clan. In some societies, certain responsibilities—such as performing religious rituals or leading war parties—were associated with particular clans, and important positions in the community could be held only by members of a specific clan. All clans offered their members benefits and expected them to meet certain obligations, such as offering hospitality to other members of the clan who visited their village. If an individual from one clan murdered someone from another clan, the killer's clan provided compensation to the family of the victim.

Clan members regarded themselves as kin and called each other brother and sister. Membership gave Native Americans an additional level of identity and support that was larger than family but smaller than the community as a whole. One rule followed by almost all Native Americans was that members of the same clan could not marry each other.

British Colonial Families

The people who settled the British colonies of North America came from a variety of backgrounds. The new arrivals included members of such religious groups as PURITANS, QUAKERS, and Anglicans, as well as indentured servants*. Not all of them were English. Beginning about 1720, large numbers of immigrants arrived from Scotland and Ireland, often settling in the backcountry and on the western frontier. Many Germans made their homes in Pennsylvania and the southern backcountry. Throughout the colonial period, however, most families in the British colonies shared and were shaped by certain traditional ideas. Aside from these ideas, family structures differed from region to region because of religious, economic, and cultural variations in the population.

* ***indentured servant*** person who agreed to work a certain length of time in return for passage on a ship to the colonies

Traditional Family Structure. Most families throughout the colonies shared certain "English" views about marriage and the family. The most basic of these was that the family was the central unit of the community and the state. People did not think it desirable to remain unmarried, and forming a family was considered the ideal.

A traditional family consisted of a man, a woman, and their children. This nuclear family lived in a house of its own, apart from other relatives, whenever possible. Yet many households included various nonrelatives, such as servants and apprentices. Marriage was a lifetime contract, and divorce was extremely rare (although married couples did sometimes separate). Sexual activity was mostly limited to married people. When a woman wed, she gave up her personal rights and property to her husband and became dependent on him for everything. This meant, in most cases, that she could no longer conduct business in her own name.

The husband and father was the head of the household. He could discipline children, wife, and servants as he saw fit, although society disapproved of brutality. He controlled the family's money and assigned the work to be done by family members. In matters of inheritance, fathers generally divided land among all their sons instead of leaving it all to the oldest son, as was common in Britain. Daughters usually received a share of other wealth, such as money or slaves. Patterns of inheritance varied greatly from colony to colony, however, and fathers could dispose of property in any way they chose.

Children were expected either to live with their parents or to place themselves under another adult's supervision—perhaps by becoming a servant or

Charles Willson Peale's painting of his family includes his wife and child, their servant, his two brothers, his mother, and his sisters.

apprentice—until they could afford to marry. It was not customary for young single adults to set up households of their own. Most elderly widows and widowers, on the other hand, lived alone if health and finances allowed them to do so. Those who could not manage on their own might share a residence with an unmarried child or grandchild.

Regional Variations. Many of the people who settled in the Chesapeake Bay region in the 1600s were young, unmarried laborers and indentured servants who had come to America in search of work and other opportunities. Family life in the region was shaped by two important factors: a high death rate and a shortage of women. The Chesapeake region proved unhealthy for English settlers—many died of malaria and other DISEASES. A third of all indentured servants failed to live out their period of service, and less than half the babies born in the region survived to reach adulthood. Many children lost one or both parents. A surviving parent generally remarried, which meant that households often included stepsiblings* and half siblings.

* ***sibling*** brother or sister

In a society where so many parents died early, childhood was brief. Young people married earlier in the Chesapeake region than in other parts of the British colonies. Yet many men could not find wives because far more men than women settled in the region. It took several generations before American-born girls began to even the balance between men and women in the population.

Later generations of families in the Chesapeake region and other parts of the South faced the same difficult conditions as the early immigrants. But they had the advantage of a large network of siblings and other relatives. Members of extended families often lived near one another and helped each other through illnesses, financial problems, and other difficulties. Respect for family helped shape the tradition of southern hospitality, which required people to come to the assistance of relatives in need and to take orphaned kinfolk into their homes.

Unlike the Chesapeake region, New England was settled primarily by families with children. The people of New England tended to live longer than those in the Chesapeake—and to marry later, at the age of 25 or 26 for men and 23 or 24 for women. Because parents lived longer, households with stepsiblings and half siblings were uncommon, and most adults lived to see their grandchildren. Families were generally larger than in the Chesapeake region—often up to eight or nine children, of whom perhaps six or seven managed to survive to adulthood.

The Puritans of New England kept the basic structure of the English family but changed it slightly to reflect their religious beliefs. New Englanders enforced rules against sexual misbehavior, such as unwed pregnancy, more strictly than in England. At the same time, they allowed married couples to divorce more easily under certain circumstances. Family life was closely linked to religious life, and church leaders took an active interest in how parents were educating their children. In turn, parents felt that their most important responsibility was to give their children moral, spiritual, and religious guidance.

The Quakers of Pennsylvania and other middle colonies had a slightly broader idea of family than their neighbors to the north and south. Aunts, uncles, and cousins played an important role in family life, and parents frequently turned to relatives and neighbors for help in raising children. Older members of Quaker communities often counseled families and provided guidance—even in matters that most people today regard as private. Young Quaker men and women, for example, had to gain the approval of community elders before they could marry, and the process could take months.

By the mid-1700s, family life throughout the British colonies had begun to change. An increase in nonfarming jobs made it easier for young people to find work away from home and to start new lives elsewhere. The authority of fathers declined somewhat because they could no longer control children by withholding the land or money young adults needed to become independent. Along with a weakening of parental authority came an increase in sexual freedom among young people. In the 1600s, fewer than 10 percent of brides were pregnant when they married, but by the mid-1700s, the number of pregnant brides had increased to about 40 percent. At the same time, open displays of affection among family members became more common, and married couples increasingly called each other "dear" and "honey" rather than "Sir" or "Madam" as in earlier times.

Public documents—birth and death records, wills, and law codes—provide the basic facts of family life in the British colonies. Other documents, such as letters and diaries, offer more intimate glimpses of family relationships. Although the quality of family life undoubtedly varied from household to household, the British colonists knew the same joys and troubles that families experience in most places and times.

Dutch Colonial Families

Dutch colonists in NEW NETHERLAND followed the model of family life in their homeland. By the 1600s, the Netherlands had the most urbanized* and educated population in Europe. Dutch women possessed greater rights and freedoms than women in other countries, including the right to own property and carry on business in their own names even after marriage. Male and female children in the Netherlands tended to receive equal shares of family inheritances. Prenuptial agreements—contracts that spelled out the rights of each partner in a planned marriage—were common.

* ***urbanized*** concentrated in cities and towns

Men and women in the Netherlands tended to marry between the ages of 24 and 29, and the average family had two children. Households usually consisted of a nuclear family, and Dutch parents were less likely than other Europeans to allow in-laws and relatives, church elders, or the community to interfere in their lives. People cherished the right to educate their children as they thought best and to attend the church of their choice.

This orderly family life was missing from New Netherland in the early years of settlement. Although the colony's first wave of immigrants in the 1620s included some families, most of the early settlers were young, single men interested more in wealth than in marriage and family. Women were in short supply. The turbulent and rather primitive society of early New Netherland made it difficult to establish stable families, and domestic violence was not unknown.

Because New Netherland was largely agricultural, life in the colony centered around the home. This farmhouse, painted by John Heaten in the early 1700s, belonged to the Van Bergens, a Dutch colonial family who remained after the English took over New Netherland.

Immigration to New Netherland began to increase in the mid-1640s. From that time on, the majority of immigrants were families, usually young couples with small children. The dangers, hardships, and diseases of frontier life contributed to a high death rate, and it was not uncommon for a wife or husband to lose a spouse. The surviving partner usually remarried, which meant that families might include stepsiblings or half siblings. As the population grew, the colonists focused more on families. One official wrote in 1653, "Children and pigs multiply here rapidly and more than anything else." Colonial families tended to be larger than those in the Netherlands. One scholar estimates that Dutch marriages of the late 1600s produced an average of six children. Because New Netherland lacked networks of schools, churches, and social clubs, family became even more important in the colony than in the home country. The home was not only the basic economic unit of a largely agricultural society; it was also the place where young people received much of their education and religious training.

Women and children were respected in society because their labor played a significant role in family survival. Colonial wives and daughters enjoyed more rights and freedoms than women in the Netherlands. They not only managed the household but also were actively involved in the family's business and finances. Sometimes women continued farming, trading, or practicing the family craft after their husbands or fathers died.

When the English took over New Netherland in 1664, many Dutch colonists remained. Under the agreement covering the transfer of power, these colonists were permitted to keep their traditional ways of dealing with

> ### *The King's Girls*
> The French royal government wanted to turn the rowdy bachelor society of early New France into an orderly, family-based colony. Royal officials tried to encourage marriage in the colony, but New France had few women. To solve the problem, the French crown sent 774 young women to the colony between 1663 and 1673. The king paid for the voyages and presented each woman with a dowry, a sum of money for her future husband. These women—called the *filles du roi* (the king's girls or daughters)—were orphans from religious charity houses in France. All were married soon after arriving in Quebec.

property rights and patterns of inheritance. As a result, Dutch families in New York were in some ways more modern—with a higher degree of equality between men and women—than the English families around them.

French Colonial Families

As in other parts of colonial America, men at first outnumbered women in NEW FRANCE and LOUISIANA and thus had difficulty finding wives. An official count of the French settlement of Montreal in 1681, for example, showed that more than 20 percent of the households belonged to single people—nearly all of them men. The same census showed that bachelors outnumbered unmarried women by ten to one. With such a shortage of European women, many men in New France lived with Indian women. In Louisiana they formed relationships with both Indian and African women. Although the French authorities disapproved of marriage between races, local Catholic priests often married mixed-race couples to prevent people from engaging in sexual activity outside of marriage.

Both the church and the government wanted to encourage the development of stable, law-abiding families in the colonies. The government tried to encourage population growth by imposing fines on bachelors and rewarding parents who had ten or more living children. But such measures had little effect on the formation of families. More important were the availability of women and the influence of French laws and customs.

French family law was based on a code of law known as the Coutume de Paris (Custom of Paris). This legal code, which applied throughout the French colonies, spelled out the rights and obligations of all family members in matters concerning property and personal relationships. The French believed that a family should ensure the financial security of its members. For this reason, the Coutume de Paris provided for a "community of property" between husband and wife in which they shared all property. Although the husband was head of the household and managed the property, he had to consult with his wife and other relatives before making important decisions. If he managed the family estate badly, his wife could sue him. The wife's rights to her portion of shared property were generally guaranteed in a marriage contract.

Disagreements between husband and wife rarely led to the breakdown of a marriage. But the Coutume de Paris allowed couples to divorce if their marriages fell apart. Women applied for divorce far more often than men, often complaining of drunkenness, abusive violence, or "familial irresponsibility." This last complaint usually meant that the man had failed to support his family or play his proper role in family life.

French family law gave parents a great deal of control over their children. Individuals were not considered adults until they reached the age of 25. Before that time, they needed the approval of their parents or guardians to manage property on their own. A daughter needed permission to marry before age 25, while a son could not marry without his father's consent before age 30. But permission to marry before those ages must have been fairly common because the average age for marriage in the French colonies was 22 for women and 28 for men.

The Coutume de Paris mattered a good deal to members of the colonial upper classes—merchants, public officials, and military officers. For these

* ***status*** social position

educated and prosperous groups, marriage was much less a question of individual choice than a social and financial alliance between two families. Concerned with maintaining their status* and property, families exercised considerable control over the selection of spouses for their children. Marriages were accompanied by careful negotiations over property and wealth. The relatives of both the bride and the groom wanted to make certain that family wealth and property would not pass to the other family in case of death.

Such concerns were less important to the great majority of the colonists who lived by farming. Although the law granted authority to husbands and fathers, the practical demands of farm life meant that women often helped make decisions and manage property. Their labor, as well as that of children, was vital to the proper running of the farm. Children shared in farmwork until they could establish homes and families of their own. They often had more influence in choosing a marriage partner than the children of the upper classes, and they usually shared more equally in inheritance when their parents died.

A notable exception to settled family life in New France could be found among the fur traders, where single men worked as trappers or boatmen. Some men involved in the fur trade married, had children, and lived in settled communities. Many, however, spent a good part of their lives on the frontier, often maintaining families with Indian women.

Spanish Colonial Families

Remember: *Words in small capital letters have separate entries, and the index at the end of Volume 4 will guide you to more information on many topics.*

The Spanish idea of family was shaped by two forces: ancient Roman law and the ROMAN CATHOLIC CHURCH. The Spanish had incorporated many Roman legal principles into their law, including the idea of *familia,* or family. In ancient Rome, a family included slaves—and anyone else over whom the head of a household had legal control—as well as people linked by ties of marriage and kinship. The idea of family had more to do with authority than with blood relationship.

The Roman view of *familia* affected Spanish law and also shaped Spanish ideas about the nature of families. In 1611 a Spanish scholar defined a family as "the lord and his wife, and the rest of the individuals under his command, such as children, servants, and slaves." First and foremost, the Spanish family was a structure of authority, not of affection—though normal emotional ties certainly existed within families. People thought of a family household as a type of domestic kingdom, with the father at its head like a king. When children married, they left the father's authority and started new families of their own.

The Church and the Family. The second major influence on the Spanish family was the Roman Catholic Church. Church leaders disapproved of the great power a father had under the law of *familia*—in part because they believed the church should have greater control over people's lives. They tried to limit this power by emphasizing the idea of a "spiritual" family, with the church as its final authority.

Marriage was a common source of conflict between the church, which tried to restrict parental authority, and the law of *familia.* Many parents tried to control the timing of their children's marriage and choice of partner. As in New France, the upper classes tended to regard marriage as a political or economic alliance between families. They often pressured their children to marry against their will or prevented marriages considered unsuitable. The church, however, said that individuals must enter a marriage willingly. As a result, priests might marry couples—sometimes secretly—who had failed to receive parental approval, and they might refuse to unite couples if they believed the individuals were being forced into marriage against their wishes.

One of the most difficult issues faced by church and civil authorities in the Spanish colonies concerned the role of Native Americans. For years they struggled to answer such questions as these: Should Indians be allowed to form families under Spanish law? Should the union of non-Christian Indians be considered a proper marriage? Eventually, Spanish family law was extended to cover the Indians, who then had to give up their own traditions of marriage and family and adopt Spanish customs. Perhaps realizing that relationships between Spanish colonists and Indians would occur with or without the church's blessing, the church made interracial marriage legal.

Spiritual Families. Spanish culture included two forms of kinship based in religious ideas. One was "godparenthood" and the other, open only to men, was brotherhood. Both types of relationship provided emotional support, a sense of identity, and help in times of need. They were especially important in the Spanish Borderlands*, where communities were isolated and the hazardous conditions of frontier life could leave people orphaned or penniless.

* ***Spanish Borderlands*** northern part of New Spain, area now occupied by Florida, Texas, New Mexico, Arizona, and California

Godparenthood, or *compadrazgo,* was a form of spiritual parenthood that often had no connection to blood relationships. Parents chose a set of godparents for each child. The parents and godparents referred to each other as *compadres,* or co-parents. The godparents took part in important religious ceremonies in a child's life, including baptism, confirmation*, and marriage. Their main responsibilities were moral and spiritual—to guide their godchildren toward the right beliefs and behavior and to make sure they followed the laws of the church. Yet the *compadrazgo* relationships often took on other dimensions as well. Godparents generally gave their godchildren gifts on birthdays and other special occasions, and they sometimes provided them with a home, an education, or money to get started in life.

* ***confirmation*** ceremony marking admittance to church membership

Men in the Spanish colonies belonged to brotherhoods, or *cofradías.* These organizations began in Europe in the 1100s as voluntary associations of Christians that helped the poor, the sick, and the homeless. The brotherhoods operated with the consent of the church. Each *cofradía* had rituals*, dues, and rules about who could join. All members were required to perform good works and to celebrate certain religious holidays. The common thread that bound the members of most brotherhoods was the obligation to lead lives of Christian virtue* and to care for the poor, the sick, and the elderly. Because government gave almost no aid to those in need, *cofradías* provided an important social service.

* ***ritual*** ceremony that follows a set pattern

* ***virtue*** moral goodness

Almost every man in the Spanish colonies—whether soldier, colonist, or slave—belonged to one or more brotherhoods. As soon as a church was

built in a settlement, the men of the community formed brotherhoods. Some of these *cofradías* included individuals from different social classes: rich and poor, Spanish and Indian, slave and free. By bringing these different groups together, such brotherhoods helped unite communities and release social tensions that could lead to conflict. Other *cofradías* were open only to people of the same social or economic class. Yet whatever their membership, the *cofradías* created a sense of kinship. They were a family beyond the family.

Remember: *Consult the index at the end of Volume 4 to find more information on many topics.*

African American Families

One of the greatest losses Africans suffered in colonial America was the destruction of their traditional patterns of family life. Most communities in Africa consisted of numerous overlapping networks of family relationships. The families were generally large, and men often had more than one wife. Africans also maintained close relations with all their aunts, uncles, and cousins. In addition, they honored the memories of their ancestors and could trace their families back for many generations.

Blacks in America, whether free or enslaved, were separated from these family networks. Africans brought to America as slaves sometimes tried to replace lost kinsfolk with friendships formed during the terrible voyage across the Atlantic. Deep and lasting relationships begun on slave ships provided much needed emotional, spiritual, and physical support. Children honored such relationships and considered these close friends kinfolk, calling them "aunty" and "uncle" and using other terms of respect.

Relations between black men and women in colonial America were influenced both by African tradition and by the practices of European colonists. In Africa, women entered into marriage with guidance and protection from their extended families. This was not the case in America. European marriage did not give black women the protection they had enjoyed in Africa, such as the right to protest a husband's mistreatment and the right to control their own property. For this reason, some black women were reluctant to enter into European-style marriages.

Yet family relationships lay at the heart of the African way of life. As much as possible, African Americans tried to reproduce the close-knit African village culture. They formed new extended "families," consisting of friends and fellow laborers as well as actual kinfolk. They linked their children to their African heritage and kinship traditions by naming them after relatives who had died. They also honored elderly people, who were considered closest to their ancestors.

Tragically, families made up of enslaved blacks faced a danger other colonial families did not—that of being broken apart by a master's decision to sell slaves. Separations caused by the sale of spouses or children seriously damaged the stability of African American marriages and families. Although many colonists experienced hardship, poverty, and the early deaths of parents or siblings, only enslaved blacks experienced the loss of the family in this cruel way. (*See also* **Childhood and Adolescence; Courtship; Death and Burial; Gender Roles; Land Ownership; Marriage; Old Age; Women, Roles of.**)

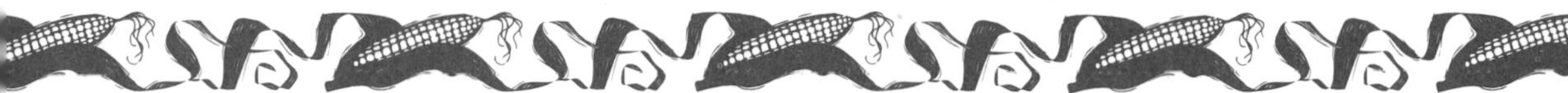

Farming

See *Agriculture.*

Festivals

Festivals—community celebrations of holidays, annual events, or other special occasions—were an important part of life in the North American colonies. People eagerly awaited them. But conflicts sometimes arose between those who organized the festivals and church or government authorities who wanted to control the celebrations.

Dutch, British, French, and Spanish colonists brought the traditional festivals of their homelands to the "New World." Some of these customs were very old, dating from the Middle Ages or even earlier, and many had become linked to Christianity. European colonists also borrowed elements from Native American and African American festivals. Over time, as the North American cultures mixed and blended, some colonial festivals assumed distinctive new shapes, becoming truly American events.

The Dutch. Dutch settlers in NEW NETHERLAND held a variety of festivals throughout the year. The colony's governors and religious leaders repeatedly tried—and failed—to stamp out these often riotous events. One of the liveliest celebrations was on New Year's Eve, when colonists usually drank a great deal of alcohol, made music long into the night, and fired guns into the air. One year the guns set fire to the house of the colony's director. Soon afterward the director banned drinking and shooting on New Year's Eve.

Many Europeans have festivals on Shrove Tuesday, a Christian holiday that comes just before the season of Lent. The Dutch colonists celebrated the day with a custom called "riding the goose," in which people on horseback tried to pull the head off a greased goose hanging on a rope. Although condemned by the Dutch Reformed Church and outlawed by the local authorities, this custom remained popular.

Another occasion for a festival was Whitsunday, or Pentecost, a Christian holiday that occurs several weeks after Easter. Among the Dutch, Pentecost had become linked with the ancient tradition of carnivals marking the return of spring. The Dutch called their festival Pinkster and celebrated by dressing in their finest clothes, making music, dancing, and eating colored, hard-boiled eggs. The colonists' black slaves joined in the celebration, and gradually Pinkster took on some qualities of an African festival, with drumming, African dancing, and parades. Blacks in New York and New Jersey celebrated Pinkster into the 1800s.

Dutch colonists also made merry on market days, when they gathered to buy and sell furs and farm produce. In addition to the weekly market days, every autumn they held a ten-day market fair as well as separate cattle and hog fairs. The fairs provided an occasion for shooting contests, drinking, and dancing. Dance contests among the colony's African Americans became a market-day tradition. Competitors performed on a wooden board, keeping time by tapping their heels.

The British. In England the festivals celebrated in the 1600s had grown out of a blend of traditions from the many ethnic groups that had settled the

country. Sometimes religious clashes affected festivals. When the PURITANS controlled the English government, for example, they took steps to abolish holidays with either Roman Catholic or pagan* origins.

* ***pagan*** relating to religion with more than one god; non-Christian
* ***May Day*** the first day of May, celebrated as a festival of springtime and fertility
* ***ritual*** ceremony that follows a set pattern

In North America in the 1600s, the Puritans of New England outlawed the celebration of Christmas and May Day* because of their link to pre-Christian rituals* and their emphasis on merrymaking. In other parts of the English colonies, however, people continued to celebrate these holidays. Children were told that Christmas would bring visits from St. Nicholas, who delivered gifts to good children, and from Old Nick, a devil who gave coal to bad children. A flying demon called the Hobby Horse also had a role at Christmastime. Parents warned that the Hobby Horse would carry bad children away. Another Christmas tradition involved groups of masked beggars who went from house to house performing short plays. One of the most popular plays showed St. George, England's patron saint, killing a dragon.

The English held festivals of thanksgiving for important events such as the annual wheat harvest. The colonists continued this custom in North America. In New England they established the Thanksgiving holiday, a celebration of the Native American foods—the turkey and the pumpkin—that had saved the early Pilgrims. Colonists in other parts of North America also held THANKSGIVING CELEBRATIONS following their autumn harvests.

Christmas celebrations were prohibited in New England during the early colonial period. But Virginians enjoyed them with great enthusiasm, as shown in this woodcut by E. Lentze.

Guy Fawkes Day

Guy Fawkes Day, November 5, was a holiday on which British citizens celebrated the failure of a plot by an Englishman named Fawkes to blow up Parliament in 1605. Festivities included bell ringing, sermons on patriotism, bonfires, and fireworks. The participants also burned effigies, dummies made to look like the plot's villains. In the colonies, Guy Fawkes Day took on new meaning as the revolutionary spirit grew. Outraged by British policies, colonists burned effigies of British officials as an act of protest.

Festivities marked many public occasions in the colonies: royal birthdays, college graduations, elections or appointments of local officials, even hangings. The activities might include bonfires, parades, banquets, dancing, drinking, and sports such as horse racing. Communities also celebrated after group efforts such as hunting trips or large agricultural projects. Festivals helped bind the community together and relieved the stresses of frontier life.

The French. French colonists in North America, from Canada to Louisiana, preserved traditional festivals of France that dated from the Middle Ages. Scattered in small communities across great distances, the French settlers kept their cultural identity alive through these holidays.

Every French colonial community celebrated MARDI GRAS, a Shrove Tuesday festival. Among the traditions of Mardi Gras was the custom of groups of costumed men going from house to house, singing and dancing in exchange for food or money. In New Orleans this old French custom blended with African and Caribbean traditions to create the Mardi Gras carnival.

Not all festivals in the French colonies came from France. Some developed in America to meet the special needs of frontier settlements. As early as the winter of 1606–1607, for example, one of the leaders of the settlement of Acadia started a tradition that called for the colonists to take turns preparing special banquets for the community. These winter feasts not only ensured that the colonists would eat well but also lifted their spirits.

Contact with Native Americans introduced the French to new festivals. The Europeans observed and eventually joined in such Indian celebrations as the monthly feast in honor of the new moon. Missionaries who had come to convert the Indians to Christianity often complained that instead the French were being converted to "heathen"* practices.

* ***heathen*** not believing in the God of the Bible

* ***Spanish Borderlands*** northern part of New Spain, area now occupied by Florida, Texas, New Mexico, Arizona, and California

The Spanish. Festivals in the Spanish Borderlands* revolved around Roman Catholicism. For the Spanish, one of the main goals in the region was to convert the Native American inhabitants to Christianity. But the Spanish had learned that it was easier to blend Native American religious beliefs and customs into Christian ones than to stamp them out. Thus many festivals celebrated in Mexico and the Borderlands combined Native American and Roman Catholic traditions. For example, the missionaries added gift giving to some Christian festivals because giving gifts was an important custom for many Indian groups. They also incorporated the Indians' traditional midsummer celebrations into the Catholic holiday known as Corpus Christi.

In every Spanish settlement, the biggest festival was the annual celebration of the community's patron saint. Each year a priest or community group selected the *mayordomos,* citizens who would be in charge of the festival. During the year, the *mayordomos* gathered contributions to pay for the celebration and then supervised the church's decoration—the walls, benches, and floors were washed, and the altar was adorned with seasonal fruits and flowers. The day before the festival, the members of the community attended religious services in the church, lit bonfires, and carried images of the saint in processions around town. On the festival day, they celebrated with feasting,

music and dancing, games for children, and horse races. Like many colonial festivals, the saints'-day celebrations were based in religion but also served the purpose of uniting and refreshing the community. (*See also* **Missions and Missionaries; Religions, Native American; Roman Catholic Church; Religious Life in European Colonies.**)

First Continental Congress

In the early 1770s, the opposition of American colonists to the policies of the British government was growing stronger. In 1774 representatives from 12 of the 13 colonies met in Philadelphia to discuss what course they should follow. While not yet ready to declare independence, the delegates to the First Continental Congress expressed outrage at British policies that they considered a violation of their fundamental rights. They also took steps to organize their resistance to the British.

The Congress Meets. After the end of the FRENCH AND INDIAN WAR in 1763, Great Britain tried to raise funds to help cover the cost of defending their American colonies by imposing various taxes on the colonists. Each tax met with loud protests. The colonists claimed that the British PARLIAMENT—which had no colonial representatives—did not have the right to tax them. The protests climaxed in December 1773 in the BOSTON TEA PARTY, at which colonists demonstrated their opposition to a tax on tea by dumping barrels of British tea into Boston harbor. Angered by this defiance of British authority, Parliament passed laws to punish Boston. The colonists called these harsh measures that restricted their freedom the INTOLERABLE ACTS.

In response to the Intolerable Acts, patriots* in Boston asked all colonists to stop buying British goods. The idea received wide support, but colonial leaders feared that unless a plan was developed, the boycott* would fail—as had happened in 1768. For this reason, they invited colonial representatives to meet in Philadelphia. On September 5, 1774, 56 delegates from every colony but Georgia gathered in the city. They called their meeting the Continental Congress to distinguish it from the congresses of individual colonies.

* ***patriot*** American colonist who supported independence from Britain
* ***boycott*** refusal to buy goods as a means of protest

The Work of the Congress. One of the first issues the congress had to consider was voting procedure. Should it allow each delegate a separate vote or have the delegates vote collectively by colony? The representatives decided on voting by colony, establishing a pattern for decision making that lasted throughout the period of the American Revolution.

Soon after the delegates assembled, patriots in Massachusetts issued a document called the Suffolk Resolves, which urged colonists not to obey the Intolerable Acts because they violated the British constitution. The document also advised towns in Massachusetts to begin collecting taxes and to organize colonial militia*. Paul REVERE, a Massachusetts delegate, delivered the Suffolk Resolves to the Continental Congress, which adopted them on September 17, 1774.

* ***militia*** army of citizens who may be called into action in a time of emergency

Some delegates to the congress, particularly those from New England, called for drastic measures against Britain. Many other delegates, however, were more cautious. They wanted to protect the colonists' rights, but they hoped to resolve differences peacefully and maintain the basic relationship between Britain and the colonies. Pennsylvania delegate Joseph Galloway drew up a plan of union that featured a council, elected by the American colonies, that would be a branch of the British Parliament. The congress defeated Galloway's plan by just one vote.

On October 14, delegates approved a Declaration of Rights and Grievances. This document contained ten points summarizing the colonists' position on British rule. One point proclaimed the right to "life, liberty, and property"—a demand that would reappear in slightly different form in the DECLARATION OF INDEPENDENCE. Other points stated that the colonists had the right to meet in assemblies, to send petitions* to the king, and to have jury trials. The declaration also expressed opposition to the Intolerable Acts and the QUEBEC ACT, which had banned settlement beyond the Appalachian Mountains. Another point protested the stationing of British troops in the colonies. Finally, the declaration challenged every measure to raise revenue that Parliament had forced on the colonies since 1763 and proclaimed that only colonial assemblies—not Parliament—had the right to tax the colonists.

* ***petition*** formal statement asking a person in authority to address a problem

After approving the Declaration of Rights and Grievances, the congress took an important step as it turned to the issue of the boycott that had prompted the meeting in the first place. On October 20, the delegates approved the creation of the CONTINENTAL ASSOCIATION, a program to halt all trade with Britain. The delegates promised not only to boycott British goods but also to stop shipping colonial goods to Britain and British colonies in the West Indies. They also pledged to end the SLAVE TRADE. The Continental Association relied on local COMMITTEES OF CORRESPONDENCE to use public opinion to persuade colonists to observe the ban.

To explain their intentions and actions, the congress issued a series of pamphlets and documents. These were sent to the king, the people of Great Britain, the people of Canada, and the American colonists. The last session of the First Continental Congress took place on October 26, 1774. Before leaving, the delegates agreed to meet again the following May, if Britain had not taken action to satisfy colonial complaints. The delegates did reassemble—in a new body called the SECOND CONTINENTAL CONGRESS. (*See also* **American Revolution; Independence Movements.**)

Fish and Fishing

The first Europeans to visit North America regularly were fishermen. They sailed to the waters off the northeastern coast, especially the Grand Banks near the island of NEWFOUNDLAND. Here the Gulf Stream and the Labrador Current came together to create rich feeding grounds for fish. Fishing soon became an important and profitable industry in the region.

Early Fishermen. Portuguese, Spanish, French, and English fishermen began making the transatlantic voyage before 1500. The earliest European fishing ships may have reached the North Atlantic before Christopher Columbus's first voyage to the Caribbean in 1492. Each summer some 350

vessels, carrying 8,000 to 10,000 men, gathered around the Grand Banks and the mouth of the St. Lawrence River. Here the mariners found many kinds of fish, as well as seals and whales. The most valuable was cod, which could be eaten fresh or preserved by drying or salting, and its liver yielded oil.

The French dominated the fishing industry in North America during the 1500s. In the early 1600s, the English established a number of small fishing stations along the coast from Cape Cod to what is now Nova Scotia. North American colonists soon entered the industry as well, and in time fishing became New England's single most important economic activity.

Methods of Fishing. There were two ways of fishing, depending on whether the fish was to be salted or dried. Some fishermen drifted along the banks, salting their catch as they went along. Those who used the drying process camped on land because they needed space to spread the fish out in the sun.

The French, Spanish, and Portuguese often brought large supplies of salt on their ships to preserve their catch. In many cases, they returned to their home ports without ever setting ashore. The English developed the technique of drying the fish because they lacked a cheap, abundant supply of salt. On arriving in North America, the ship's crew set up camp on shore. Some sailed out to the fishing banks in small boats, returning every day or so with their catch. Others remained on shore to process the fish, splitting them and spreading them on wooden frames to dry in the sun. The English were very aggressive in seizing land along the coast for their fish-processing camps. Although fishermen of different nations competed

Fish could be preserved either by salting or by drying. In Newfoundland, fishermen often set up camps onshore to dry the fish. Many of these camps later became permanent villages.

for the choicest Atlantic fishing grounds, the French and English managed to dominate in the area.

Fishing and Colonization. Fishing played a role in settling the North American coast. The French and English set up fishing camps in the harbors and bays dotting the coasts of Newfoundland, the Gulf of St. Lawrence, and New England. Many of the camps became permanent villages. Some settlements started by the French and Portuguese on Nova Scotia and Newfoundland still exist. The English government recruited experienced fishermen to serve on its early voyages of trade and colonization.

The land-based fishermen began trading with local Indians, exchanging mirrors, combs, and hatchets for pelts*. Returning to Europe with their ships loaded with pelts, they launched an extremely profitable trade in furs. Fishing may have brought the French to the American coast, but it was the FUR TRADE that kept them there.

* ***pelt*** skin and fur of an animal

Some settlements in British North America were planned and founded by English fishing companies. For example, Gloucester, Massachusetts, was established in 1623 by a company that needed a base in New England. These company-founded communities often grew into independent towns whose citizens built their own boats and fished on their own behalf.

New colonists in North America often learned about the best local fishing grounds from Native Americans. The English who settled around the Chesapeake Bay discovered that the region's waters had rich supplies of fish, crabs, and oysters. Chesapeake fishing remained mostly local, feeding the ever growing population around the bay. In New England, by contrast, the colonial fishing industry produced a surplus of dried and salted fish for export to Europe and the Caribbean. By the 1700s fishing produced one-third of New England's exports and employed one out of every ten men in the region. (*See also* **Animals; Whaling.**)

Five Nations

See ***Iroquois Confederacy.***

Florida

The first area within the present-day United States to be settled by Europeans, Florida never developed into a large colony. Its main value was its location near the principal route of Spanish treasure ships carrying gold and silver to Europe. Other European powers wanted Florida, and Spain had to defend it numerous times. The colony thus played a key role in the European struggle for empire in North America.

See map in Spanish Borderlands (vol. 4).

Exploration and Early Settlement. Spanish explorer Juan PONCE DE LEÓN arrived in Florida in 1513. As the first European visitor, he named the region La Florida (Spanish for "the land in bloom")—probably because he arrived at Easter time (*Pascua Florida* in Spanish).

The Spanish explored the region further over the next few decades. In 1528 Pánfilo de Narváez led an ill-fated expedition along Florida's Gulf

The Spanish settlement at Pensacola, shown here in 1743, was one of the two that survived when British forces destroyed Florida's mission settlements in 1704.

coast. Storms, disease, and hostile Indians killed most of the Spaniards. Only 4 out of more than 400 survived, including Alvar Núñez CABEZA DE VACA and an African named ESTEBAN. In 1539 Hernando DE SOTO began a four-year exploration of the Southeast in Florida. A number of other adventurers came to the region in search of Indian slaves and resources.

The Spanish, alarmed at the actions of French privateers* off the east coast of Florida, made two attempts in the 1550s to found settlements in the region. Both failed. Several years later, however, the Spanish did establish a permanent presence in Florida in response to other French activities.

* ***privateer*** privately owned ship authorized by the government to attack and capture enemy vessels; also the ship's master

In 1564 French Protestants had built Fort Caroline (near present-day Jacksonville) as a haven from religious persecution. The Spanish considered the French presence a serious threat to their territorial claims and to their ships carrying gold and silver to Europe. For this reason, in 1565 Spanish forces under the command of Pedro MENÉNDEZ DE AVILÉS laid the foundations for ST. AUGUSTINE, about 50 miles south of Fort Caroline. Then they marched north to destroy the French fort. The military base of St. Augustine became the first permanent Spanish settlement in Florida. Over the next few years, Menéndez de Avilés built several other forts, or PRESIDIOS, along the east and west coasts of Florida, but none was as important as St. Augustine.

See color plate 2, vol. 4.

Spanish Occupation of Florida. The territory of La Florida claimed by Spain included the Florida peninsula and lands stretching north to Virginia and west to the Mississippi River. But the Spanish settlement was concentrated in the northern part of the Florida peninsula and the coastal regions of

GEORGIA and SOUTH CAROLINA. Florida's importance came from its role in defending Spanish interests in the Caribbean region and providing a base for missionary activities among the Native Americans. Nevertheless, Florida remained one of the least developed Spanish regions in North America, and it relied heavily on money and supplies from NEW SPAIN.

In 1566 Menéndez de Avilés invited Catholic missionaries to come to Florida to convert the Indians of the region to Christianity. In the following years, the JESUITS established a chain of MISSIONS along the coast from Florida to Virginia. But in 1572 they were forced by Indian rebellions to abandon all these sites. The next year, Franciscan friars* arrived and began missionary work among the Indians. The Franciscans had more success among the Indians than did the Jesuits, and their missions remained active for more than a hundred years.

*friar member of a religious brotherhood

Spanish Florida struggled for many years. From the beginning, the chief settlement of St. Augustine had problems with local Indians, and the Spanish did not manage to make peace with them until about 1580. By that time, the Indians had been seriously weakened by European diseases, but as they recovered their health, they renewed hostilities. Then in 1586 the British mariner Francis DRAKE attacked St. Augustine and burned it to the ground. Although the Spanish quickly rebuilt the town, a devastating hurricane struck in 1599 and destroyed it again. As a result, St. Augustine had only a few hundred inhabitants by 1600.

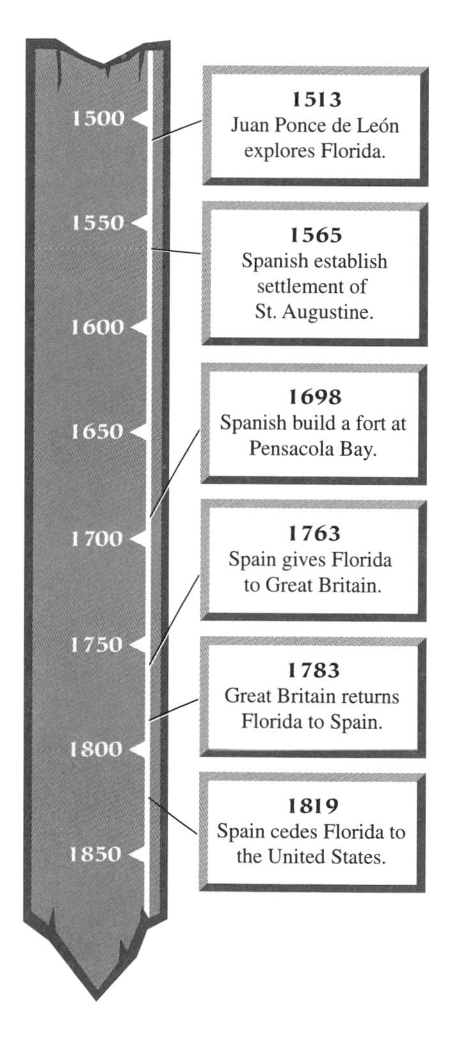

Florida recovered from these setbacks and began to make some progress in the 1600s. The efforts of the Franciscans led to the founding of 40 missions in Florida and neighboring Georgia by 1650. St. Augustine grew during this period as well, reaching a population of between 500 and 700. Spanish settlers established ranches inland from the coast and raised cattle or wheat for export. Spanish farmers also grew vegetables and citrus fruits such as oranges, lemons, and limes. Despite occasional setbacks caused by Indian revolts, bad weather, and pirate raids, ranchers and farmers achieved moderate success, and Florida's economy began to expand slowly. Even so, Florida still remained dependent on supplies from other areas of New Spain.

Conflict Between Empires. The situation began to change in the late 1600s. The establishment and growth of English colonies along the Atlantic coast to the north alarmed the Spanish, and they responded by erecting more forts in Florida. The Spanish also strengthened existing defenses by increasing the number of soldiers stationed in St. Augustine and replacing the old fort there with a stone fortress, the Castillo de San Marcos.

The spread of English settlement in the Southeast created serious problems for Spanish Florida. English colonists established commercial relations and alliances with various Indian tribes. Goaded by the English, Indians in Georgia rebelled against Spanish missionaries. By the 1680s, Indian hostilities had forced the Spanish to abandon most of their northernmost missions and pull back toward St. Augustine. Spain did not abandon its claims to those areas, however, and conflicting territorial claims by the Spanish and English disturbed the Southeast for decades.

The Spanish struck back at the English by offering safety and freedom to any slaves who escaped to Florida from the Carolinas. Hundreds of African

Americans took advantage of the offer over the years. In the early 1700s, the Spanish organized these former slaves into a military force to help defend Florida from the British.

The Spanish faced another rival in the west. When the French explorer René-Robert Cavelier de LA SALLE landed in Texas in 1685, the Spanish renewed their interest in the northern Gulf coast area of Florida. In 1698 they built a new fort on Pensacola Bay to block French expansion in the region. Plagued by food shortages, Indian raids, and unrest spread by convict laborers, the Pensacola settlement struggled to survive. It served its purpose, though. When a French expedition arrived in the area in 1699 and found the Spaniards, it headed farther west.

The Citrus Industry

The Spanish brought oranges, lemons, and limes to St. Augustine for planting. They found Florida's warm climate well suited to growing these delicate fruits that cannot tolerate frost. Though rare, frost can strike in Florida—and with devastating effect. In 1895 a severe frost damaged citrus trees across the state. The citrus industry recovered, and today Florida is the nation's top producer of oranges, grapefruit, and tangerines. Recognizing the importance of its citrus industry, Floridians chose the orange blossom as the state flower.

North American Wars. Between 1702 and 1763, Europe and North America went through several wars as France, Great Britain, and Spain competed for power. During QUEEN ANNE'S WAR (1702–1713) France and Spain joined forces against England. In 1702 English colonists from Carolina attacked St. Augustine, burned the town, and laid siege* to the Castillo de San Marcos. This stone fortress withstood the attack for two months, then the English gave up and left. They returned to Florida two years later, however, and destroyed all the Spanish mission communities. Only the settlements at St. Augustine and Pensacola survived. Pensacola was captured by the French in 1719, but the Spanish regained it three years later.

During KING GEORGE'S WAR (1744–1748), the British again tried to take St. Augustine—and once again they failed. After the war ended, Florida enjoyed almost two decades of relative peace. The population of St. Augustine expanded to more than 3,000 people, and both St. Augustine and Pensacola began to develop industries based on lumber and products for shipbuilding. The standard of living also improved as colonists began to trade with British merchants.

The battles of the FRENCH AND INDIAN WAR (1754–1763) left Florida untouched, largely because Spain did not ally with France until late in the war. But the TREATY OF PARIS, which ended the war, had a dramatic effect. According to the terms of the treaty, Spain gave up Florida for Cuba, which the British had captured. Florida was no longer a Spanish colony.

British Control. When the British took over Florida in 1763, more than 3,000 Spanish settlers left for other areas of New Spain. The British tried to rebuild the population by offering grants of land to settlers. Some of those who received these grants established PLANTATIONS and brought agricultural laborers to work the land. The plantation settlement of New Smyrna (near present-day Daytona Beach) became home to about 1,500 workers from southern Europe.

Despite these efforts, the population of British Florida grew very slowly until the American Revolution. Thousands of Loyalists* left the 13 colonies during the conflict, and about 19,000 of them settled in Florida. Many of these Loyalists fought with the British and directed raids from Florida into Georgia and the Carolinas.

Spain became an ally of the United States during the Revolution and launched successful attacks on the western region of Florida from 1779 to

* ***siege*** prolonged effort by armed troops to force the surrender of a town or fort by surrounding it and cutting it off from aid

* ***Loyalist*** American colonist who remained faithful to Britain during the American Revolution

1781. Under the Treaty of Paris of 1783, which ended the war, Britain returned Florida to Spain. Just as Spanish settlers had left when the British arrived in 1763, now British settlers abandoned Florida.

Last Years of Spanish Control. Several thousand Spanish colonists settled in Florida in the next few decades. St. Augustine and Pensacola remained the principal settlements. As time passed, several hundred American settlers also moved into Florida—many illegally. The presence of these Americans led to tensions with the Spanish in the region.

Florida became a source of controversy when the United States purchased LOUISIANA from France in 1803. Americans argued that the Louisiana Purchase gave the United States the rights to the western part of Florida. Spain disagreed, and this led to boundary disputes with the United States. But Spain's hold over the region was very weak. Between 1810 and 1814, the United States successfully extended its control over portions of western Florida. American forces invaded eastern Florida in 1814 and 1818, supposedly to punish Indians who had raided American settlements from bases there. In 1815 the United States and Spain began negotiations over Florida. Under the Adams-Onís Treaty of 1819, Spain ceded* Florida to the United States. It officially became part of the United States in 1821, when the U.S. Senate approved the treaty. (*See also* **American Revolution; Cities and Towns; Exploration, Age of; Government, Provincial.**)

* ***cede*** to yield or surrender

People consumed a wide variety of foods and beverages in North America. Native Americans, Europeans of various nationalities, and Africans had their own traditions and preferences when it came to eating and drinking and wanted to maintain their customary ways. Yet they also tried new foods—sometimes out of necessity when there was nothing else to eat. Gradually, the food habits of different peoples living in New England, the South, and the Southwest mingled to form regional cuisines*.

* ***cuisine*** style of cooking

Although the first European colonists brought livestock and seeds for crops with them, they soon added new items to their diets. Indians taught them about foods that were native to North America, saving some early settlers from starvation. Later, when trade became established between Europe and the Americas, the colonial diet included many imported foods such as tea, wine, and spices. Wealthy colonists could enjoy meals as lavish as those served in the finest European homes. At the same time, colonists exported some of the foods native to the Americas, introducing Europeans to such exotic items as tomatoes, potatoes, beans, peanuts, squash, and chocolate.

Food was more abundant in colonial North America than it was in Europe. After the terrible "starving times" that some of the early settlements endured at first, shortages were rare. Most colonists could heap their plates with large quantities of food, even if variety was sometimes lacking. The ample supplies contributed to a population that tended to be healthier and to live longer than the people in Europe.

Corn, or maize, was an important part of the diet of most Native Americans. This 1585 drawing by John White shows corn "meale" being cooked in an earthenware pot.

An Indian Feast

John Bartram, an English colonist of the 1700s, studied the customs of the Native American tribes, especially their use of plants. In his journal, he described a meal he shared with the Iroquois in 1748:

> This repast consisted of three great kettles of Indian corn soup, or thin hominy, with dry'd eels and other fish boiled in it, and one kettle full of young squashes and their flowers boiled in water . . . [L]ast of all was served a great bowl full of Indian dumplings, made of new soft corn, cut or scraped off the ear . . . [W]ith the addition of some boiled beans, lapped well up in Indian corn leaves, this is good hearty provision.

Native American Foods

Many Native Americans, especially those who combined farming with hunting for game and gathering wild grains and fruits, had remarkably healthy and balanced diets. They had learned to make the best possible use of the plant and animal resources of each region and each season.

The principal crops of the Indians were corn, beans, and squash, which the Iroquois called the "three sisters" because, like sisters, they grew side by side in the fields. Of these, the most important was corn, or MAIZE. Over the centuries, Native Americans had developed many different varieties of maize, including popcorn, which they cooked until the kernels exploded. Eaten when immature, sweet corn contained a high proportion of sugar. Flour corn had kernels with soft hulls, or shells. The Indians ground this corn to make the cornmeal used for breads and porridge. Two other varieties, flint corn and dent corn, produced hard, sturdy kernels that were stored for winter use.

Native American farmers grew a wide variety of beans, including lima, butter, navy, and kidney beans. In combination with corn, the beans added protein to the Indians' diet. This was especially important in areas that lacked large game animals to provide meat protein. Indians of the Northeast boiled corn and beans together to make a dish they called succotash, which the colonists adopted.

The Indians also made good use of wild plants. In the Northeast, they learned to make syrup and sugar from the sap of maple trees, a skill they shared with European colonists. In the Northwest, they gathered the edible roots of the camas plant, a type of lily, and ground them into flour. In areas of the west coast where oak trees were plentiful, the Indians made flour from acorns. They gathered many kinds of seeds and nuts, including sunflower seeds and pine nuts, as well as huckleberries, blueberries, and other fruits.

Most Native Americans who raised crops also hunted. In the Eastern Woodlands, deer was the main game animal, but the Indians also pursued smaller animals such as squirrels, rabbits, and raccoons as well as ducks, geese, and pigeons. Those who lived in the northern and western parts of the continent relied on hunting and fishing for most of their food, gathering plants and berries when these were available. In the Great Plains and the interior of Canada, Indians depended on meat from large game animals such as BUFFALO, caribou, moose, and elk. To preserve meat, they cut it into strips and smoked it over fires or dried it in the sun. European colonists later called these strips of dried meat jerky, a term still used today. In cold climates, some Indians preserved meat for the winter simply by allowing it to freeze outdoors, then hacked off chunks as needed.

Indians of the Pacific coast, the northern Atlantic coast, and the southern part of present-day Florida turned to the sea for their primary source of food. They ate fresh and dried fish such as grouper, cod, and salmon, and along the far northern coasts, whales, walruses, and seals.

British Colonial Foods

The PILGRIMS who established Plymouth colony escaped starvation in the winter of 1620 because they found stores of corn that local Indians had

Beverages, especially alcoholic ones, varied throughout the British colonies. Rum, a popular drink, was made from molasses imported from the West Indies.

buried. The following spring a Patuxet Indian named SQUANTO showed the new settlers how to plant corn. The Pilgrims and other colonists tried to grow the wheat and rye they had brought from Europe, but these grains did not do well in the areas first settled by Europeans. As a result, corn became the basic grain of the North American colonists, just as it had long been the basic food of many Native Americans. Nearly every colonist ate cornbread, often baking or frying it in flat cakes called johnny cakes.

Throughout the British colonies, settlers changed their eating habits to fit their new circumstances. Women substituted cornmeal for wheat flour in traditional European recipes and began to rely on other Indian foods, such as maple sugar and pumpkins. Men learned to hunt wild turkeys and other native game to supplement the yield from their livestock. Pork was cheaper and more widely available than beef. The colonists dried, pickled, or salted both beef and pork to preserve them for year-round use. They also caught or gathered fish, lobsters, crabs, and oysters, often learning about the best fishing grounds from local Indians.

Some European crops thrived in North America. These included carrots, peas, turnips, and certain kinds of fruit. In time, colonists brought beehives across the Atlantic and began producing honey. By combining European foods with local produce, the different regions of the British colonies created their own culinary* traditions.

* ***culinary*** having to do with preparing foods

New England. Settlers to New England brought cattle, chickens, hogs, and fruit trees to the colonies. Despite a plentiful supply of many foods, New Englanders favored a plain style in cooking as in other areas of life, reflecting their Puritan heritage. For this reason, the New England diet leaned toward simple foods with little or no seasoning. The New England boiled dinner—a

piece of salted meat cooked in water with carrots, potatoes, and cabbage—is an example of this plain style of cookery. Baked beans, which could be prepared one day and eaten the next, became a local specialty because they allowed Puritans to obey their rule against cooking on Sundays. The colonists found an abundant supply of cod in the waters off New England, and they soon invented ways to mix the fish with cornmeal to create codfish balls and codfish cakes. As in England, beer was the most common beverage, and most households brewed their own from barley.

Many of the foods now regarded as typical of New England were borrowed from the Native Americans. They introduced the colonists to the main ingredients of the traditional THANKSGIVING feast—turkey, baked pumpkins, and cranberry sauce. The New England clambake also originated with Native Americans living along the coast, who cooked large quantities of clams, crabs, and other foods on the beach in sand pits heated with hot rocks.

Beginning in the mid-1600s, New Englanders also used molasses, which came from the sugar plantations of the West Indies, to make rum. The colonists drank this highly alcoholic beverage and also used it for trading with the Indians.

The Middle and Southern Colonies. Like the Puritans, the QUAKERS who settled in the middle colonies of New Jersey and Pennsylvania preferred plain, unseasoned food. They regarded food as a necessary fuel for the body, provided by God, and disapproved of attempts to make it more appetizing or enjoyable. They used their favorite culinary technique, boiling, to prepare such specialties as dumplings and puddings. Quakers avoided the use of sugar, which was produced by slave labor. They opposed slavery on moral grounds.

The prosperous planters of Virginia and the Carolinas enjoyed the most elaborate meals in the British colonies. They dined on roast meat and fowl, wheat bread, baked desserts, and imported wines and fruits. Throughout the colonies, such meals were signs of wealth and status, especially if they included out-of-season ingredients and complicated recipes.

Poor southerners, like poor folk in all the colonies, ate boiled preserved meat, cooked with dried peas or beans, parsnips, turnip greens, onions, or wild herbs. They had locally grown vegetables such as sweet potatoes and served chicken as an occasional treat. Southerners created one of their staple dishes from cornmeal, first making a cornmeal porridge, then frying the porridge lightly to make cornmeal mush. Southerners generally added more salt, HERBS, and other seasonings to their food than did people in the northern colonies.

Spoon Bread

Spoon bread, a kind of cornbread, was part of many colonial meals. To make spoon bread, start by preheating the oven to 400 degrees. Lightly coat the inside of a baking pan with butter and set it aside.

In a saucepan, boil **2 cups of water,** and slowly add **1 cup white or yellow cornmeal** and **½ teaspoon salt.** Cook and stir for 1 minute. Remove pan from heat. Add **2 tablespoons butter.** Beat well. Now stir in **4 beaten eggs** and **1 cup milk.** Pour this mixture into the baking pan. Bake for 25 minutes.

Serve with butter. Or do what colonial Americans often did—top the spoon bread with molasses, maple syrup, or maple sugar.

The Backcountry. The backcountry was the western frontier of settlement in the hills and mountains away from the coast. Many of the people who settled there came from Scotland or northern Ireland, regions that were frontiers by European standards. These settlers were accustomed to simple ways of life in rural surroundings, and they adapted their farming and food traditions to the conditions they found in America. When oats, their staple grain, did not flourish in the woodlands of North America, they switched to corn. Using traditional recipes for oatcakes, they substituted cornmeal and made flat cornmeal cakes on broad iron pans called griddles.

Table Manners

In the 1700s, some colonists turned to books of manners for advice on how to behave politely. Some of these books tried to improve children's table manners. In 1715 New Englander Eleazar Moody published *163 Rules for Children's Behavior,* which instructed: "Eat not too fast, or with greedy behavior" and "stuff not thy mouth so as to fill thy cheeks." Pennsylvanian Christopher Dock, in *100 Necessary Rules of Conduct* (1764), said that children should "avoid everything that indicates excessive hunger, such as looking greedily at food." He also warned them not to lick their plates.

People in the backcountry also switched from raising sheep, their principal livestock in Europe, to pigs, which were better at seeking out food in forested country. These settlers successfully transplanted white potatoes—originally from South America—to North America. They also specialized in making whiskey from corn and other grains.

African American Foods

The majority of Africans in North America were slaves, mostly on southern plantations. Because their masters determined the amount and kind of food they received, blacks had little freedom to follow their own preferences in food and cooking styles. Nevertheless, they managed to keep some African culinary traditions alive. African Americans who worked in their masters' kitchens soon learned to cook in various European styles as well. People throughout the colonies regarded blacks as the best chefs, partly because of their knowledge of seasonings.

The basic ingredients of the slaves' diet were salted pork and cornmeal. From time to time, masters also provided sweet potatoes or other vegetables, rice, fruit, and molasses. On Christmas and other holidays, they might make gifts of coffee or candy for the slaves. Some slaves supplemented their diets by fishing, hunting, raising chickens, or tending small gardens of their own. On large plantations, they received cooked food from a central slave kitchen. More often, however, each slave received a daily or weekly supply of food, and individuals and families cooked their own meals. Instead of eating from individual plates as Europeans did, Africans generally ate from bowls that everyone shared.

A number of foods and methods of food preparation came to America with the Africans. In the 1500s, European explorers and traders had carried peanuts and yams from South America to Africa. These foods had become part of the cuisine of west Africa, and Africans from that region brought them to North America. *Goober,* the southern term for peanut, comes from the African word *nguba.* Other African words that entered the English language were *ngombo*—which became gumbo, a thick soup or stew—and *nkru*—okra, a nutritious seedpod that can be eaten fried or cooked in gumbo. These and other foods that were once associated with black slaves became part of the southern regional cuisine.

Dutch Colonial Foods

Like the British colonists, the people who settled the Dutch colony of New Netherland borrowed crops from the Indians. These included corn, which the Dutch called "turkey wheat," and pumpkins. In his 1655 description of the Dutch colony, Adriaen van der Donck noted that in Europe pumpkins were "generally despised as a mean and unsubstantial article of food." North American pumpkins, however, were of such good quality that the colonists regarded them as a tasty and valuable food source.

In addition to corn, the Dutch colonists raised European grains such as wheat, rye, and barley. Their gardens contained turnips, large gray peas called "old wives," cabbages, parsnips, carrots, beets, spinach, onions,

This illustration of a Dutch woman cooking over an open fire is taken from *Wercken (Work)*, a book by Jacob "Father" Cats of the Netherlands.

radishes, several kinds of beans, and a wide variety of herbs, such as rosemary, tarragon, lavender, and chives. Housewives used some of these herbs to season food and made others into teas and medicines. Van der Donck noted that the Dutch loved fruit and that the colonists had brought several varieties of apple and pear trees to North America. They also found that watermelons, which did not grow in northern Europe, flourished in New Netherland.

The colonists brought Dutch breeds of cattle from Europe, and their dairy cows were famous for producing large amounts of milk, which women made into butter and cheese. The Dutch settlers also kept goats and used their milk to make cheese. Pigs were numerous in the colony. According to van der Donck, the Dutch breeds of pig were larger than the English breeds and produced "thicker pork."

The people of the Netherlands had earned a reputation as highly productive gardeners and farmers, and that reputation followed them to

America. Food shortages were never a problem in New Netherland. Soon after arriving in North America, the Dutch colonists were producing a surplus of milk, butter, cheese, grains, and root crops such as turnips. They sold these goods at weekly markets or used them in trading with other colonies and the Indians. They also shipped some produce back to the Netherlands.

Unlike the Puritans and Quakers, who disapproved—at least in public—of hearty appetites, the Dutch colonists openly enjoyed eating and drinking. Births, weddings, and funerals provided occasions for feasts. Alcoholic beverages such as beer and rum were popular and widely consumed in the colony, in spite of attempts by some authorities to curb the use of liquor.

French Colonial Foods

Settlers in NEW FRANCE, the French colony based in present-day Canada, did not rely heavily on corn. Their lands were too far north for corn to grow well, but wheat thrived there. Wheat became the colony's principal crop, and wheat bread was an important part of the diet.

Most of the French colonists lived on bread, beans or peas, root vegetables such as carrots and potatoes, and preserved meat or fish. In summer they added apples and berries to their diet. Although they brewed beer, most French settlers preferred wine or brandy made from grapes. Wealthy colonists drank only wine and consumed more beef and milk than did other colonists.

Although some prosperous households had cast-iron stoves, everyone else cooked in the fireplace, as did most rural colonists throughout North America. French colonial houses often had a stone or brick oven built into a side wall of the fireplace or in a separate lean-to kitchen behind the house. Women used this oven to bake bread, cakes, and fruit and maple syrup pies and to cook meat and casseroles of beans and salt pork.

New dining customs arose in New France as in other colonies. In Europe poor rural families usually ate their meals sitting along one side of a narrow table with their backs to the fireplace. In New France, however, members of such families generally sat on both sides of a folding table that had been covered with a cloth. They drank from tin cups and ate from pewter*, bronze, brass, or pottery plates, using pewter spoons and iron forks. After the meal, the family would push the table against one wall of their main room until it was time to eat again. Only the wealthy had special rooms just for dining.

* ***pewter*** metal made of tin and lead

The French settlers mastered the Native American practice of making maple sugar and turned it into an industry. They tapped sugar maple trees with tubes and pipes to collect sap, boiled the sap to make syrup, and poured the syrup into molds where it hardened into lumps of maple sugar. By 1706 the region around Montreal was producing 30,000 pounds of maple sugar a year. People throughout the colony used maple sugar as a sweetener.

Food shortages occurred from time to time in New France. During the 1700s, there were poor harvests in at least 17 years. At these times, bread became expensive, and people rioted against the colonial government, which was considered responsible for providing enough food. In 1749, for example,

a crowd of angry settlers marched to Quebec to demand assistance. Similar protests took place whenever the price of bread or salt rose sharply.

Spanish Colonial Foods

* ***Spanish Borderlands*** northern part of New Spain, area now occupied by Florida, Texas, New Mexico, Arizona, and California

The Spanish Borderlands* of North America had a rich and complex cuisine. Some of the colonists who settled in the region came from Spain. Others were mestizos, people of mixed Spanish and Indian blood, from NEW SPAIN. The mestizos brought foods and cooking methods that combined European and Indian traditions.

The diet of the Spanish Borderlands was based on the Native American staples of corn, beans, and squash plus a great variety of chile peppers. It also included European wheat and chickpeas, which grew well in some parts of the Borderlands. Other important European agricultural products introduced by the colonists were peas, fava beans, grapes, melons, figs, apples, peaches, pears, and apricots.

Women made flat round breads called tortillas out of wheat flour or cornmeal. They used the tortillas for many local dishes, including tacos, enchiladas, and burritos. Although wheat tortillas were easy to make, only families with servants ate corn tortillas, which were complicated and time-consuming to prepare. Spanish colonists also ate baked bread, fried bread, and sweet biscuits of wheat flour.

Everyday meals generally consisted of cornmeal mush, tortillas, beans, goat or cow cheeses, and soup made of any available meat and vegetables. The most common beverage was *atole,* water in which cornmeal had been boiled, seasoned with salt. Coffee, chocolate, and sugar were costly imported treats for special occasions. One of the few sweets in the Spanish colonial diet was a sprouted-wheat pudding called *panocha.*

Festive Foods

At Christmastime, colonists in the Spanish Borderlands enjoyed *posole,* a stew made with pork and white hominy (hulled corn). To make *posole,* cut **1 onion** in half and place each half in a separate saucepan. To each pan, add **peppercorns,** a **clove of garlic,** and **3 cups of water.** Then put **6 chicken thighs** in one pan and **1 pound of lean pork,** cut into 1-inch cubes, in the other. Bring both pans to a boil, cover, and simmer for 50 minutes.

Transfer the meat and broth to a large pot, and add a **1-pound can of hominy,** drained. Bring to a boil, cover, and simmer for 30 minutes. Add **salt** to taste. This dish can be served with lettuce, salsa, onions, radishes, avocado, or wedges of lime.

People preserved food by drying it in the plentiful sun of the Borderlands. They made strips of meat into *carne seca,* or jerky. To preserve pork, which spoiled easily, they soaked it in *adobo,* a mixture of chilies, salt, and garlic. They sliced many varieties of fruit into small pieces, which when dried they called *orejones,* or "little ears." People also dried melons and pumpkins in strips and round slices of squash into *rueditas,* or "little wheels." Travelers and soldiers often lived on *pinole,* ground dried corn, as well as dried fruits and vegetables.

The Spanish colonists enjoyed their most elaborate meals at the Christmas season. Pork was the favorite meat of this time of year, and when a pig was butchered, the whole community feasted. Spring brought Lent, a period when Christians ate lightly and gave up favorite foods such as meat. During this time, cooks prepared fish, meatless stews of corn and beans, and side dishes of greens and dried vegetables.

In observing special FESTIVALS, Spanish settlers held food exchanges that enabled everyone to share the land's bounty. In Texas and other ranching regions, people celebrated by preparing food in a style called *barbacoa,* or barbecue, which the Spanish had learned in the Caribbean. It involved cooking whole sides of beef and other meats in a pit. Throughout the year, Spanish colonists used special ingredients, seasonings, and cooking methods that survive today in the cuisines called Mexican, Tex-Mex, and Southwestern. (*See also* **Agriculture; Animals; Puritans; Ranching.**)

Forests

When the first colonists arrived in North America, they found vast, seemingly endless forests. Pines, firs, spruce, and other evergreens grew in the forests of the continent's northern climates. Farther south, throughout much of the Atlantic coastal region, the forests contained a mixture of evergreens and deciduous trees—such as maples, oaks, and beeches—that lose their leaves in the fall.

These early European colonists brought with them two conflicting ideas about forests. On the one hand, they viewed the woods as sources of fuel and material for construction. On the other hand, they saw forests as fearful places where hideous man-beasts, trolls, and other creatures lurked among the trees. But both ideas made clearing wooded areas seem necessary and desirable to the colonists. Not only did cutting trees create farmland and provide fuel and building material; it also reduced dangers. In clearing away

As soon as European colonists arrived in North America, they began cutting down trees to make room for farmland. The clearing of the forests had a dramatic impact on the environment in colonial areas.

forested land, the settlers felt they were gaining control of the environment and increasing their security.

Soon after establishing settlements, Europeans began cutting trees for their own needs and for export. As early as the 1630s, English colonists began building sawmills to produce lumber for construction. The shipping of lumber became an important business at nearly every major port along the Atlantic coast.

The colonists cut different types of trees for different purposes. They chose red and white oak to make barrels for transporting sugar. They used red and white cedar for fence posts and shingles for houses. Pine was the wood of choice for building ships, and pine trees of 200 feet or so became ships' masts. The colonists also consumed enormous amounts of wood as fuel. As the population expanded, the demand for fuel increased, and more and more trees were cut. In addition, settlers continued to open up land for farming. A colonial family might clear as much as 10 to 15 acres of forest per year.

The growth of colonial settlements led to a dramatic reduction in the size of American forests. Assuming the wood supply to be unlimited, most colonists cut down trees without a thought for the future. Clearing the forests had a significant impact on the environment. Tree roots help absorb water, and as trees disappeared, water runoff increased and contributed to soil erosion. In addition, the runoff carried large amounts of silt—topsoil—into streams and rivers, making them shallower and more difficult to travel by boat. Changes in rivers also altered the temperature of the water, which harmed some types of fish.

Loss of forests affected animal populations as well, leading to a reduction in the number of deer, rabbits, wild turkeys, and other animals. As these animals became rarer, so did the animals that hunted them, such as wolves, foxes, hawks, and eagles. The destruction of forests also caused some lakes and streams to dry up, which meant that animals living around them—mink, otters, and muskrats—also decreased in number.

By the end of the colonial period, many forests in the eastern part of North America had been replaced by fields and meadows. The landscape bore little resemblance to what the earliest European explorers and colonists had seen when they arrived on the continent. (*See also* **Environmental Impact of Colonization; Housing; Ships and Shipbuilding.**)

Fort Duquesne

Located at the site of present-day Pittsburgh, Fort Duquesne was built by the French in 1754 to extend their influence into the Ohio Valley—an area claimed by both Britain and France. The fort had great strategic* importance because it controlled the place where the Allegheny and Monongahela rivers join to form the mighty Ohio River.

* ***strategic*** key part of a plan; of military importance

See map in French and Indian War (vol. 2).

In 1753 the Marquis de Duquesne, the governor of New France, ordered French troops to build a series of FORTS that would link the Great Lakes region to the Ohio River. Meanwhile, Governor Robert Dinwiddie of Virginia sent a group of colonists to establish a military base at the headwaters of the Ohio River to protect the site from the French. Before the Virginians finished the fort, however, French troops seized it and then built their own stronghold, Fort Duquesne.

Shortly thereafter, British colonial forces led by Lieutenant Colonel George WASHINGTON tried without success to recapture the French fort. In 1755, at the beginning of the FRENCH AND INDIAN WAR, the British sent regular troops under the command of General Edward BRADDOCK to take Fort Duquesne. The French again triumphed, gaining a firm hold on the Ohio Valley. They used the fort as an administrative center, as well as a base from which to encourage Indian raids on the British colonies.

French control of Fort Duquesne lasted only a short time. In 1758 British general John Forbes led a large army to the stronghold. Faced with overwhelming forces, the French abandoned and burned the fort and retreated to the north. The British rebuilt the base and renamed it Fort Pitt, after William Pitt, the British prime minister. The fort continued to play a strategic role, helping the British secure control of the Ohio Valley and defend the frontier from Indian attacks. (*See also* **European Empires; Frontier.**)

* ***strategic*** key part of a plan; of military importance

* ***patriot*** American colonist who supported independence from Britain

* ***siege*** prolonged effort by armed troops to force the surrender of a town or fort by surrounding it and cutting if off from aid

See map in French and Indian War (vol. 2).

Located in New York on the western shore of Lake Champlain, Fort Ticonderoga controlled a strategic* route between French Canada and the British colonies. Built by the French, the stronghold passed into British hands and played an important role in the American Revolution.

The French began construction of Fort Carillon in 1755 during the FRENCH AND INDIAN WAR as part of their defense against a possible British invasion of Canada. The British attacked but failed to capture the fort in 1758. The following year, they had more luck. Led by Sir Jeffrey Amherst, they took possession of the site, but not before the French had blown up the fort and retreated. After rebuilding, the British called it Fort Ticonderoga.

During the American Revolution, the fort changed hands several times. In May 1775, it was seized without a fight by American patriot* Ethan ALLEN and his GREEN MOUNTAIN BOYS and Captain Benedict ARNOLD. Later that year, the stronghold's cannons were sent to Boston to help colonial American troops maintain their siege* against the British. The Americans abandoned Fort Ticonderoga in 1777, when faced with a large British army under the command of General John Burgoyne. After Burgoyne's defeat at the Battle of Saratoga later that same year, American forces reoccupied the fort. Never used again after the Revolution, Fort Ticonderoga was restored and became a museum in the early 1900s. (*See also* **American Revolution; Forts.**)

* ***strategic*** key part of a plan; of military importance

* ***outpost*** frontier settlement or military base

Forts were among the earliest and most important structures that Europeans built in North America. The French, British, Dutch, and Spanish erected forts to protect their settlements from Native Americans and to secure harbors, river mouths, and other strategic* locations from attack by rival powers. Many of these military bases also became important outposts* of trade between Europeans and Indians.

The Spanish and French, who began building defensive structures in North America in the late 1500s, often found themselves in competition

Fort Caroline in Florida was one of the earliest military bases in North America. Jacques Le Moyne painted the building of the French fort in 1564. A year later, the fort was destroyed by the Spanish.

See map in Spanish Borderlands (vol. 4).

for the best locations. Soon after the French built Fort Caroline (near present-day Jacksonville, Florida), the Spanish responded by founding ST. AUGUSTINE about 50 miles to the south. Similar competition for prime locations occurred in other parts of the continent and involved the British and Dutch as well.

For more than 200 years, European powers built forts along both coasts of the continent and throughout the frontier regions of the interior. Often in the forefront of colonization efforts, these strongholds played a vital role in the survival of settlements and in establishing territorial claims of rival nations.

Types of Forts. The design and strength of colonial forts varied greatly. Some were small enclosures with crude earthen walls thrown up quickly as protection against Indians. Stockades were larger, more solid structures with walls of logs that could withstand well-organized attacks and sieges*. The strongest and largest forts, built of stone, were designed to survive massive assaults by artillery and troops.

* ***siege*** prolonged effort by armed troops to force the surrender of a town or fort by surrounding it and cutting it off from aid

Log stockades were the most common type of fort on the frontier. Most had blockhouses—two-story structures at the corners—which provided a place from which defenders could fire along the walls and prevent a direct offensive on the fort. When faced with the threat of enemy attack, settlers from the surrounding countryside gathered in the stockade for protection.

Stockade forts could usually stand up against Indian assaults because the Indians lacked heavy weapons that could bring down the walls. These forts were less effective against well-armed European troops because even armies with light artillery could easily destroy stockade walls. For this reason, colonial powers often built large, stone fortresses at strategic locations, such as at the mouths of important rivers and along major invasion routes. Many of these strongholds began as wooden stockades and were later rebuilt and made stronger.

Dutch Forts. When early Dutch colonists established the settlement of NEW AMSTERDAM (present-day New York City), they had specific plans and measurements for a defensive structure. Begun in 1627, their fort had four earthen bastions* on which to mount artillery. But the earthworks deteriorated, leaving little besides mounds of dirt. Rather than rebuild the fort, Peter STUYVESANT, the governor of New Netherland, decided to put up a wall in the 1650s that would separate New Amsterdam from the rest of Manhattan Island.

* ***bastion*** part of a fortress that sticks out beyond the walls

See map in New Netherland (vol. 3).

Farther up the Hudson River, near present-day Albany, New York, the Dutch built Fort Orange on the site of an earlier, abandoned military post. Constructed of wood, Fort Orange had four bastions and a moat that surrounded it. After a flood swept the fort away during the winter of 1647–1648, the Dutch rebuilt it with stone. Fort Orange included several houses and a brewery and was used primarily as a place for conducting trade with the Indians.

French Forts. The French had the most extensive network of defensive structures in colonial America. These forts served both military and commercial purposes. The early settlements in QUEBEC were protected by large garrisons—compounds that included a fort, barracks for soldiers, and other buildings. As the French extended their territorial claims, they established many military posts throughout North America. At strategic locations, they often constructed large, heavily fortified garrisons. In other places, they built stockades, used at times as administrative centers. Some French forts functioned primarily as TRADING POSTS and had only limited fortifications and few if any troops in residence.

Many of the forts built in the 1600s served as commercial centers in the FUR TRADE. These fortified trading posts provided a safe place where merchants, fur trappers, and Indians could gather and conduct business. In the late 1600s, the French began to invest huge amounts of money to construct forts primarily for military purposes. This shift occurred largely as a result of the continuing conflict with Britain over control of North America.

See map in French and Indian War (vol. 2).

Some of the French forts of the 1700s were built to provide a line of defense against the British. Several guarded strategic sites. Fort LOUISBOURG on Ile Royale, begun in 1720, protected access to the St. Lawrence River. FORT DUQUESNE (1754) was built to increase French strength in the Ohio Valley, a region claimed by both Britain and France. Fort Carillon (1755), later renamed FORT TICONDEROGA by the British, was designed to guard an invasion route between the British colonies and Canada.

Remember: *Words in small capital letters have separate entries, and the index at the end of Volume 4 will guide you to more information on many topics.*

English Forts. All early English settlements, including ROANOKE ISLAND in present-day North Carolina and JAMESTOWN COLONY in Virginia, had some type of fortification. Even the Pilgrims put up a crude stockade of logs and branches after landing in Massachusetts in 1620.

As settlement expanded, the British built forts of various types from Maine to northern Florida. Some served as trading posts. Others protected settlements from Indians. Still others helped establish British territorial claims and provide defense against France, Spain, and other colonial powers. The forts ranged in size from small stockades to large, heavily fortified garrisons.

During the 1700s, Britain responded to the growing number of French military bases by constructing rival forts throughout frontier areas. Among these was Fort Necessity, built near Fort Duquesne by George WASHINGTON to challenge French claims in the Ohio Valley. Other rival forts included Fort William Henry in northern New York—near the French Fort Carillon—and Fort Cumberland in Nova Scotia.

* ***Spanish Borderlands*** northern part of New Spain, area now occupied by Florida, Texas, New Mexico, Arizona, and California

See map in Missions and Missionaries (vol. 3).

Spanish Forts. Forts, or PRESIDIOS, played a major role in the defense and settlement of the Spanish Borderlands*. Spain established claim to territory by founding MISSIONS and then protecting the missionaries and settlers by building forts. These presidios provided defense against both Indians and rival colonial powers. Settlements often grew up around the Spanish forts, which served as marketplaces and government centers as well as military outposts. San Marco in Florida, Santa Fe in New Mexico, San Antonio in Texas, and San Diego and Monterey in California were among the most important presidios.

Almost all presidios were garrisons that included barracks for troops, plus a kitchen and storerooms, a jail, blacksmith and carpenter shops, and even a chapel. Presidios that were located at a seat of government also contained a governor's house and governmental offices. In design, presidios often were quite different from Dutch, French, or British forts. Most were built either of stone or adobe—sun-dried bricks—a common building material in desert areas of the Southwest. (*See also* **Construction and Building Techniques; Frontier; Military Forces; Spanish Borderlands.**)

Fox Indians

See second map in Native Americans (vol. 3).

In the early 1700s, the Fox Indians lived in the western Great Lakes region. French colonists gave the name Fox to the tribe, but the people have always called themselves the Mesquakie, which means Red Earth People.

The Fox were both a hunting and an agricultural society. During the warmer seasons, they lived in permanent lodges made of poles and bark. The women raised corn, beans, squash, pumpkins, and melons and gathered nuts, berries, honey, and other wild foods. The men hunted deer and other animals, both for food and for the skins, which they used for clothing and for trading. In the fall and winter, the Fox migrated to the prairies to hunt. There they built small, oval-shaped lodges that could be easily moved as they followed the game.

In 1712 the commander of the French fort at Detroit heard rumors that the Fox Indians were planning to destroy the fort, and he convinced neighboring tribes to attack them. The Fox attempted to flee but were pursued and forced to fight. About 800 of them died in the battle, and they became bitter enemies of the French and their Indian allies.

Conflict between the French and the Fox continued for many years, marked by an occasional truce. In 1730, after losing a battle against the French, the Fox sought shelter with the Sauk, a closely related tribe. The Sauk stood by the Fox and refused to surrender them to the French. Soon afterward, the two tribes migrated west to what is now Wisconsin and then south to an area in present-day Iowa and Illinois. In 1804 the U.S. government tried to force the Sauk and Fox to leave Illinois so white Americans could settle there. Some Fox moved out of the area, but others refused. Finally, in 1832 U.S. soldiers drove the remaining Fox across the Mississippi River after a short but bloody war.

France

During the Middle Ages, the area of present-day France was divided into several regions ruled by powerful nobles. Over time, strong kings united these regions into one nation and ruled with almost unlimited power. These monarchs helped make France one of the leading powers in Europe—and a major player in the contest for colonial empires in North America.

A Powerful Monarchy. King Louis XI, who reigned from 1461 to 1483, used marriages, wars, and political schemes to take control of lands that had been ruled by nobles. He built a strong national army and gained power from the Estates-General—a representative assembly similar to the English PARLIAMENT. By tradition, the Estates-General had to approve all taxes, but Louis won the right to tax without the assembly and to pass any laws he desired. This new royal power was an important step in the creation of an absolute monarchy* in France.

* ***absolute monarchy*** rule by a king or queen who possesses unlimited power

The trend toward absolute monarchy continued under Louis's successors. Francis I, king from 1515 to 1547, gained significant power over the Catholic Church when the pope allowed him to appoint religious officials in France. Thereafter, church and state were closely linked, and French kings claimed that their right to rule came directly from God.

Throughout the 1400s and 1500s, French kings also made efforts to increase their power in Europe. They tried to gain control of Italy in a series of wars that began in the late 1400s, and they resisted the expansion of Germany along France's eastern borders. This focus on European affairs prevented any serious effort by France to explore or colonize the Americas. However, as the French saw gold and silver flowing to Spain from its American empire, they became interested in acquiring American territory and riches themselves. In the early 1500s, France sent Giovanni da Verrazano and Jacques CARTIER on expeditions that provided the basis for claims to large portions of North America. But finding no gold in these regions, the French did not pursue colonization at that time.

See third map in Exploration, Age of (vol. 2).

Religious Conflict and Colonization. Starting in the mid-1500s, France was torn apart by religious wars between Catholics and Protestants, who were known as HUGUENOTS. The wars led to the country's first attempts to settle in the Americas. Huguenots fleeing persecution tried to create colonies in Brazil and Florida. But opposition from Portugal and Spain, which already claimed those lands, forced the Huguenots to abandon their plans.

The religious wars in France ended when Henry IV became king in 1589. Raised as a Huguenot, Henry became a Catholic to overcome opposition to his rule, but he issued the Edict of Nantes, a law that granted Huguenots freedom of religion. Under the edict, Huguenots gained political control of some

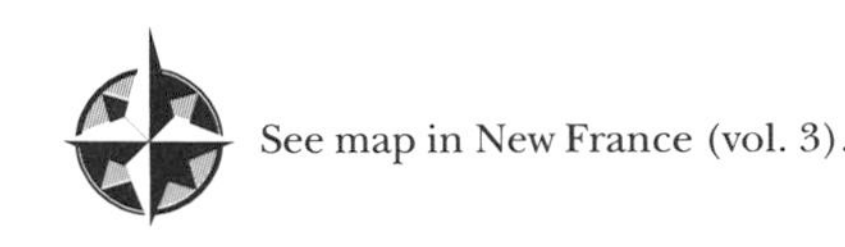
See map in New France (vol. 3).

regions of France. A period of peace followed, during which France began its first major efforts to colonize North America. In 1608 Samuel de Champlain founded Quebec, the first permanent French settlement in North America. In 1627 France formed a trading company known as the Company of One Hundred Associates to speed the colonization of New France.

Rising Power of France. Civil war raged again in France in the mid-1600s as nobles struggled for power. Hoping to restore order, the French people gave even greater power to the king. During his reign from 1643 to 1715, Louis XIV gained control over all aspects of government. He used his power to build France into one of the mightiest nations of Europe. His government raised taxes to finance vast building projects and wage war against other European nations. He canceled the Edict of Nantes in 1685 and began to persecute the Huguenots.

During his long reign, France gained a reputation as the cultural center of Europe. French architecture, painting, and literature were greatly admired throughout Europe, and Louis became known as the "Sun King" because of the splendor of his reign.

As France's power and prestige grew, so did its empire in North America. New France expanded to include the area around the Great Lakes, the Mississippi River valley, and Louisiana. At the same time, France often clashed with its chief rival, Great Britain. Between the late 1600s and mid-1700s, the two nations fought a series of wars in both Europe and North America. The last of these wars, known as the French and Indian War in North America and the Seven Years War in Europe, resulted in a serious defeat for France. In the Treaty of Paris of 1763, the nation lost important parts of its overseas empire, including most of its North American territories.

See second map in European Empires (vol. 2).

France sought to gain some revenge for this defeat when Britain's 13 American colonies declared their independence. The French came to the assistance of the rebels and in 1778 signed a formal alliance with the new American nation. French military and financial aid played a vital role in helping the Americans win the Revolutionary War.

Revolution and the End of Empire. Frequent wars—and the aid to the United States—eventually drained the French treasury and led to serious financial problems in the late 1700s. Moreover, high taxes and poor harvests spread hunger and unrest throughout France. Many French people began to lose confidence in the monarchy, and the success of the American Revolution inspired them to demand change. The Marquis de Lafayette, a French officer who had fought in the American Revolution, was one of the first to urge the French to pursue democracy. Tensions rose, and in 1789 the nation plunged into a bloody revolution that resulted in the overthrow of the monarchy. King Louis XVI and his queen, Marie Antoinette, were killed—along with thousands of nobles.

Remember: *Consult the index at the end of Volume 4 to find more information on many topics.*

Out of the ashes of the French Revolution arose a brilliant general named Napoleon Bonaparte. Napoleon won victories over European nations that invaded France to restore its monarchy. He also won back Louisiana and lands west of the Mississippi River, giving France a North American territory once again. Napoleon, however, needed funds to pursue his wars in Europe. For

that reason, he sold the vast Louisiana territory to the United States in 1803, ending forever all dreams of a French empire in North America. (*See also* **American Revolution; Colonial Administration; European Empires; Exploration, Age of; Roman Catholic Church.**)

Franciscans

See *Missions and Missionaries.*

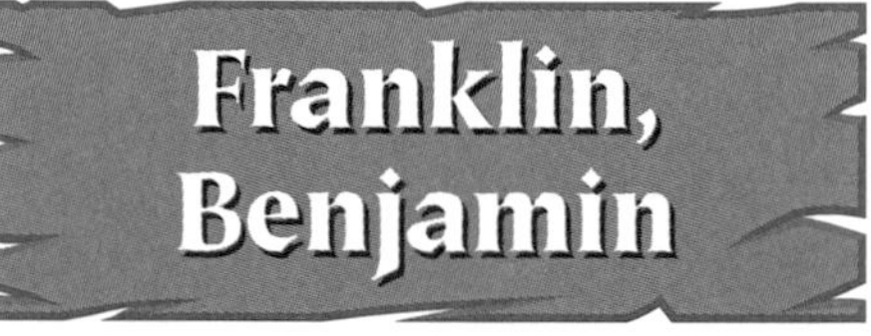

Franklin, Benjamin

1706–1790

Statesman, scientist, printer, author

Gifted with intelligence, wit, and charm, Benjamin Franklin rose from humble origins to become one of the best-known and most admired Americans of his day. A successful businessman, Franklin retired early to pursue his wide-ranging interests. He read extensively, made important discoveries in science, and invented several useful devices. Franklin was also a patriot* and statesman who spent years furthering the cause of American independence, serving as a member of the SECOND CONTINENTAL CONGRESS, a peace negotiator, and a diplomat to France.

* ***patriot*** American colonist who supported independence from Britain

* ***apprentice*** to place in the care of a merchant or crafts worker to learn a profession

Early Life. Josiah Franklin, Benjamin's father, came to North America from England around 1682 and settled in Boston. Benjamin, the youngest of Josiah's ten sons, was born in 1706. At age 12, he was apprenticed* to his half brother James, a printer and later a newspaper publisher.

While learning the printing trade, Franklin read every book he could find. He practiced writing, modeling his style on the work of famous essayists of the time. One day he wrote a short piece, signed it "Silence Dogood," and slipped it under the door of James's print shop. It appeared in his brother's newspaper the following day, prompting Franklin to write several more "Dogood" pieces.

The two brothers frequently quarreled, and in 1723 Franklin left the print shop—and Boston—and sailed south. He landed in Philadelphia, only 17 years old and ready to begin a new life.

Benjamin Franklin was already well known as an author and a scientist before he became involved in politics. In later life, he spent years working to secure independence for the British colonies.

Printer and Public Figure. For the next few years, Franklin worked in a series of jobs, sometimes in a printer's shop, sometimes as a merchant's clerk. In 1730 he married and became the sole owner of a print shop and a newspaper called *The Pennsylvania Gazette.* Over the next 20 years, Franklin devoted much of his time to making his business profitable. His friendly nature, good business sense, and clear style of writing gained him many friends and admirers.

In 1732 Franklin wrote *Poor Richard's Almanack,* a book filled with short and often humorous sayings advising people how to live wisely, thriftily, and morally. The almanac became a huge success, selling about 10,000 copies, and he published a new edition every year for the next 25 years. "As poor Richard says" became a common phrase throughout the colonies whenever a speaker wished to add authority to his or her point.

While working as a printer, Franklin also pursued his passion for self-improvement. He taught himself to read French, Spanish, Italian, and Latin.

He established a debating club in which he and his friends could exchange views on leading issues of the day. He also drew up a list of useful virtues*—including sincerity, justice, and moderation—and tried to practice one of them each week.

* ***virtue*** moral goodness

Along with improving himself, Franklin contributed greatly to his community. He outlined plans to establish a police force in Philadelphia and to pave, clean, and light the city streets. In 1731 he started a circulating library, the first in the colonies. In 1736 Franklin formed a volunteer fire company, another first for the colonies. A few years later, he launched the AMERICAN PHILOSOPHICAL SOCIETY, and in 1751 he founded a city hospital. Franklin also helped create the Academy for the Education of Youth, which later became the University of Pennsylvania. In addition, he served in the Pennsylvania assembly and was one of two deputy postmasters for the 13 British colonies.

Scientist and Inventor. Franklin became fascinated with scientific matters as a young adult and pursued this interest throughout his life. In 1744 he invented the "Pennsylvania stove," a cast-iron stove that heated rooms better and more cheaply than did other stoves of the day. He also invented a more efficient clock. In order to spend more time on his scientific studies, Franklin made the foreman of the print shop his partner and left the daily operation of the business to him.

During this period, Franklin used a kite to perform his famous experiment in which he proved that lightning was a form of electricity. Though others had suggested the connection between electricity and lightning, Franklin deserves credit for inventing a method to test the idea. His report on his work made Franklin famous in the European scientific community. Three leading American colleges—Harvard, Yale, and William and Mary—awarded Franklin an honorary master of arts degree.

Statesman and Patriot. Franklin's success—and his resulting fame—reinforced his desire to devote himself to science. But events interfered with his plans, and politics became his main occupation for the next 30 years. At the ALBANY CONGRESS in 1754, which included representatives from seven colonies, Franklin presented a plan for uniting all the colonies under one government. Although the congress supported the proposal, the colonial assemblies and the British government rejected it. Franklin's plan would later provide a model for colonists seeking an independent American government.

Franklin also became involved in politics on a local level. The Pennsylvania colonial assembly had an ongoing dispute with the family of William PENN about taxes. As proprietors* of the colony, the Penns appointed its governor and received an exemption* from paying taxes on their property. The assembly sent Franklin to London in 1757 to persuade the British government to force the family to pay taxes on their holdings. After almost three years, the British government ruled in the colony's favor.

* ***proprietor*** person granted land and the right to establish a colony
* ***exemption*** excused from an obligation

Enjoying his time in London, Franklin stayed for two more years and even considered making England his home. He reluctantly returned to America in 1762, but a new dispute between the assembly and the Penns sent him back to Britain. While in London, he advised British political leaders not to

enact a proposed law that placed a tax on paper products and documents in the colonies. When the British PARLIAMENT went ahead and passed the STAMP ACT in 1765, however, Franklin urged the colonists to obey it. The law provoked great opposition in the colonies, and Franklin's position hurt his popularity. Later he testified before the House of Commons* and asked them to repeal* the Stamp Act. Widely published, his eloquent testimony helped repair his damaged reputation in the colonies and gained him new admirers abroad.

* ***House of Commons*** one of two houses that make up the British Parliament

* ***repeal*** to undo a law

In the next few years, Franklin took a stronger position on American rights. While he had once believed that Parliament had the right to tax the colonies, his views gradually changed. By 1768 he commented: "Parliament has a power to make *all laws* for us, or . . . it has a power to make no laws for us; and I think the arguments for the latter [position] more numerous and weighty, than those for the former." He remained in Britain and served as an agent for Massachusetts, New Jersey, and Georgia, representing the colonies' interests in discussions with British officials. He did not return home until May 1775. The day after his arrival, the Pennsylvania assembly named him as a member of the Second Continental Congress.

Politics and the fight for independence from Britain kept Franklin occupied during the next year and a half. He drafted a plan of union for the colonies, organized the post office, joined a commission to CANADA to try to persuade Canadians to take part in the rebellion against Britain, served on the committee that drafted the DECLARATION OF INDEPENDENCE, and helped open diplomatic relations with FRANCE. In 1776 the congress sent Franklin and two other diplomats to France to negotiate an alliance. Before leaving, Franklin loaned the congress several thousand pounds.

Remember: *Words in small capital letters have separate entries, and the index at the end of Volume 4 will guide you to more information on many topics.*

Although the French government could not receive Franklin without officially recognizing the colonies as an independent nation, the French people treated him like a hero. Franklin's popularity and his close relationship with the French minister, Comte de Vergennes, played a large part in the success of the American mission to form an alliance with France. The two countries signed treaties—one for trade and one for mutual defense—in February 1778. Later that year, the American congress named Franklin as the sole representative to France. He spent the next three years strengthening the alliance and obtaining much needed money, troops, and supplies for the new nation.

In 1781 an American delegation made up of Franklin, John ADAMS, and John Jay met with British diplomats in Paris to discuss ending the Revolutionary War. Franklin's diplomacy helped smooth the sometimes heated negotiations that led to a series of treaties formally granting the colonies independence from Britain. After finally returning to Pennsylvania in 1785, Franklin—by then almost 80—was named president of Pennsylvania's executive council. Two years later, he served in the Constitutional Convention, which produced the Constitution of the United States.

In his final years, Franklin wrote, met with friends, and enjoyed his grandchildren's company. He continued to tinker with inventions, creating a device to lift books off high shelves. His last public act was to send a message urging Congress to end slavery. When he died, at age 84, 20,000 people paid honor to him at his funeral.

Free Blacks

Although most African Americans in colonial North America were slaves, a sizable number were free. The status* of these free blacks varied according to where they lived. But throughout the colonial era, most had to struggle to maintain their few rights and privileges.

* *status* social position

The Origin of Free Blacks. Some African Americans gained their liberty by escaping from SLAVERY in one colony to freedom in another. As early as the 1680s, Africans who worked as slaves on South Carolina plantations found freedom by fleeing to Spanish Florida. Many of them served in a militia* unit formed to protect the Spanish colony. In the 1730s, these black troops were stationed at Gracia Real de Santa Teresa de Mosea, a base just north of the town of St. Augustine that became the center of free black life in Spanish Florida.

* *militia* army of citizens who may be called into action in a time of emergency

The French in Louisiana also used black militia troops to protect the colony. When European rivals or Indians threatened the colony, French officials recruited both free and enslaved blacks. The slaves who served in the army were liberated, thus adding to the number of free blacks. After Spain took over Louisiana in 1763, black soldiers played an important role in the colony's defense. By 1770 more than 300 free blacks served in the militia.

Fewer African Americans took this path to freedom in the British colonies, where the large white population filled the need for militia service. Even there, though, emergencies could persuade colonial officials to enlist black soldiers. Feeling threatened by its Spanish neighbors and by Indians, Georgia invited free blacks to settle in the colony in 1765. During the American Revolution, the British—and some colonies—offered freedom to any slaves who enlisted in the army.

Some free blacks were the children of white settlers and African women. In early colonial times, the number of male settlers often exceeded the number of females. White men sometimes formed relationships with African women and liberated children born of the union. This practice was especially common in Louisiana. Under both French and Spanish rule in that colony, the majority of the African Americans freed from slavery were children of mixed white and black ancestry.

Some slaves managed to purchase their liberty, and others were freed by slaveholders. African Americans who worked as artisans*—especially in towns and cities—might save money to buy their own freedom. In some cases, free blacks paid for the liberation of other blacks. During the 1700s, an ANTISLAVERY MOVEMENT developed in the British colonies. QUAKERS decided that it was immoral for any Quaker to have slaves, and several northern states banned slavery after the British colonies won independence. By 1790 the United States had about 60,000 free blacks, 8 percent of the total African American population.

* *artisan* skilled crafts worker

Treatment of Free Blacks. Free blacks generally lived in a halfway zone—enjoying more rights than slaves but fewer privileges than whites. Their status and treatment tended to be better in areas where plantation agriculture and slavery did not dominate the economy. In such places, they could buy land, increase their wealth, and pass estates on to their children. Even in slaveholding Virginia, free blacks could prosper. Anthony Johnson came to

Virginia as a slave in about 1621, before slavery had become widespread in the colony. He managed to win his freedom, marry, and acquire a 250-acre farm. Building on this foundation, his sons established prosperous farms of their own. But such success stories were extremely rare in slaveholding colonies.

Similar stories occurred in French Louisiana and the Dutch colony of New Netherland. The DUTCH WEST INDIA COMPANY—the holder of most of the slaves in New Netherland—created a status called "half-freedom." This position allowed slaves to work for themselves as long as they paid a certain sum to the company every year. Under half-freedom, blacks enjoyed many privileges, including registering their marriages and baptizing their children, that were denied to slaves. Some blacks used the benefits of half-freedom to earn enough to become fully free.

As slavery became more fully developed in the British colonies, life became more difficult for free blacks. They enjoyed better treatment in the 1600s than in the 1700s. Over time, many colonies passed laws relating to the status of African Americans. Some restricted the opportunity of slaves to purchase their liberty and of slaveholders to grant it. Others limited the rights of free blacks. Rumors that Virginia would actually enslave free blacks led the Johnson family to leave the colony. By the time of the American Revolution, most colonies banned free blacks from voting, holding office, joining the militia, serving on a jury, or testifying against a white person in a trial. Free blacks who committed crimes often suffered more severe punishments than whites for the same offense.

Still, there was a great deal of variation in the treatment of free blacks during the colonial period. While the British colonies passed laws to limit the rights of free blacks, the Spanish in Louisiana took steps to expand their privileges. By 1723 Virginia and the two Carolinas had prohibited voting by free blacks. However, by the time Georgia passed a similar law in 1761, North Carolina had reversed its policy. Many restrictions on the lives of free blacks remained in place through the end of the colonial period. (*See also* **African American Culture; Race Relations.**)

Freedom of Religion

Many colonists came to North America in the 1600s seeking freedom of religion—but only for themselves. They did not respect the right of other people to worship in their own way. This situation gradually changed as colonies adopted policies allowing citizens some freedom in their choice of religion.

Religious groups such as the PILGRIMS, PURITANS, Catholics, and QUAKERS had all come to America to escape persecution for their beliefs. Throughout the 1600s, though, most colonial governments favored one religion over others. Some even established an official religion for the colony and denied rights to people of other faiths. In early Massachusetts, citizens who were not Puritans could not vote or hold public office.

Several colonies did allow considerable religious liberty. Roger WILLIAMS founded Rhode Island as a haven for people who left Massachusetts because of its restrictions on religious freedom. Rhode Island did not

have an official religion, and the colony kept CHURCH AND STATE separate. The founder of Maryland, Cecil CALVERT, hoped to create a refuge for Roman Catholics who faced persecution in England. But when Protestants entered the colony in large numbers, he assured them that they would be free to practice their religion as well. He convinced the colonial assembly to pass an ACT OF TOLERATION in 1649 that allowed most Christians the right to worship freely. Although the Protestant-led assembly repealed* the act five years later, the Calverts continued to support a policy of toleration* for many years.

* ***repeal*** to undo a law
* ***toleration*** acceptance of the right of individuals to follow their own religious beliefs

The colonists of the middle colonies enjoyed considerable liberty to worship as they pleased. New York and New Jersey consisted of settlers of many different faiths, and this religious diversity encouraged a spirit of toleration. In Pennsylvania and Delaware, the policies of William PENN promoted religious freedom. In 1682 he issued a Charter of Liberty that allowed anyone who believed in God the right to worship in his or her own way.

From the 1730s to 1750s, the GREAT AWAKENING spread throughout the British colonies. This religious revival created new Protestant groups, and the increased number of different faiths made the existence of an official church difficult. At the same time, another movement sweeping Europe and North America helped broaden the idea of religious liberty. Followers of the ENLIGHTENMENT thought that governments should not interfere with people's beliefs. They also argued that citizens should respect the rights of others, including the right to practice one's faith freely and openly. These Enlightenment ideas had a great influence on American political leaders. In 1776 Virginia passed a Declaration of Rights, which proclaimed that laws should not limit an individual's "liberty of conscience." The First Amendment to the United States Constitution, adopted in 1791, prohibits the establishment of an official religion and guarantees freedom of religion to all Americans. (*See also* **Jews; Protestant Churches; Roman Catholic Church.**)

Freedom of the Press

See *Press in Colonial America.*

French and Indian War

For almost a century, France and Great Britain fought for dominance in North America, carrying their long, bitter rivalry in Europe across the Atlantic to the "New World." This struggle included four major wars. The last of these conflicts, the French and Indian War, lasted from 1754 to 1763. The war began in North America but extended to Europe, where it was called the Seven Years' War. In winning the war, the British expelled the French from North America—a victory that set the stage for the American Revolution.

Background of the War. Between 1688 and 1748, England and France fought three major wars. Each began in Europe but included combat in North America. The peace that followed the third war in 1748 was a fragile and uneasy one.

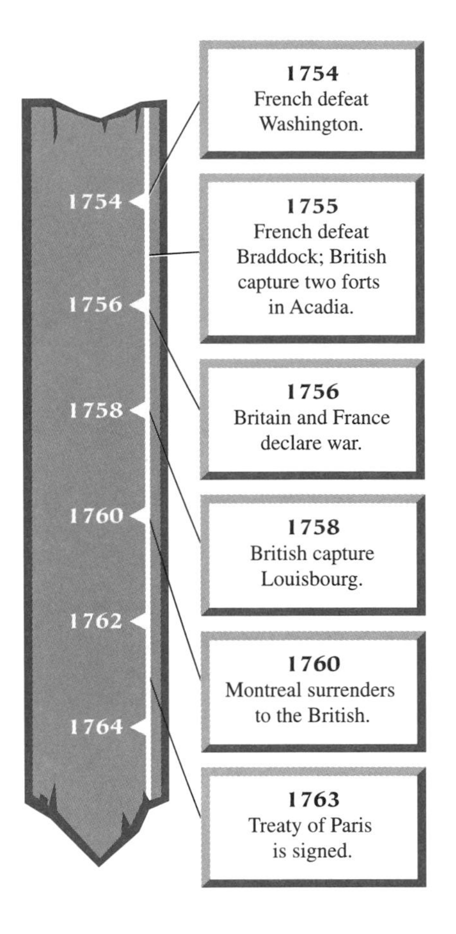

Three sources of conflict remained in North America after 1748. First, the British and French competed for fishing areas in the rich waters off the coast of eastern Canada. Second, both sides wanted to control the profitable trade in furs. The main source of conflict, however, arose over possession of land. Once the British colonists had settled much of the Atlantic coastal region, they began to push westward over the Appalachian Mountains into the Ohio River valley. But the French also claimed that region as part of New France. If the French controlled the Ohio Valley—as well as the St. Lawrence River, the Great Lakes region, and the Mississippi River—the British would not be able to expand their settlements beyond the Appalachian Mountains.

In terms of numbers, the British had a clear advantage over the French. About 1.5 million people lived in the British colonies, while New France had only about 70,000 inhabitants. The French, however, enjoyed better relations with several powerful Native American groups. If a war broke out, the French could count on these Indians for help in fighting the British.

Conflict Begins. In the 1750s, the governor of New France, Ange Duquesne de Menneville, began building a series of forts from the Great Lakes to the Ohio Valley in order to strengthen French claims in the region. The move angered British colonists in Virginia, who claimed the Ohio Valley region themselves. In 1753 Virginia governor Robert Dinwiddie sent a colonial militia* under George Washington to order the French to abandon Fort Le Boeuf near Lake Erie. The French not only ignored the Virginians' demand but also began building a new fort at the site of present-day Pittsburgh. They called it Fort Duquesne in honor of their governor.

The British government then authorized Dinwiddie to use force to expel the French from the Ohio Valley. Once again, the governor sent Washington and the militia westward. Early in 1754, while on their way to the Ohio River, Washington's troops ambushed a group of French soldiers, killing ten of them. News of the attack outraged France, and a large army of French troops and Indian warriors pursued Washington and his militia. Unable to escape, the British hastily erected "Fort Necessity." The French captured the fort and forced Washington and the militia to retreat to Virginia.

* ***militia*** army of citizens who may be called into action in a time of emergency

French Successes. The conflict resumed in 1755, although neither side had formally declared war. The British undertook several actions that year. They sent a fleet to prevent additional French troops from landing in Canada. The fleet seized two French ships off the coast of Canada but failed to stop more than 3,000 French troops from reaching Quebec. Meanwhile, British troops under General Edward Braddock prepared to attack Fort Duquesne. French and Indian forces surprised Braddock, routing his troops and killing the general. British attacks on two other French strongholds also ended in failure. The only British success that year came in the province of Acadia, where British troops captured two French forts.

While this fighting took place in America, Britain and France scurried to build alliances with other European nations. In 1756, with their allies in place, the two nations formally declared war. France and Britain were now at war in North America, in Europe, and in other territories around the world.

The French military success in America continued in 1756. General Louis-Joseph de Montcalm captured Fort Oswego, a British stronghold on Lake Ontario, and began to threaten British settlements throughout western New York. The British had difficulty fighting in the heavily forested areas of the frontier, where France's Indian allies had the advantage. They began to look for other strategies. Lord Loudoun, the British commander, came up with a plan to use the British navy to take control of the St. Lawrence River and then capture Quebec, the capital of New France.

In the summer of 1757, Loudoun prepared to attack the French fort of LOUISBOURG, which guarded the mouth of the St. Lawrence River. On arriving, however, he discovered a superior French fleet protecting the site. Loudoun withdrew. In the meantime, General Montcalm captured an important British military base, Fort William Henry in upstate New York, and

The battles of the French and Indian War took place throughout the disputed border region between New France and the British colonies. After early French victories in upstate New York, Britain gained the upper hand, eventually capturing the key French cities of Montreal and Quebec.

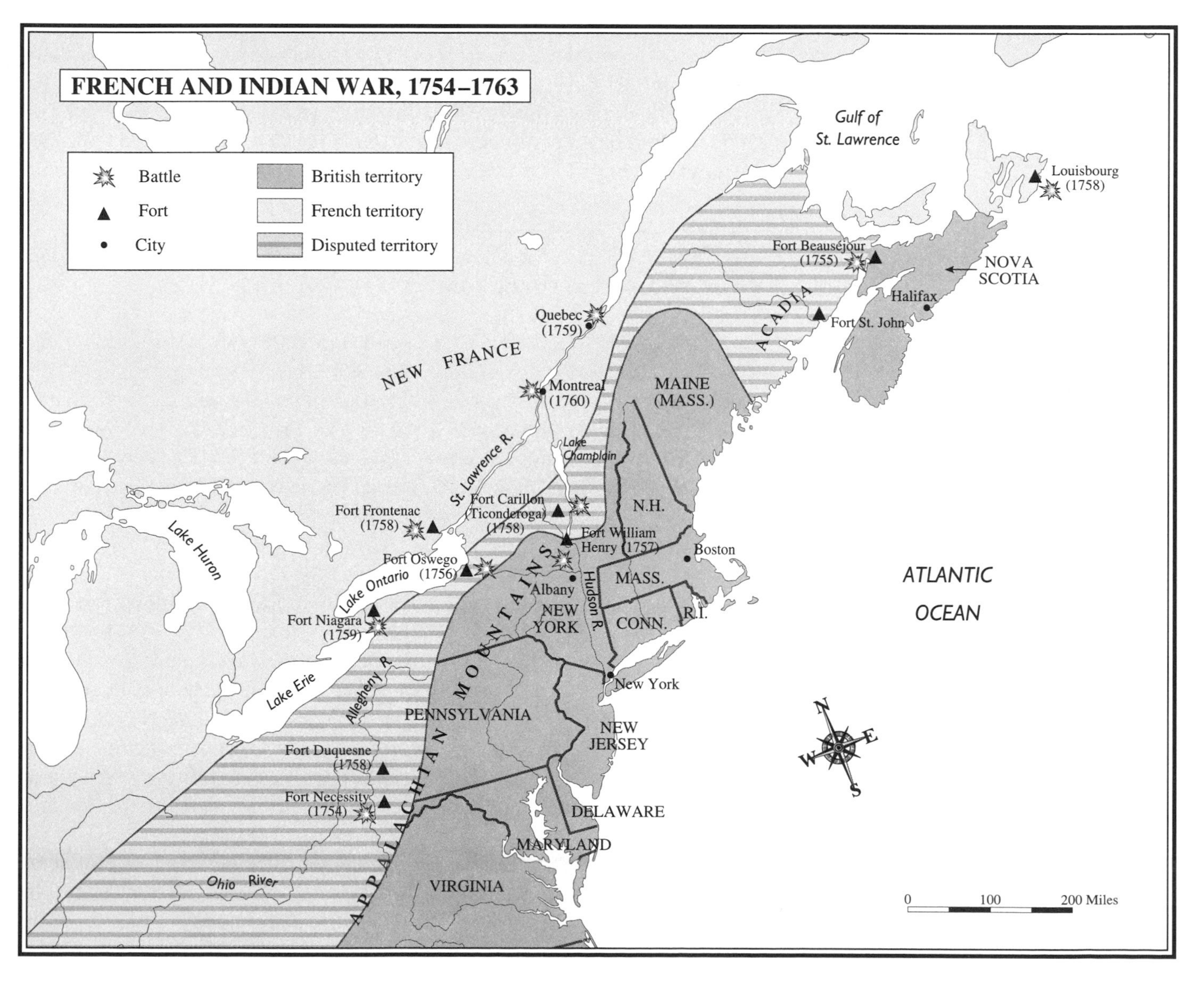

British colonists in New York City and New England felt threatened. But at this crucial time, France's Indian allies withdrew, leaving Montcalm's forces too weak to undertake any new campaigns in the region.

British Victory. Troubled by losses in North America and Europe, King George II named a new prime minister—William PITT—to head the British government. Pitt pursued the war more aggressively, sending large numbers of troops to North America and launching new offensives.

In 1758 the British captured Louisbourg and Fort Frontenac, an important outpost* on Lake Ontario. They also forced the French to leave Fort Duquesne. The following year, the French suffered even worse setbacks. They had to abandon two important forts on Lake Champlain in New York. They also lost Fort Niagara, a strategic* base on Lake Ontario that guarded approaches to and from the Great Lakes region.

* ***outpost*** frontier settlement or military base

* ***strategic*** key part of a plan; of military importance

The capture of Fort Niagara gave the British a staging area from which to launch an attack on MONTREAL. The French countered this threat by sending troops from Quebec to Montreal. This move helped save Montreal from the British, but it weakened Quebec. In 1759 British commander James Wolfe led an assault on the French colonial capital. After months of siege*, Quebec finally surrendered to the British in September of that year. Both Wolfe and the French commander Montcalm died in the battle.

* ***siege*** prolonged effort by armed troops to force the surrender of a town or fort by surrounding it and cutting it off from aid

In the spring of 1760, French troops from Montreal tried to recapture Quebec. But when British reinforcements arrived, the French had to retreat to Montreal. Later that year, the British forced the French in Montreal to surrender. Soon after, other French outposts in the Great Lakes region fell to the British, bringing the American part of the war to an end.

Peace and the Aftermath. Between 1760 and 1763, France and Britain worked out the details of a peace treaty. With the TREATY OF PARIS of 1763, France ceded* to Britain all its North American territory except for St. Pierre and Miquelon, two small islands in the Gulf of St. Lawrence, and several islands in the West Indies. The British thus gained all of Canada and all land east of the Mississippi River. France ceded its land west of the Mississippi to Spain, which had become involved in the conflict the previous year. Spain gave Florida to Britain in return for Cuba, which the British had captured toward the end of the war.

* ***cede*** to yield or surrender

See second map in European Empires (vol. 2).

By 1763 most British troops had returned to Europe. The few thousand that remained were insufficient to meet a new threat that loomed. The Treaty of Paris had angered Native Americans because it gave Britain lands that the Indians felt belonged to them. Chief PONTIAC, a leader of the Ottawa Indians, organized a siege of several frontier forts. To restore peace, the British agreed to regulate trade and place a temporary ban on the sale and the settlement of Indian lands west of the Appalachian Mountains. But this new ruling, the Proclamation of 1763, outraged many Americans whose colonies claimed portions of the western lands. These western claims had played a role in the French and Indian War. Anger over this policy contributed to the strained relations between the colonies and Britain that led 13 years later to the American Revolution. (*See also* **American Revolution; European Empires; King George's War; King William's War; Queen Anne's War.**)

See *New France.*

The French West Indies Company was one of several European trading companies formed during the colonial period. Made up of wealthy investors, it took over the management of the colony of NEW FRANCE from another French enterprise, the COMPANY OF ONE HUNDRED ASSOCIATES.

Jean-Baptiste Colbert, a high official in the court of King Louis XIV of France, formed the West Indies Company in 1664. He gave it a monopoly* of trade between France and its possessions in West Africa and the Americas. The company's main focus was the WEST INDIES, France's most valuable territory in the Western Hemisphere.

* ***monopoly*** exclusive right to engage in a certain kind of business

* ***charter*** written grant from a ruler conferring certain rights and privileges

The charter* of the West Indies Company gave it a broad range of economic powers and the right to own forts and lands in France's American colonies. The king, however, reserved the right to appoint the colonies' governors. The French government hoped the new company would make New France less dependent on the FUR TRADE, promote colonization and agriculture, and help the colony become more self-sufficient. However, the enterprise found few investors and never became a financial success, despite the many economic advantages granted by the crown. It did build a large commercial fleet, but continuous warfare with other European nations brought heavy losses. The French West Indies Company was dissolved in 1674, just ten years after its founding. (*See also* **European Empires; Trade and Commerce.**)

Frontier

For the colonists of North America, the frontier was a broad zone on the outer edges of white settlement. Isolated from the centers of colonial power, the frontier was an area beyond European control, where the line between civilization and wilderness became blurred. This was also the area where Europeans and Native Americans met and mingled—for what the settlers considered "the frontier" was "home" to the Native Americans. Throughout the colonial period, the European frontier continually shifted as colonists left established settlements and pushed deeper into lands occupied only by Native Americans.

Two factors affected European and Native American relations on the frontier. The first was DISEASE. Between 1600 and 1700, thousands upon thousands of North American Indians—according to some estimates, up to 90 percent of the population—died of measles, smallpox, and the flu introduced to the continent by Europeans.

The second factor was the Europeans' attitude toward the land and its people. They believed they had every right to make full use of the resources they found in North America. The English colonists expanded their settlements continually, even when it meant pushing Indians off their lands. The Spanish pressed Native Americans into forced labor—a practice that provoked strong resistance from the Indians.

Native Americans who lived in frontier regions developed new ways of life as a result of their contact with Europeans. They adopted European goods such as metal pots for cooking or storage and firearms. They joined European trading networks and helped with the development and operation of the FUR TRADE. The introduction of the horse by the Spanish transformed the lives of some Native Americans, especially the PLAINS INDIANS. Many Indians who had contact with European MISSIONS AND MISSIONARIES converted to Christianity. Many, too, had their lives changed by addiction to alcohol, which the Europeans traded or sold to them.

The lives of Europeans were also affected by contact with Native Americans on the frontier. Colonists grew corn and other Indian crops and adopted Indian items such as canoes and moccasins. Some colonial settlements arose on the ruins of Indian villages, and settlers followed Indian trails through the forests.

While contact between Europeans and Native Americans affected both groups, Indian life suffered the most profound effects of this interaction. Traditional ways of life deteriorated and led to the breakdown of Native American societies and cultures. Moreover, conflicts between whites and Indians ultimately resulted in the defeat of the Indians and their domination by whites.

British Colonies

Remember: *Words in small capital letters have separate entries, and the index at the end of Volume 4 will guide you to more information on many topics.*

For the early English settlers in North America, the frontier was the land along the ATLANTIC COAST. As late as 1660, settlements were concentrated on the coast or inland along major rivers. The frontier was located at the outer edge of these areas. One hundred years later, colonial settlement had expanded all along the coast and into the interior as far west as the APPALACHIAN MOUNTAINS, and the frontier moved along with it.

Life on the Frontier. At first the Indians and settlers who met on the frontier often got along well. The early settlers of JAMESTOWN and the Pilgrims at PLYMOUTH survived largely because of local Indians, who helped provide food during the crucial early years of each colony. Within 15 years, however, cooperation had changed to conflict. The interaction of colonists and Indians led to the same result throughout the colonies. As more and more colonists arrived, they grew stronger. Feeling pressures building against them, the Indians fought to protect their lands and ways of life. Eventually, unable to contain the colonists, many Indians simply moved farther west.

Colonists expanded into the frontier by forming settlements in areas vacated by the Indians. Movement into the frontier differed by region. In New York and New England, settlement generally extended to the north and west, and pioneers tended to make relatively short moves to nearby frontiers. By contrast, settlement in Pennsylvania and the southern colonies generally expanded to the west and south, and colonists often relocated to frontier areas as far as 100 miles away from their homes. Pioneers rarely entered an area before the Indians had abandoned it. Forests covered much of the land, requiring the new inhabitants to clear the trees to make way for homes and farms. The settlers could sometimes take advantage of the land clearing that Indians had done over hundreds of years.

This painting of the frontier shows settlers clearing forested land. First they girdled the trees by cutting out a narrow strip of bark all around the trunk to kill the trees. Then they burned the fallen trees.

While some of the people who moved to the frontier were single men or women, most were young couples who wanted land to establish their own homes and farms. These people left their families behind and relied on their own skills and resources to begin new lives. In many cases, the frontier settlers did not remain isolated for long. The success of early pioneers led others to follow. Occasionally, parts of communities moved together. Sometimes owners of large tracts of land on the frontier encouraged settlement, inviting settlers to clear the land and raise crops in exchange for the payment of rent.

Mix of Cultures. The expansion of colonial settlement in the early 1700s brought new groups to the frontier and increased the mix of different cultures. Hoping to establish a buffer zone* between coastal settlements and Native Americans in the interior, British colonial leaders encouraged Scotch-Irish people to come to America to settle in the "backcountry," particularly in the South. These settlers were seen as proud and independent minded, aggressive in seizing land from the Indians, and loose in their standards of sexual behavior. It appears that they generally married young, and many had large families.

* ***buffer zone*** neutral area between two enemy areas

The frontier attracted African Americans as well. Some escaped slaves sought refuge and freedom in the unsettled areas of the frontier. Some lived in Native American villages, while others banded together in their own settlements. FREE BLACKS also came to the frontier in search of greater opportunities. African Americans contributed to frontier society in various ways. They applied their knowledge of European agriculture to frontier life. They also drew on their African tradition of using plants for healing, experimenting with the new plants they found. Black settlers adopted Indian practices—

often more rapidly than did white settlers. In some parts of the frontier, influences flowed in the opposite direction as well, with Indians adopting African American practices and plants.

Interracial communities developed in some parts of the frontier, most notably in the South. These MAROON COMMUNITIES generally remained beyond the reach of colonial law. They included people who wanted to escape established white society—Indians, blacks, people of mixed race, white indentured servants*, and poor whites. One of the most notable maroon communities, established by runaway slaves, was located in the Great Dismal Swamp on the border between Virginia and North Carolina. The large size of the swamp and its junglelike growth helped hide the community. Yet the swamp offered opportunities for hunting and fishing and numerous islands on which to build homes and create fields. Because the swamp lay between two colonies, it fell beyond the boundaries and authority of both. The maroon community grew to about 2,000 people and lasted more than 150 years.

* ***indentured servant*** person who agreed to work a certain length of time in return for passage on a ship to the colonies

The End of the Frontier. The British colonists believed that the frontier would continue to extend westward indefinitely, providing opportunities for new settlement. In the 1750s and 1760s, the OHIO RIVER valley became the focus of frontier activity. However, dreams of expanding into that region were cut short after the FRENCH AND INDIAN WAR. In 1763 Britain promised Native Americans living in the Ohio Valley that colonial settlements would be restricted to areas east of the Appalachian Mountains. The decision outraged colonists and contributed to the growing split between the colonies and Great Britain.

As the conflict between the colonists and Britain increased in the 1770s, tensions between the colonists and Indians in frontier regions rose to the breaking point. Memories of clashes during the French and Indian War combined with colonists' frustration over the British decision to limit settlement. Scattered outbreaks of violence by both Indians and whites occurred throughout the frontier.

In this atmosphere of mounting conflict, many Indians simply moved farther west. Some eastern tribes joined with the Americans during the American Revolution. Most, however, tried to remain neutral or sided with the British. After winning independence and signing the Treaty of Paris with Britain in 1783, the United States acquired all the land east of the Mississippi River. Neither the British nor the Americans invited Native Americans to sign the treaty, and neither side recognized Indian rights to that land. Within a few decades, almost all Indians would be gone from the frontier regions of the East. Many fled, while others were killed or removed forcibly from their lands. Once again, the frontier began to push westward.

Frontier Games

People on the frontier loved to take part in competitive sports—foot races, jumping contests, tugs of war, and the tossing of heavy objects such as quoits (stones) or cabers (heavy poles). Some frontier sports were violently aggressive. Bare-knuckle boxing and "gouging"—a bloody contest in which fighters bit, butted, choked, kicked, or stomped each other, sometimes ripping off noses and ears or tearing out tongues and eyeballs—were popular forms of combat. Colonial officials passed laws against such violent sports. But many frontiersmen laughed at rules they considered too "delicate" for the rugged backwoods and the strong, hardy people who lived there.

Spanish Colonies

Like the frontier in the British colonies, the Spanish frontier changed over time. During the late 1500s, the Spanish founded a handful of small isolated settlements in present-day Florida, Georgia, and South Carolina. Most of these were later abandoned. In the early 1600s, the Spanish began to colonize what are now New Mexico and Arizona. It took another hundred years before

See map in Spanish Borderlands (vol. 4).

the Spanish frontier extended into Texas, and it was not until the late 1700s that the Spanish started moving into California.

Character of the Spanish Frontier. The Spanish frontier differed from the British frontier in several ways. The first was size. The Spanish Borderlands* covered an enormous area that stretched from Florida to California. The vast expanses of this territory made communication and control difficult.

* ***Spanish Borderlands*** northern part of New Spain, area now occupied by Florida, Texas, New Mexico, Arizona, and California

The second difference was the reason for settlement. In the British colonies, settlers moved to frontier areas to start farms, build homes, and create new lives for themselves. They did this voluntarily and generally without needing encouragement from colonial officials. The Spanish frontier served a different purpose. Colonial authorities of NEW SPAIN ordered the construction of PRESIDIOS, or forts, in the Borderlands to provide defense for the main colonial settlements to the south. Presidios in Florida helped protect sea routes traveled by Spanish treasure ships from the Americas to Europe. Those in New Mexico and Arizona served to defend settlements in northern Mexico from Indian raids. In Texas the forts helped counter a French threat from the Mississippi River valley, and in California they were built to discourage Russian advances down the coast from Alaska. Settlement slowly followed the founding of presidios, with authorities actively encouraging colonists to move to the frontier.

Remember: *Words in small capital letters have separate entries, and the index at the end of Volume 4 will guide you to more information on many topics.*

The huge size of the Spanish Borderlands and the defensive purpose of its frontier settlements together explain a third difference between the British and Spanish frontiers. Although many fewer people lived in the Spanish Borderlands than in the British colonies, they tended to cluster together in groups. The land was simply too vast to fill, and settlers felt more secure living near each other because of the threat from Indians and other European powers.

These patterns of population distribution in the Spanish and the British colonies resulted in different relations with the Indians in the two arcas. In the British colonies, ever growing numbers of settlers posed an increasing threat to Indians, causing periodic outbreaks of hostilities and the eventual departure of Indians from their lands. In the Spanish colonies, the Indians greatly outnumbered the settlers and remained a powerful presence throughout the colonial period. From Arizona to Texas, the constant threat of raids from some Indian groups combined with the possibility of trade with others. In California, missions founded to convert Indians to Christianity and Spanish culture became important economic centers because of the work of Indian laborers.

Challenges on the Frontier. The Spanish presidios that guarded the frontier were staffed by small groups of soldiers, often accompanied by their families. Some presidios protected nearby missions, while others defended strategic* locations. The fort at ST. AUGUSTINE, for example, helped prevent raids on Spanish shipping off the coast of Florida.

* ***strategic*** key part of a plan; of military importance

In New Mexico, the PUEBLO REVOLT of 1680 revealed the weakness of Spanish defenses in the face of Indian attacks. While trying to address the growing problem of Indian raids and facing the additional threat of possible

French expansion from the Mississippi Valley into Texas, some officials began urging changes along the frontier. At the same time, however, Spanish colonial authorities wanted to reduce military expenses and cut the number of troops at the presidios.

With defenses along the frontier weakened by troop reductions, Indian attacks became more serious during the mid-1700s. In an area covering northern Mexico, southern Arizona, and western Texas, raids by APACHE INDIANS killed hundreds of Spanish settlers and destroyed millions of dollars' worth of property from 1749 to 1763. A new set of measures followed, involving the relocation of some presidios and a strengthening of troops.

In addition to making changes in the presidio system, the Spanish also forged closer ties to the COMANCHE INDIANS—the traditional enemies of the Apache. By making peace with the Comanche, the Spanish reduced the Indian threat and gained an important ally. At the same time, the Spanish took other steps that affected the frontier. They sent engineers to map the frontier regions of New Mexico and Arizona and to look for possible sites for mines, and they considered building new roads across the northern regions of the frontier.

The new defense policy calmed the situation along much of the frontier regions of New Mexico and Arizona. With peace came population growth—and growing prosperity. Trade with local Indians increased, as did trade with Mexico and other regions. Although the changes improved conditions for many settlers on the frontier, soldiers at the presidios continued to lead a difficult life. Many chose to leave the presidios and seek opportunities elsewhere. A good number of them simply deserted, vanishing into the wilderness outside Spanish control.

Settlers in Texas also faced the problem of Indian raids, but far fewer colonists lived there than in New Mexico or Arizona. Only in California did peace prevail throughout the entire colonial period. The CALIFORNIA INDIANS never mounted large organized campaigns against the Spanish, and the California frontier remained a stable area unmarred by the violence that had plagued the Southwest. (*See also* **Migration Within the Colonies; Native Americans.**)

The Fundamental Orders of Connecticut, adopted in 1639, established a framework for government in CONNECTICUT. The document is often regarded as the first written constitution in the English colonies. The royal charter* that replaced the Fundamental Orders in 1662 included many of the original document's provisions. The charter formed the basis of Connecticut's government until the state adopted a new constitution in 1818.

A few groups of colonists settled in Connecticut in the mid-1630s, founding the towns of Windsor, Hartford, and Wethersfield. In the spring of 1638, representatives of each town—plus Springfield, which later became part of Massachusetts—gathered to draw up a plan for governing the colony. The following January, a similar meeting approved adoption of the Fundamental Orders, an outline of government written by colonist Roger Ludlow.

* ***charter*** written grant from a ruler conferring certain rights and privileges

Patterned after the Massachusetts charter, the document included 11 orders, or points. The orders established a colonial assembly, listed the powers of the assembly, and specified who would sit on it and how they would be elected. The inhabitants of each town would elect four deputies to send to the assembly. These deputies, as well as the governor and judicial officials, were required to be property owners. Two of the orders established an important principle of representative government. If the governor failed to hold an assembly meeting, the deputies could call a meeting themselves. (*See also* **Colonial Administration.**)

Fur Trade

The fur trade played a major role in the history of the North American colonies. Although early explorers were disappointed to find that most of North America contained little gold, they discovered another source of wealth there—an abundant supply of animal life. The quest for valuable furs and hides led traders deeper and deeper into the heart of the continent, spurring the exploration of the interior and the West.

* ***pelt*** skin and fur of an animal

Trading companies in North America shipped millions of pelts* to Europe, creating a far-flung commercial enterprise that involved thousands of people on both sides of the Atlantic. Trappers, guides, shipowners, sailors, bankers, merchants, leather workers, hatmakers, and shoemakers all worked in the fur trade. It created unlikely alliances and fierce rivalries and made fortunes for some merchants. The fur trade also resulted in long-term damage to the ecology of North America and to the Native American way of life.

Origins of the Fur Trade. The fur trade grew out of the FISHING industry. In the early 1500s, European fishermen camped on the Atlantic coast of North America to dry their catches. They traded with Indians they encountered in the area, exchanging pieces of cloth or metal hardware such as nails and knives for the pelts of beavers, mink, and foxes. By the end of the century, the fur trade had developed from a sideline of the fishing industry to an important economic activity in its own right.

Furs were the most important item in the trade between Europeans and Native Americans. The fur trade developed first in the parts of present-day Canada that were colonized by the French.

In Europe people had cleared and cultivated much of the land. As the population expanded and took over the continent's forests and fields, fur-bearing animals such as the beaver all but disappeared. Yet the demand for pelts remained strong. Leather workers used hides to make cloaks, slippers, boots, harness pieces, and other goods. The wealthy wanted fine furs such as mink, otter, and ermine for decorative collars or trimmings on their clothing. Most desirable was the beaver, whose fur could be used to make fashionable hats that were sturdy and waterproof.

Europeans regarded furs as an ideal item for trade. North America appeared to contain an endless supply of animals, and the pelts were easy to transport and store. Best of all, furs were cheap. Native Americans exchanged them for hardware, cloth, blankets, mirrors, bells, beads, kettles, needles, and inexpensive jewelry. Many of these items were produced in large quantities especially for the Indian trade. Other major trade goods included guns and ammunition and liquor.

French Trade. The French were the first to begin acquiring furs systematically. In 1603 King Henry IV of France granted the first of several fur monopolies* in North America. By the mid-1600s, the French had established QUEBEC and several other settlements in the St. Lawrence River valley to support the fur trade. The HURON INDIANS, allies of the French, acted as middlemen between the Europeans and the Indians of the interior who trapped and hunted the animals. This connection gave the French control of most of the fur trade in the GREAT LAKES region.

* ***monopoly*** exclusive right to engage in a certain kind of business

In the early years of French colonization, young men sometimes abandoned the settled areas to become COUREURS DE BOIS. These "woods runners" were often unlicensed, and therefore illegal, fur traders who spent years living in the wilderness. In the late 1600s, there were perhaps 200 to 300 of these traders in Canada. Although the government and the monopoly holders opposed them, coureurs de bois played an important part in exploring and developing the region west of the Great Lakes.

In the early days, Indians brought furs directly to the French trading posts. As the demand for furs increased, however, trading companies began to send agents to seek out furs in the interior. For this task, they hired voyageurs, who skillfully navigated Canada's many rivers and lakes in birchbark CANOES as they ventured into the wilderness.

Hoping to link their Canada and Louisiana colonies, the French built a series of trading posts from the Great Lakes south along the Mississippi River. French traders based at these posts gathered pelts from this vast region. In 1763, when the French lost Canada and the lands east of the Mississippi following the FRENCH AND INDIAN WAR, British fur traders quickly moved into the territories previously controlled by the French.

Dutch and English Trade. In 1614 the Dutch established Fort Orange—later called ALBANY—on the Hudson River in New York. At the same time, they formed an alliance with the IROQUOIS, who served as their middlemen in the fur trade. The trade quickly became NEW NETHERLAND's chief source of income. When the English took over the Dutch settlement in 1664, they continued the Iroquois alliance.

Rivalry between the Dutch and English and their allies on one side and the French and their Indian allies on the other led to a series of Indian wars in the mid-1600s, resulting in the near-destruction of the Huron. In 1670 the English crown granted a monopoly on all trade, including the fur trade, to the HUDSON'S BAY COMPANY, a trading firm that established posts on Hudson Bay in northeastern Canada. For the next century, the French and the English clashed as they competed to win the loyalty—and the furs—of Indian tribes across central and western Canada.

English colonists also participated in the fur trade. For the PILGRIMS and PURITANS of New England, furs provided a source of income until their farms or other economic activities could support them. By about 1700, however, the growth of settlements and excessive hunting and trapping had exhausted the population of fur-bearing animals in the region to the point that it could no longer support trade. Farther south, in the Carolinas and Georgia, colonists bartered with the Indians of the interior for deerskins, an important part of the region's economy. By 1700 Carolina planters were taking caravans of 25 to 100 horses, each capable of carrying 150 pounds of skins, on trading expeditions into the APPALACHIAN MOUNTAINS and beyond.

Remember: *Words in small capital letters have separate entries, and the index at the end of Volume 4 will guide you to more information on many topics.*

Spanish Trade. The Spanish did not trade extensively in furs. Their territories lay in the southern part of the continent, where fur-bearing animals were rarer than in the North. Spanish colonists in New Mexico did, however, trade with the local Indians for deerskins and buffalo hides. The COMANCHE and other tribes brought hundreds of hides to gatherings such as the annual fair at Taos, New Mexico, in the mid-1700s. The colonists shipped most of these hides to New Spain using packs of mules.

Consequences of the Fur Trade. The extent of the North American fur trade is difficult to measure because it took place across a vast geographic region over a period of several hundred years. However, some records have survived. In the mid-1600s, for example, the French exported about 30,000 pounds of furs every year. When the French captured three of the Hudson's Bay Company's trading posts in 1698, they found 50,000 top-quality beaver pelts. Between 1730 and 1748, South Carolina exported 16,000 deerskins, despite the fact that frontier wars interrupted trade several times during this period.

The large-scale slaughter of animals had a devastating effect on North America's ecology. Many fur-bearing animals, especially beavers, vanished from the eastern part of the continent and from many regions in the West. Their loss affected other animals who depended on them for food. The disappearance of the beaver meant that ponds that had been created over the years by beaver dams were destroyed, along with the fish and other creatures that lived in the ponds.

The fur trade also greatly affected Native Americans. The new goods introduced by Europeans forever changed their way of life. Some changes were minor—for example, the Indians' replacement of traditional handmade clothing with garments made of European cloth and blankets. Others seemed beneficial, such as the introduction of kettles, needles, and knives that made domestic tasks easier. Yet even these simple changes played a role in turning once self-sufficient communities into dependent ones. Indians involved in the fur trade no longer hunted just to meet their basic needs for food, clothing, and shelter. They moved away from their traditional beliefs in the harmony and equality of all living things and toward the European view that the natural world was meant to be used for the benefit of humans.

Some changes brought by the fur trade were visibly and immediately destructive. Traders introduced alcohol, with which Indians had no previous experience. It had a devastating effect on their health, family life, and social structures. The DISEASES traders brought with them to North America—such as influenza, measles, and especially smallpox—caused even greater damage. Although Europeans had developed resistance to these illnesses, the Indians had no such immunity. Countless Native Americans died as a result.

The fur trade also altered long-standing relationships among Indian tribes as various groups of Europeans competed for Indian allies and trading partners. In the early 1700s, for example, British colonists from South Carolina clashed with French and Spanish traders beyond the Appalachian Mountains. The British colonists accused the French and Spanish of giving weapons to the CREEK and YAMASSEE INDIANS and encouraging them to attack British settlements. In retaliation, the British armed the CHEROKEE and the CHICKASAW INDIANS, inciting an Indian war.

Not all encounters between Europeans and Native Americans were negative, of course. French, English, and Scottish traders, especially those who spent long periods of time away from their settlements, often married or formed long-term relationships with Indian women and raised families. In French colonies, the practice was so common that a new population of mixed Indian and European ancestry emerged, known as the métis. The fur trade also played a vital role in increasing Europeans' geographical knowledge. It is unlikely that the interior of North America would have been explored and mapped as rapidly as it was without the efforts of the European fur traders and the cooperation of their Native American partners. (*See also* **Animals; Economic Systems; Trade and Commerce.**)

Furniture and Furnishings

When colonists arrived in North America, they attempted to create homes and furnishings similar to those of their native lands. Their furniture reflected traditional designs, but it also took on new features to suit colonial life.

British Colonies. During the 1600s and most of the 1700s, British colonists generally lived in small one-room houses. The poorest residents furnished their houses only with chests and coarse bedding. They cooked their meals in a common pot and ate from bowls using spoons or their fingers. Some one-room houses contained such additional furniture as a bed, chairs, stools or benches, and a table. These items were often simple, made of boards nailed together by house carpenters.

Prosperous colonists tended to fill their houses with many other pieces of furniture and with fairly elaborate pieces. They might possess low rectangular

This house in Salem, Massachusetts, has been preserved to reflect the way it looked in the 1600s. Early homes in the British colonies typically had simple furniture but were not as large as the house shown here.

chests, tables, chairs, bedsteads, and cupboards that were crafted by joiners, skilled woodworkers who used techniques handed down from the Middle Ages. Black, red, and earth-tone were popular colors. One Pennsylvania resident, who lived in a single-room house, had a bed, three tables, a half-dozen chairs, a chest, cooking utensils, and various other pieces. Such crowded quarters left little space for the family, which typically included six or more people.

See color plate 2, vol. 1.

In the early 1700s, only the wealthiest colonists lived in two-room houses. As the century progressed and the colonies prospered, such homes became more common. A two-room house typically consisted of a hall, also called the common room or kitchen, and a parlor. The hall was furnished with a large cooking hearth, tables, boxes and chests, seating, and often a built-in bake oven. Cooking utensils included a kettle, frying pan, iron pot, earthenware storage jars, milk pans, and baking dishes. The parlor usually served as a sleeping room and private sitting room. It held the best furniture, including the most expensive bed and items such as tea tables, caned and upholstered chairs, curtains, and mirrors.

As colonists became more prosperous, the demand for finer goods increased. In the early 1700s, cabinetmakers turned out lighter, more elegant pieces than the heavy chests and tables of the 1600s. New items included tall clocks, high chests of drawers with matching dressing tables, and chairs finished with cane, leather, or upholstery. Native walnut and maple were the most commonly used woods.

In the late 1700s, upholstered chairs and sofas, tea and card tables, desks and bookcases, and firescreens became popular. Americans knew

about the latest fashions in Europe because they imported British furniture. They also received information and ideas from British cabinet-makers who came to the colonies and from pattern books such as Thomas Chippendale's *The Gentleman and Cabinet Maker's Directory.* Much of the stylish new furniture was made of mahogany, a more expensive wood than oak, walnut, or maple. Wealthy colonists were able to outfit their houses with other luxury goods imported from England, including china, silver, glassware, draperies, and paintings. The lower classes also improved the furnishings in their homes, adding better cookware, beds, and chairs.

While American crafts workers continued to imitate British furnishings, they adapted many of the styles to their own taste. The quality of the best American work was equal to that of the finest European pieces. Philadelphia, New York, and several New England cities developed their own special styles of furniture.

French Colonies. Only the wealthiest immigrants to the French colonies brought their furniture with them. Even beds were a luxury in the 1600s, but most households had plenty of furniture by the 1700s. Although the French colonists made many of their own items, some were produced by professional carpenters. Crafts workers of New France were known for their skill at wood carving.

The most important household furnishings were the armoire—a large, ornate wardrobe or cabinet—and the marriage bed. Other items included chests, buffets, tables, and chairs. The colonial furniture tended to be simple copies of French styles.

Dutch Colony. The Dutch colonists lived much like their ancestors had lived since the Middle Ages. Their homes usually had a large fireplace on one wall. They whitewashed the walls and painted the window frames red or blue-gray. A typical house had a *groot kamer* (great room), similar to the parlors of British colonists, and a kitchen for cooking, eating, entertaining, and sleeping. The cellar and second floor were used mostly for storage. The kitchen contained one or more tables and several chairs. Against a wall stood a cupboard of shelves for holding and displaying pottery, dishes, and pewter* utensils. The wall might have a spoon rack on which each member of the household hung his or her spoon between meals. Since the Dutch tended to have large families, beds were often placed in every room.

* ***pewter*** metal made of tin and lead

Spanish Borderlands. Spanish and Native American carpenters used the local ponderosa pine wood to build simple furniture such as chests, chairs, stools, tables, cabinets, and shelves. They painted some of their furniture and decorated various pieces with carved designs of rosettes or wheels. Most homes, even those of the well-to-do, contained little furniture, as this was the custom in Spain. The adobe—baked clay—homes of the Southwest often had mud-plaster benches, shelves, cabinets, and fireplaces built into the walls as well as a few wooden pieces. Poor people had almost no wooden furniture. (*See also* **Architecture; Housing.**)

Gálvez, Bernardo de

1746–1786
Governor of Spanish Louisiana

Bernardo de Gálvez led the Spanish colony of LOUISIANA and influenced Spain's colonial policies. During the American Revolution, he played an important role in driving the British from the lower Mississippi River and the eastern Gulf coast.

Born in the province of Malaga in Spain, Gálvez belonged to a distinguished family. He entered the army and served in Portugal, Algiers, and NEW SPAIN. He became governor of Spanish Louisiana in 1777, and he married the daughter of a prominent Louisiana family. The marriage won him the support of Louisiana's CREOLES—French people born in the Americas.

Soon after taking office in Louisiana, Gálvez allowed American rebels who were fighting for independence from Britain to set up a supply base in NEW ORLEANS. In 1779, when Spain entered the war against Britain, Gálvez joined the fighting and took West Florida from the British. He captured Baton Rouge, Manchac, and Natchez on the east bank of the Mississippi River, then Mobile and Pensacola on the Gulf of Mexico.

Pensacola was so heavily defended that Gálvez requested additional troops from Cuba. Ships carrying these reinforcements finally arrived, but the Spanish admiral refused to sail under the guns of the British fort. Gálvez embarrassed him by sailing under the guns up to the fort in his own small ship, the *Galveztown.* For his bravery, he was made Count de Gálvez and captain-general of Louisiana and the Floridas. Gálvez displayed his coat of arms on his ship, with the proud words *Yo Solo* (I alone).

Gálvez's success gave Spain control of the mouth of the Mississippi River and the Gulf of Mexico. It also caused Britain to cede* East and West Florida to Spain in 1783 in the Treaty of Paris. The Spanish government appointed Gálvez viceroy* of New Spain in 1785. He died there the following year. (*See also* **American Revolution.**)

* ***cede*** to yield or surrender

* ***viceroy*** person appointed as a monarch's representative to govern a province or colony

Gama, Vasco da

See *Exploration, Age of: Portuguese.*

Gender Roles

Every culture has its own gender roles—a set of expectations about how males and females can and should behave. Some societies tolerate a great deal of variety in the way people adapt to these roles. Others interpret gender roles very strictly and enforce them through custom and law.

The population of North America in colonial times was quite diverse. In addition to many different Native American tribes, it also included colonists from several European countries and blacks from various parts of Africa. Each of these groups assigned men and women a set of rights and responsibilities based on their sex.

Native Americans. Gender roles among the Indians varied from tribe to tribe. Some tribes were patriarchies, which means that fathers had authority over family members and that people traced their ancestry through their fathers. Besides controlling the family's resources, fathers arranged the marriages of their children, and newlyweds often lived with the husband's family.

Other tribes were matriarchies, in which people traced their ancestry through their mothers. Mothers held authority within families, and the mother's brother, not the father, was responsible for disciplining the children. Mothers arranged matches for their children, who after marriage lived with the bride's family. Even in matriarchal societies, women did not usually serve as tribal or community leaders—though they did have great influence. In some cultures, elder women chose men to represent them in tribal councils. Among the IROQUOIS, for example, women elected male elders and could remove them from power. They also produced and controlled most of the food supply.

Native Americans generally divided work along gender lines. Men hunted, fished, and fought in wars. Women farmed, cleaned and prepared the game and fish the men brought, and made household items such as clothing. Patriarchy was commonly practiced by groups who lived mainly by hunting, such as the PLAINS INDIANS. Many of the matriarchal societies, on the other hand, were tribes that lived in settled villages and relied primarily on agriculture.

European Colonists. The colonists who came to North America from England, the Netherlands, France, Spain, and other European countries shared certain ideas about gender roles. Most believed that women were less intelligent than men and should accept male authority. Women seldom received an education beyond the basics of reading and writing, which was considered sufficient for their role as homemakers. Although women were expected to attend church and to give their children religious training, most faiths did not allow them to preach or to play a role in church business. Except in the Netherlands, husbands had complete control of their wives' property and earnings and the right to speak for their spouses in legal matters.

Women in colonial North America usually performed household chores. J. E. Laughlin created this woodcut of women spinning thread and weaving fabric around 1750.

These attitudes shaped the development of gender roles in the colonies. Women were responsible for household chores, whether performing the tasks themselves or supervising their children, servants, or slaves. They cooked, cleaned, sewed, gardened, built fires, carried water, raised children, cared for the sick, and taught the young to read. Some made goods such as candles, cheese, or wool and traded the surplus with neighbors and shopkeepers. Farm women often helped when it was time to hoe the family's fields or harvest the crops. City women sometimes assisted their husbands in running inns, taverns, shops, and other businesses.

Men seldom performed household chores. In the countryside, where most colonists lived, men cleared land, built houses and barns, tended livestock, raised crops for market, maintained buildings and equipment, bought and sold land, and hired workers. Urban artisans* ran workshops, often in their homes. Men dominated the professions, as women were not allowed to serve as lawyers and judges, become doctors, or teach in secondary schools and colleges. Men also controlled public life, except in the few rare cases where a woman—such as Margaret BRENT—held a responsible position in the community.

National, religious, and economic factors created many exceptions to these broad gender roles. German women in the British colonies, for example, customarily worked in the fields with men as they had done in Germany. QUAKERS and some Methodists and Baptists allowed women to teach, preach, and take part in church government. Gender roles in the Dutch colony of NEW NETHERLAND reflected those of the Netherlands, where women had more rights than women in other European countries. Dutch colonial women owned property, ran businesses, and enjoyed more freedom than women in other colonies.

Beliefs about appropriate behavior for women were somewhat flexible in NEW FRANCE, the French colony in what is now Canada. Because men in the fur trade or in military service often left home for long periods, women took over some traditionally male activities, such as running businesses and operating trading posts. Female entrepreneurs* helped create the colony's textile and lumber industries.

Colonial women in the Spanish Borderlands* had few opportunities to become involved in activities outside the family and the church. Under Spanish colonial law, however, they could own property, go to court, and sign legal documents. Some women assisted their husband in business or ran the family ranch if their spouse died. In the Spanish colonies, a man's role was to support his family and to safeguard its good name and status* in the community. Because fathers took responsibility for the family honor, they held ultimate authority over all family members.

*** artisan** skilled crafts worker

*** entrepreneur** person who organizes, manages, and takes the risks of a business venture

*** Spanish Borderlands** northern part of New Spain, area now occupied by Florida, Texas, New Mexico, Arizona, and California

*** status** social position

The Deputy Husbands

Despite the limits of custom and law, colonial women sometimes managed to step outside the boundaries of what was considered "a woman's place." When men fell sick or were away from home on long journeys or in wartime, their wives or daughters might take on certain responsibilities, such as signing a contract or running a business. Although these women had power, it was only temporary. In society's eyes, they were merely filling in for men who could not carry out their usual duties. One historian called these women "deputy husbands." Their communities saw them not as independent women but as stand-ins for the missing men.

African Americans. The blacks who lived in North America created a culture that blended African traditions with those of the European colonists. Because of the values of the European society that surrounded them, black women lost much of the independence they had enjoyed in Africa. However, slave women were less dependent on their husbands economically than white women were because they received food and clothing from their masters, not their mates. A black woman could also leave an unsatisfactory marriage more easily than a white woman could because African Americans viewed marriage as a social contract that could be broken rather than as a religious institution. In the early days of slavery, male slaves often lived on different plantations away from their families, giving their wives the responsibility of raising the children.

Enslaved African women and men worked side by side in tobacco, corn, and rice fields. In terms of other work, though, their masters enforced traditional European gender roles. Only black men could become drivers or artisans, while black women were given such tasks as cooking and sewing. No matter how great their workload, slave women were also responsible for cooking, sewing, cleaning, and otherwise taking care of their own families. (*See also* **Childhood and Adolescence; Courtship; Education; Family; Labor; Marriage; Wills and Inheritance; Women, Roles of.**)

Genízaros

Genízaros were enslaved Indians in the Spanish colony of New Mexico. Although outlawed in Spain's American territories, slavery continued with little interference from authorities in remote areas such as New Mexico, where the colonists relied on Indian slaves for various kinds of labor.

According to local practice, Native Americans who refused to submit to Spanish rule could be captured as slaves and kept for 10 to 20 years. The Spanish raided Indian territory on a regular basis, seizing men, women, and especially children and bringing them back as slaves. They also acquired slaves from the PLAINS INDIANS, who sometimes captured members of other tribes. In New Mexico, these slaves became known as *genízaros.* The word may have come from the Turkish for "new troops" or from the Spanish for "children of different nations."

The Spanish often employed the *genízaros* as defense troops in wars against Indian tribes such as the APACHE, Ute, and COMANCHE. The *genízaros* also served as domestic slaves and as goods to be exchanged. In 1761 one Spanish priest claimed that slaves "are the kingdom's gold and silver and the richest treasure." Some *genízaros* worked on farms or in silver mines.

By 1800 as many as one out of three people in New Mexico had come to the colony as a slave. Many of these Indians learned the Spanish language and became Christians. They eventually formed a distinct ethnic group in Spanish society. (*See also* **New Mexico; Slavery.**)

Geography of North America

Geography is the study of place. It includes both physical geography—which focuses on such features as landforms and CLIMATE—and cultural geography—which examines how those features shape the lives of the people who live in a particular area. North America's physical and cultural geography reflect the continent's great size and diversity.

North America contains the world's largest expanse of temperate* climate zones, those well suited to human use. Over the centuries, the people living here have hunted, farmed, fished, mined, and built villages, towns, and cities.

* ***temperate*** not extreme; in climate, midway between polar cold and equatorial heat

Pennsylvania is part of the Temperate Woodland region, which covers all the eastern part of North America except southern Florida. Because of its rich soil and long growing season, the area is well suited to agriculture.

Physical Geography. North America covers a total area of about 9.4 million square miles, making it the third largest continent on earth. It extends from the Arctic regions of Canada in the north to Central America in the south, a distance of approximately 5,300 miles. At its widest, the continent measures about 4,000 miles from Newfoundland in the east to Alaska in the west.

Within this vast area is an immense diversity of natural environments, with many different ecological zones* in mountains, deserts, forests, grasslands, marshes, and the like. Each of these zones is created by a complex combination of factors, including temperature, rainfall, elevation above sea level, distance from the oceans, and type of soil. Much of the ecological diversity of North America comes from its wide range of climates. They vary from the polar climate of the Arctic region, to the hot, dry climate of the Southwest, to the hot, humid subtropical and tropical climates of southern Florida and southern Mexico.

* ***ecological zone*** natural environment that supports a particular combination of plant and animal life

Geographers divide North America into several broad regions. The Arctic region includes the northern areas of Canada and Alaska. The Boreal region covers much of central Canada. The Rocky Mountains region contains the continent's highest mountains, some of which support permanent ice sheets called glaciers. These regions are unsuitable for agriculture because they have thin soils and short growing seasons.

The Cool Temperate Woodland region extends through the Great Lakes and the St. Lawrence River. Just south of it is the Temperate Woodland region, which covers all of eastern North America except southern Florida, which is classified as the Subtropical Swamp region. Agriculture thrives in these regions, with the richest soils and longest growing seasons in the south. The center of the continent is the Plains Grasslands region. There trees are scarce and soils are rich, but rainfall is unpredictable, especially in the western area.

The Dry Southwest region, located between the two southern arms of the Rocky Mountains region, is the most arid part of the continent. This dry, rugged landscape of mountains, plateaus, and basins stretches into northern Mexico. The wettest part of the continent is the Pacific Maritime region, a narrow strip between the Rocky Mountains region and the Pacific Ocean. Mexico has extensive mountain and plateau regions, as well as hot and wet subtropical and tropical regions along its Atlantic and Pacific coasts and in the south.

Cultural Geography. The first European explorers and colonists often described North America as a "natural" environment or a "virgin" land. They failed to recognize that Native Americans had lived in complex relationships with the land for thousands of years. An important aspect of Indian life throughout North America was the harmony that existed between the physical environment and the methods people developed to survive in each region. Although ways of living varied from place to place and from culture to culture, they can be grouped into four main kinds of economic activity based on the geography and available resources of a region.

Farming was the principal economic activity in some parts of eastern North America, generally in river valleys with flat areas of fertile soil. However, forests covered sections of the east, and Indians who farmed generally hunted game animals as well. In the Dry Southwest region, some Indians who lived along river valleys also practiced agriculture. They learned to use irrigation canals to carry scarce water to their fields of corn, beans, and squash. Other groups in that region lived by gathering wild food, particularly seeds. In the Pacific Northwest, the main economic activities were fishing and gathering. HUNTING was the primary means of obtaining food everywhere else on the continent. Game included whales and seals in the far north, BUFFALO on the Great Plains, and deer, wildfowl, and small animals such as rabbits in many regions.

Fishing and gathering had little long-term effect on the environment, but hunting and agriculture changed the landscape. Native American hunters regularly set fires, sometimes to trap game and sometimes to transform dense forest into open woodland where deer would gather. The fires affected plants and trees, destroying some species* and favoring the regrowth of others. Indian farmers changed the environment as well, removing trees in some areas and replacing natural plants with cultivated ones.

* ***species*** group of plants or animals with similar characteristics

The cultural geography of Native Americans—the way they lived on the land—was shaped by the physical environment, but at the same time, it changed that environment. However, the Indians had much less of an impact on the land than did the European colonists and their descendants. When Europeans settled in North America, they immediately began to shape the land to their own needs and gave no thought to the long-term effects of their activities. By the end of the colonial period, the environment of many parts of North America had been dramatically altered. The cultural geography of the continent was changed as well, as Europeans tried to conquer the environment rather than live in harmony with it. (*See also* **Agriculture; Animals; Climate; Environmental Impact of Colonization; Fish and Fishing.**)

George III

1738–1820
King of Great Britain

George III enjoyed the longest reign of any English king. An honest, well-meaning, but stubborn individual, his rule was marred by political disputes in Britain, by the loss of the 13 British colonies in North America, and by his own illness and insanity late in life.

George William Frederick Hanover became heir to the throne at age 12, upon the death of his father, Frederick, the Prince of Wales. Although a poor student, George prepared himself for the day he would rule Britain by working very hard and adopting a strict standard of morality.

George became king in 1760 upon the death of his grandfather, George II. He began his reign with high hopes, including plans to make the political system less corrupt and to reduce the power of the aristocracy* in PARLIAMENT. During the first years of his rule, George III named—and dismissed—several prime ministers, as he tried to find a head of government he could trust and who could control Parliament. These changes in leadership resulted in political instability at home and contradictory policies toward the colonies.

* ***aristocracy*** people of the highest social class, often nobility

In disputes with the American colonies, Parliament generally followed a hard line. At first the king did not take an active role and simply supported each new minister and change in colonial policy. Finally, in 1770 George found a strong and capable prime minister, Frederick, Lord NORTH, who held the office for 12 years. North gained the support of both Parliament and the king with his tough colonial policies.

In the early stages of the conflict with Britain, the American colonists blamed Parliament for their difficulties. As crisis loomed in 1775, they appealed to the king to help settle matters peacefully. Instead, George III proclaimed that the colonies were in a state of rebellion and sent additional troops to America, ending all hopes of peace. George III did not imagine, however, that British royal and parliamentary policies might lead to the loss of the colonies.

King George III of England had a long and troubled reign. His strict policies toward the American colonies contributed to the Revolutionary War, and the loss of the colonies greatly damaged his popularity at home.

Britain's war against the colonies had public support for the first few years. By 1779, however, many members of Parliament wanted to end a conflict they believed the nation could not win. But George III insisted on continuing the fight. To back down, he said, would allow disobedience to go unpunished—and could lead Ireland to rebel against British control. The king also argued that the war would weaken France, Britain's traditional enemy, which had formed an alliance with the United States.

George's popularity fell sharply with his continued support of the war. The low point of his rule came in 1783, when Britain signed the Treaty of Paris, confirming the independence of the United States. At about the same time, he also suffered political defeat at home when a longtime political enemy took over leadership of Parliament. Facing these setbacks, George considered giving up the throne.

By 1784 George III had regained popularity by choosing a new, well-respected and capable prime minister, William PITT the Younger. Four years later, the king experienced the first of several attacks of physical and mental problems. He suffered from severe pain, periods of paralysis and of hyperactivity, and occasional loss of mental balance. His distress was worsened by the actions of his son—the future King George IV—who allied himself with his father's political enemies. Young George also adopted a lifestyle that the king found distasteful and immoral.

After 1801 George III suffered increasingly from bouts of illness and mental breakdowns. He was declared insane in 1811, and his son became regent*. George III lived for another nine years at Windsor Castle, cared for by his devoted wife, Charlotte Sophia. (*See also* **American Revolution; Colonial Administration; Great Britain.**)

* ***regent*** person appointed to govern while the rightful monarch is too young or unable to rule

Georgia

Georgia, the last of the original 13 British colonies in North America, was founded in 1733 by James OGLETHORPE as a haven for debtors and poor people. The new colony also served to protect the British colonies from Spanish FLORIDA.

Early Exploration and Settlement. In 1526 the Spanish attempted to establish a colony on present-day Sapelo Island along the coast of what is now Georgia. Indian attacks, disease, and hunger forced the settlement's 600 Spanish and African residents to leave after only three months. Then in the 1540s, the Spanish explorer Hernando DE SOTO visited the interior of Georgia while on an expedition in search of gold and other riches. He encountered several Native American tribes, including the CHEROKEE and the CREEK.

Twenty years later, the Spanish founded several MISSIONS on the Sea Islands along the Georgia coast. The missions flourished until the 1600s, when the English founded the colony of Carolina. The new colony's traders and settlers provoked local Indians into attacking the Spanish missions, leading Spain to abandon the missions in the 1680s. But Spain still claimed the region, and this remained a source of conflict with the British for almost 100 years.

English Colonization. In the early 1700s, Great Britain wanted to create a buffer zone* between the Carolinas and Spanish Florida as protection against possible invasion. The proprietors* of North and South Carolina supported the idea and decided to grant land in the area to a Scottish nobleman in 1717, but the plan eventually collapsed.

* ***buffer zone*** neutral area between two enemy areas
* ***proprietor*** person granted land and the right to establish a colony

The idea of a buffer zone remained, however. In 1732 King George II granted a charter* to James Oglethorpe to establish a colony in the region between Florida and the Carolinas. The colony was named Georgia in honor of the monarch. The charter provided for the formation of a board of trustees* to manage the colony for 21 years, after which time the British crown would take control. The grant also required the proprietors to establish a silk industry to reduce Britain's dependence on Asian silk.

* ***charter*** written grant from a ruler conferring certain rights and privileges
* ***trustee*** person appointed to administer the affairs of a company or institution

See map in British Colonies (vol. 1).

Oglethorpe led the first group of settlers to Georgia in February 1733 and began laying out plans for the town of SAVANNAH. He negotiated a series of treaties with the Creek Indians that allowed the British to establish a colony on the Indians' land. Oglethorpe and the trustees had an idealistic vision for Georgia. They hoped to create a haven for debtors, who faced imprisonment in Britain, and for Protestant groups that were persecuted.

To further their goals, the trustees imposed a series of regulations on Georgia colonists. They limited the amount of property that settlers could

own or rent to ensure that poor individuals would have adequate land to farm. They prohibited rum and other spirits, fearing the effects of alcohol on both the colonists and the local Indian population. The proprietors also banned slavery, believing that slaves might revolt and aid the Spanish enemy. To promote the colony's financial development, they required settlers to plant mulberry trees, which were needed for the cultivation of silkworms.

Early Problems. Soon after the colony was settled, the conflict known as the War of JENKINS'S EAR erupted between Spain and Great Britain. Much of the fighting between the two powers occurred along the Georgia-Florida border. In 1740 Oglethorpe led an unsuccessful attack on the Spanish settlement of ST. AUGUSTINE. The Spanish retaliated the following year but were defeated by the British in the Battle of Bloody Marsh. This defeat ended Spain's claim to the lands north of Florida.

By the late 1740s, it became clear that Oglethorpe's ambitious plan for Georgia had failed. The silk industry was a disappointment, and the economy had not grown significantly. The area attracted few new settlers, and many colonists complained bitterly about the restrictions on landowning, slavery, and liquor. In the face of such opposition, the trustees lifted the ban on slavery in 1750 and allowed the sale of rum in the colony a year later. They handed control of the colony over to the British crown in 1752, a year earlier than required by the charter.

Growth and Development. After becoming a royal colony, Georgia began to grow and prosper. With restrictions on landowning and slavery abolished, large PLANTATIONS developed. Rice and indigo* became important cash crops*, and exports of these and other products, including deerskins, increased rapidly. The availability of cheap land attracted increasing numbers of settlers from Europe and other British colonies. Georgia's leaders also encouraged free blacks to settle in the colony and offered free people of mixed racial ancestry the same rights as other colonists, except for voting and participating in the colonial assembly. Despite this population growth, Georgia remained lightly settled in comparison to other British colonies.

* ***indigo*** plant used to make a blue dye

* ***cash crop*** crop grown primarily for profit

In the mid-1700s, conflicts frequently arose between colonists and Native Americans, largely over the expansion of white settlement into Indian territory. During the FRENCH AND INDIAN WAR, the Cherokee launched attacks on settlements along the frontier, but the colonists eventually drove them back into the mountains. In 1773 Governor James Wright signed a treaty with the Indians in which they ceded* more than 2 million acres to the colony. Thereafter, settlers began pouring into the backcountry.

* ***cede*** to yield or surrender

Georgia and the Revolution. Georgia was slow to join the other colonies in protesting British policies in the 1760s and 1770s. During the STAMP ACT CRISIS, for example, Georgia was the only colony to obey the new British law. After Britain passed the INTOLERABLE ACTS, however, support for independence began to increase in the colony. Georgia did not send delegates

in 1774 to the FIRST CONTINENTAL CONGRESS, a meeting called to consider taking action against Britain. But by June 1775, Georgia patriots* had begun to organize, and the colony sent representatives to the SECOND CONTINENTAL CONGRESS the following month.

* ***patriot*** American colonist who supported independence from Britain

During the American Revolution, perhaps half the Georgians remained loyal to Great Britain. British forces captured Savannah in December 1778, and by the end of 1779, they had gained control of every major town in the colony. They used Georgia as a base from which to launch attacks on the Carolinas. By 1782 a series of American victories forced the British to evacuate Georgia. (*See also* **American Revolution; British Colonies; Colonial Administration; Economic Systems; Government, Provincial.**)

German Immigrants

German immigrants began arriving in the British colonies in the 1600s. Most of them came from the Rhine Valley of southwestern Germany, an area that was overcrowded and torn apart by war. By the time the American colonists declared their independence in 1776, people of German ancestry accounted for more than 10 percent of the population.

The first group of German immigrants arrived in Pennsylvania in 1683, seeking religious freedom. Under the leadership of Francis Daniel Pastorius, they founded the settlement of Germantown. Large-scale immigration began in 1709, when nearly 3,000 Germans fled to New York and North Carolina after suffering through a particularly harsh winter in Europe. Like the Germantown settlers, some Germans moved to America to escape religious persecution, particularly members of such PROTESTANT groups as the Amish,

Although most German immigrants were farmers, some found work in manufacturing. This 1747 engraving by Charles Grignion shows German immigrants at work in a glass factory.

Mennonites, Moravians, and Quakers. The majority of the immigrants, though, belonged to the mainstream Lutheran and Reformed churches and came to America for economic reasons.

German immigrants continued to arrive throughout the 1700s. Most of them traveled to the colonies as "redemptioners," immigrants who made the voyage on credit. If they failed to pay for their ship passage within a certain period after arrival, they could be sold into servitude for up to seven years. But as German communities in America grew and prospered, they often helped these new arrivals "redeem" the cost of their passage, find work, and adjust to life in America.

Over three-quarters of the Germans arrived in family groups. About one out of three entered America through Philadelphia and settled in Pennsylvania. By 1790 more than one-third of Pennsylvania's inhabitants were German. Connected by their language and culture, the Germans tended to settle together in their own communities. This increase in the German population seemed to annoy Benjamin FRANKLIN and others, who feared that Pennsylvania would lose its "American" character. Franklin complained about the German immigrants and their failure to learn English. In 1753 he wrote, "they will soon so out number us, that all the advantages we have will not, in My Opinion, be able to preserve our language, and even our government will become precarious [threatened]."

However, by the 1770s, the German immigrants had established a reputation as thrifty and hard-working farmers. The people known as the Pennsylvania Dutch trace their origins to groups of German farmers. Germans also settled in the rich farmland of New York, New Jersey, and Maryland. While many Germans farmed, others became artisans*, merchants, and traders. Each fresh group of immigrants worked its way farther westward and southward, with later arrivals reaching the backcountry of South Carolina and Georgia before the American Revolution.

* ***artisan*** skilled crafts worker

German immigration slowed during the Revolution and did not pick up again until about the 1820s. Over time the German population began to speak English and to blend into American society. (*See also* **Immigration; Pennsylvania.**)

Gilbert, Sir Humphrey

ca. 1539–1583

English soldier and explorer

Sir Humphrey Gilbert helped promote the idea of English exploration in North America. Although Gilbert made only one voyage to the "New World," he wrote a book on the NORTHWEST PASSAGE, *A Discourse of a Discoverie for a New Passage to Cataia [China],* that inspired later explorers to seek this water route through the Americas.

In 1578 Gilbert sought and received from Queen ELIZABETH I the right to colonize lands in North America not claimed by other European nations. Gilbert and his half brother, Sir Walter RALEIGH, planned an expedition to North America. They ran out of money, however, and none of their ships completed the voyage across the Atlantic. Gilbert then devised a plan to raise funds for a new expedition. He offered large tracts of land in North America to anyone who put up a reasonable sum of money and promised the investors complete control over their affairs in America.

By 1583 Gilbert had obtained the money he needed for his second voyage. He sailed for NEWFOUNDLAND, intending to continue south along the coast of North America to what is now New England. In August he formally claimed Newfoundland for the English crown. While there, he made laws and began to collect fees from fishing vessels.

Gilbert never made it any farther south. He lost his main ship and decided to sail back to England. Unfortunately, he never reached England either, drowning on the voyage home. Gilbert's grand plan for settling North America came to an end. (*See also* **Exploration, Age of.**)

Glorious Revolution in America

Throughout the 1600s, religious conflict tore England apart. Catholics and Protestants battled for control of the country—and the English crown. In 1688 PARLIAMENT replaced King James II, a Catholic, with his Protestant daughter Mary and her husband, William of Orange. This event, known as the Glorious Revolution because it was achieved without bloodshed, sparked a series of uprisings in North America.

King Charles II, who ruled before James, had expanded royal control over the colonies, removing governmental powers the colonies had enjoyed for many years. When Massachusetts failed to obey English trade laws, the monarch punished the colony by taking away its charter*. In 1685 Charles's brother James became king and continued to tighten royal control over the North American settlements. James united all the English colonies from New York northward and placed them under a single government, calling it the DOMINION OF NEW ENGLAND.

* ***charter*** written grant from a ruler conferring certain rights and privileges

Colonists opposed this plan fiercely. Many disliked Sir Edmund ANDROS, the new governor of the dominion because he had failed to come to their aid during KING PHILIP'S WAR. Furthermore, his strong support of the Anglican* Church offended Massachusetts PURITANS. When the colonists heard that Parliament had removed James from power, they acted swiftly. Boston residents seized Andros, who had tried to flee the city dressed as a woman, and jailed him and several other officials. The colonists sent the former governor back to England for trial.

* ***Anglican*** of the Church of England

Revolt broke out in New York as well. Jacob LEISLER, a captain in the local militia* and a prosperous merchant, captured New York City's fort with a small band of rebels. Leisler proclaimed himself head of a new colonial government. Conflict soon broke out among the rebels, and Leisler was unable to establish a stable government. The new English monarchs dispatched another governor, who hanged Leisler for treason and restored order.

* ***militia*** army of citizens who may be called into action in a time of emergency

MARYLAND colonists also revolted. Protestant settlers feared that the CALVERT family, Maryland's Catholic proprietors*, planned to turn the colony over to Catholic France. The Protestant colonists overthrew the government of the Calverts and asked William and Mary to make Maryland a royal colony.

* ***proprietor*** person granted land and the right to establish a colony

Massachusetts and New York received new charters that placed them under royal authority as well. Although the charters gave the crown the power to appoint governors, they did allow the colonies to elect their own colonial ASSEMBLIES.

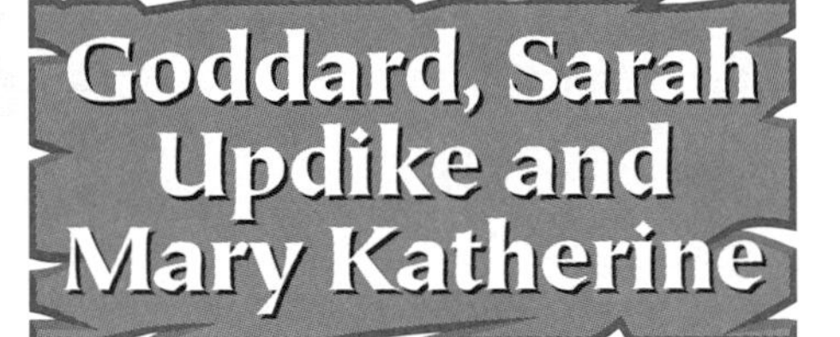

Goddard, Sarah Updike and Mary Katherine

Sarah Updike
ca. 1700–1770
Printer

Mary Katherine
1738–1816
Printer

The Goddards, Sarah Updike and her daughter, Mary Katherine, were influential printers and publishers in the British colonies. They were among the very few women who achieved professional success in colonial America. Supporters of rights for the colonies, they used their publishing skills to further the cause of American independence.

Born into a prominent family in Rhode Island, Sarah Updike was educated by private tutors. In 1735 she married Dr. Giles Goddard. After his death in 1757, Sarah Goddard used her inheritance to help her son, William, set up a printing shop in Providence. He began publishing a newspaper, the *Providence Gazette,* in 1762. His mother and sister worked in the shop and learned the printing business. Articles on colonial rights appeared frequently in the paper, and a special August 1765 issue of the *Gazette* helped organize colonists against the STAMP ACT.

When William Goddard left to start a newspaper in Philadelphia, his mother reorganized the business as Sarah Goddard and Company and continued publishing the *Gazette* and books with her daughter, Mary Katherine. William Goddard sold the business in 1768, and his mother moved to Philadelphia.

Mary Katherine Goddard learned the publishing business by working with her mother and managing her brother William's newspaper in Philadelphia. When William started the *Maryland Journal,* she went to Baltimore to run it. She also served as Baltimore's postmaster, a position she held for 14 years.

A respected publisher, Mary Katherine Goddard printed the first copy of the DECLARATION OF INDEPENDENCE with the names of the signers in 1777. Her publishing career ended in the 1780s, when she and her brother quarreled over control of their publishing business. She also lost her position with the post office on the grounds that a woman could not travel enough to do the job properly. However, she received the support of some 200 Baltimore business leaders in her effort to hold onto the postal position. Mary Katherine Goddard spent the remaining years of her life operating a bookshop in Baltimore.

Gold

The Spanish discovery of gold and other riches in MEXICO and Peru in the early 1500s sent European adventurers to the "New World" in search of treasure. At the time, European powers measured their wealth and power in gold and SILVER, following an economic theory called MERCANTILISM. Later expeditions to North America failed to uncover great quantities of gold, but they gathered valuable information about the geography and peoples of the continent that helped pave the way for establishing colonies.

Mexico was a major source of gold in the early years. When Spanish explorer Hernando CORTÉS conquered the Aztecs in 1521, he seized the vast stores of gold they had mined over the centuries. By 1540, however, the Mexican gold mines were almost exhausted.

Spain launched numerous other North American explorations to look for gold and to establish territorial claims. An expedition led by Hernando DE SOTO in 1539 was supposed to lay the foundations of an empire. Instead, it became a haphazard search for gold that took the explorers from Florida northward to present-day North Carolina and westward to what is now Arkansas. De Soto found no gold, but his expedition located the Mississippi River and learned much about the southeastern part of the continent.

Hearing tales of great treasures in a place known as the SEVEN CITIES OF CÍBOLA, Francisco Vásquez de CORONADO set out in 1540 to explore the region north of Mexico. What he found were some poor villages of the PUEBLO INDIANS, which offered no riches other than semiprecious turquoise. During their travels, Coronado and his men came upon the Grand Canyon and crossed the Great Plains as far as present-day Kansas. Like de Soto, Coronado failed to find gold but collected important information about the interior of North America.

Spaniards continued to look for gold on the continent, digging mines in the Southeast and Southwest. The remains of mine shafts and mining tools in what are now Georgia, the Carolinas, Arizona, Texas, and California provide evidence of their searches. But the Spanish unearthed very little gold or other metals in those regions. Though they did find some additional gold in Mexico, its value was small in comparison with the stores of silver. In the late 1500s, however, about 20 percent of Spain's annual revenues came from the gold and silver produced by Mexico and Peru. This treasure was considered the foundation of Spanish power in Europe.

Other European nations had little luck in their search for gold in North America. In 1576 English explorer Martin Frobisher discovered some promising rocks in the northern reaches of present-day Canada, but a large shipment of the rocks sent to England proved to be worthless. In the 1620s and 1640s, the DUTCH WEST INDIA COMPANY hired mineral experts to look for gold and other metals in the colony of New Netherland. Two ships loaded with ore samples sank on the voyage to Europe, postponing what would, in any case, have been bad news—the ore contained no gold or silver. The French did not strike gold in their colonies either, though they did locate small deposits of copper and lead.

The passion for gold intensified the rivalries among European nations. Spanish ships carrying treasure from Mexico and South America to Europe became the target of PIRATES and privateers*. France tried to build bases in Florida and the Carolinas from which to launch attacks on the treasure ships. England mounted official expeditions to chase down Spanish ships, led by adventurers such as Francis DRAKE.

* ***privateer*** privately owned ship authorized by the government to attack and capture enemy vessels

The desire for gold and other riches contributed to the competition for empires, causing a flurry of European exploration and colonization in North America in the 1500s and 1600s. The first English colonists in JAMESTOWN devoted more energy to searching for gold than to finding and growing food. As time passed, though, the European powers realized that their colonies would bring them greater benefits through trade and other economic activities than as sources of gold and silver. (*See also* **European Empires; Exploration, Age of; Money and Finance.**)

Government

See *Colonial Administration; Government, Provincial.*

Government, Provincial

European settlers in North America needed institutions and procedures to handle local matters. In many colonies, the settlements were far apart, and not all issues could be brought to the attention of the officials who headed the COLONIAL ADMINISTRATION. Conflict inevitably arose between the colonists and the European nations over control of local policy and government.

British Colonies

See map in British Colonies (vol. 1).

The BRITISH COLONIES can be divided into three broad regions: the New England colonies, the middle colonies, and the colonies of the Chesapeake region and the lower south. Each of these regions developed distinct patterns of local government. In New England, local government centered on towns. In the Chesapeake and southern colonies, it developed around counties, and in the middle colonies, it involved both towns and counties. English colonists began to establish these systems with the early settlements of the 1600s. With few exceptions, the forms of government they created remained unchanged throughout the colonial period.

New England. New England followed the traditions of England, where towns had charters* that gave them the right to set up their own governments. From the start, New England settlers established self-governing towns. Every community had a TOWN MEETING, which assembled regularly

* ***charter*** written grant from a ruler conferring certain rights and privileges

Both the governor's council and the Virginia House of Burgesses met in the capitol building in Williamsburg during the 1700s. The burgesses were elected, but the governor appointed his own council.

to discuss local issues and elect officials. Only white male property owners—and in some places white male property owners who were church members—had the right to vote and hold office. Though very limited by today's standards, the amount of political participation allowed in New England was high for the time. All qualified voters could attend town meetings, speak out, and hold office.

Town meetings were held at least once a year so that voters could elect town officials. As towns increased in size, they generally held fewer meetings and instead turned over most decision making to elected officials. Even in larger communities, however, town meetings kept the power to make decisions on any issue.

New England communities had a variety of officials. These included selectmen, constables, tax officials, road supervisors, and the town clerk. Not all officials were elected by the town meeting. Justices of the peace, who presided over local trials, were chosen by the governor or the colonial council. In Massachusetts, Connecticut, and New Hampshire, which had official churches established by the government, parishes* also served as a form of local government. They provided assistance for the poor and education for children.

* ***parish*** church district

The Chesapeake and Southern Colonies. The form of local government in the Chesapeake region and the southern colonies was more varied than in New England. Appointed officials played a larger role in governing, and most power lay with county officers called magistrates or justices of the peace rather than with town officials.

In Virginia and Maryland, colonial GOVERNORS appointed justices of the peace, who served as judges in minor civil and criminal cases. The justices assembled regularly to act as a county court and, in this capacity, performed the three main functions of government—legislative (making laws), executive (carrying out laws), and judicial (enforcing laws). The county court licensed taverns, registered deeds*, supervised elections, settled disputes, and presided over serious criminal cases.

* ***deed*** formal document showing lawful ownership of property

Local government included a number of other officials. The sheriff and constables were law enforcement officers who carried out the orders of the county court, serving warrants* and arresting criminals. Clerks maintained local records, highway officials supervised road construction and maintenance, and coroners conducted investigations into suspicious deaths. Local Anglican* church officials called vestrymen also performed certain duties associated with community government, such as collecting taxes to help the poor.

* ***warrant*** formal court paper allowing a search of property or an arrest

* ***Anglican*** of the Church of England

South Carolina did not have county courts, and the power of the justices of the peace was more limited than in Virginia and Maryland. Aside from such duties as imposing fines for minor offenses and issuing licenses for taverns, the justices had little control over white colonists—though they did have the power of life and death over blacks. As a result, Anglican officials played a greater part in local government. The role of church vestrymen expanded beyond helping the poor to enforcing laws and supervising schools. South Carolina also had an organization called the commission. Appointed by the colonial ASSEMBLY, commissions supervised roads, regulated markets,

organized military defense, and provided fire protection. The commissions gave the colonial government a direct role in local matters.

Both North Carolina and Georgia had weak local governments, with most officials appointed rather than elected. In North Carolina, vestrymen of the Anglican Church possessed considerable power. But because much of the population was not Anglican, many colonists resisted their authority. In Georgia the proprietors* who ran the colony appointed all local officials. Their tight control kept local government weak, and this situation did not change after Georgia became a royal colony in 1752.

* ***proprietor*** person granted land and the right to establish a colony

The Middle Colonies. When the English took NEW NETHERLAND from the Dutch in 1664—renaming it New York—they found several different types of local government. They reformed all levels of government and established a more uniform system of local administration. The county emerged as the main unit of local government, and the sheriff became the most powerful county official. County judges had limited judicial authority—not the broad range of powers enjoyed by justices in the Chesapeake region. The governor appointed both county sheriffs and judges. New York and Albany also had town and city governments with various appointed and elected officials. Both enjoyed a considerable degree of independence.

Pennsylvania had four basic units of local government: county, township, borough, and city. The county was the most important of these; township and boroughs were subdivisions of the county. Each county had three commissioners—appointed until 1722 and then chosen by election—who exercised executive power for the county. County government included other officers such as sheriffs, constables, coroners, clerks, and assessors, whose duties involved estimating county expenses and collecting taxes. Township governments did not enjoy the independence of New England towns.

Pennsylvania had three boroughs, which contained larger village centers than townships. Governed by elected officials called burgesses, the boroughs possessed greater powers and more independence than townships. The colony's chief settlement, PHILADELPHIA, had a government unlike any other in the British colonies. Run by a common council, the city was independent of county government and, in many respects, of the colonial assembly as well.

Though officially part of Pennsylvania after 1691, Delaware enjoyed a great deal of independence in local matters. The governors of Pennsylvania appointed justices of the peace for each of Delaware's counties. The justices possessed great power—more than in any other British colony—including the authority to raise taxes and hear both civil and criminal cases. The governor of Pennsylvania named sheriffs, coroners, assessors, and other officials for each county, but they were chosen from lists of nominees elected by the citizens of Delaware.

New Jersey also had strong local government. Justices of the peace, appointed by the governor, served individually as local judges and collectively as a county court. Local officials called selectmen, also elected by voters, governed the townships of the colony with the assistance of clerks, assessors, tax collectors, and others.

Duties of Town Officials

Many officials of local government today date from colonial times. Selectmen acted as the town's chief executives, making day-to-day administrative decisions. Sheriffs and constables maintained law and order, tax officials collected taxes, and surveyors of highways supervised the building of roads. Town clerks recorded the minutes of town meetings and registered official documents. The functions of some colonial officials—fence viewers, church sweepers, and grave diggers—have disappeared or been taken over by other organizations. The fence viewer's job was to make sure that property owners built secure fences and put them in the right place.

Dutch Colony

The colony of New Netherland never developed an organized system of local government. The DUTCH WEST INDIA COMPANY maintained strict control of the colony at first, but over the years, the settlers struggled to gain a greater role in running their communities. In the last decades of Dutch rule, town residents won increasing powers.

Early Period. Between 1624 and 1639, New Netherland had no local government at all. The colony's main settlements functioned as both forts and fur trading posts. The directors of the West India Company regulated all affairs, acting as government officials, business leaders, and military commanders.

Remember: *Consult the index at the end of Volume 4 to find more information on many topics.*

The company allowed one exception to its centralized rule. To encourage colonization, it offered certain individuals—called patroons—large estates in unsettled areas. Patroons who could bring 50 adults to the colony won the right to own and govern vast areas of land. Only one patroonship, Rensselaerswyck in the upper Hudson Valley, lasted throughout the Dutch period, and it never developed a system of government.

Later Years. In 1640 the West India Company tried a new approach to promoting settlement. Under an order called the Freedoms and Exemptions of 1640, colonists who organized villages or towns could name nine candidates for local office. From this list of candidates, the company's director and council would choose one sheriff and two justices of the peace. These local officials had the authority to hear minor civil and criminal cases, but the company reviewed all their decisions. Between 1641 and 1664, settlers created 14 towns under these rules. From the start, however, the West India Company tried to limit the power of the local officials, leading to constant friction with the colonists.

See map in New Netherland (vol. 3).

Towns achieved more self-government through the efforts of New England colonists who migrated to New Netherland. Before making the move, these English colonists insisted that the Dutch West India Company give them greater control over local affairs. Company officials reluctantly agreed because they were desperate for colonists. Once the towns founded by English colonists won the right to pass their own laws, Dutch settlers demanded—and gained—the same privilege.

The Dutch colonists pressed further. In 1647 they gained the right to establish a committee of residents—the Board of Nine—to advise the company on local matters. Although authorized only to provide advice, the committee began to act independently and to demand more authority in community affairs.

The government of NEW AMSTERDAM differed from other local governments in New Netherland. In theory, the city had a great deal of independence. But to exercise that right, the residents of New Amsterdam had to struggle constantly with the colonial governor, Peter STUYVESANT, who resisted any decisions that would lessen his power.

French Colonies

In its early years, the colony of NEW FRANCE was run by trading companies. In 1663 the French government took over and established a strong central

administration. While this colonial administration contained no structure for local government, colonists developed informal arrangements to deal with central authorities.

Centralized Control. Under royal control, the colonial administration of New France became well organized and efficient in a military style. Army commanders governed forts and other outposts* scattered across North America. None of these settlements had local government, though some commanders allowed residents to manage their own affairs.

* ***outpost*** frontier settlement or military base

Canada, the most populated region of New France, did develop a system of local government. Two officials, the governor-general and the intendant, ran Canada's colonial administration. At the head, the governor-general served as overall military commander and handled relations with other colonies and with Native Americans. The intendant dealt with the day-to-day concerns of the colony. He maintained law and order, administered justice, and managed the colony's budget and economy. Most importantly, he provided a link between royal officials in France and the colonists.

See map in New France (vol. 3).

The intendant lived in QUEBEC, the capital of New France. He presided over a council that included the governor-general, the colony's Roman Catholic bishop, and other high officials. While council members offered opinions on current issues, the intendant made all final decisions. In the 1600s, the council played a major role in passing laws. During the 1700s, however, the intendants adopted many laws simply by issuing executive orders, and the council became more involved in enforcing the laws.

Local Structures of Government. The royal colonial government reached outside Quebec. The intendant appointed deputies in Trois-Rivières, MONTREAL, and Detroit to carry out his orders and report to him. Montreal and Trois-Rivières also had town councils. Settlers in other areas formed merchant or parish councils. While these councils had no authority to make or enforce laws, they played a vital role by keeping the colonial government informed of settlers' needs and concerns. Most colonial laws originated in requests for action made at council meetings.

In rural areas, officials called *capitaines* acted as a link between local residents and the intendant. They sent reports from local council meetings to Quebec and passed on the intendant's orders to residents. Originally assigned responsibility for defense, the *capitaines* gradually assumed a government function. Yet they also kept their military role and led the local militia*.

* ***militia*** army of citizens who may be called into action in a time of emergency

Landowners called seigneurs also exercised power in rural areas. Like Dutch patroons, seigneurs received large grants of land and the right to administer justice on them in exchange for promoting settlement. Few exercised this right, however, letting the *capitaines* run local affairs.

Spanish Colonies

Forms of local government developed throughout the Spanish Borderlands*—except in FLORIDA. This small colony remained primarily a military outpost, governed by colonial officials in New Spain*. Local government emerged first in New Mexico and later spread to Arizona, Texas, and California.

* ***Spanish Borderlands*** northern part of New Spain, area now occupied by Florida, Texas, New Mexico, Arizona, and California

* ***New Spain*** Spanish colonial empire in North America; included Mexico, the area now occupied by Florida, Texas, New Mexico, Arizona, California, and various Caribbean islands

See map in Spanish Borderlands (vol. 4).

The Spanish Borderlands had certain characteristics that influenced local government. First, the region was lightly populated with settlements spread out over a vast area. Colonial officials had difficulty communicating with and controlling these widely scattered communities. Second, Spanish authorities accepted responsibility for the Native Americans living within the Borderlands and had to devise ways of dealing with these people. Perhaps most important, colonial officials had to work with other powerful institutions. The Catholic Church played a major part in settling the Borderlands, and conflicts arose between CHURCH AND STATE over their proper areas of authority. The military also had a key role in the Borderlands.

Three distinct types of settlement developed in the Borderlands: PRESIDIOS, MISSIONS, and towns, each governed in a different way. In addition, the Spanish established a system of provincial government that had authority over broad areas.

Military Government. Presidios were fortified settlements built to defend Spanish territory in North America from other European powers and to protect colonists from hostile Indians. Controlled by colonial authorities in Spain and New Spain and governed by military commanders according to military law, presidios offered no opportunity for residents to participate in decision making.

Mission Government. Missions, the most common type of settlement in the Spanish Borderlands, affected more people than towns did. The number of Indians living on missions was greater than the number of Spanish colonists in towns or in the countryside. For the first 100 years or so of Spanish rule, the Catholic Church had complete control over the missions. But after 1693, the Spanish government took a greater role in running them.

*** *friar*** member of a religious brotherhood

The church believed that Native Americans should participate in mission government. Each year, the friars* who ran the missions held elections for governor, sheriff, and other minor posts. All adult Indians could vote for candidates. They held most offices, and they usually supported the friars in disputes with the colonial government. The frequent conflicts between church and colonial officials prompted Spain to change the way missions were administered. After 1693 colonial governors appointed their own representatives to live on the missions and serve as middlemen between the government and the Indians.

The Spanish government had originally planned to close the missions once the Indians converted to Christianity and adopted the Spanish way of life. But the missions continued to operate, increasing in size and power. Settlers argued that they should be closed, and this demand grew when Mexico gained its independence from Spain in 1821. By the 1840s, few missions remained open.

Town Government. The *cabildo,* a town council with six to eight members, was the most important institution in town government. It had the power to impose taxes, regulate markets, provide law enforcement, and pass some laws. The *cabildo,* which reported directly to the Spanish crown, enjoyed considerable independence from colonial governors.

Only the leading citizens could vote for council members, and meetings of the *cabildo* were usually closed to ordinary townspeople. SANTA FE was the first town to have a *cabildo.* In the late 1700s, colonial authorities set up town councils in San Antonio, Los Angeles, and a number of other places.

The *cabildos* helped create a balance of power in Spanish colonial society between *peninsulares,* colonists born in Spain, and CREOLES, Spanish colonists born in America. *Peninsulares* had the highest social rank and usually held the most important political positions, commanding presidios and controlling high-level courts. But Creoles, despite their lower position in society, dominated the *cabildos* and took a leading role in town affairs.

Provincial Government. Spanish officials divided the Borderlands provinces into districts, each ruled by an *alcalde mayore* appointed by the governor. Like justices of the peace in the British colonies, these officials had legislative, executive, and judicial powers. They supervised trade with Indians, regulated travel, announced royal decrees, kept records, maintained law and order, and conducted trials. If a district had no presidio, the *alcalde mayore* assumed responsibility for defense as well.

The districts were subdivided into smaller units led by officials called *tenientes alcaldes,* who answered directly to the *alcalde mayore.* Although these junior officials had broad power, their authority was actually limited to fairly minor matters. The term of office for both *alcaldes mayores* and *tenientes alcaldes* was supposed to be three years. But because of a shortage of qualified candidates, they generally served for life. (*See also* **British Colonies; Class Structure in European Colonies; New Spain; Roman Catholic Church; Seigneurial System; Spanish Borderlands.**)

Governors, Colonial

The British, French, Dutch, and Spanish colonies in North America all had governors as their highest officials. However, the power held by these governors and the roles they played varied. Most colonial governors were dependent on officials in Europe for their authority. But to carry out the policies of these officials, the governors needed the support of leading groups within the colony.

* ***charter*** written grant from a ruler conferring certain rights and privileges

* ***proprietor*** person granted land and the right to establish a colony

British Colonies. In colonies established by charter*, the governor was chosen by a council elected by the colonists. In other colonies, the proprietor* named the governor. By the 1700s, however, the crown appointed the governors of most British colonies. These royal governors, who served as the monarch's direct representatives, held considerable authority. Besides enforcing the laws, the governor could call together or dismiss colonial ASSEMBLIES, approve or veto laws passed by the assemblies, and issue proclamations that served as law. In judicial matters, the governor could establish civil and criminal courts, appoint judges, and pardon criminals. In time of war, the governor served as commander in

Edward Winslow served three one-year terms as governor of Plymouth colony—in 1633, 1636, and 1644. He wrote several accounts of the colony's progress and of its dealings with the Indians. This painting of Winslow is the only surviving portrait of a Pilgrim.

chief of the colony's military and naval forces, with the authority to appoint lower-ranking officers.

The power held by these British governors was not absolute. They received detailed instructions from the crown and its councils in Great Britain, and they could be removed from power for failing to carry out the instructions. The governors also lacked one very important power: taxation. Only the elected legislatures could impose taxes on colonists. Because the governor needed tax money to run the colony—and to pay his own salary—he often had to yield some power to the assembly.

French and Dutch Colonies.

In NEW NETHERLAND, the governor was known as the director general. Appointed by the DUTCH WEST INDIA COMPANY, the trading company that controlled the colony, the director general focused primarily on keeping order. A council made up of investors of the company proposed laws and assisted the director general in enforcing them. Although the director had only one vote in council meetings, he could cast a second vote in case of a tie.

The governors of NEW FRANCE were known as governors-general. Until the 1660s, they were appointed by the COMPANY OF ONE HUNDRED ASSOCIATES—the commercial enterprise that managed the colony—and approved by the French king. During that time, governors-general held supreme authority over military affairs, colonial administration, and the law. They also judged civil and criminal cases. After the French crown took over the administration of New France in 1663, it appointed the governors-general and greatly reduced their power. While still the most important colonial official, the governor-general retained complete authority in only two areas: military affairs and diplomatic relations. He oversaw all fortifications* and served as commander in chief of the colony's military forces. He also directed negotiations with the Indians and administered the vast fur-trading regions of the interior. But all policies required the approval of royal officials in France.

* ***fortification*** defensive structure

Spanish Colonies.

The first governors of NEW SPAIN—explorers and conquerors such as Christopher COLUMBUS and Hernando CORTÉS—held considerable political and military power. Concerned that these men might threaten royal control of the region, the Spanish crown gradually reduced their authority. The VICEROY, who represented the king's interests, became the highest position in New Spain. Thereafter, the title of governor applied to local officials, appointed by the monarch, who administered small districts.

These local governors issued ordinances*, supervised the founding of settlements, assigned land and water rights to colonists, regulated travel, appointed local officials, and collected taxes. They served as chief judges in their districts, commanded local military forces, defended the legal rights of Indians, and exercised religious authority for the Spanish crown. Although they reported to the viceroy, the governors in the Spanish Borderlands* often had a great deal of independence because of their isolation from Mexico City, the capital of New Spain. (*See also* **Colonial Administration; Government, Provincial; Laws and Legal Systems.**)

* ***ordinance*** law or regulation usually made by the government of a city or town

* ***Spanish Borderlands*** northern part of New Spain, area now occupied by Florida, Texas, New Mexico, Arizona, and California

Art and Architecture

Plate 1

Art and crafts of European colonists were shaped by traditions brought from home. This wooden box of the 1700s was made by the Pennsylvania Dutch, who were actually German settlers. Confusion over national origin arose because these people referred to themselves as *Deutsch,* meaning German.

Plate 2

Mark Catesby, an English naturalist, traveled to North America in the mid-1770s to study the continent's exotic plants and animals. Focusing on the southern colonies, he spent many years making sketches and collecting samples. This drawing of a bison appeared in *The Natural History of Carolina, Florida, and the Bahama Islands,* a collection of Catesby's watercolor drawings purchased by King George III.

Plate 3

Most Native American art had either a practical or a spiritual function. This Pueblo mural in New Mexico decorated the wall of a kiva—an underground room used for religious ceremonies. It dates from about 1500.

Plate 4
"The Old Plantation," a painting of the 1700s by an unknown artist, reveals slaves in a moment of relaxation. Music and dance gave African Americans a way to express their hope and faith and to share their African heritage.

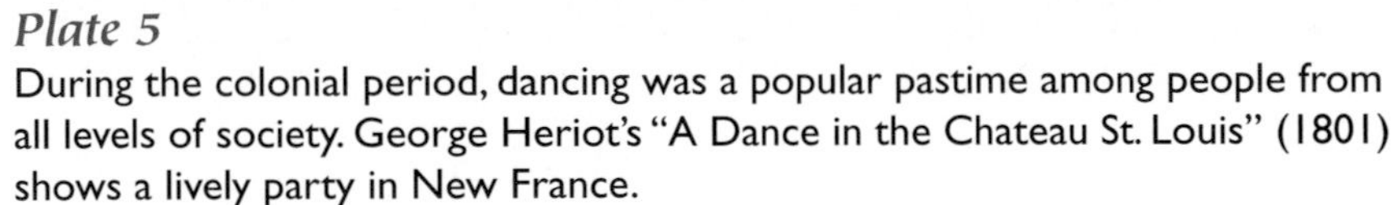

Plate 5
During the colonial period, dancing was a popular pastime among people from all levels of society. George Heriot's "A Dance in the Chateau St. Louis" (1801) shows a lively party in New France.

Plate 6

Well-brought-up colonial women were often skilled at needlework. This beautiful piece by Hannah Otis of Massachusetts creates an idyllic image of life in the country. John Hancock, the American patriot, can be seen on horseback in the foreground.

Plate 7

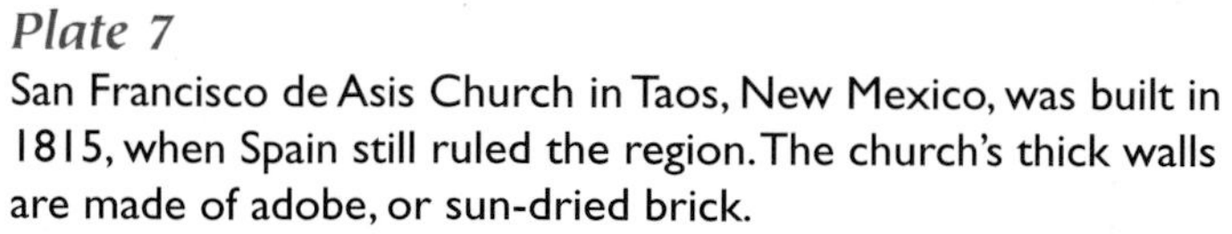

San Francisco de Asis Church in Taos, New Mexico, was built in 1815, when Spain still ruled the region. The church's thick walls are made of adobe, or sun-dried brick.

Great Awakening and Revivalism

Between 1739 and 1745, a wave of religious feeling swept through the British colonies of North America. Called the Great Awakening, this movement promoted a more emotional religious experience and had important and lasting effects on American religion, education, and politics.

Revivalism Before the Great Awakening. The PURITANS who settled New England in the early 1600s believed that only certain people could belong to the church. To become members, people had to live moral lives. But more importantly, they had to convince other members that they had experienced a conversion—a moment when they accepted salvation through the love of God. Over the years, fewer people seemed willing or able to describe such an experience, and church attendance declined.

Ministers began to seek ways of attracting new church members. In the early 1700s, a group of preachers in the Connecticut River valley, led by Solomon Stoddard, emphasized the minister's role in awakening—or reviving—people's religious feelings. They adopted a highly emotional style of preaching, describing in great detail the horrors of eternal punishment for those who did not accept Jesus Christ as their savior. After frightening their listeners, the ministers then created a glorious picture of the wonders of God and the joy of accepting salvation.

Stoddard's grandson, Jonathan EDWARDS, became the leading minister of the Connecticut River valley in the 1730s. His powerful sermons moved many people to experience a conversion. Similar movements arose in the middle colonies. In the Raritan River valley of northern New Jersey, a Dutch Reformed minister named Theodorus Frelinghuysen gave passionate sermons on the importance of conversion. In Pennsylvania, Gilbert Tennent preached in similar style to his Presbyterian congregation.

Whitefield and the Great Awakening. At the same time, several Anglican* ministers in Great Britain began an evangelical* movement known as Methodism. Methodist leaders such as Charles and John Wesley and George WHITEFIELD rejected the dry, reasonable style of preaching of most Anglican pastors and delivered passionate sermons about hell and salvation, often without any preparation. They stressed the individual's personal relationship with God and the importance of a conversion experience. In 1739 Whitefield brought the Methodist message to North America.

* ***Anglican*** of the Church of England

* ***evangelical*** Christian movement emphasizing the importance of personal faith in leading to salvation

Over the next several years, Whitefield made six trips to America, preaching his message of repentance and pardon to huge crowds throughout the British colonies. His popularity stemmed from several factors. He acted out the biblical story of creation, human sin, and God's salvation with dramatic flourish. He spoke in simple language and illustrated his sermons with examples from everyday life. He was also a master of self-promotion, using advertising to generate excitement and build audiences.

Whitefield would speak anywhere—in Anglican and Presbyterian churches and in Baptist and Puritan meetinghouses. If local authorities denied him the right to meet in a church, he preached outdoors. When he returned to Britain, other ministers such as Edwards continued his work. Like Whitefield, they often traveled from place to place, spreading the evangelical message.

Members of many congregations enthusiastically embraced the emotional character of these religious meetings. They met in small groups to discuss their experiences and beliefs and sang hymns that became a central part of the evangelical service. Some cried out at the powerful words of the sermon, while others fainted, overcome with emotion. The movement's emphasis on the individual particularly appealed to the members of colonial society who had little power—women, young people, and the poor.

Although most ministers welcomed the new revival of religion, some—called "Old Lights" or "Old Side"—came to distrust the excessive emotion of the movement. They disapproved of the fact that many of the new ministers lacked formal education and training. The evangelical preachers—"New Lights" or "New Side"—began to criticize the formal style of the Old Lights. Many Protestant groups split, including the Baptists and Presbyterians. Believers in the evangelical way rejected Old Light ministers, while those who preferred traditional religion scorned the New Light preachers.

The most notable figure of the Great Awakening was George Whitefield. His simple but passionate style of preaching drew huge crowds throughout the British colonies in the mid-1700s, helping revive public interest in religion.

Consequences of the Great Awakening. Jonathan Edwards believed that the conversion experience revived people's basic instinct to do good and that the minister's task was to promote conversion. Those who had experienced conversion then demonstrated their faith by helping improve the moral character of society. Edwards attracted many followers, and his writings influenced social reform movements that developed in the early 1800s in the United States.

* ***clergy*** ministers, priests, and other church officials

The Great Awakening changed the character of the American ministry as well. The established clergy* argued that training and education—not the ability to rouse a congregation—were the essential requirements for a pastor. Their experience with the evangelicals did teach them, however, that a minister won the loyalty of church members not by relying on their respect for his position and knowledge but by developing a close relationship with them. As a result, clergymen began to emphasize a spirit of humbleness and active service to their congregations.

The movement had other effects. The spread of the evangelical movement to the South converted large numbers of African Americans there to Christianity. Committed ministers undertook missionary work among Native Americans. To ensure a supply of qualified ministers, evangelicals founded several colleges, including the College of New Jersey (later Princeton) and Queens College in New Jersey (later Rutgers), the College of Rhode Island (later Brown), and Dartmouth College in New Hampshire.

The Great Awakening had a significant impact on individuals as well. In helping people feel closer to God, the revival increased their sense of their own worth. It brought converts together, uniting communities. It renewed interest in spiritual matters in an age when many members of society were becoming increasingly interested in acquiring money and possessions.

Though a religious movement, the Great Awakening also had political consequences. Disagreements about proper religious teaching and church membership opened debate on the relationship between CHURCH AND STATE. Many evangelical congregations refused to pay taxes that supported the state-sponsored churches. Some who protested served time in jail or paid fines. Many evangelicals urged the end of official state religions, arguing that the church and the government should be separate.

The Great Awakening also affected obedience to authority. The movement emphasized the power of the individual conscience, making people less likely to follow those in power blindly. Arguments between congregation and minister or church leaders and minister also weakened the hold of established church authority. (*See also* **Protestant Churches.**)

Great Basin Indians

The Great Basin Indians lived in parts of present-day Nevada, Utah, Colorado, Wyoming, Idaho, Oregon, and California. Because of their isolated location, they had little contact with Europeans before the 1800s. The Indians developed a culture adapted to the harsh environment of the Great Basin, where summers are very hot and winters can be extremely cold in the northern sections and in the mountains. Much of the land has little vegetation besides sagebrush and thin grasses.

See second map in Native Americans (vol. 3).

The major tribes of the region—the Ute, Paiute, and Shoshone—had similar cultures. The Ute and Southern Paiute lived in the area now occupied by Nevada, Utah, and Colorado. The Northern Paiute and the Shoshone, often called the Snake Indians by white settlers, made their home in the northern part of the region.

The most important foods of the Great Basin Indians were pine nuts and acorns, which they used to make porridge, flour, and cakes. They also gathered wild plants, seeds, berries, and roots. The region had few native animals, and the tribes depended on fish, squirrels, rabbits, and gophers for meat, occasionally finding antelope or BUFFALO. They even ate grasshoppers.

To make the most of the region's poor resources, tribes divided into family groups, each with its own territory. These groups were always on the move so that they could be where food was most plentiful during each season. In the southern part of the Great Basin, the people built huts. Men wore loincloths—pieces of animal skin that hung from their waists—and women dressed in animal skin skirts. The northern tribes constructed brush shelters in summer, and in winter they lived in cone-shaped huts built of pine poles that were covered with animal skins or sod. In the north, clothing consisted of leggings and fringed shirts for the men and dresses and leggings of animal skin for the women. Both men and women wore moccasins. During the winter, Indians throughout the region wrapped themselves in robes made of rabbit fur.

* ***shaman*** person with spiritual and healing powers

The Great Basin Indians believed that spirits inhabited the world. Their shamans* conducted ceremonies to heal the sick and to ensure a good supply of game animals. Three times a year, tribes held the Round Dance, their most important ceremony. Men and women danced in a circle around a pole to pray for rain, good hunting, and plentiful food.

During the 1600s, some Great Basin Indians obtained HORSES from Spanish settlers or from other tribes. Owning horses changed the culture of many tribes. By the 1700s, the Shoshone had become buffalo hunters like the PLAINS INDIANS. They also adopted some elements of Plains Indian culture, such as the Sun Dance. (*See also* **Religions, Native American.**)

Great Britain

The modern nation of Great Britain consists of England, Scotland, and Wales—originally three separate, independent countries—and Northern Ireland. Wales became part of England in the 1500s, and England and Scotland combined to form the United Kingdom of Great Britain in 1707. In the 1700s, Great Britain was one of the leading powers in Europe and in colonial North America.

The Middle Ages. During the Middle Ages, English kings frequently struggled for power with the country's nobles. The conflict came to a head in 1215 during the reign of King John I. The nobles rebelled against the king's treatment of them and against his heavy taxes. They forced John to sign the Magna Carta, a document that limited his power and listed certain rights of the nobles. The Magna Carta made it clear that even the king must obey the law, and it became the foundation of the legal rights of the English people.

The Stuart monarchy, overthrown in 1649, was restored in 1660. This print shows Charles II, the heir to the throne, being welcomed back to England as king.

The Middle Ages also saw the beginnings of the English PARLIAMENT. In 1295 King Edward I summoned nobles, church leaders, and representatives from counties and towns to a meeting to discuss government issues. Previous kings had called similar meetings, but this one, later called the Model Parliament, set the pattern for future English assemblies. Over time Parliament continued to gain authority and power.

The early 1400s were marked by a struggle for the throne that pitted two noble families, the Yorks and the Lancasters, and their supporters against each other. Begun in 1455, this long and bitter war ended in 1485, when the Tudor family, part of the Lancaster faction, took the throne.

Tudor England. Under the leadership of the Tudors, from 1485 to 1603, England changed dramatically. Tudor rulers used their power to strengthen the monarchy and the nation. During the Renaissance*, literature, the arts, and science flourished in England. The European discovery of unknown lands on the other side of the Atlantic led England to develop new trade routes and rapid economic growth.

* ***Renaissance*** intellectual and artistic movement that began in Italy in the late 1300s and lasted until the 1600s

The first Tudor monarch, Henry VII, supported the voyages of John Cabot to North America in 1497 and 1498 to discover and claim new land for England. But the English did not pursue further exploration in the Americas because their next king, Henry VIII, had other interests.

See second map in Exploration, Age of (vol. 2).

A popular and talented ruler, Henry VIII strengthened England's navy and brought about the political union of England and Wales in 1536. He is best known, however, for ending his country's ties to the ROMAN CATHOLIC CHURCH. The king desperately wanted a male heir to the throne, but his first wife produced only a daughter. Henry asked the pope in Rome for permission to divorce and take a new wife. When the pope refused, Henry broke with Rome and established the Church of England as the country's official

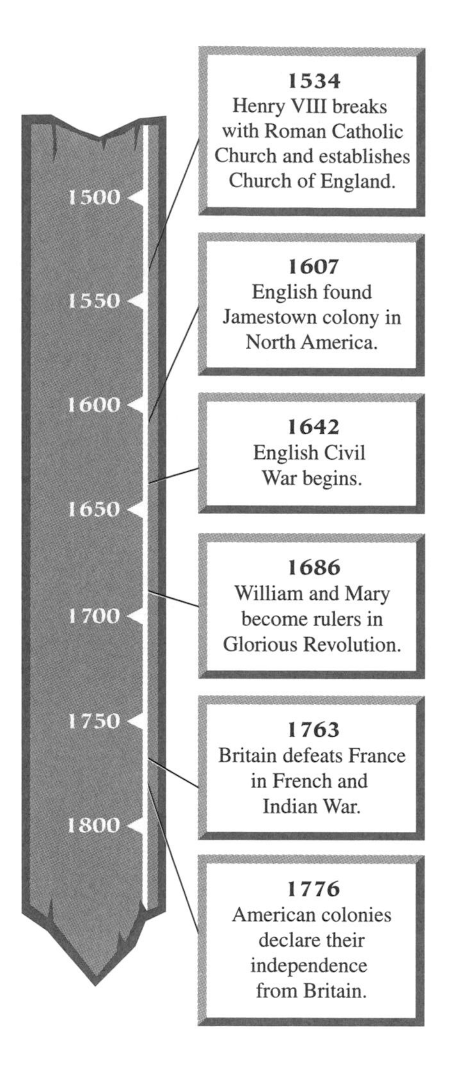

religion. This break with the Catholic Church would affect English politics for many years. Henry eventually married six times and fathered another daughter and a son. His son, Edward VI, and his daughter Mary both occupied the throne briefly, but the last and most notable of Henry's children to rule England was Elizabeth, his younger daughter.

Queen ELIZABETH I became one of the country's most powerful monarchs. When she began her reign in 1558, England and Spain were bitter rivals. A Protestant country surrounded by Catholic nations, England had long been isolated from European politics and had made little attempt to take advantage of opportunities in the "New World." Spain already possessed settlements throughout the Americas, and France had established trading posts in North America.

Elizabeth sought to advance England's interests overseas and encouraged exploration and colonization. Adventurers such as Francis DRAKE explored the coasts of the Americas. Merchants formed companies, such as the BRITISH EAST INDIA COMPANY, to create new trade routes and overseas markets. Sir Walter RALEIGH and others made the first, brief attempts to establish English colonies in North America. Elizabeth's reign was also marked by growing conflict with Spain, caused largely by the rivalry over territory in the "New World." England triumphed over Spain in 1588, when it defeated the great naval fleet called the Spanish Armada and brought an end to Spain's domination of the seas. The victory opened the way for England to become more involved in North America.

The Stuart Kings. Elizabeth died in 1603, leaving no children to succeed her. The throne passed to King James VI of Scotland, Elizabeth's cousin and a member of the Stuart family. As JAMES I of England, the new king ruled the two countries separately.

The Stuart rulers were highly unpopular with the English people. The Stuarts believed in the divine right* of kings and tried to exercise full authority over all aspects of government, including Parliament.

During the reigns of James and his son Charles I, tension increased between the government and the PURITANS, people who sought to reform the Church of England. In 1620 the first of many groups of Puritans left England for North America, hoping to establish their own Christian community. While the JAMESTOWN COLONY in Virginia had been founded to promote trade, the PLYMOUTH COLONY and Massachusetts Bay colony were established by people seeking religious freedom.

Religious conflict and the struggle for power between the Stuarts and Parliament intensified, leading in 1642 to the English Civil War. In 1649 the monarchy was overthrown, Charles I was beheaded, and England became a republic—the Commonwealth of England—ruled by Parliament. In 1653 Oliver Cromwell, a powerful member of Parliament, dissolved the Parliament and took control of the country as Lord Protector. Under Cromwell, England conquered Scotland and Ireland. The nation was also engaged in the first of a series of wars with the Dutch and another war with Spain.

By 1660 many English people had become dissatisfied with the government and wanted to bring back the monarchy. Supporters of the royal family overthrew the government and elected a new Parliament, which invited Charles I's son, Charles II, to take the throne.

* ***divine right*** idea that monarchs get their right to rule from God, not the consent of the people

See map in British Colonies (vol. 1).

The return of the Stuarts to power, known as the Restoration, did not resolve the issues of religion and royal authority. When James II, the brother of Charles II, became king in 1685, he ignored Parliament and tried to restore the Catholic religion and absolute monarchy* in England. Parliament responded by asking James's Protestant daughter Mary and her husband, William of Orange of the Netherlands, to become England's rulers. William invaded with an army, forcing James to flee to France. In what is known as the GLORIOUS REVOLUTION, William and Mary became joint monarchs of England in 1686. First, however, they agreed to a bill of rights that guaranteed certain basic liberties to the English people and confirmed the sovereignty* of Parliament. In 1701 King William signed the Act of Settlement, which barred Catholics from the throne, ending the religious conflict that had long troubled the country.

* ***absolute monarchy*** rule by a king or queen who possesses unlimited power

* ***sovereignty*** supreme power or authority

Empire and Revolution. The late 1600s and 1700s were marked by economic prosperity and growth. In 1707 the Act of Union joined England and Scotland into the nation known as Great Britain. Having largely resolved the religious struggles and conflicts between Parliament and the monarchy, the government of Great Britain could now devote full attention to the growing empire.

In the late 1600s, England had became involved in a series of wars with France and its allies over commercial and colonial supremacy around the world. After defeating France in the last of these conflicts—the Seven Year's War, or the FRENCH AND INDIAN WAR (1754–1763), as the fighting in North America was known—Britain emerged as the leading European colonial power. It had enlarged its empire to include all of French CANADA and the French territory east of the Mississippi River.

Not long after winning the struggle with the French, Britain faced an even greater threat to its rule in North America. In the 1760s and early 1770s, the nation took advantage of the peace in Europe to tighten its hold on its 13 American colonies. Up to that time, the colonies had been left to manage local affairs without much interference from authorities in London. Then Parliament passed a series of laws that took away some colonial rights and imposed new taxes. The American colonists began challenging British authority, and the conflict between the colonies and the colonial power grew into the AMERICAN REVOLUTION. Britain lost the war and was forced, in the 1783 Treaty of Paris, to recognize the independence of the 13 colonies. (*See also* **British Colonies; Colonial Administration; European Empires; Exploration, Age of; Trade and Commerce.**)

England's Irish Colonies

England's first attempts to establish colonies were not in North America but in Ireland. The English had claimed parts of Ireland for many years but had allowed local authorities to govern. When England tried to gain a tighter hold on the country in the mid-1500s, the Irish—who were Catholic—resisted. They were particularly opposed to England's royal family—which was Protestant. The English responded by seizing land and giving it to loyal settlers from England, Scotland, and Wales. The English sought to conquer Ireland by replacing the native population with their own people, a practice they would follow again in North America.

Great Lakes

The Great Lakes—the largest group of inland bodies of water in the world—consist of Lakes Superior, Huron, Michigan, Erie, and Ontario. Located in central North America, they served as important highways of trade and travel during the colonial period and afterward.

French explorers discovered the Great Lakes while searching for a NORTHWEST PASSAGE, a waterway across North America to Asia. Samuel de CHAMPLAIN was the first to provide descriptions and maps of the lakes. The

French were kept away from the lower Great Lakes (Erie and Ontario) by Indians of the IROQUOIS CONFEDERACY, but they reached the upper Great Lakes easily by way of the Ottawa River.

During the 1600s, the French built a series of FORTS in the Great Lakes region, and Jesuit priests founded MISSIONS there. The area became a great fur-trading center. The French established close ties to the HURON INDIANS, who supplied them with pelts*. French woodsmen known as COUREURS DE BOIS settled in the region, and many of them married Indian women. This strengthened the bonds between the French and their Huron allies and promoted further settlement of the "upper country," as the area became known.

* ***pelt*** skin and fur of an animal

Beginning in the late 1600s, the Great Lakes region played a role in the long series of wars that France and Britain fought for control of North America. The British gained access to Lake Ontario during these conflicts because of their alliance with the Iroquois. But the French maintained their hold on the other lakes.

When Britain won the FRENCH AND INDIAN WAR in 1763, France had to surrender all its territory in present-day Canada. The British thus became masters of the Great Lakes—but their control was short-lived. Under the terms of the Treaty of Paris of 1783, which ended the American Revolution, Britain agreed to share the lakes with the United States. Today the Great Lakes form part of the boundary between the United States and Canada. (*See also* **Canada; Fur Trade; Geography of North America.**)

Green Mountain Boys

The Green Mountain Boys were a group of VERMONT settlers who banded together to defend their right to certain lands against competing claims made by New York. They achieved fame for the part they played in the early years of the American Revolution.

In 1749 the governor of New Hampshire began giving land to settlers in the region west of the Connecticut River (present-day Vermont). New York promptly objected, claiming the region under the terms of its charter*. In 1764 the British king upheld New York's authority over the disputed area. Six years later the New York Supreme Court ruled that the New Hampshire land grants were not valid. As a result, those who held property in the "New Hampshire Grants," as the region was called, would have to buy it again from New York.

* ***charter*** written grant from a ruler conferring certain rights and privileges

Residents of the New Hampshire Grants were determined to keep their lands, by force if necessary. Some of them formed a local militia* known as the Green Mountain Boys, electing Ethan ALLEN as their leader. The Green Mountain Boys terrorized New Yorkers who had moved to the region, tearing down their fences, stealing their cattle, and burning their cabins. They also ignored New York laws and officials. The British government refused to use military force against the rebellious band and ordered New York to stop making land grants until the disagreement could be settled.

* ***militia*** army of citizens who may be called into action in a time of emergency

The American Revolution brought a temporary halt to the dispute, as the Green Mountain Boys quickly joined forces with the patriots*. They

* ***patriot*** American colonist who supported independence from Britain

helped capture FORT TICONDEROGA from the British in May 1775 and played a leading role in the colonial victory at the battle of Bennington in August 1777. That same year, the Green Mountain Boys declared their region the independent republic of Vermont and adopted a constitution that banned slavery and allowed all male residents to vote. New York finally abandoned its claim to the region in 1790, and Vermont became a state the following year. (*See also* **American Revolution.**)

Grenville, George

1712–1770
British prime minister

George Grenville led the British government from 1763 to 1765, a period of mounting tension between Great Britain and its North American colonies. His policy of raising revenue through taxation caused widespread protests among the colonists.

Grenville's political career began in 1741, when he became a member of PARLIAMENT. He went on to hold a series of other public offices. In 1763 King GEORGE III appointed Grenville prime minister, the head of the British government.

At the time, Britain had a large army stationed in North America to protect the colonies. Believing that the colonists should pay part of the cost of their own defense, the new prime minister began proposing methods of raising revenue. In 1764 he introduced the SUGAR ACT, which revised the colonial trade laws and placed a tax on sugar and certain other items that were shipped to the colonies from foreign ports. Though it was unpopular, the Sugar Act primarily affected those involved in trade with the West Indies. But the following year, Grenville infuriated a large part of the population with the passage of the STAMP ACT. The measure required the colonists to purchase government-issued stamps for various legal documents and printed materials. The colonists refused to buy the stamps, arguing that the British government did not have the right to tax them because they had no representatives in Parliament. To protest the Stamp Act, they organized a series of riots and a boycott* of British goods.

* ***boycott*** refusal to buy goods as a means of protest

As opposition to the new laws grew and political problems erupted in Great Britain, Grenville began losing the support of the king. In 1765 he was dismissed as prime minister. Grenville remained in Parliament, often defending his earlier policies, until the last year of his life. (*See also* **Colonial Administration.**)

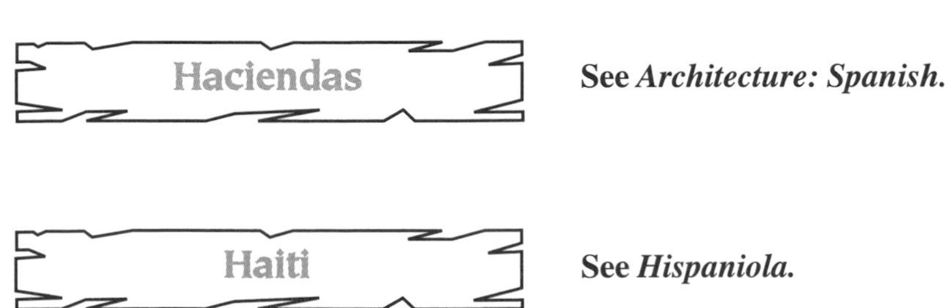

Haciendas

See ***Architecture: Spanish.***

Haiti

See ***Hispaniola.***

Hakluyt, Richard

ca. 1552–1616
English historian and promoter of exploration

Although Richard Hakluyt never set foot in the Americas, he influenced the course of English expansion in the "New World." A trained geographer, he recognized early that North America would bring greater profit to England through colonies and trade than through gold and other precious materials. In addition, Hakluyt collected detailed accounts of the voyages of many explorers of his day, including Francis Drake and Jacques Cartier.

Hakluyt became a clergyman, but he was fascinated by geography and gave lectures on the subject at Oxford University. Through his work, he met several of the explorers who had traveled to North America to search for a Northwest Passage, a water route to Asia. Convinced that a Northwest Passage could be found, Hakluyt urged the English government to increase its efforts to explore the continent. In 1582 he published *Divers Voyages Touching the Discoverie of America,* in which he argued for English colonization of North America.

In 1583 Hakluyt went to France as chaplain to England's ambassador to that country. English authorities wanted him to find out about French activities in the Americas. Hakluyt returned to England to present this information and to lend support to Sir Walter Raleigh's proposal for a colony in North America. In an effort to convince Queen Elizabeth I of the economic and political benefits of Raleigh's plan, Hakluyt wrote a document entitled "A Discourse of Western Planting." The queen showed little enthusiasm for the project, but the clergyman's passion for exploration remained undiminished.

Hakluyt turned his energies to collecting the firsthand accounts of the adventurers who risked the voyage overseas. The resulting three-volume work, *The Principall Navigations, Voiages and Discoveries of the English Nation* (1598–1600), became a valuable source of information on both English and foreign exploration. It included the journals of participants as well as official documents and private letters. (*See also* **Exploration, Age of.**)

Hallam, Mrs. Lewis

died ca. 1774
Actress

Mrs. Lewis Hallam was the leading actress in the Hallam company, the most important theatrical company in colonial America. During the mid-1700s, she traveled widely with the company, appearing in performances in such cities as Williamsburg, New York, Philadelphia, and Charleston.

Few details are known about Mrs. Hallam's early life and background—not even her first name. It is known that her husband, Lewis, came from a large theatrical family in Great Britain. In 1751 his older brother organized a theater company to tour America, with Mrs. Hallam and her husband as the principal actors. The Hallams arrived in the colonies the following year.

In America the theater company staged many of the plays of William Shakespeare, and Mrs. Hallam often performed the leading female roles. She also appeared in works of other playwrights. Few records exist of her acting talents, though one English visitor noted with surprise that the actors in the Hallam company were as good as many British performers.

Touring the colonies was difficult. When the members of the company arrived in a city, they had to prepare or build a playhouse. In addition, they often faced opposition from people who regarded the theater as immoral. In 1754 the company went to Jamaica, where Mrs. Hallam's husband died. She married the actor David Douglass, and a few years later the company returned to the northern colonies, changing its name to the American Company of Comedians. Mrs. Hallam died in about 1774, probably in Philadelphia. (*See also* **Drama.**)

Hamilton, Andrew

See *Zenger, John Peter.*

Hammon, Jupiter

ca. 1720–ca. 1800
Writer

An African American slave, Jupiter Hammon wrote poems, essays, and sermons while working as a clerk for his masters. Although his first poem appeared in print 12 years before any by Phillis WHEATLEY, Wheatley rather than Hammon is usually considered the first black voice in American literature.

Hammon was a dutiful and trusted slave to three generations of the Lloyd family of Long Island and Connecticut. The family regarded him so highly that they helped get his poems published. Hammon's first published poem, *An Evening Thought: Salvation by Christ, with Penetential Cries,* appeared in 1761 as a broadside*. The poem emphasized Christian religious feeling, as did much of his writing.

* ***broadside*** large sheet of paper, printed on one side, that was handed around or posted on buildings and walls

Hammon's writing frequently dealt with slavery. One of his most influential works, *An Address to the Negroes of the State of New York,* was presented to members of the African Society in New York City in 1786. Published the following year in New York and Philadelphia, the address reflected Hammon's belief that it was his duty to bear slavery with patience. Yet at the same time, he expressed strong disapproval of the institution and urged that young slaves be set free. The address may have influenced his masters. A will made by John Lloyd, Jr., in 1795 directed that certain of his slaves be freed when they reached age 28. (*See also* **Slavery.**)

Hancock, John

1737–1793
American Revolutionary leader

John Hancock, a wealthy Boston merchant, played a leading role in the American colonies' fight for independence. In Massachusetts he helped organize resistance to the British, and as a delegate to the Continental Congress, he was the first to sign the Declaration of Independence.

Hancock was born in Braintree (now Quincy), Massachusetts. After the death of his father, he was adopted by his uncle, Thomas Hancock, a successful merchant and one of the richest men in Boston. John Hancock graduated from Harvard in 1754 and went to work for his uncle. He inherited the family business and fortune when his uncle died nine years later.

In 1768 the young merchant imported a large shipment of wine without paying taxes on it. British customs officials accused Hancock of smuggling and seized his ship *Liberty.* Enraged by the incident, a large crowd gathered on the docks and harassed the customs officials, who fled the city. The British sent troops to Boston to prevent further rioting.

The *Liberty* affair made Hancock a popular hero in Massachusetts. He was elected to the colony's legislature in 1769. Several years later, he became chairman of Boston's Committee of Safety, the organization that controlled the local militia*. Hancock used his considerable wealth and influence to support the patriots*—a fact that did not escape the notice of the British. He was charged with treason, and in 1775 the British general Thomas Gage attempted to capture Hancock and Samuel ADAMS during their march on LEXINGTON AND CONCORD. But the two men received a warning from Paul REVERE and escaped.

* ***militia*** army of citizens who may be called into action in a time of emergency

* ***patriot*** American colonist who supported independence from Britain

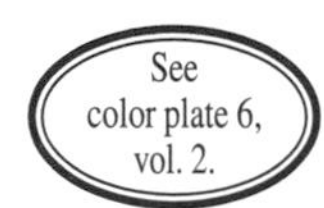
See color plate 6, vol. 2.

A delegate to the SECOND CONTINENTAL CONGRESS, Hancock served as its president for the first two years. When the congress issued the DECLARATION OF INDEPENDENCE in 1776, he signed the document in bold letters. According to one story, he explained that he wrote his name so large so that the king of England would be able to read it without his glasses.

A man of limited military abilities, Hancock nonetheless sought the position of commander in chief of the Continental Army. When Congress appointed George Washington to the post, Hancock was disappointed, but he did lead Massachusetts troops in an attempt to free Rhode Island from the British in 1778.

Hancock turned again to public office, becoming the first governor of the state of Massachusetts. In 1788 he presided over the state convention that ratified* the U.S. Constitution. He died at the age of 56, while serving his ninth term as Massachusetts governor. (*See also* **American Revolution; Independence Movements.**)

* ***ratify*** to approve

Health and Safety

Health and safety were of great concern to the colonists of North America, where disease and accidents were everyday events. Diet, sanitation, and the environment all played important roles in the health of people in colonial America—as they continue to do in the world today.

Diet varied greatly from region to region and among different groups. Though most people had enough to eat, their food often lacked important nutrients*. For example, colonists who had no fresh fruits and vegetables might develop scurvy, a disease caused by an absence of vitamin C. Food shortages occurred from time to time, bringing the risk of malnutrition, particularly for military expeditions. While people rarely died of malnutrition or dietary diseases, they became weak and had little resistance to other illnesses.

* ***nutrient*** substance in foods that the body needs to maintain health

Poor sanitation often led to disease. The dumping of garbage and human waste contaminated the soil as well as the streams and wells that supplied drinking water. Contaminated water could spread diseases such as typhoid fever and dysentery. Colonists bathed infrequently and had few changes of clothing. Dirty clothes sometimes harbored lice and other organisms that might carry disease. At the time, people knew little about the causes of disease.

Very few towns in the colonial period had any laws or organizations to protect public health and safety. An exception was New York City, which boasted a fire brigade known as the Hand-in-Hand Fire Company. This picture comes from a poster created around 1750 to announce a meeting of the company.

The environment affected health in many ways as well. Hot, humid climates provided a breeding ground for the mosquitoes that carry malaria and yellow fever. In many areas, inadequate shelter presented a health risk. Houses were often small, poorly ventilated, and overcrowded. People in rural areas might share their homes with animals. Such conditions contributed to the spread of disease.

Accidents occurred frequently in colonial America. People fell from buildings and broke bones. They cut themselves working with axes, saws, and other sharp-bladed tools. Carriages and carts hit people walking in the streets. Colonists were kicked by horses or fell while riding. Because few people could swim, drowning was common. People suffered from exposure to severe cold in the winter and sometimes even froze to death. In crowded homes, people often got burned or scalded in kitchen accidents. Settlers in frontier areas were sometimes attacked by bears or bitten by poisonous snakes. Accidents such as these killed many people or left them permanently deformed, scarred, or disabled. Safety precautions to prevent accidents were rare.

Medical knowledge was limited in colonial times, and doctors rarely practiced outside of settled areas. To treat illness, people relied on a few drugs and medicinal HERBS, bloodletting*, and quarantines. Colonists paid little attention to sanitary conditions. Some towns did adopt measures such as cleaning streets

* ***bloodletting*** opening of a vein to take blood, a procedure that was believed to aid healing

and regulating waste disposal. But they usually took these steps to improve the appearance of the town rather than to prevent illness. It was not until the 1800s that communities and local governments began making efforts to improve the health and safety of their populations. (*See also* **Diseases and Disorders; Medical Practice.**)

Henry, Patrick

1736–1799
Orator and patriot

Patrick Henry was a lawyer, a politician, and one of the most powerful orators of the American Revolutionary period. He is best remembered for his stirring words, "Give me liberty or give me death," which urged the colony of Virginia to arm itself against Great Britain in 1775.

Henry was born in Hanover County, Virginia, to a family of comfortable means. His father, a well-educated man, taught young Patrick at home. His mother often took Patrick to hear the fiery, tearful sermons of the great southern preacher Samuel Davies.

After brief attempts at farming and business, Henry turned his efforts to law. Within three years, the young lawyer had handled more than 1,000 cases, winning most of them. He displayed his remarkable powers of persuasion in 1763 during the famous Parson's Cause case. Henry argued that the king forfeited the right to obedience when he acted against the good of his people. Henry's performance brought him fame throughout the colony and established his reputation as a dedicated supporter of colonial rights.

In 1765 Henry was elected to the Virginia House of Burgesses, where he repeatedly spoke out against British authority. During his first year there, Henry proposed a set of resolutions protesting the STAMP ACT, declaring that the British government had no right to tax the colonists because they were not represented in Parliament. His dramatic speech concluded with some of his most famous words: "Caesar had his Brutus—Charles the First, his Cromwell—and George the Third—may profit by their example. If this be treason, make the most of it." Henry's statement shocked some of the representatives, but the house nevertheless passed several of the resolutions. The *Virginia Resolves,* a pamphlet containing all of the resolutions, was published and read throughout the colonies.

Patrick Henry was one of the first colonial politicians to promote complete independence from Britain. After the Revolutionary War, he continued to fight to ensure greater freedom for individuals in America. This portrait of Henry is based on an 1815 painting by Thomas Sully.

Henry served as a delegate to the FIRST CONTINENTAL CONGRESS in 1774 and to the SECOND CONTINENTAL CONGRESS in 1775. Virginia asked him to command the colony's military forces, but he resigned the post in 1776, after disagreements with political opponents. That same year, Henry was elected governor of the new state of Virginia. While in office, he recruited soldiers for the CONTINENTAL ARMY and provided supplies such as clothing, shoes, and food for the troops. He served as governor until 1779 and again from 1784 through 1786.

The following year, Henry attended the Virginia convention called to approve the U.S. Constitution. He strongly opposed the document, believing that it endangered the rights of individuals and states. After supporters of the Constitution won out, he led the fight for adoption of the ten amendments that became the Bill of Rights.

In 1788 Henry returned to his private law practice until ill health forced him to retire six years later. Although President George Washington offered

the famous speaker several important positions, including that of the chief justice of the United States, Henry declined them all. In 1799 Washington finally convinced him to run for the Virginia state legislature. Henry won the election but died before he could take office. (*See also* **American Revolution; Independence Movements.**)

Herbs

Herbs played an important role in the lives of people in North America. While European colonists commonly used chives, mint, rosemary, thyme, and sage to flavor food, many also relied on herbs to treat illness and injury. In some rural and frontier areas, herbs and roots were the only remedies available.

Europeans colonists discovered that Native Americans used many plants medicinally, treating everything from coughs and fever to headaches, numbness, insomnia, and snakebites. The plants might be mixed with grease and rubbed on the body, inhaled in steam, chewed, or boiled and drunk. Each had certain specific applications. The Indians' knowledge of herbal medicine was enormous.

Spanish colonists quickly learned herbal remedies from the Indians and adopted various herbs that were unknown in Europe. One of the favorites was *oshá* (wild celery), used for everything from curing colds to repelling rattlesnakes. Other European colonists, however, preferred imported drugs and the familiar herbal medicines of Europe to Indian remedies. Some colonial doctors tried to treat various conditions with native plants such as sassafras, ginseng, and jimsonweed, but none of these became as popular as European remedies.

Unlike European colonists, black slaves relied primarily on herbal medicine. African American healers experimented with many plants and gained great knowledge of the properties of various herbs and roots. They had a plant remedy for every illness. Herbs commonly used for medicinal purposes included comfrey, sage, catnip, mustard weed, tansey leaves, and snakeroot.

Among both black slaves and white colonists, women played a major role in herbal medicine. Many grew herbs in gardens and gathered wild herb plants to make their home remedies. Such herbal medicine was an important part of colonial health care, especially in rural areas. (*See also* **Food and Drink; Medical Practice.**)

Hidalgo y Costilla, Miguel

1753–1811
Mexican priest and revolutionary leader

Miguel Hidalgo y Costilla was a Catholic priest who helped lead a revolt against the Spanish rulers of MEXICO. His role in the independence movement earned him the title "Father of Mexican Independence."

Born and raised in central Mexico, Hidalgo was the son of an administrator of a hacienda, or large estate. He became a priest in 1778 and was sent to the town of Dolores a few years later. There he devoted his energies to improving the physical as well as the spiritual welfare of the people. He helped expand the town's industry by introducing a pottery works, brick factory, olive grove, and vineyards.

* ***philosophy*** study related to ideas, the laws of nature, and the pursuit of truth

* ***Creole*** person of European ancestry, born in the Americas

* ***mestizo*** person of mixed Spanish and Indian ancestry

Hidalgo, who loved philosophy* and music and spoke French, spent much of his time among educated people in Guanajuato, a city near Dolores. It was there that he probably first met with Creoles* and others who supported the idea of Mexican independence. Hidalgo began planning a revolution with them.

The colonial government learned of the revolutionary plans and arrested several leaders. Faced with possible arrest, Hidalgo took a bold step. On September 16, 1810, he rang the bells of his church in Dolores to summon the people and then delivered an emotional speech urging Mexicans to revolt against their Spanish rulers. This call to arms, known as the *Grito de Dolores* (Cry of Dolores), was answered. Within a short time, tens of thousands of Indians and mestizos* joined the revolutionary cause.

Hidalgo and his followers—estimated at 60,000 strong—marched through the Mexican countryside armed with machetes, farm tools, slings, and stones and captured town after town. They arrested Spaniards and threatened to execute those who resisted. By October 30, Hidalgo and his army had reached the capital of Mexico City, where they faced well-trained Spanish colonial troops. After some fighting, the Spanish army withdrew. But the inexperienced rebel forces had suffered heavy losses, and Hidalgo abandoned plans to take the city.

In the end, Hidalgo's peasant army could not stand up against the well-armed Spanish troops. In late 1810 and early 1811, the rebels suffered defeat after crushing defeat, and they fled north toward the United States. Captured along the way, Hidalgo was dismissed from the priesthood and executed by a firing squad.

The rebel priest had set out to end colonial rule and reform Mexican society by improving the lives of Indians and the lower classes. Although he made little progress toward that goal, he became a symbol of the independence movement. Mexico finally gained its freedom in 1821. Today Mexicans celebrate September 16 as Independence Day. A church bell is rung in Mexico City and the Mexican president repeats the *Grito de Dolores* in honor of Hidalgo. (*See also* **Independence Movements; Mexican Independence.**)

Hispaniola

See first map in European Empires (vol. 2).

Hispaniola, a large island in the Caribbean Sea, was the site of the first European colony in the Americas. Hispaniola had another, more important role in colonial history, though. It served as a starting point for Spanish expeditions to other islands in this area known as the West Indies and to the mainlands of North and South America.

Spanish Settlement. In the autumn of 1492, the Taino Indians who lived on the island were surprised by the appearance of strangers on the north coast. The newcomers were Spanish explorers led by Christopher Columbus, then on his first voyage to the Americas. Columbus named the island Hispaniola. The Spaniards noticed that some of the Taino wore gold ornaments and also discovered a little gold in the rivers that ran down

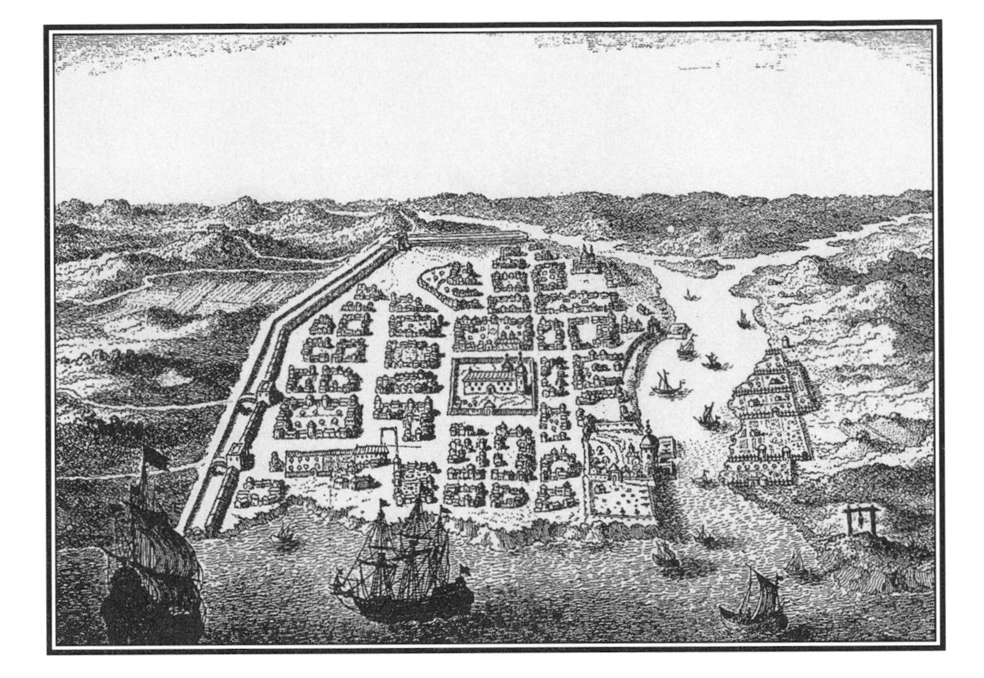

The city of Santo Domingo, on the southeastern coast of Hispaniola, was the center of Spanish exploration in the early 1500s. Later it became a port for Spanish treasure ships.

to the sea from the inland mountains. They saw these bits of gold as a sign of great riches. One of Columbus's ships, the *Santa Maria,* ran aground while sailing along the coast of Hispaniola on December 24, 1492. Columbus returned to Spain with his other two vessels, leaving some of his crew at a small settlement the Spaniards had established—Navidad. When Columbus came back to Hispaniola 11 months later with a large force, he found Navidad ruined and empty. The first European colony in the Americas had failed.

Columbus and his men built another community, which they called Isabella after the queen of Spain. Other settlements followed as the Spaniards spread out in search of gold. They found little of the precious metal—just enough to arouse their appetites. But while stripping Hispaniola of gold, the Spanish enslaved the Taino Indians and forced them to work in gold mines. Slavery devastated the Indians. Many died from overwork and outright brutality. Others perished from new DISEASES, including measles and smallpox, that the Europeans introduced to the Americas. Within a period of about ten years, the Taino had almost disappeared. The Spanish replaced them with slaves brought from Africa.

A few years later, the Spanish crown took control of Hispaniola away from Columbus and his brothers Bartolomeo and Diego. The brothers had proved to be ineffective governors. Santo Domingo, a settlement founded on the southeastern coast of the island in 1496, became the center of Spanish operations. From this port, the Spanish military commanders and explorers known as CONQUISTADORS set out to gain knowledge and control of the Americas. From Santo Domingo, Juan PONCE DE LEÓN left to explore PUERTO RICO. Vasco Núñez de Balboa sailed to the isthmus* of Panama, crossed it, and found the Pacific Ocean. Francisco Pizarro went to Peru and conquered the Inca empire.

See first map in Exploration, Age of (vol. 2).

* ***isthmus*** narrow strip of land connecting two larger land areas

Santo Domingo remained an important port throughout most of the colonial period. When Spain began obtaining massive amounts of gold and silver from Peru, Mexico, and the Philippines, the treasure ships that carried the riches back to Spain always stopped there. In 1585 the English mariner Francis DRAKE attacked and devastated Santo Domingo. But he failed to capture the Spanish treasure fleet or to establish a permanent English base of operations on Hispaniola.

Power Struggles. The Spanish considered Hispaniola a disappointment because it yielded little gold or silver. Still, the island occupied a strategic* position in the West Indies trade routes, and Spain wanted to hold on to it. The English tried to gain control of the Spanish West Indies in 1655. Although they captured the island of JAMAICA, they failed to take Hispaniola, which had a larger population than Jamaica and was better fortified.

* ***strategic*** key part of a plan; of military importance

* ***cede*** to yield or surrender

Most Spanish colonists lived on the eastern part of Hispaniola, as the island's western half was rugged and almost impossible to police. PIRATES of many nations used this region as a hideout. In 1697 Spain ceded* the western part of the island to the French, who called it St. Domingue. Hispaniola remained divided between Spain and France for nearly 100 years. During that time, colonists of both nations imported thousands of slaves from Africa to work on the island's vast sugar plantations.

A time of enormous conflict and change began in 1791 as black slaves across Hispaniola began rebelling against their owners. The British used the slave uprising as an excuse to invade the island and strike a blow against the French. The British occupied the French portion of Hispaniola from 1793 to 1798, when blacks led by a former slave named Toussaint-Louverture drove them out. In 1801 Toussaint's forces conquered the eastern part of the island, which Spain had ceded to France several years earlier. In 1804 Hispaniola became the republic of Haiti.

The inhabitants of the eastern part of Hispaniola declared their independence from Haiti in 1844 and formed the Dominican Republic. Today the island of Hispaniola remains divided between Haiti in the west and the Dominican Republic in the east, with the border between the two nations marking the old colonial border between Spanish and French territory. (*See also* **Slave Trade; Slavery.**)

Haitian Hero

Toussaint-Louverture, a former slave, became governor-general of Hispaniola in 1801. During his brief rule, he outlawed slavery and brought order to the island. Fearing that this powerful black leader had plans for independence, the French sent a large army to regain control of the island and return the blacks to slavery. The army captured Toussaint and he died in prison in France in 1803. But Toussaint-Louverture triumphed in the end. The people of Hispaniola for whom he had fought defeated the French and declared their island the independent nation of Haiti.

Hohokam and Mogollan Indians

See *Native Americans: Early Peoples of North America.*

Holidays

See *Festivals.*

Hooker, Thomas

1586–1647
Puritan leader and a founder of Connecticut

Thomas Hooker was a Puritan minister whose religious beliefs brought him into conflict with church leaders. A founder of CONNECTICUT, he helped draft the FUNDAMENTAL ORDERS OF CONNECTICUT, a plan of government for the colony.

Hooker was born in England and educated at Cambridge University. He became a minister in about 1620 and soon attracted great public attention because of his forceful preaching and Puritan ideas. Ordered to appear before a church court in 1630 because of his views, Hooker fled to the Netherlands, fearing that he would be persecuted.

While in the Netherlands, Hooker learned that some members of his former church planned to move to North America. He decided to join them. Arriving in Massachusetts in 1633, Hooker settled in New Towne (present-day Cambridge) and became a popular preacher.

Before long, Hooker found himself at odds with Puritan leaders such as John COTTON. Hooker argued that church members should have a

In 1636 Thomas Hooker and a group of followers left Massachusetts and settled in the Connecticut River valley. The new colony they founded adopted a more democratic government than that of Massachusetts.

greater role in church affairs. Dissatisfied with conditions in Massachusetts, he left the colony with a group of followers in 1636. They moved west to the Connecticut River valley, where Hooker founded the settlement of Hartford.

The Puritan minister became an influential leader in Connecticut. In 1637 he began discussing the possibility of forming a confederation with Massachusetts. Nothing came of the idea, mainly because Hooker and Massachusetts governor John WINTHROP disagreed on a number of issues. In particular, Winthrop opposed democracy, while Hooker wanted to give people a greater voice in government.

In 1639 Hooker helped organize Hartford and other towns in the Connecticut River valley into a colony. The Fundamental Orders of Connecticut, a framework of government for the colony adopted in 1639, contained many of Hooker's democratic ideals.

Hooker continued to pursue the idea of a colonial alliance. His plan was finally realized in 1643 with the formation of the NEW ENGLAND CONFEDERATION, the first union of colonies in America. Connecticut, Massachusetts, the PLYMOUTH COLONY, and the New Haven colony joined in a loose alliance for the purpose of mutual defense. Hooker died four years after this dream was fulfilled. (*See also* **Puritans.**)

See *Native Americans: Early Peoples of North America.*

Hopi Indians

The Hopi, one of several groups of PUEBLO INDIANS in the Southwest, are probably descendants of an ancient people known as the Anasazi, who moved to the region about 3,000 years ago. During colonial times, the Hopi remained fairly isolated from Europeans. As a result, colonization had less of an impact on them than on many other Native Americans.

The Spanish were the first Europeans to encounter the Hopi. In 1540 an expedition led by Francisco Vásquez de CORONADO came upon Hopi villages while searching for gold and the SEVEN CITIES OF CÍBOLA, Indian towns rumored to be fabulously rich. The Spanish did not return for several decades after Coronado's expedition. The explorer Antonio de Espejo visited the tribe in 1583, and Juan de OÑATE followed in 1598.

See second map in Native Americans (vol. 3).

Spanish missionaries began arriving among the Hopi in 1629, establishing MISSIONS in a number of villages. The Hopi accepted the Catholic faith of the missionaries but only because of the presence of Spanish soldiers. The Hopi had very strong beliefs of their own and continued to practice their religion as much as they could.

In 1680 growing tensions between the Spanish and Pueblo Indians in NEW MEXICO erupted in an Indian uprising known as the PUEBLO REVOLT. The Hopi joined in the rebellion by destroying the missions in their villages. After the revolt, the Hopi moved many of their villages to the top of high mesas*, which were easier to defend against attack. The Spanish reconquered the Pueblo Indians in New Mexico in the 1690s, but they did not regain control of the Hopi.

* ***mesa*** flat-topped hill or mountain with steep sides

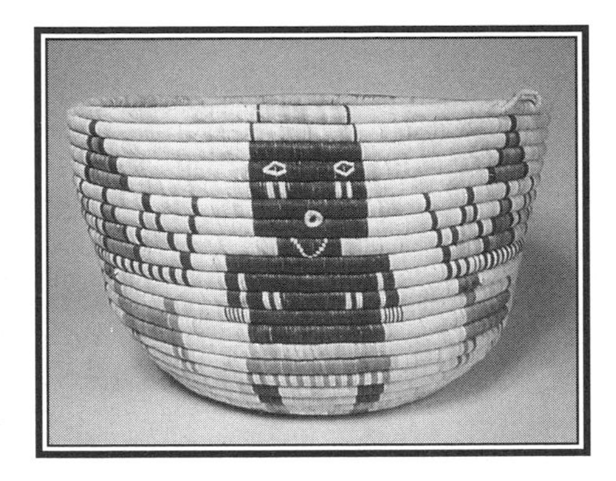

The Hopi were more successful than most Native Americans in preserving their culture in the face of European colonization. Through the years they have continued to practice their traditional crafts, producing fine silver jewelry, pottery, and baskets.

* ***clan*** related families

* ***ritual*** ceremony that follows a set pattern

Those Indians remained independent, free to follow their religion and traditional ways of life.

The Hopi economy was based on agriculture. The main crops included corn, beans, squash, and cotton. Although the harsh desert climate of the Southwest made farming difficult, the Hopi had learned techniques for adapting to the environment. They planted crops at the base of cliffs and other places where natural features of the land helped them gather rainwater. They also built small dams in streams to create ponds and dug irrigation systems to channel water into their fields.

Hopi villages consisted of multilevel houses built of adobe, a sun-dried clay brick. Within each village were several kivas—underground chambers used for religious ceremonies and as meeting places. Hopi villages contained a number of clans*, each with specific political and religious responsibilities. Women played a key role in the clans. Individuals traced their kinship through women, and each clan was headed by a "clan mother." Ownership of houses and land passed from mother to daughter, while political authority in the clan passed to men through the women.

Hopi religion had a strong relationship with nature. Religious rituals* occurred throughout the year in connection with such events as the changing of seasons and the planting and harvesting of crops. Some of the most important rituals centered on kachinas—guardian spirits associated with annual cycles of the birth, death, and rebirth of all living things. In many ceremonies, Hopi men impersonated kachinas by wearing colorful costumes and masks. They then participated in dances and other ceremonial activities.

The Hopi generally have been a peaceful people. In fact, their name comes from a Hopi word meaning "the peaceful ones." Yet they did not hesitate to use force against the Spanish, and even against other Hopi who were friendly to the Spanish.

After the colonial period, the Hopi came into contact more frequently with white Americans. Yet they remained geographically isolated. As a result, these Indians have one of the best-preserved native cultures in North America today. They continue to live in their traditional homelands in northeastern Arizona. The Hopi village of Oraibi, established around 1100, may be the oldest continuously inhabited site in the United States. (*See also* **Native Americans; Religions, Native American; Spanish Borderlands.**)

Horses

The ancestors of modern horses originated in North America millions of years ago and eventually spread into Asia, Europe, and Africa. Sometime between 7,000 and 10,000 years ago, these animals disappeared from their original homeland. They only returned to the continent with the arrival of Europeans in the late 1400s. Horses came to play an important role in the lives of European colonists and many Native Americans.

On Christopher COLUMBUS's second voyage to the Americas in 1493, he brought 25 horses to the West Indies. In 1519 Hernando CORTÉS took horses along on his expedition to Mexico. Other Spaniards shipped horses from

Europe, and the number of animals in North America gradually increased. By the early 1600s, ranchers in various parts of NEW SPAIN were raising horses for their own use and for sale to others.

Over the years, many Spanish horses escaped into the wild and multiplied. In time these wild horses spread throughout the Spanish Borderlands*. They continued moving northward until, by 1800, millions of them roamed the west. Small herds of wild horses also appeared in some of the English colonies in the southeast. In addition English and French colonists imported domesticated* horses from the Spanish colonies, brought some from Europe, and traded or bought horses from Indians.

* ***Spanish Borderlands*** northern part of New Spain, area now occupied by Florida, Texas, New Mexico, Arizona, and California

* ***domesticated*** tamed and raised for human use

At first North American colonists used the animals primarily for riding or carrying small loads. The Spanish breeds were too small for heavy work. By the late 1700s, however, horse breeders in the British colonies had begun to develop new, larger horses capable of pulling wagons, carriages, and farm equipment, such as plows.

As horses spread throughout North America, many Native American groups realized their value and adopted them for their own use. Indians probably acquired horses first from the Spanish, who taught them how to ride. Indians later learned how to tame wild horses. They built their herds through trade and by raiding white settlements and other Indian tribes.

These animals had a tremendous impact on Native American cultures, especially in the Great Plains and the Southwest. With horses, the nomadic tribes of those regions could travel farther, faster, and with less effort. Hunting BUFFALO was easier on horseback as well, and the lives of most PLAINS INDIANS revolved around the buffalo. Some eastern tribes abandoned farming, moved to the Great Plains with horses, and became nomadic hunters and gatherers. The animals also changed the nature of Indian warfare, enabling tribes to conduct swifter and more effective raids on their enemies.

Horses thus played a significant role in the colonial period of North America. They made it easier for early European explorers to penetrate the interior of the continent and helped colonists settle and occupy the land. They also dramatically changed the lives of many Native Americans. In the 1800s, the horse became an important symbol of the American West because of its role in cattle RANCHING and its association with the Indians and their struggle to hold on to their lands. (*See also* **Animals; Hunting.**)

They're Off!

People have raced horses since ancient times. A popular sport among the Greeks and Romans, horse racing became known as "the sport of kings" during the Middle Ages because many monarchs and nobles owned racing horses.

The early colonists in North America raced horses on flat, straight courses. Races became a common attraction at market fairs. The first racetrack was built in 1665. Known as New Market, it was located near the site of present-day Belmont Park racetrack in New York State.

Hospitals

The earliest hospitals in colonial North America were built in the 1500s and early 1600s by the Spanish and French. Many years later, British colonists established hospitals to care for people in their growing communities.

Beginning in 1521, the Spanish developed a highly organized and well-funded hospital system centered in Mexico City in New Spain. Run by the Spanish crown and staffed by religious orders*, these colonial hospitals served the health needs of both colonists and Native Americans.

* ***order*** religious organization whose members live according to certain rules

New France also had a well-run hospital system. Financed by the Roman Catholic Church, the government, and wealthy individuals and staffed by religious nursing orders, the hospitals provided medical and surgical care for the sick, the elderly, and the insane. The *Hôtel-Dieu* (house of God) of QUEBEC, established in 1639, is the oldest hospital in North America. The French also had hospitals in the towns of Montreal and Trois-Rivières and at major forts along the frontier.

The British colonies did not develop a system of hospitals until much later. The early health-care facilities of the mid-1600s were no more than small infirmaries connected to local poorhouses. Run exclusively for poorhouse residents, they hired local doctors only when needed. In the following years, many British colonial towns began to set up temporary infirmaries during epidemics to care for infected people. But the first permanent hospital established exclusively for the care of the sick was the Pennsylvania Hospital in Philadelphia, founded in 1751 by Benjamin Franklin and physician Thomas Bond.

During the American Revolution, the colonists created temporary military hospitals to care for the wounded and for soldiers recovering from surgery or disease. Many of these were set up in large private homes or public buildings. After the Revolution, American cities began to establish permanent general hospitals to care for people who could not afford private nursing care at home. (*See also* **Health and Safety; Medical Practice.**)

House of Burgesses

See ***Virginia House of Burgesses.***

Housing

Shelter is a basic human need. The different groups of people who lived in North America during the colonial period met this need by building a wide variety of homes. Americans and European settlers all required protection from rain, cold, wild animals, and other perils. Their dwellings gave them that protection. But as in today's cities and towns, their homes also served as the framework of family life and the building blocks of communities.

Housing in colonial North America was shaped by three factors. The first was climate. People who lived in the chilly northern regions of Canada and New England, the flood-prone lowlands of Louisiana, and the hot, dry Spanish Borderlands* of the Southwest required different kinds of housing for the particular conditions of their environment. The second factor was the building materials that were available. For example, in the heavily forested northeastern region with its plentiful timber, people built wooden houses. Trees were much scarcer in the Southwest, so the Indians and Europeans who lived there built houses of stone and sun-dried brick called adobe.

* ***Spanish Borderlands*** northern part of New Spain, area now occupied by Florida, Texas, New Mexico, Arizona, and California

The third factor that influenced colonial housing was tradition. The European colonists brought building methods and housing styles from their homelands. Often, however, settlers had to adapt these traditions, changing them to fit new conditions. In doing so, they borrowed techniques and styles from the

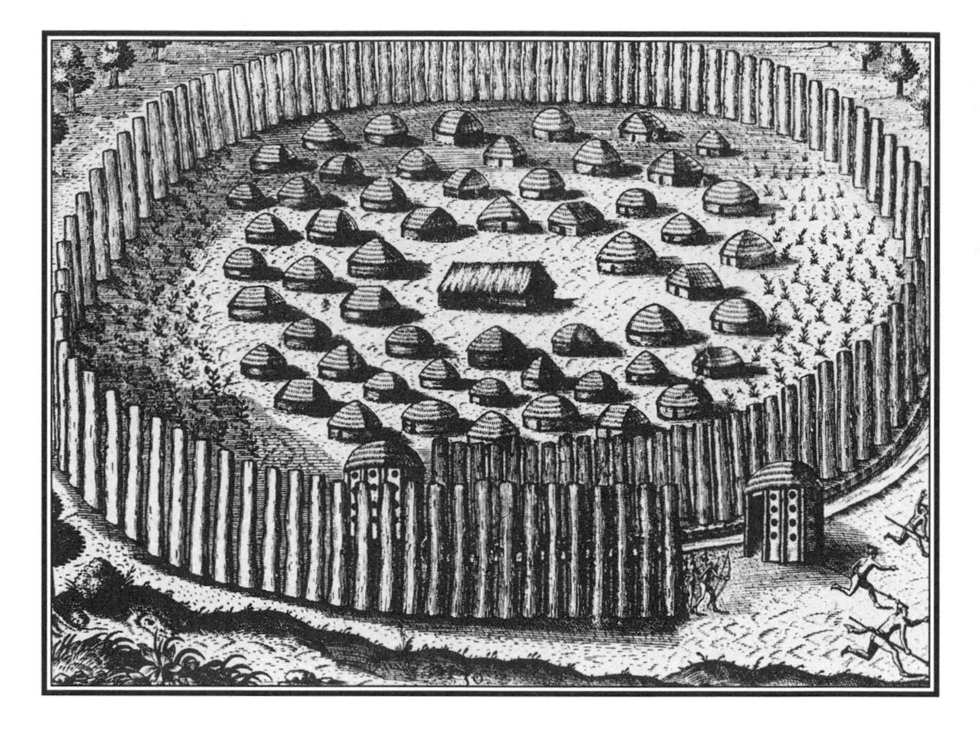

This 1594 engraving was based on Jacques Le Moyne's paintings of a Timucua Indian village. The settlement was protected by a log palisade, and guardhouses stood near the entrance.

Native Americans and from other European groups. Over time, colonial housing blended traditions from many cultures, all adapted to meet American needs and building materials.

Native American Homes

The Indians of the Atlantic coast were farmers and hunters who divided their time between temporary wigwams in seasonal hunting camps and larger dwellings in more permanent settlements. Some coastal Indians built oval homes that were partly underground. Basically pits dug in the ground, these structures had cone-shaped roofs of poles covered with skins or bark. Inside, sleeping benches formed a ring around the walls.

In the Hudson Valley of New York and in southern New England, many Native Americans lived in longhouses—group buildings that sheltered as many as 18 families. The largest longhouses in the region were 100 feet long and 25 feet wide. These warm, watertight, and sturdy structures were made of thick layers of bark attached to frames of wooden poles. Longhouses also provided shelter for the Iroquois tribes of the St. Lawrence River valley and what is now central New York and the Huron Indians of the Great Lakes region. These tribes built longhouses close together in communities surrounded by wooden palisades*. Interior walls divided the buildings into separate compartments for each family.

In the far north, many Native Americans built dwellings all or partly underground, using the earth for insulation from the cold. Tribes in the Southeast generally constructed wood-framed houses covered with straw, reeds, or leaves. The Chumash Indians on the California coast lived in dome-shaped grass huts. The nomadic tribes of the Great Plains used a

* ***palisade*** fence of stakes forming a defense

variety of portable dwellings, such as tents made of hide and wooden poles, as well as more permanent earthen lodges that had wooden frames covered with sod.

In the Southwest, Native Americans such as the Tewa, Zuni, and Hopi lived in settlements that the Spanish called pueblos. Instead of individual freestanding houses, these Indians built structures similar to modern apartment houses, with large blocks of many small rooms. The term *pueblo* refers both to a village and to these apartmentlike buildings—and to the Indians who lived in these structures. The dwellings were made of adobe or stone. Their flat roofs consisted of heavy wooden timbers, often brought from forests many miles away. Over these beams, the Indians laid smaller poles, branches, and mud to form a solid surface. The thick walls of the pueblos provided insulation, keeping the interior cool in summer and warm in winter. The pueblos had no doors at ground level. Entrances were placed on the second or third level and could be reached only by wooden ladders, making the dwellings easy to defend. The pueblos were the largest Indian buildings in North America. Spanish settlers adapted the construction methods used in the pueblos to meet their own needs.

Homes of European Settlers

The first structures that European settlers built in North America were forts—clusters of buildings within protective walls or palisades. Throughout the colonial period, people who lived in dangerous areas, such as the frontier regions, continued to build forts and flee to them for safety in times of peril. Nearly all settlers built private, freestanding houses as soon as they could do so.

The early colonists arrived in a land with no sawmills or glassworks and no sources of familiar building supplies such as bricks, nails, and plaster. For this reason, many settlers built temporary shelters patterned on the dwellings of the local Indians. First homes were often a hole in the ground sheltered with branches or tepees of poles and bark. But as soon as they could fell trees and cut logs into rough timbers, the colonists began building square-framed, above-ground houses that resembled those of their home countries.

After the European settlers had met their immediate need for shelter, housing acquired other values. In the North American colonies, as elsewhere in the world, a home reflected its owner's wealth, social class, and status* in the community. As communities became more settled, differences in housing increased, reflecting the widening range of social classes. By the mid-1700s, colonial dwellings included the small and often crowded slave quarters on southern plantations, the dirt-floored log cabins of the frontier, the sturdy wooden and brick two-room houses of colonial cities, and the two- and three-storied mansions of wealthy landowners and merchants.

* ***status*** social position

British Homes. The most common dwelling in the British colonies in the 1600s and 1700s was a one-room house measuring about 18 by 20 feet. The single room served as kitchen, living room, workshop, and bedroom. Toilets were in separate buildings called outhouses. People who lived in one-room houses cooked outside when the weather permitted. Often, they later added a roofed extension to the back of the building and used that new room as a kitchen. These one-room structures might house six or more people. Privacy was rare, even for such events as birth, illness, and death.

Colonists built these one-room homes using a method called earthfast construction. They drove wooden posts into the ground, constructed a timber frame between the posts, and covered the frame and the roof with wooden timbers and shingles. The best one-room houses had a few glass windows, a wooden floor, inside walls coated with plaster, a chimney, and a floored loft under the ceiling that served as a sleeping and storage space. Furniture generally included a bed, a table, and some chairs, stools, or benches.

The most primitive one-room houses were windowless and had dirt floors. Instead of fireplaces and chimneys, they had open cooking fires and holes in the roof to let smoke out. Such structures were badly lit, smelly, hot in summer, bitterly cold in winter, and dangerous at all times because of the open fires. The furniture in these houses might consist of simple chests for storage and sitting and coarse bedding, perhaps a straw mattress on the floor.

Colonists who could afford somewhat larger houses built two-room structures with a "hall" and a "parlor." The entrance of the house led directly into the hall, which was used for cooking, eating, and domestic work, such as spinning and sewing. Behind the hall was the parlor, where the family displayed its best furniture and household goods, such as a mirror or tea set. The parlor also served as the sleeping area. Sometimes a loft or second story provided additional sleeping and storage space. In cities two-room houses often consisted of a hall behind the family workshop or store and a parlor above it.

The difference between one-room and two-room houses was more than just additional space. A two-room house allowed people to separate their activities and possessions. The hall sometimes was called the "common room" because it was the scene of common, everyday life. The parlor, or "best room," was used to impress visitors. Three-room houses offered families even more choices for dividing their goods and activities. But such houses were still entered by a door that led directly into the heart of the dwelling—generally the hall or kitchen.

A new kind of residence appeared in the British colonies in the 1700s. In this two- or three-story house built in a style known as Georgian—after the reigning kings of Britain—the front door opened into a passage leading to various rooms rather than into an actual room. Georgian houses introduced separate rooms for sleeping, eating, and living. But such houses belonged only to a wealthy minority.

Remember: *Consult the index at the end of Volume 4 to find more information on many topics.*

Dutch Homes. The Dutch colonists built houses much like the traditional homes of the Netherlands. They generally consisted of two good-sized rooms—a kitchen and a *groot kamer,* or "big room." Many also had cellars and attics or second stories for storage.

The Dutch kitchen, with a large fireplace dominating one wall, was used for cooking, eating, entertaining visitors, and often sleeping, especially in cold weather. Against one wall stood the *pottebank,* a cupboard of shelves for

storing and displaying pottery and dishes. The *lepelrekje,* a spoon rack where family members placed their spoons between meals, hung on another wall.

The family displayed its most valuable possessions—such as a family Bible, upholstered chairs, or a painting—in the *groot kamer.* The room also contained the family's best bed, generally reserved for the home owners, and a *kas,* or cupboard, with fine china and silver.

French Homes. Rural colonists in New France* grouped their houses with other buildings, such as barns and sheds, to form an enclosed courtyard. A French colonial house generally consisted of a single room, perhaps with wooden partitions to divide it into smaller areas for sleeping. It might have a large, central stone fireplace or smaller ones at each end of the room for cooking and heating. A narrow stairway against one wall led to a trapdoor in the ceiling that opened to an attic. Houses usually had high, steeply sloping roofs, so attics tended to be large. Colonists often extended the roof out past the walls of the house and supported it with posts to form a veranda, or porch. Wealthy rural landowners generally built larger stone houses and decorated them with fancy woodwork and ironwork.

* ***New France*** French colony centered in the St. Lawrence River valley, an area known as Canada; included the Great Lakes region and, until 1713, Acadia (present-day Nova Scotia)

Houses in urban areas were narrow, two- or three-story structures crowded closely together along streets. In Quebec the residences were often built of stone. In Montreal and other towns, most colonists lived in wooden houses. The typical urban home had a workshop (many town dwellers were artisans), a kitchen-living room, and one or more bedrooms, which were subdivided with partitions or curtains as a family grew. The homes of wealthy individuals might also have separate parlors and dining rooms. In both urban and rural homes, furniture included various tables, chairs, beds, chests, cupboards, and armoires, or wardrobe cabinets.

In the colony of Louisiana, settlers sought protection from the heat by building broad, shady verandas and by putting kitchens in separate structures away from the living quarters. They also built their houses above ground level, often on a raised foundation of brick or stone, as protection from floods.

Spanish Homes. The first homes of Spanish colonists in the Southwest were pueblo dwellings borrowed from the Indians. When the settlers built their own communities, they used the same basic principles for their houses—thick adobe walls for insulation and flat roofs that served as outdoor "rooms" or work spaces in mild weather. But the Spanish constructed individual homes rather than group dwellings, adding European features such as chimneys and windows. They also plastered or whitewashed the adobe walls to make them smooth and white and included decorative features such as carved wood and fancy ironwork.

A Spanish colonial home resembled a small fort, with thick, windowless walls on the outside. A two-story tower at one corner served as a lookout post from which the family could keep an eye on the surrounding countryside. The rooms of the house had windows opening onto a protected inner courtyard—the center of family life. Spanish dwellings had larger rooms than those in Indian pueblos. Using metal tools and wagons, the Spaniards could cut large trees and haul them great distances. The long roof beams allowed them to increase the size of their rooms. Many homes had a *sala,* or great room, for large family gatherings and public events such as dances.

Not all Spanish colonists lived in pueblo-style housing. Those who settled high in the mountains of New Mexico and Arizona could find plenty of big trees. They built their homes and outbuildings of logs, sometimes plastering over them with adobe.

Because wood was scarce in most of the Southwest, Spanish homes had little furniture. Instead, the colonists had niches in walls and adobe benches for sitting and sleeping and built-in cupboards for storage. Wealthy families, especially in New Mexico, might own some rustic furniture—perhaps a table, several chairs or benches, a few trunks, and a freestanding wooden cupboard for the kitchen. (*See also* **Architecture; Furniture and Furnishings.**)

Howe, Sir William

1729–1814
British general

Sir William Howe was commander of British troops fighting the Americans in the early part of the Revolutionary War. During the same period, Howe's brother Richard served as commander of the British fleet in America.

William Howe joined the British army in 1746. During the FRENCH AND INDIAN WAR of 1754 to 1763, he fought in the Battle of Quebec, commanded troops at Montreal, and also took part in battles in Europe. He became a major general in 1772 and was knighted four years later.

In June 1775, Howe led his troops against the Americans in the Battle of BUNKER HILL. In October he replaced General Thomas Gage as the commander of the British army in America. When colonial troops attacked Howe's army in Boston, the British commander retreated to New York and occupied the city. He led his forces against American troops in several battles during 1776 and 1777, defeating them at Long Island, White Plains, and Brandywine. Yet despite these victories, Howe failed to destroy the American army.

Resigning as commander in 1778, Howe was replaced by Sir Henry Clinton. He returned to England, where he later became a full general. (*See also* **American Revolution.**)

Hudson, Henry

died ca. 1611
English explorer

See second map in Exploration, Age of (vol. 2).

Henry Hudson, an English navigator, explored the waters around North America for the Dutch and the English. His voyages into the HUDSON RIVER established claims that led to Dutch settlements in present-day New York. His exploration of Hudson Bay in Canada enabled the English to set up trading ventures there.

Nothing is known of Hudson's early life. In 1607 an English trading company sent him to find a route to Asia across the North Pole. Hudson failed to locate such a route, but his reports of the many whales in the waters off Greenland brought great numbers of English ships to the area. In 1609 the DUTCH EAST INDIA COMPANY hired Hudson to sail around Europe to the north coast of Russia. The expedition encountered such cold weather that the crew rebelled. Hudson decided to turn his ship—the *Half Moon*—around, crossed the Atlantic Ocean, and explored the coast of North America. He sailed up the Hudson River to the present site of ALBANY, giving his Dutch sponsors a claim to that area.

In 1610 Hudson returned to North America, this time for English merchants. They wanted him to find a NORTHWEST PASSAGE, a sea route through the continent to Asia. The explorer entered a huge waterway on the northeastern coast of Canada, hoping it was the passage. The waterway turned out to be an immense bay, and Hudson and his crew spent a miserable winter on the frozen shore, eating frogs and moss to stay alive. In the spring, he proposed to continue exploring the western part of the great bay, but his men had had enough. They organized a mutiny and set Hudson adrift in a small boat with seven loyal crew members and his son. The mutineers returned to England in Hudson's ship, avoiding punishment by turning over the maps and charts he had made of the bay that still bears his name. No trace of Hudson was ever found. (*See also* **Exploration, Age of.**)

Hudson River

The Hudson River, a major waterway in present-day New York State, flows about 315 miles from its source in the Adirondack Mountains to the Atlantic Ocean. Named after the explorer Henry HUDSON, the broad, deep river provided a key route for travel and trade during the colonial period.

Henry Hudson did not actually discover the great river that bears his name. That honor belongs to Giovanni da Verrazano, an Italian explorer

In 1609 Henry Hudson sailed up the river that bears his name. It led into the fertile valleys of present-day New York, which Hudson claimed for the Dutch.

working for France. While exploring the Atlantic coast in 1524, Verrazano entered the mouth of the river and sailed a short way inland. During the 1500s, French fur traders from Canada frequently crossed the upper reaches of the river.

In 1609 Henry Hudson became the first European to explore the river. Sailing for the Dutch East India Company, Hudson found what he thought might be a water route through North America—the Northwest Passage. He ventured upriver as far as present-day Albany and claimed the land for the Dutch. The Dutch founded the colony of New Netherland in 1624, establishing settlements on both sides of the river. They used the Hudson River as a highway connecting these communities with the city of New Amsterdam and the Atlantic coast.

See map in New Netherland (vol. 3).

After the English took control of New Netherland in 1664, colonization along the river increased rapidly. The rich soil and mild climate of the Hudson River valley made the region ideal for farming. The river's deep channel allowed large merchant ships to travel inland for trade.

During the 1700s, the Hudson River was the site of much bloodshed. Indians frequently raided white settlements along the river, and New England colonists searching for better land often came into conflict with Hudson Valley landowners. During the American Revolution, both the British and the American colonists fought for control of the river because of its strategic* importance as a line of separation between New England and the other colonies. (*See also* **Exploration, Age of; Transportation and Travel.**)

* ***strategic*** key part of a plan; of military importance

Hudson's Bay Company

The Hudson's Bay Company, an English fur-trading company, played an important role in the history of Canada. At the height of its power in the early 1800s, the company had economic and administrative control over a vast area that stretched from the Atlantic Ocean to the Pacific.

Founded in 1670, the Hudson's Bay Company received a charter* from King Charles II of England that granted exclusive trading rights and the authority to govern in the lands surrounding Hudson Bay. The area became known as Rupert's Land after the king's cousin, Prince Rupert, a founding member of the company.

* ***charter*** written grant from a ruler conferring certain rights and privileges

The Hudson's Bay Company built forts and trading posts in Rupert's Land and developed an active fur trade with the Cree Indians. It forged close relations with the Indians, depending on them for food and other supplies, and company fur trappers often married Indian women. Unlike other trading companies of the time, however, the Hudson's Bay Company made little effort to colonize. No settlers moved to the area until the early 1800s.

See first map in European Empires (vol. 1).

The French challenged British claims to Rupert's Land, a region just north of New France. French traders competed for furs with the Hudson's Bay Company, and several times French forces captured company forts. With the Treaty of Utrecht in 1713, France abandoned all claim to the Hudson Bay region. But the company faced a new challenge to its trade in

1783, when a group of independent fur traders formed the North West Company. The rivalry that developed between the two companies spurred Hudson's Bay to establish new trading posts farther inland and to the west. It also led to the founding of the Red River colony (in present-day Manitoba) in 1812.

In 1821 the two rivals merged into one company, keeping Hudson's Bay as its name. The company now had a trade monopoly* and complete rule over an enormous territory that reached to the Pacific Ocean. By the mid-1800s, though, the company had lost its exclusive trading privileges because of strong opposition from rivals. Then in 1869 control of the territory was transferred to the government of Canada.

* ***monopoly*** exclusive right to engage in a certain kind of business

Despite the loss of its trade monopoly and territory, the Hudson's Bay Company continued to be successful. It became a large corporation with many different business interests. Still in existence today, it is one of the oldest companies in the world.

Huguenots

See color plate 2, vol. 4.

Huguenots were French Protestants. During the 1500s and 1600s, religious struggles in France between the majority Catholics and minority Protestants drove thousands of Huguenots out of their homeland. Many fled to North America and settled there.

Huguenots tried to found colonies in SOUTH CAROLINA and FLORIDA in the 1560s. Both attempts failed, partly because of conflicts among the French settlers and partly because of attacks by the Spanish, who did not want the French to establish a foothold in territory claimed by Spain.

In the early 1600s, many Huguenots immigrated to the Dutch colony of NEW NETHERLAND, forming communities at Fort Orange (Albany), Kingston, and New Paltz. The population of NEW AMSTERDAM included numerous Huguenots as well. Among them were the parents of Jean Vigne, the first child born to European colonists on the island of Manhattan, now part of New York City.

Throughout the 1600s, groups of Huguenots settled in Connecticut, Delaware, New York, Rhode Island, Pennsylvania, and Virginia. One named Nicholas Martiau, a resident of Virginia in 1620, was an ancestor of George Washington. Most of these French Protestants lived among English colonists and intermarried with them. Between 1670 and 1764, they established several French communities in South Carolina and played a key role in the settlement of CHARLESTON. The Huguenots who lived in South Carolina preserved more of their French customs, religious beliefs, and identity than those settling in other colonies.

Some Huguenots went to NEW FRANCE as fur traders and fishermen, but they made no attempt to establish communities there. French rulers wanted to restrict the colony to Roman Catholics. In the early years, officials simply discouraged the settlement of Huguenots, but after 1625 they barred them altogether. A few French Protestants immigrated to Canada after the British took control in the 1760s. (*See also* **Immigration; Protestant Churches.**)

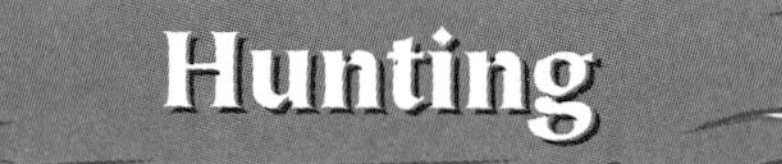

Hunting

All over North America, Indians hunted to obtain food. Even groups that relied primarily on agriculture sought game to supplement their diets. European colonists, especially those living in frontier areas, also pursued ANIMALS for food. For many colonists, however, hunting was a sport rather than a necessity.

Native Americans. Native Americans sought and killed many kinds of animals. The species* hunted depended largely on the location. In the far north, Indians in the interior went after moose and caribou*, while those along the seacoasts pursued seals, walruses, and whales. In the eastern forests, the most important game included deer, bear, and small animals such as squirrels, rabbits, and raccoons. On the Great Plains, some tribes followed the BUFFALO, a task made much easier after the introduction of HORSES by the Spanish in the 1500s and 1600s.

* ***species*** group of plants or animals with similar characteristics
* ***caribou*** large deer, similar to reindeer

In almost all Indian societies, the men hunted while the women tended crops and gathered nuts, berries, and other plant foods. This division of labor was not always clear-cut, however. In some societies, men helped with gathering and farming, and women participated in hunting activities, most generally in hunts involving small game such as rabbits and squirrels.

Native American hunting generally involved a religious relationship between people and animals. In preparing for the hunt, Indians performed certain rituals* to make a spiritual connection to the animals they chased. They believed that such ceremonies, which often included dancing and drama, were essential for the success of the hunt. Usually a shaman*, credited with influence over animals, supervised the rituals and directed the hunt.

* ***ritual*** ceremony that follows a set pattern
* ***shaman*** person with spiritual and healing powers

To be successful, hunters also needed to know about animal behavior, hunting territories, and environmental conditions. Indians observed and learned about the patterns of different kinds of animals. They became familiar

Among the Native Americans of the eastern coast, deer were an important source of meat and hides. This engraving, based on a painting by Jacques Le Moyne, was printed in 1591.

with their hunting territories and knew where game was most likely to be found. They also studied the effect that the season, time of day, and weather conditions had on animal populations. Native Americans began learning these things at an early age, and training was based on generations of observation and experience.

Success in hunting also involved skill in the use of bows and arrows, lances, and other weapons. Weapons were prized possessions, and Indians took care to maintain their sharpness and accuracy. The introduction of European weapons had a tremendous impact on hunting. The Indians found that guns were superior to bows and arrows for pursuing deer and other large game and that steel knives and axes were stronger and more easily sharpened than similar Indian tools. The new weapons made it possible to kill more game with less effort and time. This greater efficiency, along with use of European steel traps, led many Indians to focus on hunting animals for their furs—which could be traded to Europeans—rather than for food.

European Settlers. For the early European colonists, hunting played an important role in survival. They quickly adopted Indian techniques, and game animals helped supplement farming as a source of food. But as the colonies grew, hunting for food became less important, except in frontier areas. One reason was that animal populations declined because of the FUR TRADE and the impact of colonization on the environment.

Many colonists now hunted for recreation. They took to the woods and fields for raccoon, rabbit, and squirrel hunts and turkey shoots. Hunting for sport became especially popular in the South. Many wealthy southern colonists attempted to imitate the lifestyle of the upper classes in England by engaging in fox hunts. Organized hunting parties, whether they involved a group of people tramping through the woods or more formal events with lavish equipment and ceremonies, became an important social event in colonial America. (*See also* **Economic Systems; Environmental Impact of European Colonization.**)

Huron Indians

The Huron were a confederacy* of Indian tribes who spoke an Iroquoian language. At the time of their first contact with Europeans, these Indians lived in what is now the Canadian province of Ontario. They became an important ally of the French and a primary source of pelts* during the early days of the FUR TRADE.

The French called these people the Huron, from the French word for "boar's head," because of the bristly haircut of the Huron men. But the Indians referred to themselves as *Wendat,* meaning "Dwellers of the Peninsula"—their land was surrounded by water on three sides.

The Huron were farmers who grew corn, beans, squash, and tobacco and supplemented their crops with hunting and fishing. Women cultivated the food crops, while men tended the tobacco. The Indians built their villages close to each other and surrounded them with enormous cornfields, covering perhaps as many as 7,000 acres. Living at the crossroads of the region's trading

* ***confederacy*** alliance or league of peoples or states
* ***pelt*** skin and fur of an animal

networks, the Huron routinely bartered with their Algonquian-speaking neighbors, exchanging their surplus crops for meat and furs. The Huron language was the trade language in the north.

Government in Huron society operated on three levels: village, tribal, and confederacy. Decisions were made by consensus—agreement among the group members. Socially, the people were organized into eight clans*, with members of each clan descended from a common female ancestor.

* *clan* related families

The French explorer Samuel de CHAMPLAIN first encountered the Huron in the early 1600s. He quickly established alliances with them, thereby gaining access to their extensive trading network. French traders sent interpreters to live with the Huron to learn their language and customs. French missionaries arrived soon after the traders and began trying to convert the Native Americans to Christianity. Contact with Europeans brought severe epidemics to the Huron in the late 1630s, killing well over half of their population.

Warfare with the IROQUOIS CONFEDERACY, or Five Nations, further reduced the Huron population. The two groups had long been enemies, and the Huron's monopoly* on the French fur trade increased the hostility between them. The Huron, divided by rivalry between Christian converts and those who still followed the traditional religious beliefs, were no match for the Iroquois. The Iroquois forced the Huron out of the area in 1649. Many refugees of the once-powerful Huron confederacy fled to join the Iroquois people to the south. Some already had relatives among the Five Nations, as the Iroquois had often adopted Huron prisoners of war to replace tribe members lost in wars and epidemics. Other Huron retreated to what is now northern Ohio. This group became known as the Wyandot—a variation of Wendat.

* *monopoly* exclusive right to engage in a certain kind of business

See second map in Native Americans (vol. 3).

The Wyandot quickly came to dominate politics among the Indians in present-day Ohio and southwestern Ontario. Neighboring tribes did not dispute their claim to a large part of the region. During the FRENCH AND INDIAN WAR, the Wyandot supported their old ally, the French. They backed the Ottawa chief PONTIAC in the 1763 uprising against the British in the Ohio Valley, but they sided with the British during the American Revolution. In the late 1700s, the United States government forced the Wyandot to give up much of their territory. The United States later moved the tribe to Indian Territory in present-day Oklahoma.

Hutchinson, Anne

1591–1643
Religious activist

Anne Hutchinson challenged the authority of PURITAN leaders of the Massachusetts Bay colony in the 1630s by expressing her own views about religion. Because her ideas differed from established Puritan doctrine*, authorities regarded her as a threat and cast her out of the church and the colony.

* *doctrine* set of principles or beliefs accepted by a religious or political group

Hutchinson grew up in England in a family of dissenters—people who disagreed with the beliefs and practices of the country's official religion, the Church of England. At the age of 21, she married a merchant named William Hutchinson. She became a devoted follower of John COTTON, a Puritan preacher. Cotton emigrated to the Massachusetts Bay colony in 1633, and the Hutchinson family left for North America the following year, settling in Boston.

This painting by Howard Pyle shows Anne Hutchinson preaching in her Boston home. Her weekly prayer meetings began as discussions of the sermons of John Cotton. When she started questioning Puritan beliefs, she was tried and banished.

Kind, intelligent, and experienced as a nurse, Anne Hutchinson was a welcome addition to Massachusetts. Deeply concerned with religious matters, she held weekly meetings in her home to discuss Cotton's sermons. At first she limited herself to interpreting the preacher's message, but she gradually began expressing some of her own opinions about religion.

Cotton preached the doctrine of free grace, which meant that an individual's salvation depended only on faith and God's grace, not on conduct or good works. Hutchinson believed that the "elect"—those chosen for salvation—received God's grace in their souls, so they could communicate directly with God without the need for ministers. Hutchinson criticized the Puritan clergy*, except Cotton, for preaching that good conduct and obedience to the laws of church and state also helped a person achieve salvation.

Hutchinson's views eventually brought her into conflict with church leaders, judges, and the colony's governor, John Winthrop. They argued that strict moral laws were necessary to a well-ordered society, and they would not allow the church's authority to be questioned. At first Hutchinson had several allies, including Cotton. However, in 1637, Puritan officials declared her beliefs to be false and dangerous, and Cotton came to agree with their judgment. Hutchinson was also accused of being an Antinomian—someone who believed that the elect did not need to follow the rules of church leaders. The religious uproar caused by the Hutchinson case became known as the Antinomian Controversy.

In late 1637, colonial authorities brought the dissenter to trial for criticizing the Puritan clergy. Finding Hutchinson guilty, they banished her from Massachusetts but delayed carrying out the sentence until the end of the winter. Hutchinson was also questioned by church leaders, who decided to excommunicate* her for refusing to take back earlier statements about her religious beliefs. In the spring of 1638, Hutchinson left the colony with her family and supporters—about 80 families. They settled in Rhode Island, joining Roger Williams, another dissenter who had been banished from Massachusetts. After the death of her husband in 1642, Anne Hutchinson moved to New York. The next year she and several of her children lost their lives in an Indian attack. (*See also* **Protestant Churches; Religious Life in European Colonies.**)

* ***clergy*** ministers, priests, and other church officials
* ***excommunicate*** to expel from the church

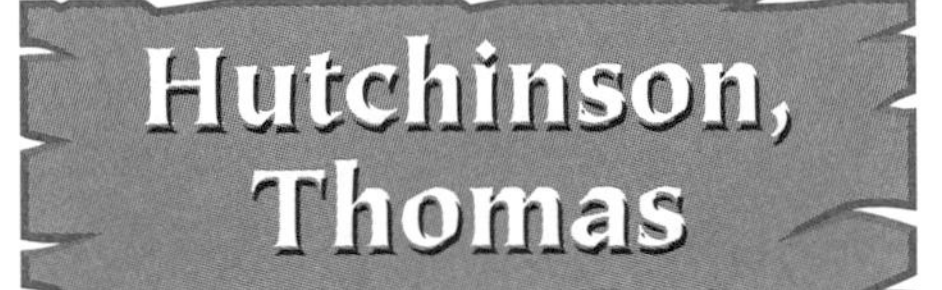

Hutchinson, Thomas

1711–1800
Colonial governor of Massachusetts

Thomas Hutchinson served as governor of Massachusetts during a time of increasing tensions between the colonies and Britain. A man of great ability, he was torn between his love for the colonies and his commitment to the British crown.

Born in Boston, the son of a prosperous merchant, Hutchinson began his political career in 1737 with election to the colonial assembly. During his years in the assembly, he made many political enemies, including Samuel Adams, because his efforts to put the colony on a sound financial basis caused some colonists heavy losses.

Hutchinson served as a delegate to the Albany Congress in 1754 and supported Benjamin Franklin's proposal for a union of the colonies under one government. As chief justice of the Massachusetts Supreme Court, a position he accepted in 1760, Hutchinson opposed a plan to allow searches without court approval.

In the 1760s, Hutchinson opposed the SUGAR ACT and STAMP ACT on the grounds that they would harm British and colonial trade. He did, however, support the idea that the British Parliament had the right to tax the colonies—a view that made him very unpopular among some colonists. During protests against the Stamp Act, local citizens looted and burned his home in Boston. Hutchinson barely escaped with his life.

Hutchinson's unpopularity increased when he became acting governor of Massachusetts in 1769 and governor two years later. In that office, he favored stern measures to deal with the growing discontent, and he became convinced that the colonies must be forced to recognize the authority of Parliament. Although against the TOWNSHEND ACTS, Hutchinson enforced them strictly after they were passed by Parliament.

Hutchinson's support for the TEA ACT OF 1773 and his refusal to allow ships loaded with tea to return to Britain led to the BOSTON TEA PARTY. In 1774 the widely despised governor left Massachusetts for England. He expected to return to America after matters quieted down, but he spent his remaining years in unhappy exile in England. (*See also* **Boston; Governors, Colonial.**)

Iberville, Pierre Le Moyne, Sieur d'

1661–1706

Founder of Louisiana

Pierre Le Moyne, Sieur d'Iberville, was fiercely loyal to France and devoted much of his life to attacking English settlers, the enemies of the French in North America. He also established the first permanent French settlements in LOUISIANA.

Born in Montreal, Iberville joined the French navy when he was 14. In 1686 he took part in a French raid on the English trading posts around Hudson Bay. He acquired a reputation for bravery and added to it in the 1690s with fierce attacks on English outposts* in New York, Newfoundland, and Hudson Bay. Despite Iberville's stunning victories, in each case the English rebuilt their settlements or trading posts and went on with their activities.

*** outpost** frontier settlement or military base

In 1697, after triumphing over three English ships in Hudson Bay, Iberville went to France. King Louis XIV gave him the task of building a colony at the mouth of the Mississippi River. The king believed that establishing French settlements there would keep other nations from claiming and colonizing the region. The French wanted to gain firm control of the interior of North America and confine the English to the Atlantic coast. They could do that, they thought, by linking colonies from the Gulf of Mexico north along the Mississippi to New France. Iberville's settlement would be a vital part of this effort. Reaching the Mississippi delta in 1699, he built a fort where the city of Biloxi, Mississippi, now stands. On his second voyage, he traveled far up the Mississippi, and on his third, he built a fort at Mobile Bay in what is now Alabama.

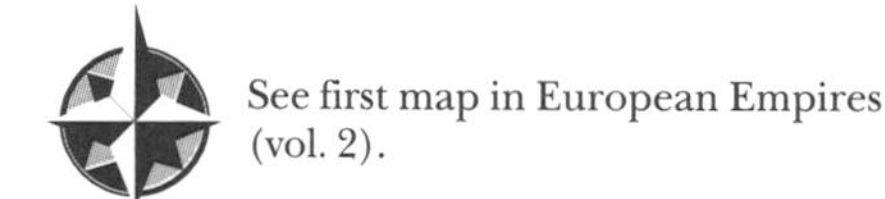
See first map in European Empires (vol. 2).

Iberville died in Cuba. He had damaged his reputation somewhat by conducting illegal trading deals in the West Indies in an attempt to build up his personal fortune. Nevertheless, he was still considered a hero for fighting the English and for the settlements he founded in Louisiana. (*See also* **New France.**)

Illinois Indians

See second map in Native Americans (vol. 3).

A group of Algonquian-speaking tribes, the Illinois Indians lived mainly along the Mississippi River in present-day Wisconsin, Illinois, Iowa, and Missouri. Longtime allies of the French, they supported the American colonists against the British during the American Revolution.

The Illinois farmed, hunted, and gathered wild foods. In spring they lived in large villages along major rivers, planting corn, beans, and other crops. In summer and early fall, they hunted buffalo and other game animals and began harvesting crops and gathering other foods. After the harvest, the Illinois moved to winter hunting camps, living in small scattered groups.

The first contact the Illinois Indians had with Europeans came in the 1670s, when French explorers and fur trappers entered their territory. French missionaries arrived soon after and established fortified mission posts among the various tribes. The Illinois became allies of the French and later helped them raid English frontier settlements.

The Illinois had a series of Indian enemies. Relations with the MIAMI INDIANS were strained throughout the 1600s. After about 1650, the Illinois were attacked by the IROQUOIS, who came to Illinois territory in search of furs to trade with the English. Then, in the early 1700s, they suffered raids by the CHICKASAW, allies of the English who lived in what is now Tennessee. Faced with threats from such enemies, the Illinois relocated their villages several times. Many eventually fled west of the Mississippi River, where they entered the territories of other tribes, including the Sioux. These tribes quickly declared war on the trespassers. By the mid-1700s, the Illinois had lost almost 90 percent of their population as a result of continual warfare and European diseases such as smallpox.

During the Revolutionary War, the Illinois provided American troops with scouts. Indian tribes allied with the British launched devastating raids on Illinois villages, killing many men and taking women and children prisoner. When the war ended, the Illinois ceded* much of their land to the new United States government. Many of the surviving Indians moved west to Kansas. A few groups, however, remained in their traditional homelands.

* ***cede*** to yield or surrender

Immigration

The North American colonies were settled mostly by immigrants, people who wanted to start their lives over in a new and largely unknown land. The immigrants arrived from many parts of Europe as well as other parts of the world, creating an extraordinary mixture of national, religious, and cultural traditions. They all contributed to the development of North America. But Britain's dominant role in colonization is reflected in the language, laws, and social structure of both the United States and Canada today.

The story of immigration to North America began in other countries. The people who emigrated from Britain, the Netherlands, France, and Spain had many reasons for leaving their homelands. Some fled because of war or famine. Others were drawn to America by the dream of greater personal and religious freedom or by the lure of jobs, affordable land, or wealth. Many emigrants were both pushed and pulled. They wanted to leave behind the worst

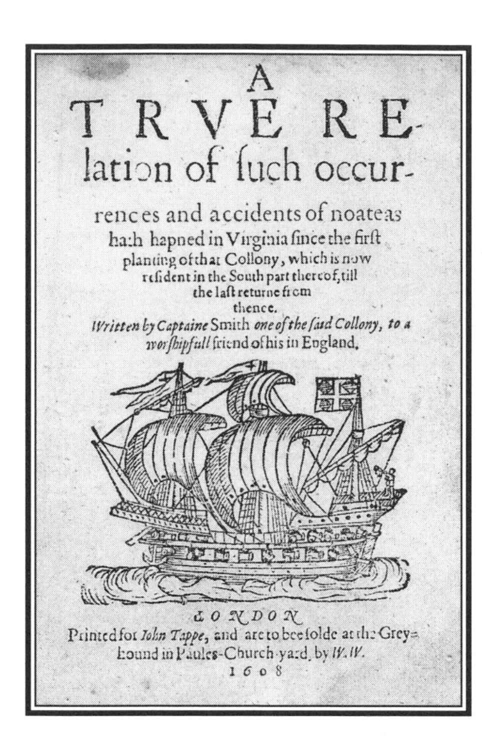

A
TRVE RE-
lation of ſuch occur-
rences and accidents of noate as
hath hapned in Virginia ſince the first
planting of that Collony, which is now
reſident in the South part thereof, till
the laſt returne from
thence.
Written by Captaine Smith *one of the ſaid Collony, to a worſhipfull* friend of his in England.

LONDON
Printed for *John Tappe*, and are to bee ſolde at the Grey-
hound in Paules-Church-yard, by *W.W.*
1608

In 1608 Captain John Smith published his *True Relation,* describing the Jamestown colony's first year of existence. Throughout the 1600s and 1700s, hundreds of thousands of immigrants followed in the footsteps of the Jamestown colonists, sailing across the Atlantic Ocean and settling in the British colonies.

part of their old lives, and they believed that life would be better on the other side of the Atlantic Ocean.

British Colonies

England's population increased from around 3 million in 1550 to more than 5 million in the 1650s. This rapid growth, combined with a series of bad harvests, caused great hardship, particularly for the poor. Land was expensive, jobs were scarce, food prices soared, and living standards began to fall. Servants, laborers, and crafts workers found it increasingly difficult to survive. Many decided to emigrate.

The journey to America was filled with hardships. The ocean voyage in cramped and crowded ships lasted six weeks or more. The food was usually scanty and of poor quality. Many passengers suffered from constant seasickness. Worst of all were epidemics of disease, which could sweep through a ship with deadly results. Some immigrant ships in the 1700s lost more than half their passengers to disease on their way across the Atlantic.

Immigration in the 1600s. During the 1600s, nearly 400,000 people left England, Scotland, Wales, and Ireland to settle in North America and the West Indies. More than two-thirds of these immigrants were English. Most of the others were Irish Catholics or Welsh settlers. Only a few thousand Scots moved to the Americas before 1707, when Scotland joined England to form Great Britain.

Many of these immigrants settled in the English colonies that produced tobacco and sugar. More than half of them went to Barbados and other islands. Almost a third emigrated to the southern colonies, especially Virginia and Maryland. The rest settled in the New England and the middle colonies.

Immigrants to New England in the 1630s generally arrived with their families. Although some were servants, the majority were skilled workers or tradespeople who paid their own passage to America. In contrast, more than two-thirds of all immigrants to the West Indies and the Chesapeake area

British Immigrants to North America in the 1600s

Destination	Number of Immigrants	Percentage of Total
New England and Middle Colonies	40,000	10%
Southern Colonies	125,000	32%
West Indies	225,000	58%

were servants or laborers. They arrived as INDENTURED SERVANTS, required to work for a certain number of years to repay the cost of their passage across the Atlantic. Many of them were young, single males. The peak years for immigration to the West Indies were 1630 through 1660. In the Chesapeake region, the growth of the tobacco industry and other plantation industries created a demand for labor that attracted immigrants throughout the 1600s and into the 1700s.

French HUGUENOTS, or Protestants, also emigrated to the English colonies. Persecuted in their Catholic homeland, they settled throughout British North America, particularly in the southern colonies. They played a role in establishing Charleston, South Carolina, in the late 1600s.

Immigration in the 1700s. Immigration to the British colonies during the 1700s differed from that of the 1600s in several important ways. Northern Ireland replaced England as the leading source of immigrants. The flow of immigrants to the West Indies declined dramatically because black slaves from Africa now filled the demand for labor there. Only one out of five British immigrants settled in the West Indies. The rest went to the North American mainland, especially to New York, Pennsylvania, Virginia, Maryland, and the Carolinas.

The Scotch-Irish lived in northern Ireland, or Ulster. In the 1600s, the English government had encouraged their ancestors to move from Scotland to Ulster to establish a Protestant population in Catholic Ireland. After several generations, however, life had grown difficult for the Scotch-Irish. Troubled by crop failures, demands from their English landlords for higher rents, and religious conflict with their Catholic neighbors, many of them headed for America.

Scotch-Irish immigrants generally landed at the busy port of Philadelphia but did not settle along the coast. Instead, they moved to the colonies' western frontiers, spreading out into the backcountry to clear small farms and build cabins. Many of the pioneers who settled the western regions of Pennsylvania, Virginia, and North Carolina came from Ulster in several waves of immigration between 1717 and 1775.

British Immigrants to North America in the 1700s

Country of Origin	Number of Immigrants
England and Wales	80,000–100,000
Northern Ireland	250,000
Scotland	50,000

After the Scotch-Irish, the next largest group of immigrants in the 1700s consisted of German-speaking people. Most of these settlers came from what is now southwestern Germany, a region repeatedly ravaged by war. Between the 1680s and the 1780s half a million people fled the area.

About 100,000 German-speaking immigrants came to British North America, usually arriving in Philadelphia. More than three-quarters of them traveled with their families. Some settled near Philadelphia, especially in the community of Germantown, founded in 1683. Some German-speaking colonists in eastern Pennsylvania belonged to minority religious groups such as the Moravians and the Mennonites. Other colonists called them "Pennsylvania Dutch"—from *Deutsch,* meaning German. German-speaking immigrants also moved into the backcountry of western Pennsylvania, Maryland, Virginia, and the Carolinas and, along with the Scotch-Irish, pushed the frontier westward.

Conflict and Acceptance. Although the population of the American colonies in the 1770s was overwhelmingly of British origin, it also included small groups of colonists who traced their ancestry to France, Finland, Sweden, Denmark, Italy, Spain, and Portugal. Most of these people lived in the middle colonies of New York, New Jersey, and Pennsylvania. In addition there were a handful of immigrants from Asia and Africa. Enslaved Africans are not considered immigrants because they did not come to North America voluntarily, but their presence greatly affected American society.

The mixture of people from so many different backgrounds created some conflict in the colonies. The great majority of the British immigrants were Protestants who distrusted and feared Roman Catholics—even those from Britain. Although Maryland and Pennsylvania were most tolerant*, Catholics throughout British North America encountered persecution. So did the JEWS, who established communities in New York City; Charleston, South Carolina; and Newport, Rhode Island.

* ***tolerant*** allowing different views and behavior

Religion was not the only cause of conflict. Some colonists disliked immigrants whose backgrounds or languages differed from their own. For example, the English and the Scots, traditional enemies in Europe, often remained hostile to each other in the colonies. In Pennsylvania some colonists feared that the growth of the German population would undermine the colony's "Englishness." Philadelphia's most distinguished citizen, Benjamin Franklin, wrote with concern: "Why should Pennsylvania, founded by the English, become a Colony of Aliens, who will shortly be so numerous as to Germanize us instead of our Anglifying them?"

In spite of these conflicts and concerns, later waves of immigrants were generally welcomed—or at least tolerated—in the British colonies. Unlike the overpopulated nations of Europe, the new land was spacious, with room for all kinds of people, customs, and beliefs. Although the majority of these later immigrants were British, the colonies continued to attract people from many nations—and would do so long after winning their independence.

Dutch Colony

The Dutch devoted far less effort and attention than the British, the French, and the Spanish to colonizing North America. During the 1600s, the inhabitants

The First Jewish Immigrants

The history of Jews in North America began in 1654, when 23 Jews arrived in the Dutch colony of New Netherland, fleeing a Portuguese takeover of the Brazilian settlement where they had been living. The director of the Dutch colony wanted to throw them out. He was overruled by investors—some of them Jewish—of the Dutch West India Company, which ran the colony. The Jews received full citizenship rights in New Netherland. Asser Levy, who became a well-known trader, remained in the colony after it passed into English hands and was renamed New York. At the time, he was one of only two Jews living in New Amsterdam (New York City).

of the Netherlands had little reason to emigrate. They enjoyed greater personal freedom and a higher standard of living than almost any other people in Europe. Those who wanted to leave could choose from many places around the world because the Dutch had established colonies in Asia, South America, and the West Indies. Finally, Dutch merchants and mariners focused their energies on trade rather than on colonization, and Asia and the West Indies offered greater business opportunities than the North American mainland. For these reasons, the Dutch showed little interest in emigrating to NEW NETHERLAND, their North American colony.

Settlement of the colony began in the 1630s. Most of the immigrants were farmers or servants, although New Netherland's sponsors managed to attract some skilled crafts workers by offering high salaries. Only about one-third of the colonists arrived with their families. The majority were single men in their late teens and early twenties, and this shortage of women and families limited the colony's growth.

By the mid-1600s, the large trading firms of the Netherlands had realized that a Dutch colony on the Hudson River could be very valuable. Such a colony would be an important stop along trade routes and a place from which Dutch merchants could sell goods and slaves to people in the other colonies. To help New Netherland grow, the DUTCH WEST INDIA COMPANY made an effort to supply the colony with stable, responsible settlers. By the late 1650s, most of the immigrants were married couples and families. However, in 1664, just when the colony seemed to be entering a period of stability and growth, the English captured New Netherland and renamed it New York.

From its earliest days, New Netherland had attracted people from many different backgrounds, and that trend continued after the colony came under English rule. By the 1670s, the Dutch made up less than half of New York's population. The colony also included a large number of Germans as well as English, French, Italian, Danish, and Norwegian immigrants.

French Colonies

The French government never managed to send as many settlers to its North American colonies as it wanted to do. The French people were reluctant to emigrate. For one thing, their country did not suffer from overpopulation. For another, reports from America were not encouraging. Settlers who had moved to NEW FRANCE, the colony along the St. Lawrence River in what is now Canada, wrote home complaining of harsh weather, bad wine, Indian attacks, and other hardships and dangers.

The French first tried to populate North America by sending convicts, beggars, and homeless vagabonds to the colonies. These people were forced settlers, not true immigrants, and they lacked the skills and the will to build a stable society.

The French government later attempted to promote settlement by handing over the responsibility for recruiting colonists to trading companies and religious orders, organizations with an interest in New France. These groups brought traders, farmers, artisans*, and workers to North America to support their activities. They offered transportation, high wages, and a cash bonus to those who agreed to work in New France for three years. Anyone who decided

* ***artisan*** skilled crafts worker

to stay on after completing the term of service would receive free land. However, unlike the English workers—who planned to remain in the colonies—most of the French who went to Canada returned to Europe when their term of service ended.

In the 1660s, the French king sent a large number of hired men to Canada. Later, to relieve a severe shortage of women, the French government arranged for transportation to the colony of almost 800 unmarried women, mostly orphans. Known as the *filles du roi* (the king's girls), these women were married in large numbers soon after arriving in the colony. Soldiers made up another important group of immigrants in the 1600s. Many of the troops on temporary duty claimed land and became permanent settlers.

Despite the best efforts of the government and recruiters, the response of the French people remained unenthusiastic. Only about 27,000 men and women traveled to Canada in the 1600s and 1700s, and fewer than 9,000 of them remained there. A few hundred others settled in Acadia, a province on the Atlantic. The British took over the province in 1713, and they eventually drove out the ACADIANS, the descendants of the French settlers.

In the early 1700s, France launched another colonial venture in North America with LOUISIANA, which the government hoped would become a wealthy center of plantation farming. About 7,000 French settlers sailed to the new colony between 1717 and 1721. About one out of five of them was a criminal, beggar, or prostitute who had been forced by the government to emigrate. Thousands of African slaves were also brought to Louisiana to work the plantations. Fevers and tropical diseases took a heavy toll on both Africans and Europeans. Small numbers of new immigrants continued to move into the area.

Spanish Colonies

The Spanish government strictly regulated immigration to the Spanish Borderlands, which included present-day Florida, Texas, Arizona, New Mexico,

The Spanish were slow to settle the desert areas of their northern frontier lands. They founded New Mexico in the late 1500s and established Santa Fe as its capital about 1609. The town is shown here in the mid-1800s, shortly before it became part of the United States.

and California. Colonists came largely from NEW SPAIN. Among the first settlers in the area were Catholic priests, who established MISSIONS to convert the local Indians to Christianity, and Spanish troops, who built and maintained presidios*.

* ***presidio*** Spanish fort built to protect mission settlements

Although most immigrants to the Borderlands were of Spanish ancestry, people of other backgrounds also settled in the area. The population of Florida included escaped slaves from the British colonies, Indians forced out of the Carolinas by colonists, and small communities of Italians and Greeks. In addition a number of French immigrants lived in Texas.

By 1800 some 28,000 settlers and soldiers of Spanish heritage lived in the five provinces of the Borderlands. Few of them had been born in Spain. Most were of mixed European, Indian, and African ancestry, though they described themselves as Spanish. In most cases, only high-ranking government officials were *peninsulares,* colonists born in Spain, and a large number of these were not true immigrants because they planned to return home after their colonial service.

The Borderlands remained thinly populated. Many of the inhabitants were soldiers on assignment or convicts from New Spain sent there by the government. However, in the late 1700s and early 1800s, English-speaking people from the United States began moving into Florida, Texas, and California. Their presence helped the United States gain control of these provinces in the mid-1800s. (*See also* **Population Growth in North America.**)

Indentured Servants

Indentured servants were people bound by an indenture, or contract, to work for a fixed number of years. During the colonial period, perhaps as many as two-thirds of the white immigrants to British North America were indentured servants. These bound workers helped populate the colonies and supplied much needed labor on PLANTATIONS and farms, in homes, and in workshops. Although they were most plentiful in the British colonies, the other European colonies had similar arrangements for obtaining labor.

Types of Indentured Servants. There were two main types of indentured servants: those who agreed to work of their own free will and those forced into indentured service because of poverty or other circumstances.

Many British people who wished to emigrate to North America could not afford to pay the price of passage on a ship, nor did they have enough money to establish themselves once they arrived. To make the move to the other side of the Atlantic Ocean, some people became indentured servants. These individuals generally signed contracts called indentures with merchants or ship captains, who paid the cost of passage in exchange for an agreement to work for a period of time. When the indentured servants reached the colonies, their contracts were sold to colonists, and they began their service.

Some servants came to America without contracts. Their services would be sold on arrival by those who had paid the passage. Instead of working for a fixed number of years, they would have to work for as many years as it took to raise the cost of their passage at the wages that were "the custom of the country." For this reason, servants without indentures were known as customary servants.

Another group of people who arrived without contracts were redemptioners. These individuals would be allowed a certain length of time to raise the money advanced for their transportation. Only if they failed to repay these costs would they become indentured servants. Entire families traveled to America in this way. Sometimes one of the children, usually the oldest son, might be indentured to pay for the whole family's transportation.

A number of the people who came to the colonies were forced into servitude. Some reluctantly became indentured because they were poor and had to pay off debts. Some were criminals and other undesirables who were deported to the colonies and compelled to work off their sentences as indentured servants. Others were tricked. Professional kidnappers called "spirits" roamed the docks of London, luring adults and children onto ships with promises of alcohol and sweets. Once aboard, the captives would be forced to travel to America, where their captors would sell their services. Many unfortunate individuals found themselves working in the colonies as indentured servants after being "recruited" in this way.

Remember: *Consult the index at the end of Volume 4 to find more information on many topics.*

Terms of Contract and Treatment. Most indentured servants worked an average of 3 to 5 years under the terms of their contracts. Customary servants and people forced into servitude to pay debts sometimes had to work for a longer period. The length of service depended largely on the amount owed. Convicts working off sentences might serve from 7 to 14 years, according to the nature of their crimes. After completing their period of labor, indentured servants received "freedom dues"—which usually included clothing, a gun, and a piece of land to start a new life.

An indenture was a contract enforceable by law, and most colonies had laws regulating it. Indentured servants who ran away from their masters before serving their contracted time could be seized and forced to return. Runaways had time added on to their service to make up for the period away from work. Colonial laws allowed masters to punish indentured servants, who needed permission to marry, to travel, or to own property. Considered property themselves, these bound laborers could be bought and sold like slaves.

At the same time, colonial laws protected indentured servants in various ways. Masters were required to give them sufficient food, clothing and shelter, as well as a day of rest on Sundays. If indentured servants were mistreated or if the terms of their contracts were violated, they could take their masters to court.

Despite such laws, the lives of indentured servants depended largely on their masters. With a kind master, a bound laborer might have a decent life. In some cases, masters even treated servants like members of the family. With a cruel master, however, a servant's life could be a nightmare.

Changes in Indentured Labor. During the early colonial period, most indentured servants were unskilled laborers. Many served on southern plantations, which needed large numbers of workers at little cost. These servants also provided an important part of the unskilled labor force in commercial centers in New England.

In the late 1600s, the supply of unskilled bound laborers in the colonies declined as economic conditions in England improved and more people could find work there. When the number of indentured servants dwindled, SLAVERY became more important as a source of cheap unskilled labor, especially on southern plantations.

By the 1700s, black slaves supplied most of the unskilled labor needed in the colonies. At this time, indentured servants with skills were in great demand, and most of them came from Scotland, Ireland, and Germany. They often served in cities rather than in rural areas.

As the population of the colonies grew, the supply of native-born laborers increased. People found that it was cheaper to pay wages to these workers than to keep indentured servants. The system of indentured service continued into the 1800s, but it ceased to be an important source of labor after the 1700s.

Other European Colonies. In the French colonies, indentured labor served a different purpose. Most of the individuals who signed contracts to work in North America hoped to earn money but not to settle there. They considered life in the colonies to be a short-term arrangement and expected to return to France after fulfilling their terms of service. As a result, indentured service never became a reliable source of settlers for the French colonies, as it had for the British.

French bound laborers were called *engagés,* a term that applied to all hired workers. Almost all *engagés* who left France for the colonies were men; families rarely emigrated under work contracts. Unlike indentured servants in the British colonies, French colonial *engagés* earned a salary. Their contracts also promised a paid passage back to France. While some decided to stay in America, the majority eventually returned to Europe.

The French were often reluctant to move to America because of the harsh climate, danger of Indian attack, and shortage of women. To overcome this lack of enthusiasm, recruiters in France tried to lure *engagés* to North America with benefits, such as a generous salary and a term of service that rarely lasted more than three years.

Indentured service did play a role in the settlement of the French colonies in the 1600s. But for the most part, the colonies were populated by self-employed farmers, fishermen, and crafts workers. To fill the demand for both skilled and unskilled labor, the colonies relied primarily on native-born workers.

* ***Spanish Borderlands*** northern part of New Spain, area now occupied by Florida, Texas, New Mexico, Arizona, and California

While indentured service existed in the Spanish Borderlands*, a similar arrangement known as debt peonage was much more common. In debt peonage, an accident, illness, or other circumstance forced a person to borrow money from another. In return, the individual agreed to work for the lender until the debt was repaid. Lenders generally provided only a small, usually insufficient, quantity of food for the debtors and their families.

Indentured service rested on a contract that specified a certain period of work, but debt peonage rarely involved contracts. With no set term of service, debtors had to continue working until they repaid their debts. For many in the Spanish Borderlands, debt peonage became a lifelong trap. Struggling to repay the initial debt, debtors generally accumulated new debts and fell farther and farther behind in meeting their financial obligations. This type of servitude provided an important source of labor for wealthy Spanish colonists. It did little, however, to encourage colonization or to develop a stable colonial society. (*See also* **Apprenticeship; Class Structure in European Colonies; Labor.**)

Independence Movements

Many forces drove the North American colonies to demand and fight for independence from the European nations that had founded them. Some of these forces were economic. Colonists wanted to choose their own trading partners and control their own resources without being limited by the rules and regulations of their parent countries. Other factors included political ideas or beliefs. In the British colonies, for example, many people became convinced that the British government did not have the right to make laws for them.

In general, independence movements arose when enough colonists came to the conclusion that their interests were no longer the same as those of the parent country. But these movements were far from unified. Not all colonists wanted independence, and those who did had different views about how to achieve it and what kind of government to establish afterward. In New Spain, some revolutionaries sought to win independence for their separate regions, while others dreamed of forming a single nation.

The 1763 TREATY OF PARIS, which ended the FRENCH AND INDIAN WAR, reshaped colonial North America and set the stage for the rise of independence movements. Under the treaty, Great Britain acquired New France and Louisiana east of the Mississippi River. France ceded* western Louisiana to Spain, while Britain gained possession of Spanish Florida. These territorial changes left Britain in control of the northern and eastern parts of North America, while Spain held the southern and western sections. Soon colonists began testing European control, first in the British colonies and then in the Spanish territories.

* ***cede*** to yield or surrender

British Colonies

Independence movements in the British colonies began as resistance or opposition to certain laws passed by PARLIAMENT. In the early stages, few colonists imagined that they would break away from Great Britain. Most expected to remain part of the British empire but under terms that gave them a greater role in government. If Parliament and King GEORGE III had compromised or agreed to some of the colonists' demands, the protests might not have grown into the full-fledged independence movement that led to the AMERICAN REVOLUTION.

Background to Resistance. From the mid-1600s to the mid-1700s, the British colonies were left pretty much on their own, with little interference from London. The British Parliament did pass colonial trade laws, but merchants in the colonies often ignored them. SMUGGLING was common. During this period, the colonies enjoyed both rapid economic

Many leaders of the independence movement in the British colonies were lawyers. Among them was Patrick Henry, shown here in 1765 protesting the Stamp Act before the Virginia House of Burgesses.

growth and considerable political freedom. Their elected assemblies made laws for the colonies and imposed taxes. Though the colonists regarded their assemblies as equal to Parliament, the British government had a quite different view.

After the French and Indian War, Great Britain was at peace with its European neighbors. The British government took advantage of this quiet period to reorganize the administration of its empire. Parliament sought to tighten its control over the colonies. It also wanted the colonies to make a larger contribution toward the costs of maintaining the empire. Britain thus took a new interest in North America—an interest that the colonists did not welcome.

Beginning in the mid-1760s, Parliament passed a number of laws, or acts, that affected its North American possessions. The QUARTERING ACTS directed colonists to provide housing for British soldiers in inns, barns, and other

The independence movement in the British colonies gained supporters rapidly after the first battles of the Revolutionary War. On July 9, 1776, colonists in New York City pulled down a statue of King George III to show he was no longer their leader.

buildings, although not in private homes. Other acts imposed duties, or taxes, on goods or services that the colonists used. The SUGAR ACT OF 1764 was the first attempt to tax the colonies. The STAMP ACT OF 1765 led to a storm of protest by American colonists, who refused to pay a tax that people in England had been subject to since the late 1600s. With the TOWNSHEND ACTS OF 1767, Parliament imposed duties on paint, paper, tea, and other goods.

The money raised by these and other taxes was supposed to help pay for colonial government and defense. Accustomed to running their own affairs, Americans resented Parliament's meddling and rejected the idea that Parliament had the right to tax the colonies. Colonial protests led to the repeal* of both the Stamp Act and the Townshend Acts. But in 1766 Parliament passed the DECLARATORY ACT, which stated that it had the authority to make laws for the colonies "in all cases whatsoever." This claim reflected the widely held belief that Great Britain owned the North American colonies. Meanwhile, new political ideas were circulating in the colonies.

* ***repeal*** to undo a law

Political Thought in the Colonies. The European intellectual movement known as the ENLIGHTENMENT had a great influence on POLITICAL THOUGHT in America in the 1700s. Among other things, it led to an examination of the relationship between rulers and the people they ruled. The Enlightenment writer John Locke argued that citizens have both the right and the duty to resist tyranny*. This idea appealed to many American colonists. In 1768 writers in a New York newspaper echoed Locke when they declared: "Good Laws and good Rulers will always be obey'd and respected."

* ***tyranny*** unjust use of power

Colonists shared a growing belief that Parliament's actions after the French and Indian War represented a violation of the British constitution and the liberties it guaranteed. At the same time, they became convinced that their opposition involved more than a dispute over Parliament's right to govern them. It was a struggle over the meaning of government itself. As resistance to Parliament grew and British rule appeared more tyrannical, colonists became increasingly committed to republican* ideals.

* ***republican*** form of government in which the people elect government officials

To these colonists, America represented a grand experiment, a chance for people to free themselves from the corrupt and worn-out systems of Europe and to create a new society based on equality and justice. There was little agreement, however, about the exact nature of that new society. Some people saw republicanism as freedom from outside interference. Others believed that it would bring an end to corrupt and powerful aristocracies. Although republicanism meant different things to different people, a belief in its basic principles unified the growing opposition to British rule in the years before the American Revolution.

Thomas PAINE summed up colonial republican thought in *Common Sense,* a pamphlet published in January 1776 that helped rouse support for independence from Britain. Paine claimed that liberty was under attack and that it was the duty of Americans to fight for freedom. Their fight, Paine said, would be more than a war for their own independence. It would be a struggle for the very survival of liberty in the world.

Toward Revolution. Parliament's acts in the 1760s caused various reactions in America. In the mid-1760s colonists formed groups called SONS OF LIBERTY to oppose the Stamp Act. They also boycotted* goods that were subject to the hated taxes. In the late 1760s, boycotts led to agreements among the colonies to ban certain goods and to the development of groups called nonimportation associations. These associations examined the financial records of merchants to see if they had imported any banned items, tried individuals suspected of violating nonimportation agreements, and punished those found guilty. Besides the use of boycotts, the colonists showed their displeasure with Parliament by rioting in the streets and burning effigies* of tax officials.

* ***boycott*** refusal to buy goods as a means of protest

* ***effigy*** dummy of a person

These violent protests disappeared between 1770 and 1773—a time sometimes called the "quiet period" of the independence movement. But the colonists had lost confidence in Parliament. Their opposition continued to grow beneath the surface of colonial life. In 1772 Bostonians formed the first of many COMMITTEES OF CORRESPONDENCE, in which colonial patriots* spread news and ideas throughout the colonies and coordinated activities aimed at resisting British policies.

* ***patriot*** American colonist who supported independence from Britain

Conflict flared again when Parliament passed the TEA ACT OF 1773, which resulted in the BOSTON TEA PARTY—a direct challenge to British authority. Parliament responded in 1774 with the Coercive Acts, a series of laws that the colonists called the INTOLERABLE ACTS. Designed to strengthen royal authority in Boston, the center of colonial resistance, these acts convinced many American colonists that Britain was determined to ignore their rights and to rule the colonies by force.

See color plate 6, vol. 4.

By late 1774, most colonists still hoped for an adjustment of their relationship with Britain, not for a complete break. They sent delegates to the FIRST CONTINENTAL CONGRESS, which rejected Parliament's right to tax the colonies and demanded individual and political liberties. The congress asked King George III to recognize their demands. The king not only failed to respond but also called the Americans rebellious traitors.

Colonial patriots now prepared to fight for their rights and liberties, assembling weapons and ammunition to defend themselves against British

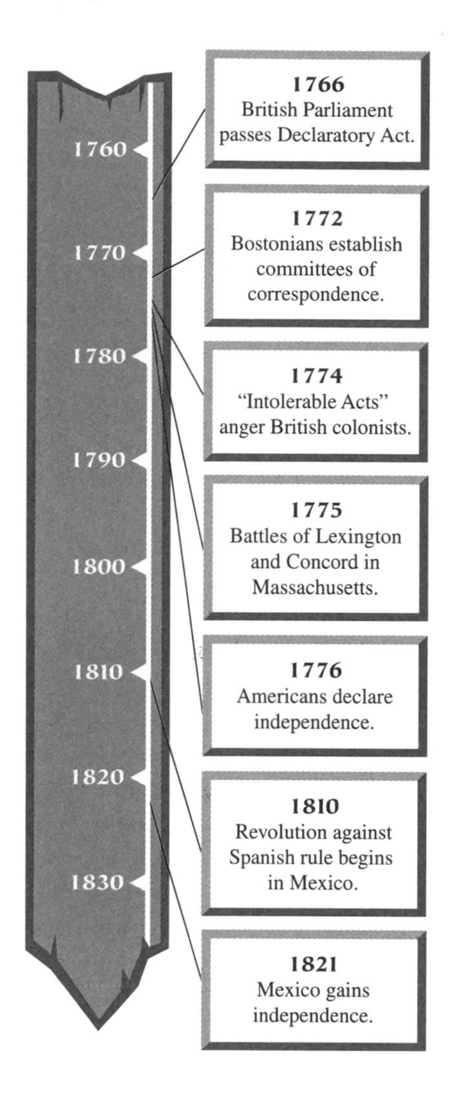

troops. In early 1775, Lord NORTH, the British prime minister, offered the colonists a compromise. He declared that Parliament would not tax any colony that paid for its own government and contributed to the cost of its defense. North did not understand that the colonists' quarrel with Britain was no longer simply about taxes. It had moved on to the broader issue of sovereignty*.

Before North's offer arrived in America, British troops fired on colonists in Massachusetts in April 1775. The resulting Battles of LEXINGTON AND CONCORD raised the stakes of the confrontation between the colonies and Britain. Fired with excitement and outrage, the colonists ignored North's offer. Patriot resistance began changing to outright rebellion, although it would be more than a year before the colonists demanded full independence in the DECLARATION OF INDEPENDENCE. The LOYALISTS—colonists who did not want to break with Great Britain—found themselves in an increasingly difficult position as that year passed and the colonies slid toward war.

During and after the Revolution, Americans had to organize new ways of governing themselves. They found inspiration not only in the republican ideals of the Enlightenment but also in groups formed during the independence movement. The Sons of Liberty, the nonimportation associations, and the Continental Congresses all provided models for government by the people.

* ***sovereignty*** supreme power or authority

Spanish Borderlands

At the time of the American Revolution, the inhabitants of Spain's American colonies showed little sign of rebellion. Two events in the early 1800s, however, challenged the colonists' loyalty to Spain. In 1805 a British fleet destroyed a combined force of Spanish and French warships. Soon afterward, French troops under Napoleon Bonaparte, the ruler of France, invaded Spain and drove the Spanish king from the throne.

These developments in Europe absorbed the attention of the Spanish crown and weakened the link between Spain and its colonies. Without consistent direction from Spain and the unifying force of loyalty to the king and the empire, the colonies began to drift toward confusion and instability. In Mexico, the center of NEW SPAIN, various groups began competing for power.

Background to Revolution. During the 1700s, the Spanish government had made many changes in the way it administered the American colonies. These reforms—called the Bourbon reforms after the royal family of Spain—were introduced to bring order and consistency to the colonial administrations of New Spain. However, the viceroys* and other colonial officials resented the changes imposed on them and resisted giving up control over their districts.

* ***viceroy*** person appointed as a monarch's representative to govern a province or colony

The Bourbon reforms also created tension between the Roman Catholic Church and the state. The church had long regarded Native Americans as its responsibility. In assuming control over the Indians, the colonial government launched a power struggle that it eventually won. This conflict between CHURCH AND STATE added to the disorder in New Spain and split the loyalties of the colonists.

Colonial society was further divided by tensions between different groups of people. The *criollos,* or Creoles, were individuals of Spanish ancestry who had been born in the Americas. They considered the colony their permanent home and wanted more control over its economy and government. The *peninsulares* came from Spain. They served in the colonial government but planned to return to Europe. For the most part, their primary concern was to please Spanish officials rather than to improve conditions of life in New Spain.

When the empire and the colonial administration fell into confusion in the early 1800s, the *criollos* saw a chance to seize more power and tried to take over government positions held by *peninsulares.* At the same time, the great mass of peasant farmers—mostly mestizos*—suffered greatly under the oppression* of both the *criollos* and the *peninsulares.*

* ***mestizo*** person of mixed Spanish and Indian ancestry

* ***oppression*** unjust or cruel exercise of authority

Revolution broke out in MEXICO in 1810, when a priest named Miguel HIDALGO Y COSTILLA led a peasant uprising against the colonial government. This was not the only rebellion. The Mexican Revolution consisted of a series of uprisings and wars over a period of 11 years. Agustín de ITURBIDE finally achieved MEXICAN INDEPENDENCE in 1821. Although little of the revolution had taken place in the frontier provinces of the Spanish Borderlands*, those provinces became part of the new nation of Mexico.

* ***Spanish Borderlands*** northern part of New Spain, area now occupied by Florida, Texas, New Mexico, Arizona, and California

* ***buffer zone*** neutral area between two enemy areas

The Frontier Provinces. Before the Mexican Revolution, the frontier provinces of Texas, Arizona, New Mexico, and California differed in several important ways from the rest of New Spain. First, Spanish law was less strictly enforced there than in other parts of New Spain. Second, the region's wealthiest families were poorer than upper-class families elsewhere in Spanish America. Finally, racial and social differences were not as sharply defined on the frontier as in older parts of New Spain.

The Borderland provinces were thinly populated, and much of the land was unmapped and unexplored. They were Spanish in name only, not yet fully under Spain's control. In fact the provinces cost more to govern than they produced in resources and trade. Spain kept them mainly as a buffer zone* between Mexico and the areas to the north that belonged to Britain and then to the United States.

The years leading up to the Mexican Revolution had brought important changes to the Borderlands. The Bourbon reforms had helped expand settlement, ranching, and trade in the area. As the population grew, conflicts occurred frequently between settlers and Indians over land. These conflicts increased in the late 1700s and early 1800s, when Spain cut back the troops and funds sent to the Borderlands because it needed them to fight European wars. Problems also arose from the spread of British and American settlers westward across the continent. Their arrival drove the Plains Indians into the Southwest, where they warred with local Indians and Spanish settlers.

Far from the center of power in New Spain, the Borderlands did not experience the full impact of Mexican independence movements. In the early 1800s, a series of colonial governors struggled to keep revolutionary influences out of Texas, stamping out a series of uprisings led by Mexicans. These rebels often fought among themselves as much as they fought against those who remained loyal to the Spanish crown. The conflicts disrupted the economy of Texas and cost many lives. California experienced a brief period of

Revolution and Counterrevolution

Early in the Mexican Revolution, Juan Bautista de Las Casas seized colonial government offices in Texas and forced Governor Manuel Salcedo to surrender. Town elders overpowered Las Casas and freed Salcedo. The next year rebel forces under Bernardo Gutiérrez de Lara invaded Texas with support from the United States. They captured and killed Salcedo but were soon overthrown by a rival rebel leader. Forces loyal to the Spanish crown later recaptured Texas. These changes, which took place between 1811 and 1813, were typical of the rapid seesaw of power in New Spain during the revolution.

revolutionary activity a few years later. But an independence movement failed to take root there as well.

For the most part, the independence movement and revolution in Mexico had little direct effect on the Borderlands. In some places, people formed local councils that assumed some government responsibilities. Most governors and other officials in the Borderland provinces remained cautious. They hesitated to join the revolution or to declare themselves against it until they knew which side was winning. The main effects of the independence movement and the Mexican Revolution were to slow down the growth of population and the economy. Frontier settlers also had more trouble with the Indians, who took advantage of the confusion brought by the revolution to increase the frequency of their raids. Order and growth returned to the Borderlands after Mexico gained its independence in 1821.

French Colonies

Remember: *Consult the index at the end of Volume 4 to find more information on many topics.*

Unlike the British and Spanish colonists, the French colonists in North America never showed any desire for independence from the parent country. The ties between the colonists and France were broken not by revolution but by treaties between France and other nations.

France ceded the western part of Louisiana to Spain in 1762 and the eastern part to Britain the following year. Although France regained possession of Louisiana for a few years, it agreed to sell the territory to the United States in 1803 for about $11 million.

After the British invaded and conquered Quebec in 1760, the days of the French colony of NEW FRANCE seemed to be numbered. The ruling officials, army officers, and wealthy merchants had fled to France just before the British attack, leaving the lower classes of crafts workers, farmers, and small traders at the mercy of the British.

At first the French settlers hoped that France would regain the colony at the end of the French and Indian War. But in the Treaty of Paris of 1763, which settled the war, France ceded its territory in present-day Canada to Britain. In 1774 the British Parliament took steps to win the loyalty of French Canadians by passing the QUEBEC ACT, which restored some forms of French law and allowed French Canadians to practice the Roman Catholic religion and to hold public office.

When the American Revolution erupted in 1776, France supported the American colonists. The French in Canada refused to join in this fight, but they still had hopes that France would retake Quebec when the opportunity arose. The rulers of France, however, had no interest in their former colony.

During the American Revolution, some 40,000 to 50,000 Loyalists fled from the 13 colonies to Canada. A much larger flood of British settlers poured into Canada afterward, and Britain created new provinces for them. People of French ancestry became a minority in Canada. But they kept their language, their faith, and their political identity alive even after all the provinces joined together to form the nation of Canada in 1867. Concentrated in the province of Quebec, the French Canadians launched a new independence movement in the late 1900s, with the goal of separation from the rest of Canada. (*See also* **Canada; Colonial Administration; Revolutionary Thought.**)

See *Agriculture: British; Pinckney, Eliza.*

Industries

Industry includes all activities—except agriculture—that produce goods or services. Any branch of manufacturing or trade can be considered an industry. Colonists in North America relied on certain basic industries, such as fishing and lumbering, to supply products for their own use and for export.

Early Industries. Even before European nations sent explorers and colonists to North America, they supported a thriving fishing industry in the waters off the continent's North Atlantic coast. By the late 1500s, the FUR TRADE had become a leading colonial industry as well. Both industries shifted large amounts of natural resources from North America to Europe. Although the industries provided European colonists with an opportunity to earn income, the intense competition to obtain fish and furs contributed to tension between England and France.

Colonists needed wood for fuel and for building houses, furniture, fences, boats, and wagons. Although farmers everywhere felled trees for their own use, access to cheap transportation—usually by water—and sawmills were required for the lumber industry to develop. The lumber was rarely exported to Europe because of the expense, but large amounts were shipped to the West Indies.

Native Americans had industries of their own before the Europeans arrived in North America. Stone was the basic material of many tools, such as

Colonists harnessed the power of rivers to run sawmills. This view of a sawmill on Fort Anne Creek appeared in Thomas Anburey's 1789 book, *Travels Through the Interior Parts of America.*

hatchets and arrowheads, so most tribes produced some form of stonework. Indians also treated skins to make leather, wove cloth from cotton and bark fibers, and made clay pottery. English, Dutch, French, and Spanish colonists had their own versions of these CRAFTS and introduced new ones such as ironworking, papermaking, and wagon building.

Industry in the colonies grew out of necessity. The European powers that had colonies wanted to import raw materials such as furs from North America and to sell manufactured goods such as tools and paper in the colonies. But the colonists could not always buy European manufactured goods. At times, war or bad weather kept merchant ships from colonial ports, and taxes and transportation costs made European items very expensive. As a result, the colonists developed their own industries, making things they needed out of local materials. The three biggest industries that developed in the colonies—shipbuilding, ironworking, and flour milling—were based on resources that were plentiful in North America.

Shipbuilding. The colonists needed boats and small ships for fishing and for river and coastal trade. Because these small craft could not be safely sailed across the ocean from Europe, the colonists built them in shipyards along the Atlantic coast. They used timber from the continent's vast forests. The construction of larger ships required more money, labor, and skill. All of these could be found in New England, which also had plenty of timber. As a result, New England became the busiest shipbuilding center, followed by Pennsylvania and the Chesapeake Bay region. At first American-built merchant vessels were used only for trade between the colonies and the West Indies. During the 1700s, however, Britain lost many ships in war, and colonial ships began carrying goods to all parts of the world. By the time of the American Revolution, one-third of the British merchant fleet had been built in the colonies.

The shipbuilding industry helped spur the growth of the fishing industry. It also stimulated the WHALING industry, which became well established in the late 1600s. Whale blubber could be made into lamp oil or candles, while whalebone was used in women's clothing. By the 1770s, several hundred American whaling ships were sailing the world's oceans. Many of them came from seaports in Massachusetts, such as Plymouth, Salem, and Nantucket. Shipbuilding also provided jobs for workers in related industries, such as rope making, sail making, metalworking, painting, and chandlery—the business of providing ships' captains with supplies.

Shipbuilding was not limited to the British colonies. New France also had an important industry. Between 1663 and 1763, French colonists launched about 230 boats and ships of various sizes. These included lifeboats, flat-bottomed troop carriers, fishing boats, ships for traders and privateers*, and warships for the French navy.

* ***privateer*** privately owned ship authorized by the government to attack and capture enemy vessels; also the ship's master

Ironworking. Iron ore was abundant in many regions, and colonists obtained it easily from shallow mines. Fuel for purifying, melting, and shaping the iron came from charcoal, a form of partly burned wood. Colonists produced a great deal of charcoal as they burned trees to clear the land for farming.

Nearly every colonial town manufactured rope. They used a ropewalk, such as the one shown here, on which fibers from the hemp plant could be twisted together into a stout coil.

Colonial ironworkers heated iron ore in large furnaces to form blocks of crude iron, called pigs because of their shape. This pig iron was then taken to forges*, reheated until it became soft, and pounded with hammers to form tough, easy-to-weld iron bars. BLACKSMITHS and iron mills used the forged iron to make tools, farm equipment, weapons, and items for the kitchen and home.

* ***forge*** special furnance or fireplace in which metal is heated before it is shaped

Ironworking became increasingly important in the British colonies after 1715. Within a short period, colonists built 80 furnaces that produced enough pig iron to supply 175 forges, most of them between Pennsylvania and Massachusetts. The colonies exported some of this iron to Britain. But most of it went to blacksmiths, gunsmiths, nail makers, shipbuilders, and other artisans* in the colonies.

* ***artisan*** skilled crafts worker

New France also had an important ironworking industry. In 1731 French colonists built a large ironworks near the town of Trois-Rivières on the St. Lawrence River. This operation had four forges and employed more than 120 workers who used local ore to make pig iron and such finished products as stoves, pots, nails, gun barrels, and cannonballs. The iron made in New France supplied the needs of French colonists; none was exported.

Flour Milling. Colonists throughout North America produced an ample supply of wheat. Before it could be used for food, though, it had to be ground into flour. Grinding wheat by hand was hard work and took time—two or three hours for grinding a day's supply of flour for one family. Most people preferred to take their wheat to a local gristmill where, for a fee, it would be ground into flour between two large millstones. The power to turn these stones came from waterwheels and moving water or, in some cases, from windmills with large wooden or cloth sails that turned in the wind. The Dutch and French were especially skilled at building and using windmills.

Small gristmills ground only a few bushels of wheat a day. They were often idle, waiting for customers or for a greater flow of water or stronger winds. Large commercial gristmills, using an elaborate system of ponds, dams, and artificial waterfalls, ground large quantities of wheat into flour for use in the colonies and for export. Most of the large gristmills were located in Pennsylvania and other middle colonies. By the mid-1700s, they were the most modern mills in the world, providing the finest flour on the international market.

Other Industries. The basic mill technology—the use of waterpower or wind power to turn a wheel—could also be used to do other kinds of work. Swedish, Dutch, French, and English colonists all built sawmills to cut felled trees into flat boards of lumber. Sawmills saved an enormous amount of labor, and they allowed colonists to build frame houses instead of log cabins and to have wooden rather than dirt floors.

The great forests of North America also provided material for the naval stores* industry. As European navies expanded their fleets to meet the threat of war, they needed tall tree trunks to serve as ships' masts and large supplies of tar and pitch—sticky substances derived from wood and used to keep rope from rotting and to seal the hulls of ships. North Carolina became an important center of the naval stores industry.

* ***naval stores*** tar and other products from pine trees that were used on ships

The manufacture of potash, a vital ingredient in glass and soap, was another wood-based industry. Obtained from the ashes of burned wood, potash became an important by-product of farming. By the end of the colonial period, colonists were supplying two-thirds of the potash used in Britain.

Another important industry was textile manufacturing. Most colonial fabric was made in homes rather than in workshops or factories. The textile industry grew slowly because colonists imported much of their cloth and clothing from Europe. Both England and the Netherlands had large, well-established textile industries. They used laws and taxes to discourage the establishment of rival industries in their colonies.

Colonists from New France to New Spain carried out many other industries in their households or in small workshops. Among these were leather working (including shoemaking), brick and tile making, papermaking and printing, and glass-making. Agriculture produced the raw materials for several additional industries, such as salting beef and pork for export to the West Indies, brewing beer, and distilling rum from West Indian molasses. (*See also* **Artisans; Economic Systems; Fish and Fishing; Forests; Ships and Shipbuilding; Technology; Trade and Commerce.**)

Intolerable Acts (1774)

In 1774 the British Parliament passed a series of laws, or acts, to punish Massachusetts for the Boston Tea Party. These Coercive Acts, known as the Intolerable Acts in the colonies because of their harshness, were intended to strengthen British authority in Massachusetts. Instead, the acts united the colonies in opposition to Great Britain and contributed to the tensions that led to the American Revolution.

The Boston Tea Party convinced the British that the time had come to bring the American colonists into line, by force if necessary. King George III and Lord North, the British prime minister, decided to make an example of Massachusetts to show other colonies what could happen if they resisted British authority. The Coercive Acts were meant to serve this purpose.

The Boston Port Act, the first of the acts, closed the port of Boston to all commerce. The port would not reopen until the Bostonians paid the British East India Company for the tea lost in the Tea Party.

The Massachusetts Government Act changed the charter of Massachusetts in ways that weakened the colonial government. The governor's council would no longer be elected by the colonial assembly but would be made up of people chosen by the British crown. Jurors would no longer be selected by local officials but by royal officials. The act also restricted TOWN MEETINGS, permitting only one annual election meeting without special permission from the governor.

The Administration of Justice Act gave governors the authority to move trials for capital crimes* to other colonies or to Great Britain. Bostonians called this the "Murder Act," arguing that it would enable royal officials to convict and execute colonists who resisted British authority. At the same time, Bostonians protested that a British official tried in Britain for the murder of a colonist would never be convicted. This act seemed particularly unfair because Massachusetts had made every effort to ensure a fair trial for the British soldiers involved in the BOSTON MASSACRE.

* ***capital crime*** crime punishable by death

The last of the Coercive Acts was a new Quartering Act. Broader than earlier QUARTERING ACTS, it allowed British authorities to house British troops in the homes of colonists if necessary.

Along with the Coercive Acts, Parliament passed the QUEBEC ACT, which also angered the colonists but for different reasons. The act established a centralized government in Canada and extended Canada's border into the OHIO RIVER VALLEY. The new border cut several colonies off from their western land claims. The act also recognized Roman Catholicism as the official religion of Quebec—an action the colonists interpreted as a threat to Protestantism and their religious freedom.

Instead of isolating Massachusetts from the other colonies and forcing it into submission, the Intolerable Acts united the colonies against Britain and provoked further resistance. COMMITTEES OF CORRESPONDENCE spread word of Boston's misfortune throughout the colonies and asked for support. Colonists responded by flooding the city with money, supplies, and food. Even those who opposed taking extreme measures against the British, a course favored by some patriots*, believed that their basic liberties were at stake.

* ***patriot*** American colonist who supported independence from Britain

In June 1774, delegates from all the colonies except Georgia met in Philadelphia to consider what action to take. The members of this FIRST CONTINENTAL CONGRESS demanded that Parliament repeal the Intolerable Acts. They hoped their grievances could be resolved peacefully but were prepared to be as stubborn as Parliament had been. When Britain ignored the colonists' demands, tensions rose. The following spring British actions led to the Battles of LEXINGTON AND CONCORD, the sparks that ignited the American Revolution. (*See also* **Independence Movements.**)

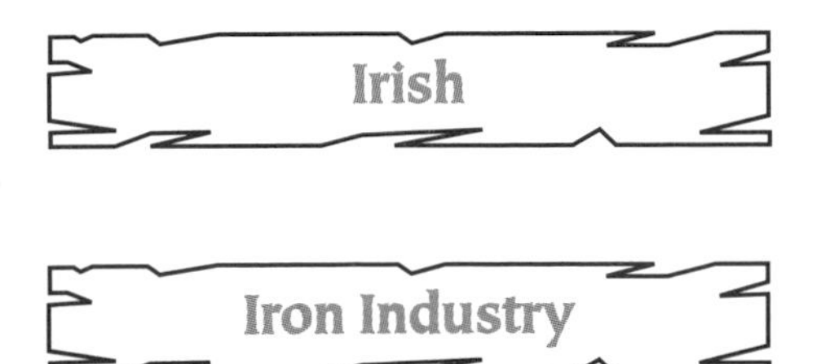

Irish

See *Immigration.*

Iron Industry

See *Industries.*

Iroquois Confederacy

See second map in Native Americans (vol. 3).

The Iroquois Confederacy, also known as the Iroquois League, was a political union of five—later six—closely related Indian tribes. The powerful alliance dominated a region that stretched through much of present-day New York. The Iroquois, fierce warriors and shrewd negotiators, played a significant role in the struggles between France and Britain for control of North America. They remained an important political force up to the time of the American Revolution.

Formation of the Confederacy. Long before Europeans came to America, people who spoke Iroquoian languages lived in small villages in

This Iroquois warrior, wielding a tomahawk and a ball-headed club, was drawn by J. Grassét de St. Sauver in 1787. By that time, the Iroquois Confederacy had lost most of its territory to the United States.

New York and the St. Lawrence region. By the 1400s, Iroquois settlements had grown quite large, with some numbering more than 1,500 people. Communities consisted of various clans*, who lived together in large dwellings called longhouses. The name the Iroquois used for themselves—*Haudenosaunee*—translates loosely as "people of the longhouse."

* ***clan*** related families

The growth of settlements caused major social change among the Iroquois people. Crowded together in villages, the different clans quarreled frequently. Their feuds often spilled over into other communities and sometimes resulted in warfare between neighboring groups. These conflicts began to threaten the stability of the tribes.

Sometime before the end of the 1500s, several Iroquois tribes joined together in a large, loosely knit alliance in an attempt to end intertribal warfare. According to legend, the founders of this Iroquois Confederacy were Hiawatha and Dekanawida (or Deganawida), a supernatural* figure who came to Hiawatha in a vision. The Iroquois believed that dreams and visions were spiritually inspired. The confederacy originally consisted of five tribes—the Seneca, Cayuga, Onondaga, Oneida, and Mohawk—and was known as the League of Five Nations. In 1722 a sixth tribe, the TUSCARORA, joined the confederacy. Related to the other tribes by language, the Tuscarora had migrated north from North Carolina because of conflicts with European settlers.

* ***supernatural*** related to forces beyond the normal world; miraculous

The confederacy helped resolve disputes among the Iroquois tribes, while allowing them to maintain separate identities. Each tribe remained independent and managed its own affairs. But the tribes also met regularly in a great council consisting of 50 sachems, or peace chiefs, representing the member tribes. All the sachems had to agree before the council took action on major issues. The council had responsibility for keeping peace among the tribes, dealing with outsiders, and planning war activities against enemies of the Iroquois.

Authority in the Iroquois Confederacy passed through the women of the tribes. Clan head women appointed the sachems of the great council, and women could speak freely on political issues. While not holding official positions of power themselves, women played a vital political role in tribal life by using their authority to put pressure on others.

Role of the Confederacy. Located between the Dutch, French, and British colonies, the Iroquois tribes were able to play a key role in the European rivalry for control of North America. In the early 1600s, the French launched military campaigns against the Mohawk Indians and denied them control of French-Indian trade in the St. Lawrence Valley region. As a result, the Iroquois became bitter enemies of the French. During the 1640s and 1650s, they launched devastating attacks on French outposts* and on Indian tribes allied to France, such as the HURON. The Iroquois succeeded in scattering the Huron and other Indians in the Great Lakes region and took over the FUR TRADE there. Through a series of alliances with friendly Indian tribes, they gained control of important fur-trading routes and the access to shared hunting territories.

* ***outpost*** frontier settlement or military base

Meanwhile, the Iroquois formed good relations with the Dutch and the English, obtaining guns and other items in exchange for furs. As the English grew more powerful, the Iroquois came to view them as possible allies against the French. In the late 1670s, the Iroquois signed a series of peace treaties with English authorities in New York. New York colonists also helped with negotiations between the Iroquois and other Indian tribes. These actions led to the creation of the Covenant Chain—a system of alliances linking the English colonies to various Indian groups throughout eastern North America.

As the competition between the English and French in North America grew more intense, the Iroquois tried to play one side against the other for their own benefit. Any peace with the French, however, was fragile and did not last long. Ties to the English remained stronger, and the Iroquois found themselves increasingly drawn into the European rivalry. During KING WILLIAM'S WAR (1689–1697), they sided with the English and attacked French forts and settlements throughout the Great Lakes and St. Lawrence regions.

Years of warfare against France and its Indian allies eventually exhausted the Iroquois. In 1700 the confederacy began to seek a more lasting peace with the French. After long negotiations, the two sides agreed to resolve their differences peacefully. The Indians also pledged to remain neutral in any future war between France and England. This peace lasted for almost 60 years, much to the frustration of the British.

In the mid-1700s, France and Britain began competing for control of the Ohio River valley. The heightened tensions in that region threatened to destroy the peace and prosperity the Iroquois had achieved. At the outbreak of the FRENCH AND INDIAN WAR, the Iroquois remained neutral. In the end, though, the confederacy joined forces with the British in return for promises of trade goods and guarantees that Iroquois land would be safe from colonial expansion.

During the American Revolution, the Iroquois Confederacy declared its neutrality. But many Iroquois warriors joined in the fighting. The Mohawk, Onandaga, Cayuga, and Seneca generally fought with the British, while the Oneida and Tuscarora sided with the Americans. The war was a disaster for the Iroquois. Divided loyalties strained their alliance, and the Americans raided Iroquois communities in revenge for their support of the British. The Mohawk and Cayuga fled to Canada, while the other tribes remained in New York. After the war, all the tribes, even those that had supported the Americans, were forced to cede* large portions of their territory. With its tribes divided and its territory largely gone, the Iroquois Confederacy lost political power. Yet it continued to serve as a source of identity for the member tribes long after the colonial period. (*See also* **Native Americans.**)

* ***cede*** to yield or surrender

Iturbide, Agustín de

(1783–1824)
Emperor of Mexico

A military leader, Agustín de Iturbide rose to power during the Mexican independence movement in the early 1800s. He helped unite different classes of colonial society against Spanish rule. For a brief period, he held the title Emperor of Mexico.

Born to a wealthy family in Valladolid (now Morelia in southwest Mexico), Iturbide joined the army at a young age. When Miguel HIDALGO Y COSTILLA launched a movement for Mexican independence in 1810, Iturbide fought against the revolutionaries, defeating their forces at Valladolid. Like most members of the upper class, he remained loyal to the king of Spain.

The Mexican independence movement was losing ground, but events on the other side of the Atlantic brought it wider support. In 1820 a new government in Spain placed limits on the power of the monarchy and the ROMAN CATHOLIC CHURCH. The upper classes in New Spain*, firm defenders of the church and the Spanish crown, felt betrayed. They broke with the new government and demanded immediate separation from Spain.

* ***New Spain*** Spanish colonial empire in North America; included Mexico, the area now occupied by Florida, Texas, New Mexico, Arizona, and California, and various Caribbean islands

Iturbide took command of the colonial army and joined forces with the revolutionaries. In February 1821, Iturbide and rebel leader Vicente Guerrero announced the Plan de Iguala. It had three goals: independence from Spain, the unity of Spaniards and Creoles*, and the supremacy of the Catholic Church. The plan quickly gained popular support, and the army took control of the country. On August 24, 1821, the Spanish viceroy* signed an agreement accepting the Plan de Iguala and recognizing Mexican independence.

* ***Creole*** person of European ancestry, born in the Americas

* ***viceroy*** person appointed as a monarch's representative to govern a province or colony

The following May, Iturbide crowned himself Emperor Agustín I of Mexico. Unwilling to share power, he angered the revolutionaries who had started the independence movement. In October he dismissed the elected congress. Iturbide soon lost all support and was overthrown in March 1823 and exiled to Italy. Hoping to regain power, the former emperor returned to Mexico the next year—unaware that the Mexican congress had sentenced him to death. He was captured and executed on July 19, 1824. (*See also* **Independence Movements; Mexican Independence.**)

Jamaica

Christopher Columbus landed on the Caribbean island of Jamaica during his second voyage to the Americas in 1494. Both Spain and England established settlements on the island in the following centuries. The English developed large plantations there that were worked by slaves.

See first map in European Empires (vol. 2).

The Spanish founded a settlement on Jamaica in 1509. They used the mountainous island as a supply base for their operations in the WEST INDIES. After the arrival of the Spaniards, the Arawak Indians—Jamaica's native inhabitants—gradually disappeared as a result of disease and harsh treatment by the colonists.

Spanish settlers introduced bananas, citrus fruits, and sugarcane, which flourished in Jamaica's tropical climate. Realizing that raising sugar could bring great profits, the English wanted to add this island to their Caribbean empire. In 1655 they invaded and captured Jamaica. Hoping to make life difficult for the English, the island's Spanish settlers freed their African slaves. The slaves fled to the mountains, establishing a base from which they raided English farms and towns. The English were never able to bring this MAROON COMMUNITY of freed slaves and their descendants under control. Spain tried several times to recapture Jamaica, without success.

The English developed Jamaica's sugar industry, creating large plantations worked by slave labor. By the end of the 1700s, Jamaica was Great Britain's main source of sugar. The SLAVE TRADE was the other leading economic activity of the island's landowners and merchants.

Port Royal, Jamaica's capital, was a lively town in its day, with a reputation for extravagant spending and wicked ways. Adventurers, PIRATES, and privateers* used the town as a base for attacks on Spanish ships. One sea

* ***privateer*** privately owned ship authorized by the government to attack and capture enemy vessels; also the ship's master

captain, Henry MORGAN, retired from privateering to become a landholder in Jamaica and even served as the colony's lieutenant governor. After an earthquake destroyed Port Royal in 1692, the English built a new capital nearby at Kingston.

Like other Caribbean islands, Jamaica was a key point in the Atlantic trade that linked Europe, Africa, and the North American colonies during the late 1600s and the 1700s. Jamaica exported sugar, molasses, and rum, a liquor made from sugarcane. It also imported thousands of African slaves each year, shaping the African heritage of the island's modern population. Jamaica remained under British control until gaining independence in 1962. (*See also* **Slavery.**)

James I

1566–1625
King of England

* ***absolute monarch*** king or queen who possesses unlimited power

* ***charter*** written grant from a ruler conferring certain rights and privileges

The first Stuart king of England, James I ruled the country from 1603 to 1625. During his reign, the English established their first permanent settlements in North America.

Born in Scotland, James became King James IV of Scotland when he was one year old, after his mother, Mary, Queen of Scots, was forced to give up the throne. James inherited the English throne in 1603 on the death of his cousin ELIZABETH I. His attempts to rule as an absolute monarch* angered the members of the English PARLIAMENT, who had grown accustomed to playing a role in government under Elizabeth.

In 1606 James granted a charter* to the VIRGINIA COMPANY OF LONDON to establish a colony on the coast of North America. The next year colonists sponsored by the company sailed three ships up the James River and established the settlement of JAMESTOWN on its banks. Although Jamestown survived, the Virginia Company saw no profit from the venture. In 1624 James broke up the financially troubled company and brought the colony of Virginia under royal control.

The PLYMOUTH COLONY was also founded during James's reign. A strong supporter of the Church of England, the king often clashed with the PURITANS—people who wanted to reform the church. In 1620 a group of Puritans, later known as PILGRIMS, emigrated to North America to establish a colony where they could practice their religion in freedom without interference from the government. James continued to persecute the Puritans who remained in England.

Jamestown Colony

Jamestown was the first successful English colony in the Americas—although less successful than its founders had hoped it would be. Jamestown's struggle to survive taught the English much about the challenges of settling North America and governing a colony.

English Interest in America. In 1585, 20 years before the founding of Jamestown, the English had tried to establish a colony at ROANOKE ISLAND in present-day North Carolina. The failure of Roanoke and the mysterious disappearance of its settlers discouraged the English from launching another colony.

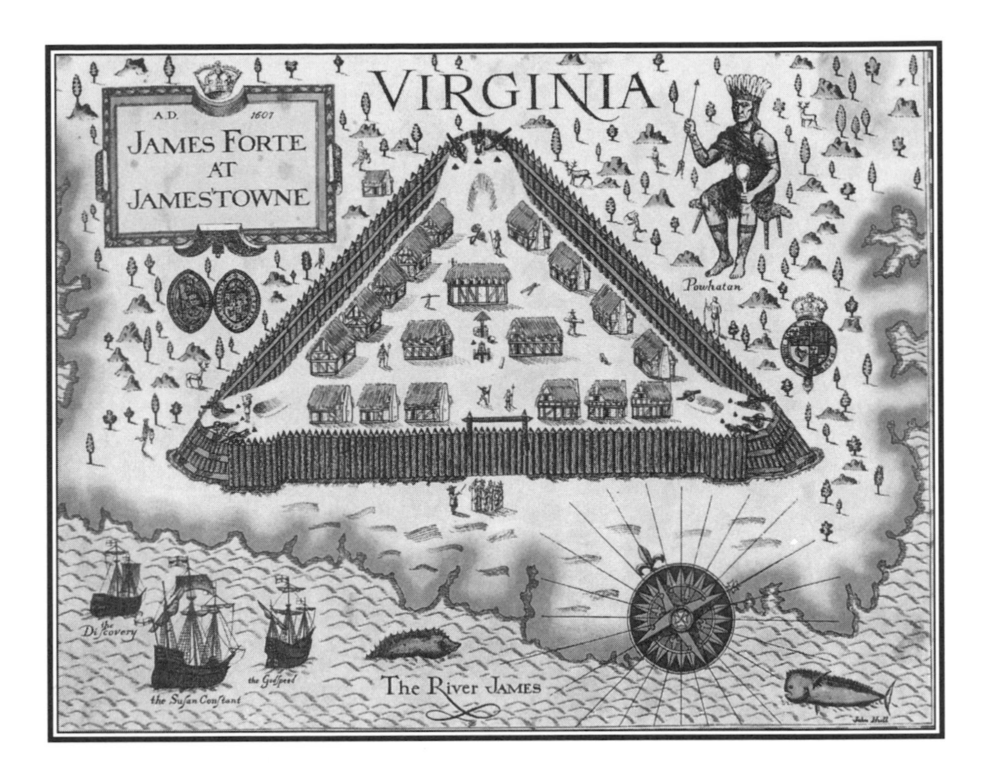

The three ships in the lower left corner of this picture—the *Discovery,* the *Susan Constant,* and the *Godspeed*—carried the first settlers into Jamestown in the spring of 1607. Powhatan, at the upper right, was the leader of the Powhatan Indians, who aided the colonists by providing them with food.

Two events in the early 1600s led England to take a new interest in the Americas. First, JAMES I became king in 1603 and made peace with Spain, ending a conflict that had drained English energy and resources for years. Second, France began making plans to colonize North America. Not wanting to be outdone by the French, a group of London merchants organized the VIRGINIA COMPANY OF LONDON to establish a colony.

The Virginia Company was a business venture, and the people who invested in it expected to make a profit. At the same time, the colonization of North America became a national mission that would bring glory to England. It was also, to some extent, a religious mission. Captain John SMITH, the military officer for the colony, wrote that one purpose of colonization was to bring the Indians "the true knowledge of God and his holy Gospell."

Founding of Jamestown. In the spring of 1606, King James gave the Virginia Company a charter* to found a colony in the region of Virginia along the Atlantic coast of North America. In December the ships *Susan Constant, Discovery,* and *Godspeed* set sail from England under the command of Captain Christopher Newport. They carried 144 colonists bound for Virginia.

* ***charter*** written grant from a ruler conferring certain rights and privileges

Even before reaching North America, the colonists ran into trouble. During the voyage, 39 people died from illness. Quarrels arose among the survivors and grew so heated that Captain Smith was charged with mutiny and arrested. When the ships reached the coast of Virginia in April 1607, Captain Newport opened a sealed box that contained instructions for governing the colony. The instructions named seven leading colonists to form a ruling council. One of those mentioned was John Smith. However, the other six members promptly voted him off the council.

The mood of discord continued as the colonists searched up and down the coast for a good place to build a settlement. In May they finally chose a point of land near the mouth of a large river that flowed into CHESAPEAKE BAY. They began building a fort and settlement, which they called Jamestown after the king.

Problems Facing the Colony. The low-lying, marshy site where the colonists settled proved unhealthy. It not only lacked a good source of drinking water but also turned out to be a breeding ground for the mosquitoes that carry the disease malaria. Illness took a high toll on the colony. By the end of 1607, all but about 40 of the Jamestown settlers had died.

The colonists faced other problems as well. Disagreements among council members continued. Three of them returned to England in June 1607, when Captain Newport went back for more settlers and supplies. Lacking strong leadership, the colonists who remained would not work together for the good of the community. Many were aristocrats* who regarded physical labor as beneath them and possessed no practical skills. Instead of hunting, fishing, and planting crops, most colonists spent their days searching for gold, playing games, or lazing around. Without meat and corn from the local POWHATAN INDIANS, the Jamestown settlement might not have survived.

* ***aristocrat*** member of the highest social class, often nobility

Captain Newport returned to Jamestown with supplies and 120 new settlers in January 1608. Soon afterward, a fire swept through the fort and storehouse, destroying much-needed supplies and housing. At this difficult time, John Smith stepped forward as the colony's leader. He visited the Powhatan Indians to patch up relations with them and obtained food. He also forced each colonist to spend a certain number of hours each day planting and tending crops or repairing buildings. His efforts enabled Jamestown to survive. But when Smith left for England to tend an injury in the fall of 1609, the colonists once again fell into bickering and laziness. They suffered horribly during the winter of 1609–1610, which came to be known as the "starving time." Only 65 colonists survived those terrible months.

Finding the Fort

The original fort of Jamestown fell into ruin and disappeared about 300 years ago. Archaeologists—scientists who study past civilizations—rediscovered the site only in 1996. First they found signs of decayed wood that marked parts of the walls of the original Jamestown fort. Digging farther, they uncovered traces of buildings within the fort and thousands of old items, including swords, armor, jewelry, beads, ceramics, coins, and a pipe, as well as the skeleton of a young man. Historians hope to learn more about life in "America's birthplace" from this important discovery.

Increasing Stability. In 1610 the Virginia Company sent a military governor to Jamestown to continue the policies of Captain Smith. Under military rule, the colony became much more stable. Colonists dug wells and planted gardens and field crops. They also began to grow TOBACCO. Although the Virginia Company made no profit, some individual colonists prospered by raising and selling tobacco.

To attract more settlers, the Virginia Company introduced a new system of land distribution, which promised grants of land to colonists and INDENTURED SERVANTS. The population increased steadily. Between 1619 and 1622, more than 3,000 new colonists arrived in Jamestown. At the same time, however, the disease rate remained very high. Three-quarters of the newcomers died within their first three years in North America.

In 1619 the Virginia Company replaced military rule with a governor, and the first assembly of elected representatives in America—the VIRGINIA HOUSE OF BURGESSES—met on July 30 in Jamestown. That same year, a Dutch ship

brought the first African slaves to Virginia. Their arrival laid the foundation for a prosperity based on tobacco PLANTATIONS and slavery. Until about 1680, however, indentured servants would outnumber slaves as the colony's main laborers.

Later Years. As Jamestown grew, colonists began to settle outside the original town. New settlements sprang up along the James and other rivers, turning Virginia from a wilderness into an English community. An Indian uprising in 1622 reversed that pattern somewhat, as colonists in outlying farms and settlements sought refuge in Jamestown.

Meanwhile, the Virginia Company faced financial ruin. The king ended the company's charter in 1624, making Virginia a royal colony under the direct control of the English crown. Jamestown became the capital of Virginia. Colonial leaders continued to hope that the town would prosper, but its unhealthy location remained a disadvantage. Fire destroyed part of Jamestown in 1676, during BACON'S REBELLION. After another fire in 1698, Virginians decided to move their capital to Williamsburg, which had a better location. Jamestown slowly shrank and died as colonists abandoned it for healthier places and more fertile land. (*See also* **Diseases and Disorders; Pocahontas; Rolfe, John; Virginia; Slavery.**)

Jefferson, Thomas

1743–1826

Statesman, author, architect, scientist, planter

One of the most admired Americans in history, Thomas Jefferson is perhaps best known as the author of the DECLARATION OF INDEPENDENCE. In clear and forceful language, he presented the colonists' reasons for breaking away from Great Britain. Jefferson spent much of his lifetime in public office, eventually becoming the third President of the United States. Outside of politics, he was endlessly curious about the world. He had a profound interest in science, loved gadgets, and was passionate about literature, music, and architecture.

Early Years. Jefferson was born on the western edge of settlement in Virginia. His father, Peter Jefferson, was a surveyor and local politician. His mother, Jane, came from the wealthy and well-connected Randolph family. Jefferson received the standard education of a young gentleman of his day, learning Latin and Greek at an early age. At 16 he entered the College of William and Mary in Williamsburg, Virginia, where he studied law and became interested in science and politics.

Achieving success as a lawyer, Jefferson began his political career in 1769 as a member of the House of Burgesses, one of the chambers of the Virginia legislature. There he joined Patrick HENRY and others who spoke out against British colonial policies.

In 1770, after his family home burned to the ground, Jefferson began building an estate on a hilltop overlooking Charlottesville, Virginia. He called the place Monticello, or "Little Mountain." During his lifetime, he was constantly modifying the design of the mansion and its gardens and reworking them. In 1772 Jefferson married Martha Wayles Skelton, who died ten years later. Only two of their six children survived to adulthood.

In 1774 Jefferson wrote an essay presenting his political views, "A Summary View of the Rights of British America." He declared that the British government had no right to make laws for the colonies because the colonists had no representatives in Parliament. Britain's only real authority in North America, Jefferson argued, came from the colonists' voluntary loyalty to the king. By emphasizing the voluntary nature of the colonists' allegiance, Jefferson implied that they could withdraw it. While many agreed with the ideas in the article, others thought that they were too extreme.

See color plate 7, vol. 3.

Revolutionary Activities. In May 1775, Jefferson attended the SECOND CONTINENTAL CONGRESS, a gathering in Philadelphia of representatives from all 13 colonies. The issue of independence became a subject of many debates and disagreements at the meeting. In May 1776, the congress selected a committee made up of Jefferson and four others to prepare a document that would set forth the reasons for separating from Great Britain. The committee chose Jefferson to draft it. In completing this task, Jefferson drew on the ideas of the ENLIGHTENMENT, a movement that exalted the power of reason and emphasized the rights of the individual. After much discussion and several changes, the congress approved the final version of the Declaration of Independence on July 2, 1776. Because it took two days to prepare a clean copy of the document, we now celebrate Independence Day on July 4.

An Enduring Friendship

Thomas Jefferson and John Adams first met at the Second Continental Congress in 1775. Over the years, the tall, soft-spoken Virginian and the short, fiery Bostonian formed an unlikely friendship. Despite their different personalities, the pair shared a deep commitment to their country and its ideals. They served together on the committee to draft the Declaration of Independence, and Jefferson was Vice President during Adams's presidency. In the following election, Jefferson defeated Adams, causing a rift between the two men. They eventually mended their friendship and began an active correspondence that continued the rest of their lives. The two men, both so involved in the founding of the United States, died within hours of each other on July 4, 1826—the fiftieth anniversary of the Declaration of Independence.

In the fall of that same year, Jefferson returned to his estate. For most of the AMERICAN REVOLUTION, he served in the government of Virginia, first in the legislature and then as governor. While in office, he proposed a number of reforms. Among his most notable achievements was the passage of a law establishing religious freedom. Jefferson believed that every individual should be free to worship—or not—according to personal choice and that the government should have no authority in religious matters.

Although a brilliant thinker and planner, Jefferson was reluctant to exercise his authority as governor. His weakness as a day-to-day leader proved to be his undoing when the British invaded Virginia during the Revolutionary War. Unwilling to take command in the crisis, Jefferson gave up his duties and fled. Although the state assembly later cleared him of any wrongdoing, the incident left a blot on his reputation for many years.

Unhappy with public service, Jefferson retired to Monticello. There he began working on *Notes on the State of Virginia.* Published several years later, the book contained detailed information about the geography, government, and culture of Virginia. *Notes* established Jefferson's reputation as a scholar and scientist.

Following the death of his wife in 1782, Jefferson was persuaded to return to government, serving as a member of the Continental Congress. While there, he helped establish the American system of currency based on dollars and cents. He also proposed plans for organizing the western territories, which included banning SLAVERY in the area.

The issue of slavery troubled Jefferson throughout his life. He often wrote about the immorality of the institution—yet he himself owned at least 100 slaves. He disapproved of slavery in principle but could think of no good

This portrait of Thomas Jefferson, author of the Declaration of Independence, was painted in 1786 for his lifelong friend John Adams by artist M. Brown.

way to end it. He did not believe that black and white people could live together in harmony as equals. Although Jefferson's ideas about liberty and equality did not include people of all races or women, his views were quite advanced for a southern slaveholder of his time.

Later Achievements. Jefferson's accomplishments did not end with the colonial period. He served as minister to France between 1785 and 1789, during that time he negotiated several important agreements. Under President George WASHINGTON, he became the nation's first secretary of state, and he served as Vice President under President John ADAMS. In 1801 he became the third President of the United States. Jefferson held the office for two terms, during which time he took steps to expand the new nation. In 1803, in an agreement called the Louisiana Purchase, he bought a huge piece of land west of the Mississippi River from France—nearly doubling the size of the United States. The following year he sent former army officers Meriwether Lewis and William Clark on their historic expedition to explore the new territory.

After leaving the presidency in 1809, Jefferson spent the rest of his life at his beloved Monticello, pursuing his many scientific and artistic interests. He sold his considerable library—more than 6,000 volumes—to the Library of Congress, doubling the size of its collection. He also founded the University of Virginia, an act that he considered one of his three great achievements—along with the Declaration of Independence and Virginia's law of religious freedom. In fact, Jefferson asked that his gravestone list only these three accomplishments. He wanted no mention of any of his political offices. (*See also* **Louisiana.**)

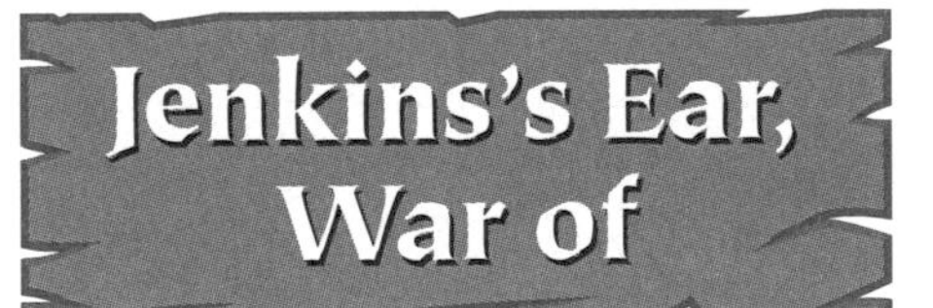

Jenkins's Ear, War of

The War of Jenkins's Ear, a colonial conflict between Great Britain and Spain in the mid-1700s, grew out of a commercial rivalry between the two nations. The fighting eventually became part of the War of the Austrian Succession, known in North America as KING GEORGE'S WAR.

During the 1730s British merchants repeatedly violated trade restrictions in Spanish America. The Spanish responded by seizing British trading ships sailing off the coast of North America. In March 1738, an English sea captain, Robert Jenkins, appeared before Parliament and displayed an amputated ear. Jenkins claimed that Spanish sailors had cut his ear off during an attack on his ship off the coast of Florida. Jenkins's story added to the wave of public sentiment against the Spanish, caused by Spain's seizure of British ships. Parliament eventually declared war on Spain in October 1739.

The War of Jenkins's Ear was fought on both water and land. Naval operations centered in the Caribbean Sea. In November 1739, a small British naval squadron commanded by Admiral Edward Vernon captured the Spanish fort of Porto Bello in Panama. The next year Vernon launched a massive attack on the city of Cartagena in Colombia. The raid was a disaster, resulting in the deaths of more than half the British forces from disease.

Warfare on land took place mainly along the frontier between Spanish Florida and Georgia. Early in 1740 James OGLETHORPE of Georgia, aided by the CREEK INDIANS, invaded Florida and seized two forts. He later led a failed mission to capture ST. AUGUSTINE. A Spanish attempt to take Georgia in 1742 met with defeat at the Battle of Bloody Marsh.

The War of Jenkins's Ear continued as a series of minor raids until the start of King George's War in 1744. Fighting intensified, and the focus of conflict shifted to Europe and Canada. (*See also* **European Empires.**)

Jesuits

Members of a Roman Catholic religious brotherhood, the Society of Jesus, Jesuits established MISSIONS throughout much of North America in an attempt to convert the Native American population to Christianity. The priests also ministered to the religious needs of Catholic settlers in the colonies.

The Society of Jesus began in 1540 in Spain. In the 1560s, Spanish Jesuits tried to establish missions in Virginia, the Carolinas, and Georgia, but their efforts met with little success. In the 1600s, however, the Jesuits became a small but important force in the exploration and settlement of North America.

In the English colonies, the Jesuits helped the CALVERT FAMILY establish the Catholic colony of Maryland in 1634. They founded Saint Mary's, the first church in the colony, and brought Christianity to the Indians of the area. The Jesuits of Maryland supported themselves by farming and even paid taxes. German Jesuits in southeastern Pennsylvania founded missions and established the colony's first Catholic church in 1733. Forty years later, during the Revolutionary War, a Jesuit founded New York's first Catholic church.

Although not the first Catholic missionaries in NEW FRANCE, the Jesuits were the most successful. They lived among the Native Americans, adopting many of their customs. They ate Indian food and preached in Indian languages. While the priests wanted to convert the Native Americans to Christianity, they tried to preserve the Indians' culture. The Jesuits refused to represent the interests of any country—unlike the Franciscan* missionaries in the Spanish Borderlands*, who worked closely with government officials.

* ***Franciscan*** member of the Order of Friars Minor, a religious brotherhood

* ***Spanish Borderlands*** northern part of New Spain, area now occupied by Florida, Texas, New Mexico, Arizona, and California

French Jesuit missionaries traveled deep into the wilderness to preach to the Indians of New York and the Great Lakes region. Father Jacques Marquette became known for his exploration of the Mississippi River in the 1670s with Louis JOLLIET.

The missionaries in the Spanish Borderlands were largely Franciscan, but one of the most influential was a Jesuit, Eusebio Francisco KINO. He founded 24 missions in Arizona between 1687 and 1711 and baptized thousands of PIMA INDIANS. He introduced wheat and other European grains to the area as well as cattle and other livestock.

Jesuit missionaries mapped much of the continent. In the course of their travels across North America, they recorded and preserved volumes of information about Native Americans and the impact of Europeans on

their culture. The priests also acted as interpreters and negotiated treaties between white settlers and Indians in an effort to promote peaceful relations between the two cultures. (*See also* **Roman Catholic Church.**)

Jews

Starting with the first voyage of Christopher Columbus, people of Jewish ancestry came in small numbers to explore and settle North America. In the "New World," they found greater freedom and acceptance than they had known in Europe. At the same time, Jews faced the challenge of establishing their faith in a new land and claiming a place in society. They met these challenges by building synagogues and becoming part of the economic and social life of the colonies.

Early Jewish Communities.

By the colonial period, Jewish communities were scattered across Europe, and smaller groups of Jews lived in parts of Asia and Africa. But anti-Semitism* frequently made their lives difficult, especially in the Roman Catholic nations of Europe.

* ***anti-Semitism*** hostility toward and discrimination against Jews

In the 1490s, the rulers of Spain and Portugal ordered all Jews to leave their countries. Jews who wished to remain had to convert to Christianity. These converts were called New Christians or *conversos.* At least six *conversos* accompanied Columbus on his first journey to the Americas. Many others later went to the Spanish colony of New Spain. Some *conversos* secretly observed Jewish religious holidays, despite the risk of severe punishment. Those discovered could be imprisoned or burned at the stake by the Catholic Church and the colonial government.

Some Jews who left Spain and Portugal settled in the Netherlands. After the Netherlands took control of the Portuguese colony of Recife in Brazil in 1629, as many as 1,000 Jews migrated there. In 1654 the Portuguese recaptured Recife, and the Jews fled. Most returned to the Netherlands. Some went to Dutch, British, and French islands in the Caribbean Sea, where they established Jewish communities. Twenty-three of the refugees from Recife landed in New Amsterdam, the capital of the Dutch colony of New Netherland. Their arrival marked the beginning of the history of Jews in North America.

Jews in North America.

Peter STUYVESANT, the director general of New Netherland, did not want the Jews to stay in the colony. But he was overruled by the directors of the DUTCH WEST INDIA COMPANY, the trading company that ran New Netherland. By 1657 the colony's Jews had won full rights of citizenship. At the same time, they struggled to maintain their religious life. They lacked a rabbi but had prayer books and prayer shawls. A man named Asser Levy, who became a leading merchant, helped keep the Jewish community in New Amsterdam alive by encouraging religious practices.

In 1664 the English took control of New Netherland and renamed it New York. English law and local custom allowed Jews to vote, hold office, and conduct public worship. The Jewish population grew slowly but steadily. In 1730 the Jews of New York City built a small synagogue, the first in British North America. Jews took an active part in the life of the colony as merchants, artisans*, public officials, and members of the militia*.

* ***artisan*** skilled crafts worker
* ***militia*** army of citizens who may be called into action in a time of emergency

Because of its commitment to religious freedom, Rhode Island attracted many Jewish settlers in colonial times. The Touro Synagogue of Newport, built between 1759 and 1763, is the oldest synagogue in the United States today.

Jewish communities arose elsewhere in the British colonies. Rhode Island, with a history of religious freedom, attracted many Jews. Most settled in and around the town of NEWPORT. With the help of New York Jews, the Jewish colonists of Newport constructed the Touro Synagogue. Completed in 1763, it is the oldest synagogue in the United States today and one of the glories of colonial architecture.

Other Jews, especially merchants and traders, settled in the bustling port of Philadelphia and formed a community there. In 1733 more than 70 Jewish immigrants arrived in Savannah in the newly formed colony of Georgia. The colony's governor welcomed them, perhaps because a Jewish doctor named Samuel Nunez had brought an outbreak of disease under control. A substantial Jewish community also developed in Charleston, South Carolina.

Very few Jews settled in the French colonies of North America. This was due largely to religious intolerance* and a lack of economic opportunity. After the British conquered New France in 1763, a small Jewish community began to form there. By the mid-1770s, the whole of Canada may have had about 50 Jewish families. A synagogue was founded in Montreal, the third in North America. Some Jewish merchants had settled in French Louisiana, but when Spain took over the region in 1763, they left. Except for *conversos,* Jews avoided the Spanish colonies because of religious persecution.

* ***intolerance*** rejecting the beliefs and practices of others

Jewish Life in America.

The Jews in North America were divided into two groups: the Ashkenazim and the Sephardim. The Ashkenazim came from Germany, eastern Europe, and Russia. The Sephardim were descended from Jews who had lived in Spain and Portugal during the Middle Ages. The Ashkenazim and Sephardim often lived and worshipped together in the early colonial period. As the Jewish population increased, however, they began forming separate congregations in order to follow their different religious traditions.

Both groups faced difficulties in America, especially in the early colonial period, when there were few established Jewish communities to help newcomers. Without rabbis and other experts in religious matters, Jews found it hard to follow the customs of their faith, and they could not always find teachers to provide religious education to the young. Although the colonies had greater religious freedom than Europe, anti-Semitism still existed, and Jews often faced intolerance and discrimination*. Jews in America also discovered a new problem—the difficulty of maintaining their religious and cultural identity in a society where they mingled freely with people of other cultures and faiths.

* ***discrimination*** unfair treatment of a group

Jews in Revolutionary America.

By the time of the American Revolution, some 2,500 Jews lived among the 3 million settlers in the British colonies. Most lived in cities and worked as shopkeepers, traders, merchants, and artisans. Few Jews became farmers. For centuries in Europe, they had been forbidden to own land and thus had little experience with agriculture.

Like other colonists, Jews were divided by the American Revolution. Some remained loyal to Britain. Most, however, favored independence. A number of Jews fought with distinction in the Continental Army. Haym Salomon, a Jew from Poland who lived in Philadelphia, made another kind of contribution. By raising money for the war effort and making loans to patriot* leaders, he helped finance the Revolution. (*See also* **Religious Life in European Colonies.**)

* ***patriot*** American colonist who supported independence from Britain

Jicarilla Apache Indians

See *Apache Indians.*

Johnson, Sir William

1715–1774
British superintendent of Indian affairs

One of the largest landholders in the British colonies, Sir William Johnson established close ties with the Mohawk Indians. As superintendent of Indian affairs, he helped keep the Iroquois on the side of the British during their struggle with the French for control of North America.

Born to a poor family in Ireland, Johnson immigrated to New York in 1738 to manage his uncle's estate in the Mohawk Valley. He began trading with the Indians and developed a close association with the Mohawk, a tribe in the IROQUOIS CONFEDERACY. He learned to speak their language and often adopted their style of dress. After the death of his wife, Johnson formed a relationship with Mary (Molly) Brant, the sister of Mohawk chief Joseph BRANT. The couple had several children. Johnson earned the trust and affection of the Indians, who gave him several large tracts of land. His landholdings and trade with the Iroquois made him extremely wealthy.

During KING GEORGE'S WAR (1744–1748), Johnson succeeded in gaining the Iroquois's support for the British. A skilled diplomat, he became colonel of the Iroquois League in 1746. His duties included holding councils with the Indian tribes and organizing attacks on the French. In one instance, Johnson dressed and painted himself like a Mohawk warrior and led a war party to Albany, New York, to join the British forces.

In 1755 the British made Johnson superintendent of Indian affairs in the northern colonies, a post he held for nearly 20 years. During the FRENCH AND INDIAN WAR (1755–1763), he negotiated an alliance between the British and the Iroquois and led a force of colonists and Indians against the French. In 1759 his troops captured Fort Niagara, and they helped take Montreal a year later. King GEORGE III rewarded Johnson for his actions with the title of baronet.

Johnson devoted much of his later years to maintaining peace between Native Americans and the colonists. He helped bring an end to PONTIAC'S War, an Indian campaign against British forts along the western frontier. In 1768 Johnson negotiated the Treaty of Fort Stanwix, which established boundaries between British settlements and Indian territory. Throughout his life, Johnson remained loyal to Britain and opposed the colonists' movement for independence.

Jolliet, Louis, and Jacques Marquette

Louis Jolliet
1645–1700
French explorer

Jacques Marquette
1637–1675
French explorer and missionary

In the 1670s Louis Jolliet and Father Jacques Marquette became the first Europeans to follow the course of the MISSISSIPPI RIVER. Their expedition served as the basis for France's claim to the Mississippi River valley, a region that the French held on to until 1763.

Born in Quebec, Louis Jolliet was educated in the Jesuit* schools of that city and later spent a year studying in France. After returning to North America in 1668, he began exploring the frontiers of NEW FRANCE. His first voyages took him into the western Great Lakes region, where he met a French Jesuit missionary called Father Marquette. The priest had come to North America a few years earlier to teach Christianity to the Indians. He had lived among the Native Americans and learned several of their languages.

In 1672 French colonial officials asked Jolliet to lead an expedition in search of a great river they had heard about from local Indians. The officials hoped that it was a NORTHWEST PASSAGE to the Pacific Ocean. Jolliet agreed

* ***Jesuit*** Roman Catholic religious order

* ***portage*** to carry goods or boats from one body of water to another

See third map in Exploration, Age of (vol. 2).

to go and requested that Father Marquette serve as the party's chaplain and Christian ambassador to the Indians.

Jolliet and Marquette spent the winter of 1672–1673 preparing for the journey. In May they set out with five men in two bark canoes. They paddled into Green Bay, an arm of Lake Michigan, and then south down the Fox River. Indians showed them where to portage* to the Wisconsin River. The Wisconsin flowed into a much larger waterway, which the explorers quickly recognized as the river they were seeking. Jolliet named it the Colbert River after the prime minister of France. But the name was soon forgotten, and the river continued to be known by its Indian name—the Mississippi.

The French explorers saw remarkable sights along their journey, including huge Native American paintings on cliffs along the river banks, enormous catfish, and wild rapids where another large river—the Missouri—flowed into the Mississippi. But they soon realized that the Mississippi was not the long-sought Northwest Passage because it flowed south, not west.

In four months, Jolliet and Marquette covered almost 2,500 miles, much of it on the Mississippi. About 400 miles from the Gulf of Mexico, in what is now Arkansas, they encountered Indians who told them about Europeans farther downriver. Realizing they were entering territory controlled by Spain, France's enemy, the explorers turned around and began paddling north against the mighty river's current.

Instead of retracing their course, the explorers followed an easier route back to the Great Lakes, which they had learned about from some Indians. They traveled up the Mississippi to the Illinois River and made a short portage to the site where the city of Chicago now stands, on the southern tip of Lake Michigan. Marquette remained at a mission on the lake while Jolliet returned to New France.

Only Marquette's written account of the journey survived. Jolliet lost his journal and maps when his canoe overturned in rapids on the way back to New France, and he had to draw maps of the journey from memory. Neither of the explorers ever returned to the Mississippi River. Marquette died in the wilderness, and Jolliet was lost at sea in the Gulf of St. Lawrence.

The "discovery" of the Mississippi was a milestone in the European exploration of North America. It paved the way for René-Robert Cavelier de LA SALLE and later explorers of the Mississippi River valley and for the colonization of the region by the French. (*See also* **Exploration, Age of; Jesuits.**)

Judicial System

See ***Laws and Legal Systems.***

Kentucky

The territory that became the state of Kentucky was a frontier region in colonial times. Bordered on the north by the Ohio River and extending west to the Mississippi River, it eventually attracted settlers migrating from the eastern colonies. Its central location between the northern and the southern colonies played an important part in Kentucky's history.

The name *Kentucky* comes from a Cherokee word with several meanings, including "dark and bloody ground," which suits some of Kentucky's past. Long before the arrival of white settlers, ancient Indian trails wound through Kentucky's forests. Colonists from the Carolinas began to hunt along the region's many streams in the 1750s, searching for skins and furs. James Harrod and Daniel Boone and other woodsmen explored the territory in the 1770s. Harrod led a group of traders up the Kentucky River in 1774 and established Harrodsburg, the first settlement in Kentucky. The following year Daniel Boone helped build a road—known as the Wilderness Road—through the Cumberland Gap, a passage over the mountains where present-day Kentucky, Tennessee, and Virginia meet. South of the Kentucky River he founded the town of Boonesborough.

The Indians of the area objected to the new settlers and fought against them ferociously. But despite the frequent Indian raids, pioneers continued to arrive, staking claims all over Kentucky. The violence continued during the American Revolution, when the British encouraged groups of Indians to attack the American settlers.

By 1790 Kentucky's rich land had attracted more than 70,000 settlers. The area was controlled by Virginia, although many residents hoped to establish a separate government. After much debate, the settlers decided to form a new state, and they drew up a constitution. In June 1792, Kentucky became the fifteenth state of the United States. (*See also* **Appalachian Mountains; Frontier.**)

Kidd, Captain

ca. 1645–1701

Pirate

* ***privateer*** privately owned ship authorized by the government to attack and capture enemy vessels; also the ship's master

Captain Kidd was hired by the English government to make the seas safe for merchant vessels. Instead, he turned to looting the ships he had been sent to protect and became one of the most notorious PIRATES of the colonial period.

Born in Scotland, William Kidd immigrated to New York, where he became the owner and captain of a ship. When England and France went to war in 1690, he joined the fight against the French privateers* who were attacking English ships off the North American coast.

In 1695 merchants complained to the English government about the pirates who threatened their vessels loaded with valuable goods from Asia. The governor of New England and several English nobles asked Kidd to raid the pirate ships. They would finance the mission in return for a share of the profits from any captured treasure. Kidd purchased an armed ship and recruited crew members from London and New York City.

In September 1696, the captain set sail from New York. After six months at sea his ship was leaking, a third of his crew had died from disease, and he had captured no pirates. The angry crew—who would receive no pay if the mission failed—threatened mutiny against the captain. Kidd then crossed the line between privateer and pirate and began raiding the very merchant ships he had been hired to protect. He also killed a crew member during a disagreement.

Outraged by Kidd's actions, English authorities declared him a pirate and sent a squadron of ships to capture him. Kidd sailed back to the colonies with his loot and tried to persuade the governor of New England to grant him a pardon. Instead, he was arrested and sent to London for trial. Found guilty

of piracy and murder, Kidd was publicly hanged in 1701. The government seized his property, including what remained of his pirate treasure. Since that time, however, rumors have persisted that Kidd buried part of his loot before his arrest.

King George's War, known in Europe as the War of the Austrian Succession, was one of many conflicts between Britain and France during the colonial period. Ending 30 years of peace, it launched a new series of clashes that concluded with the French and Indian War.

The colonization of North America had added new areas of dispute to the long-running rivalry between Britain and France. The two nations now competed for control of fishing grounds in the North Atlantic, the fur trade, and North American territory—particularly the Ohio River valley. Whenever France and Britain went to war in Europe, fighting inevitably broke out along the border between New France and the British colonies.

King George's War began as a power struggle among the European powers. Britain and France entered the conflict and declared war on each other in 1744. Fighting erupted across the Atlantic in Nova Scotia, when soldiers from the French fort of Louisbourg occupied a British fishing village in May 1744 and then launched an unsuccessful assault against the town of Annapolis Royal, formerly the French settlement of Port Royal. A year later British colonists, supported by the British navy, struck back by capturing Louisbourg in the most decisive victory in the war.

Although French ships tried to retake Louisbourg in 1746, storms and disease hampered their attempt. The British also failed that same year to carry out a planned attack on Quebec. For the remainder of the war, the conflict was limited to brutal but indecisive frontier raids by both sides and by their Indian allies.

The war ended in 1748. Under the terms of the peace treaty, the Treaty of Aix-la-Chapelle, the British returned Louisbourg to the French, and both sides exchanged prisoners. But the war had settled nothing, and the basic conflicts between Britain and France remained. Within a few years, the two nations were once again fighting for control of North America.

King Philip

See *Metacom.*

King Philip's War pitted Native Americans against New England colonists in the bloodiest conflict of the early colonial period. The war devastated many frontier settlements, but it also eliminated Indian resistance to colonization in the region.

For years the colonists and Indians of New England had lived peacefully side by side. In the mid-1600s, however, new waves of English settlers pushed more deeply into Indian land, alarming the Native Americans. Chief

King Philip's War

Metacom, called King Philip by the English, was a Wampanoag Indian chief who led members of several tribes in a revolt against New England colonists. Although the Indians had the advantage at first, they were eventually crushed by the colonists and their Mohawk allies.

METACOM of the WAMPANOAG INDIANS, known by the English as King Philip, vowed to resist further expansion by the colonists. He gained the support of some New England tribes, including the powerful NARRAGANSETT INDIANS, who shared his distrust of the colonists. But other Indians, many of whom had become Christians, joined the English side.

In June 1675, authorities of the PLYMOUTH COLONY hanged three Wampanoag Indians for murdering a Christian Indian—an informer who had reported Metacom's activities to the English. The Wampanoag sought revenge for the executions. They attacked nearby farms and raided settlements. In response, colonial militia* units launched brutal assaults on Indian villages.

King Philip's War continued for more than a year as a series of attacks and counterattacks by Indians and settlers. At first the Native Americans had the advantage because colonial troops were poorly equipped and unfamiliar with Indian-style warfare. However, by the spring of 1676, the Indians had been weakened by disease and were on the brink of starvation. Their crops had been destroyed by the colonists. Perhaps more importantly, the Mohawk of New York, members of the IROQUOIS CONFEDERACY, entered the war on the side of the English and began attacking the New England Indians from the west.

* *militia* army of citizens who may be called into action in a time of emergency

See color plate 4, vol. 4.

In August 1676, a colonial militia unit surrounded Metacom's camp. An Indian fighting on the English side shot and killed the Wampanoag chief as he tried to escape. With Metacom's death, the last Native American resistance collapsed and the war ended. Fighting continued for another year, however, in New Hampshire and present-day Maine between colonists and the ABENAKI INDIANS.

King Philip's War destroyed dozens of English settlements and killed an estimated 2,000 colonists. It devastated many Native American villages and almost wiped out several tribes. The war marked the final defeat of New England's Indians and cleared the way for English expansion.

King William's War (1689–1697)

King William's War was part of a larger European conflict, the War of the League of Augsburg. Though small in comparison with the massive struggle raging in Europe, this American war marked the beginning of a long and bitter conflict between England and France over the future of the colonies.

Trouble was brewing in North America before the war began. The French and English, rivals for control of the FUR TRADE, had been attacking each other's trading posts for years. Indians played a significant role in the frontier assaults. The IROQUOIS, allies of the English, raided French settlements in the St. Lawrence Valley. The French and their Indian allies, the ABENAKI and MICMAC, attacked English communities in the northeast. Meanwhile, the English colonists had troubles of their own to deal with. In 1686 the New England colonies were protesting the king's decision to combine them into the DOMINION OF NEW ENGLAND. Two years later, LEISLER'S REBELLION—which involved an uprising against the governor of New York—divided the people of that colony.

When word of the war between France and England reached North America in 1689, the colonial conflict immediately grew more intense. The French and their Indian allies launched bold and destructive raids on English settlements in New York and New England. In this time of danger, the quarreling New Englanders came together, formed an army, and captured the French town of PORT ROYAL in May 1690. The English colonists wanted to attack Montreal and Quebec as well, but they lacked the financial and military resources to carry out their plan.

Both England and France sent fleets to help their colonists. However, storms delayed the ships, and sickness and a shortage of supplies kept the troops from being effective. In the end, the English and French colonists had to fight with their own resources and the help of Indian allies. During the course of the war, the French generally had more success in their border raids and minor clashes. They managed to spread terror along the New England frontier.

King William's War ended in 1697 with the Treaty of Ryswick, in which the two sides agreed to exchange prisoners and territory they had captured. But the treaty did not bring a lasting peace, only a lull in the fighting. The conflict between France and England in North America continued into the next century and concluded with the FRENCH AND INDIAN WAR. (*See also* **King George's War; Queen Anne's War.**)

Kino, Eusebio Francisco

ca. 1645–1711
Missionary and explorer

Eusebio Kino was one of the first Europeans to explore Arizona and northern Mexico. A Jesuit missionary, he lived among the Pima Indians and converted thousands of them to Christianity. In 1700 he founded the mission of San Xavier del Bac near what is now the city of Tucson.

Born in Italy, Kino joined the Jesuit order in 1665, after recovering from a serious illness. Sent to New Spain in the 1680s, he helped establish settlements in Baja California, a peninsula on the Pacific coast. In 1687 church authorities assigned Kino to work in Pimería Alta, an area that is now occupied by northwestern Mexico and southern Arizona. There he founded many missions and peacefully expanded the northern boundaries of New Spain. The Jesuit approached the Indians he met with kind words and a friendly manner, often giving them small presents. He is said to have converted 4,500 to Christianity. Known as the "Black Robe" among the local Pima Indians, Kino also taught them ranching and farming skills.

The energetic priest also found time to explore mountains, plains, and canyons, covering thousands of miles on foot and on mule and horseback. The blue shells he received in some of his trades reminded him of shells along the Pacific coast. Wondering if there might be a link between Arizona and the Pacific, he set off along the Colorado River in 1699 and followed it until he reached California. He made many maps and kept detailed journals of his travels.

Kino died in Pimería Alta. A bay along the northwestern Mexican coast, Bahia de Kino, is named after him. (*See also* **California; Jesuits.**)

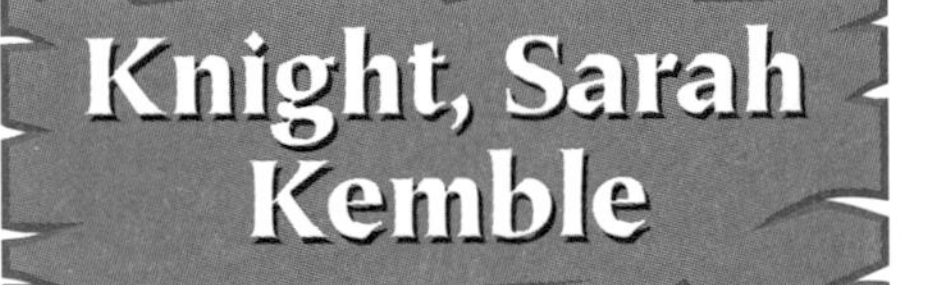

Knight, Sarah Kemble

1666–1727
Diarist

Sarah Kemble Knight is noted for her account of a journey she made on horseback from Boston to New York City in the early 1700s. Her travel diary provides a remarkable record of life and times in colonial New England.

Born in Boston, Sarah Kemble was the oldest daughter of Thomas Kemble, a merchant and landowner, and his wife, Elizabeth. Sarah received an unusually good education for a woman of her day. In 1689 she married Richard Knight, and together they had one child, Elizabeth.

In the fall of 1704, Sarah Knight set out alone on horseback for New York City to settle some family business. Travel conditions at that time were poor, and Knight had to endure many hardships. Roads—when they existed—were rocky, muddy, and uneven. Bridges were poorly constructed. One time she and her horse had to inch across a rickety wooden bridge suspended 50 feet above the water. Although she hired guides, she frequently lost her way in the wilderness.

In addition to writing about the dangers of the road, Knight described the food and sleeping quarters of the farmhouses and inns where she lodged. She also recorded in great detail the clothing and speech of other travelers. Despite the dangers and discomforts of her trip, Knight displayed a keen sense of humor in her journal. She returned safely to Boston the following spring.

After her husband's death sometime around 1706, Knight ran a store and a boardinghouse in her home. Several years later she moved to Connecticut,

where her married daughter lived. "Madam" Knight, as she came to be called, operated a shop in Norwich, Connecticut, and bought land in nearby New London. She also managed an inn at one of her farms in the area.

After Sarah Knight's death in 1727, her diary was passed along by private individuals for almost a hundred years. Finally published in 1825, *The Journal of Madam Knight* has fascinated generations of readers. *(See also* **Diaries; Transportation and Travel; Women, Roles of.**)

Labor

* ***indentured servant*** person who agreed to work a certain length of time in return for passage on a ship to the colonies

* ***Spanish Borderlands*** northern part of New Spain, area now occupied by Florida, Texas, New Mexico, Arizona, and California

Labor was scarce in the early colonial period. There were simply not enough people to do the work that had to be done. The colonists dealt with the labor shortage in various ways. They hired free workers who exchanged their time and services for some form of payment. They also depended on indentured servants* and slaves, known as bound laborers. These workers were required to serve others, either for a set number of years or, in the case of slaves, for life.

Colonists also made arrangements to help each other when work needed to be done. People in farming communities often cooperated on big projects, such as the construction of a new barn. Those who helped build a neighbor's barn knew that their work would entitle them to similar help in the future. Colonists often kept written records of labor "loaned" and "borrowed" in this way.

Women played a vital role in the colonial labor force. Few worked outside the home or received pay for their labor. However, all but wealthy women spent long hours doing housework, gardening, and making cloth and other household goods. Women also worked in the fields at busy times, such as the spring planting or the fall harvest.

Very few colonial families could get by on their own without any help in the fields or the workshop or in producing basic household goods. At some point in their lives, most colonists either worked for someone else or used the labor of others. The many people who came to America as indentured servants or hired laborers did so in the hope that one day they would be able to work for themselves instead of for someone else.

Each colonial region had its own labor system. In the Spanish Borderlands*, landowners backed by the Catholic Church and the army forced local Indians to work for them. In New France, officials hired crafts workers and laborers to come to the colony. In British North America, settlers in New England and the middle colonies relied mostly on hired labor. In the Chesapeake and southern colonies, landowners used indentured servants at first, but they later turned to slave labor.

Hired Labor. Hired laborers were free to enter or leave employment at will. In some cases they received payment in cash for their work. But cash was rare in the colonies, and hired laborers often received housing or goods as pay. One common arrangement was for an unmarried "hired man" to live with a family for a season or a year. In exchange for work in the fields or workshop, he was provided with a home, meals, laundry services, and whatever small wages the employer could pay.

Because of the labor shortage, most workers had to be able to do a variety of jobs. The famous Paul REVERE, for example, was a silversmith and an engraver, but he also manufactured cannons, sheet copper for ships, gunpowder, and dental devices. On the side, Revere served as a coroner and organized a fire insurance company. Other crafts workers often found additional employment as seasonal farm laborers. When the planting or the harvest was over, the artisans* would return to their workshops.

* ***artisan*** skilled crafts worker

Attracting hired laborers—especially skilled workers such as artisans—was a problem throughout most of the colonial period. Because labor was so scarce, wages were high—anywhere from 30 to 100 percent higher than those in England. Information about wages and living conditions in the colonies circulated freely in Europe and influenced the flow of workers to America. One reason for the scarcity of labor in New France, for example, was that people in France heard reports of the colony's harsh climate but not of the economic opportunities there.

Keeping workers could be difficult as well. Some employers used the "company store" method, selling goods to employees on credit. To repay their debts, the employees would have to do additional work. This system worked best in areas where employees had little choice about where to buy

In the plantation economy of the South, most of the labor was supplied by slaves. There were not enough free laborers available to do the amount of work required in planting and harvesting such crops as rice and tobacco.

goods. Men who sailed on New England whaling vessels, for example, often found it necessary to sign on for additional voyages to pay for goods they had purchased. Landowners in the Spanish Borderlands encouraged Indian laborers to go into debt and then used the debts to force the Indians to keep working, a system known as debt peonage.

In the early colonial period, unemployment was almost nonexistent. There was much work to be done, and almost anyone who wanted land could get it and become a farmer. By the mid-1700s, however, land was no longer readily available, especially in the heavily settled areas around cities. Colonists who did not own land had to work for wages, yet jobs were becoming scarce. The colonies had begun to import more goods from abroad, resulting in less work for local artisans. At the same time, a growing population was expanding the supply of labor. With so many people wanting to work, employers could find people who would accept lower wages. As a result, both unemployment and poverty among hired workers began to increase in the 1760s.

Bound Labor. There were three main kinds of bound labor in the colonies: APPRENTICESHIP, servitude*, and SLAVERY. Apprenticeship involved both labor and education. An apprentice was a youth, usually a boy, sent by his parents to work for a master crafts worker or professional for a certain number of years. In exchange for his labor, the apprentice received food, clothing, and housing; training in a trade or profession; and often a basic education and perhaps a small amount of money.

* ***servitude*** forced labor

Servitude covered a broad range of relationships between workers and employers. Many workers in the North American colonies were indentured servants. Most entered voluntarily into servitude because they wanted to come to America. They agreed to work for a certain length of time, generally four or five years, in exchange for their ship passage and for food, lodging, and clothing during their indenture, or work period. Indentured servants sometimes received a sum of money, known as "freedom dues," at the end of their period of service.

Some individuals—prisoners of war, criminals, and orphans—were forced to become bound laborers. European governments sent convicts and orphans into servitude in the colonies as a way of ridding their nations of undesirable citizens. Sometimes children and adults were kidnapped in Europe and forced to come to America as bound laborers.

Slavery, which also was based on force, reduced laborers to the legal status of property or possessions. Slavery became the dominant labor system in the British colonies of the South, where crops such as tobacco and rice that required enormous amounts of labor dominated the economy. However, slavery was not limited to southern PLANTATIONS. People in other regions also owned slaves.

In colonial cities, slaves sometimes worked in a "self-hire" system, in which they were allowed to find jobs but were required to pay their owners a share of their wages. In Philadelphia during the 1700s, for example, about 40 percent of the city's slaves worked for artisans or owners of craft shops such as brickyards. Female slaves in cities often hired themselves out to do laundry, cleaning, and sewing.

Child Labor

Children were an important part of the colonial labor force. Families counted on boys and girls to do chores at home or on family farms. If a family owned a business or had a workshop, the children worked there as well. Young people who earned money outside the home contributed it to the family income—an employer generally gave a young person's wages directly to the parents. Many children became apprentices, working for others as they learned a craft or profession. Children from poor families often worked as indentured servants, as did orphans and poor children who came to the colonies from Europe.

British America was the land of the unfree rather than the free. Nine out of every ten people who came to the colonies were indentured servants or slaves. Their labor was vital to the establishment, survival, and growth of the colonies. The servants among them could look forward to eventual freedom and perhaps even prosperity; the enslaved laborers had no such hope.

The Spanish colonies developed several kinds of bound labor. At first, the Spanish enslaved Native Americans and forced them to work. When the government outlawed slavery, the *ENCOMIENDA* system emerged. Colonists received large grants of land, called *encomiendas,* which included the services of the Indians who lived there. Although not considered slaves, the Indians could be forced to work for the landowner. After disease greatly reduced the Indian population, Spanish colonists began importing African slaves to do the work.

The *encomienda* system eventually gave way to *repartimiento,* a system that restricted the forced labor of Native Americans to projects approved by the government, such as planting and harvesting crops. As the colonial population grew, the need for labor increased. Indian workers began competing directly with Spanish artisans and negotiating with employers for wages. The first to receive regular wages were mine workers. Gradually, other Indian workers became free hired laborers as well. To hold and control workers, though, landowners came to rely on debt peonage, thus creating another form of bound labor. (*See also* **Agriculture; Artisans; Crafts; Economic Systems; Indentured Servants; Industries.**)

Lakota Indians

See *Plains Indians.*

By about 1600, most of the desirable land in Europe had been cleared and settled. Land was expensive, and in many places, a small group of wealthy people controlled much of the land. Few ordinary Europeans could hope to acquire property unless they inherited it.

North America was different. A huge place, it was largely uninhabited except for the Indians, whose claims to the land Europeans generally brushed aside. Moreover, America was a wilderness. Completely unlike the tame countryside of Europe, the continent bristled with dense forests and had no roads. Its vast, empty spaces provided a powerful lure to land-hungry Europeans. Not everyone who came to America wanted to own property, however, and not all of those who desired it achieved their goal. Land became a commodity* to be bought, sold, traded, and hoarded. As with any commodity, some people ended up with much more of it than others.

* ***commodity*** article of trade

Patterns of landholding in the colonies reflected the ways in which the European nations had distributed land. The parent countries—England, the Netherlands, France, and Spain—laid claim to territory by right of discovery or conquest. The land within a territory then belonged to the European monarch or governing body. In granting or selling tracts* of their North American lands,

* ***tract*** area of land

these rulers tried to find ways to encourage settlement so as to strengthen their territorial claims and to develop colonies that would quickly bring them profit. In the process of distribution, each European country tended to reproduce its particular system of landholding.

Europeans, Indians, and the Land

* ***proprietor*** person granted land and the right to establish a colony

* ***title*** legal ownership; document proving ownership

European rulers gave some individuals known as proprietors* large tracts of land in North America. Many royal land grants, though, went to companies that wanted to trade in American resources or settle and develop colonies. The proprietors and companies that held title* to the land had the power to divide it as they saw fit, usually by making smaller grants or selling property. In this way, colonial governments, landlords, and individuals acquired plots of land. These were further divided and distributed through buying, selling, and trading.

Before Europeans could settle North America, they had to arrive at some arrangement with the people who already occupied it—the Native Americans. In the early years, representatives of the monarch or colonial administrations took charge of acquiring land from the Indians. Later some colonists made individual arrangements directly. All such dealings were complicated by the fact that the Europeans and Indians had very different ideas about land ownership.

The colonists' views came from European tradition and law. To them, ownership was exclusive—no one could use property without the owner's permission. It was also permanent, meaning that land remained in the owner's possession forever unless sold or given away. In addition, Europeans believed that all land belonged to some person or organization—whether to an individual, a company, a town, or a nation—and it could have only one owner at a time.

The Walking Purchase

William Penn, the founder of Pennsylvania, was famous for his fair and friendly treatment of the Indians. By 1737 the colony's top officials, Penn's heirs, had abandoned his high standards. They made a deal with the Delaware Indians to buy as much land as a man could walk over in a day and a half. The Indians believed the distance would not be great. But the officials fooled the Indians with a misleading map, and they sent very fast walkers to pace out the purchase. The walkers covered 64 miles, and the Delaware lost the fertile Lehigh Valley. To the Indians, the Walking Purchase was a symbol of white greed and trickery.

Native Americans, on the other hand, considered themselves users of the land, not owners. They did not believe that anyone could own land in the same way that a person owned a pot or a spear. In their view, land could and often did "belong" to groups of people who shared what it produced. Thus, when Indians began selling land to Europeans, they believed they were selling the right to share in its use. They did not think they had given up all rights to the land because they did not understand the European ideas of permanent and exclusive ownership. These different views of land ownership led to tragic misunderstandings and conflicts.

British Settlements

The English colonists came from a country that was still primarily agricultural. To them, owning land meant security, the ability to feed themselves and their families, and the opportunity to become independent. To the colonists' great annoyance, one element of the English system of land ownership—a yearly payment called the quitrent—appeared in all colonies outside of New England. Colonial governments often charged quitrents on the lands they granted to settlers. Although these charges were not high and were in many cases ignored, colonists resented them as a symbol of obligation to the colonial proprietor or the English crown.

Regional Differences. New England, the Chesapeake and southern colonies, and the middle colonies developed their own patterns of land ownership. In New England, royal officials granted tracts of land to the leaders of groups who wanted to build towns. These town founders became proprietors with the power to divide up their tracts. For the most part, they distributed land according to a person's status* within the community. Well-to-do and influential people received more acres than ordinary laborers.

* ***status*** social position

Town proprietors in New England adopted either the open-field or the closed-field system. In open-field communities, much of the property remained in the hands of the town government, with only small pieces released to private control. The public land could be used by all members of the community. In closed-field communities, proprietors quickly turned most land over to private owners, who then had permanent and exclusive control over their property. By the end of the 1600s, the closed-field system had become more common, and a market for land developed as colonists bought and sold their shares.

The PURITANS of New England rejected the English tradition of primogeniture, which required that land be passed down undivided to the oldest son in a family. Because of primogeniture, the English countryside was dominated by

This 1750 Pennsylvania landscape shows the small family farms typical of the middle colonies.

large estates that passed from one generation to the next. The Puritans' practice was to divide their land among all their sons, which meant that after a few generations, many of the farms were too small to support families. People who could not buy more land became tenant farmers*, looked for other ways to earn a living, or moved to the frontier, where land was available.

* ***tenant farmer*** person who farms land owned by another and pays rent with a share of the produce or in cash

Settlers in the Chesapeake colonies of Virginia and Maryland focused on large-scale farming of export crops such as tobacco and wheat. These crops required considerable labor, which was more expensive than the land itself. Proprietors used land to attract workers to the colonies. Individuals who paid their own way to America received a headright, a grant of 50 acres of land. Colonists could also acquire headrights by paying the transportation costs for other people—each passage earned the payer one headright. Headrights became commodities in a growing real estate market, with colonists selling them back and forth repeatedly.

Under laws passed in the Chesapeake colonies, people could not buy land unless they were able to farm it. As a result, only colonists who could afford a large labor force could acquire major landholdings. By about 1650, the most desirable tracts of land in eastern Virginia belonged to large estates. People who arrived after that time had to look for land in the frontier regions to the west.

Remember: *Words in small capital letters have separate entries, and the index at the end of Volume 4 will guide you to more information on many topics.*

INDENTURED SERVANTS, who agreed to work for a set number of years in exchange for passage to America, provided the first source of labor in the Chesapeake colonies. These individuals dreamed of owning land when their period of servitude was over. Some did acquire property, but for many indentured servants, ownership remained out of reach. Either land was unavailable, or they could not afford the tools, livestock, seed, and supplies required until their farms became productive. Many former servants became tenant farmers, at least until they had saved enough money to buy their own property. Tenants provided large landholders with the labor they needed to work their estates.

The headright system benefited some early colonists in South Carolina, who built up large estates with the land acquired in payment for transporting slaves to the colony. In North Carolina, royal officials often granted larger headrights than allowed by law in an effort to help the colony grow. These tracts of land went to important colonists, such as government officials. Even so, people with small farms held most of the land in the colony.

The founders of Georgia hoped to create a population of independent farmers on small pieces of property. They also wanted to protect the colony from Indians and from the Spanish in Florida. For this reason, they carefully controlled the distribution of land and required that each plot have at least one man living on it to defend the area. Because of such policies, Georgia began as a society of small farmers. By 1750, however, colonists were free to buy and sell property as they wished, and some began building large estates.

In the middle colonies—New York, New Jersey, and Pennsylvania—the overwhelming majority of people lived off the land. Their farms were small, but generally larger than those in New England. To keep property in their families, they often tried to buy additional land for their children instead of breaking up farms into smaller and smaller plots. Land in southeastern Pennsylvania was fertile and cheap, earning the region the nickname "the best poor man's country." Even there, however, not everyone could acquire property, and many became tenant farmers. Property owners built roads and even houses on their land and kept rents low to attract tenants. Nevertheless, some people decided to take their chances on the western frontier, where settling required backbreaking work but land was still available.

Land Speculation. By the late 1600s, land speculation had appeared in the colonies. Speculators were people or companies that bought as much land as possible in the hope of making a profit by selling it later in plots. Most colonial governments tried to limit or discourage land speculation because they wanted to see property in the hands of many small owners rather than a few large landowners. But speculators ignored laws or found ways to get around them. In 1768, for example, they acquired thousands of acres of western land by arranging for groups of "settlers" to buy plots and then turn over title to the land in exchange for a small fee.

In the late 1600s, grants by English officials to certain individuals in New York resulted in the creation of huge estates of hundreds of thousands of acres called manors. Despite protests from tenants and would-be settlers about the amount of land taken up by the manors, this system of estates survived through the colonial period.

Land speculation on a large or small scale was a common feature of economic life throughout the British colonies, both in towns and in rural areas. Some of the most successful speculators were government officials. But not all speculators became rich. Many lost money when they failed to sell off lands they had bought. Still, speculators played an important role in drawing settlers to the western edges of the colonies.

Dutch Settlements

In the early days, colonists in NEW NETHERLAND were not allowed to own land or profit from working it. For this reason, Dutch farmers had little interest in leaving Europe to settle in the colony.

In the late 1620s, the DUTCH WEST INDIA COMPANY, the trading company that ran the colony, introduced a new plan to attract settlers. It offered large tracts of land along the Hudson River to anyone who equipped 50 people and brought them to the colony as tenants. Those who received the land grants were known as patroons, and they were allowed to run their estates—patroonships—as they pleased. Despite the generous terms, which included the right to tax tenants, only one patroonship flourished. Called Rensselaerswyck and owned by the Van Rensselaer family, it became a manorial estate after the colony passed into English hands in 1664. Other patroonships failed, partly because tenants were unwilling to live under conditions that gave patroons so much control over their lives.

Remember: *Words in small capital letters have separate entries, and the index at the end of Volume 4 will guide you to more information on many topics.*

Only wealthy colonists could become patroons. For humbler people, the Dutch West India Company offered a kind of tenancy called "free and common socage." Under this system, settlers could have as much land as they could use, for as long as they occupied it, in exchange for a share of what the land produced. Once again few people took the offer, largely because the land had to be returned to the company when it was no longer used. Only after the

company began granting permanent title to land in the 1630s did the pace of colonization increase. Settlers who brought five adult family members or servants to the colony received 200 acres of land.

Before claiming any land, Dutch settlers had to prove to company officials that the Indians were willing to sell it. They also had to have surveyors measure the property and mark boundaries. Founders of new communities had to survey the land, set aside plots for homes, and fence grazing land that all colonists would share. Once company officials approved these preparations, the settlers drew lots for plots of private land. This system of assigning plots provided a very fair way of dividing the land.

Land speculation became widespread in New Netherland. Large and small landowners were involved in the buying and selling, and colonists often banded together in land speculation deals. Even those with as little as one acre to spare entered the lively market for land.

French Settlements

Land grants in the St. Lawrence Valley of New France came at first from the COMPANY OF ONE HUNDRED ASSOCIATES and later from the French crown.

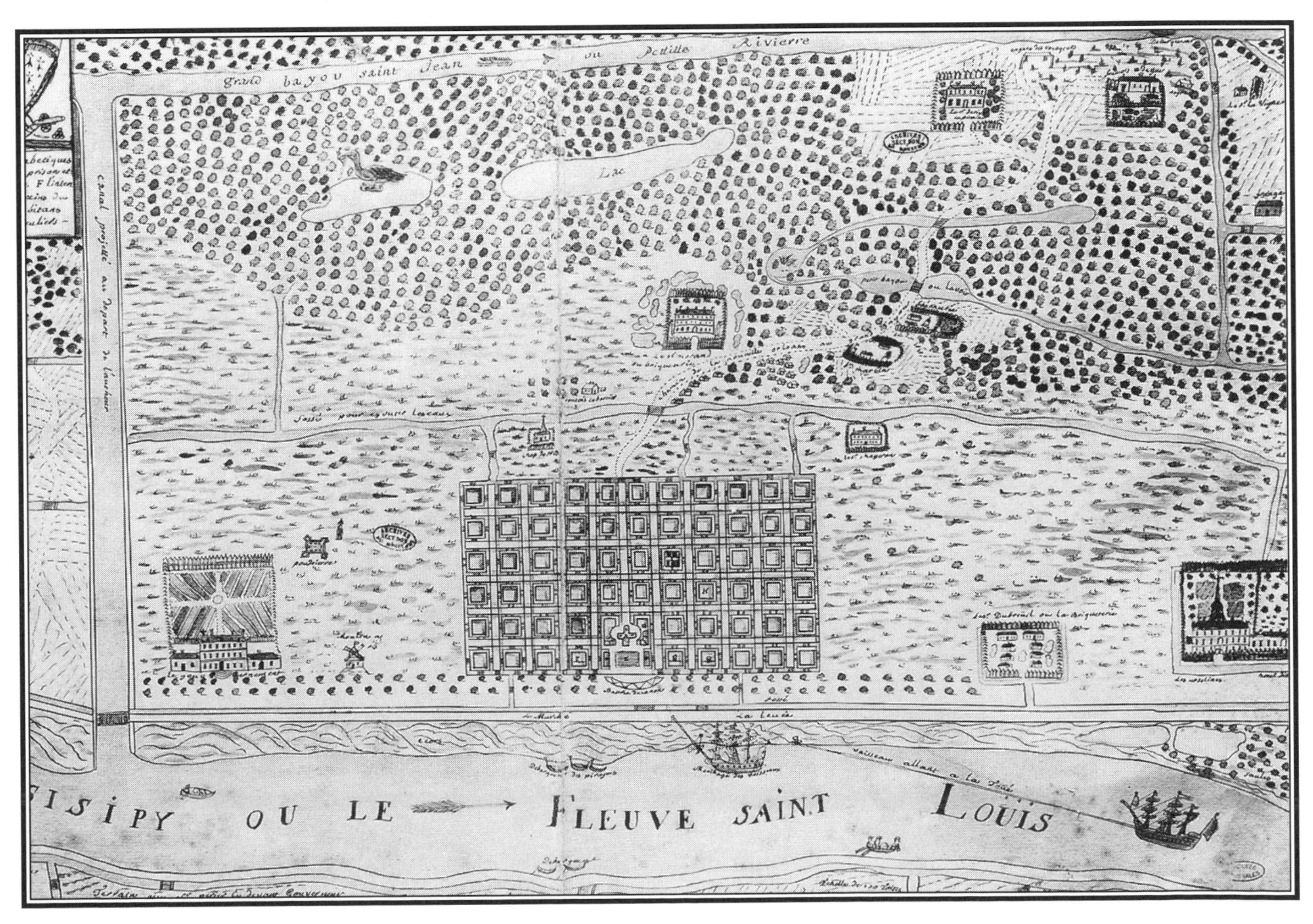

The companies that controlled French Louisiana distributed land to settlers. The population of the area grew slowly. As this map of New Orleans reveals, much unsettled woodland remained outside the city.

* *feudal* relating to an economic and political system in which individuals give service to a landowner in return for protection and the use of land

* *order* religious organization whose members live according to certain rules

The distribution of land followed a feudal* pattern known as the SEIGNEURIAL SYSTEM, modeled after the system of landholding in France. The grant holders were seigneurs, or lords. By the end of the French colonial period in the 1760s, New France contained 210 seigneuries, or estates. No settled land lay outside the seigneuries.

The Company of One Hundred Associates and the king chose seigneurs carefully from among nobles, high-ranking military officers, senior government officials, religious orders*, and a few prosperous middle-class merchants who had won royal favor. These seigneurs gave plots of their property to farmers called *censitaires.* The *censitaire* was different from a tenant farmer—he owned his land and could sell it or leave it to his heirs. But the system created a social order that placed seigneurs far above those who worked on the land.

Seigneurs had a number of rights over their *censitaires.* They received a yearly payment—*cens*—from each household. They also received a share of the profits if a *censitaire* sold land to anyone other than a legal heir. In some cases, seigneurs could request a certain number of days of labor each year from each *censitaire.* In return for these privileges, seigneurs had certain duties, including an obligation to pay the state a share of any profit made from selling property. The seigneurs also had to grant land to anyone who wished to become a *censitaire.* In the early years of settlement, the seigneuries had few inhabitants and brought little profit to their lords. As the number of settlers grew, however, the estates became more valuable.

Although seigneuries were granted in the French province of Acadia, the system never took hold there. This was probably a result of lack of population and continuing military tensions between the French and the British in the region. Seigneurial land grants ended when Britain took control of Acadia in 1713.

The French colony of Louisiana followed a somewhat different course. The crown, unhappy with the slow pace of settlement in the St. Lawrence Valley and Acadia, refused to grant seigneuries in Louisiana. During the first years of settlement in the late 1600s and early 1700s, people simply claimed what land they could. After 1717 the king gave control of the colony to several companies, including the FRENCH WEST INDIES COMPANY, which granted land to individual settlers. Because of the difficult conditions in Louisiana, the population grew slowly, and colonists were more concerned with survival than the formalities of land ownership.

Spanish Settlements

As early as the 1500s, Spain began establishing control over the Spanish Borderlands—the land now occupied by Florida, Texas, New Mexico, Arizona, and California—by giving land grants to worthy citizens. This continued until 1821, when Mexico won its independence from Spain. When the United States acquired Florida and the other Borderland regions, it inherited a pattern of public and private lands based on land grants that were, in some cases, hundreds of years old.

Spanish Land Grants. Spanish land grants took a variety of forms. Some were made to individuals and resembled traditional forms of private

property. Others, especially in Texas, were given to people who had contracts with the state requiring them to bring in settlers to occupy the land. Still other grants, particularly in New Mexico, went to communities whose members were responsible for distributing the land within the grant.

The process of gaining title to land was much the same across the Borderlands. A person filed a petition* with a colonial official, usually the governor. The petition had to show that the land in question was vacant and available and that the applicant was "proper and worthy" to become a landowner. If the governor approved the petition, he ordered the land grant to be made. In the final and most important step of the process, the governor turned the matter over to a local official, who gave the new owner actual possession of the land and sometimes mapped it as well.

* ***petition*** formal statement asking a person in authority to address an issue or problem

There was, however, an additional requirement of ownership. Grant holders had to settle on the property and live there for a certain period of time, usually from four to ten years, before gaining title to it. Only then could the owners use the land as they pleased or sell it. A lively market in land grant titles arose in New Mexico, Texas, and California in the 1700s and 1800s.

To complicate matters, Spanish and Mexican law recognized another form of land ownership—title by simple possession. This guaranteed a person who lived and worked on land the rights to it no matter what the title might say. Confusion occurred when people sold or bought land grant titles to property already occupied by others under the terms of simple possession. The highly complex system of landholding in the Borderlands led to many lawsuits.

Regional Differences. Spanish settlement in Florida began and ended earlier than in other parts of the Borderlands. Spain was never able to colonize more than a fraction of its Florida territory. Most land grants consisted of town lots in the settlements of St. Augustine and Pensacola. After 1800 the Spanish crown granted tracts of land outside these areas, hoping that settlement would help reduce the Indian threat. In many cases, the grant holders failed to occupy the land.

In the Southwest, land grants covered only about 15 percent of the total territory and were concentrated in arable* regions with good water sources. Moreover, these grants were fitted around and between tracts of land that the crown recognized as belonging to Native Americans. Unlike other colonial powers, Spain acknowledged Indian rights to land.

* ***arable*** suitable for plowing and producing crops

Spanish land grants came in many sizes and shapes. In New Mexico, for example, the government encouraged colonization in frontier areas by making small grants of land for farms. Some grants were rewards for military or government service. Other grants restricted the use of the land to certain activities, such as grazing or mining.

To create new settlements in New Mexico, the government made community land grants. Individuals received small plots of property within the communal grant, on which they built houses and dug canals to irrigate their fields. The rest of the land remained common, or shared, property that all members of the community could use for grazing livestock. New settlers could acquire private plots from this common land. These community land grants prevented the original settlers from gobbling up all the available land in a grant.

Spanish settlement in Texas and California began with presidios* and MISSIONS. The missions generally received large grants of land for use by

* ***presidio*** Spanish fort built to protect mission settlements

local Indians, who lived and worked on the mission property. The Spanish government recognized Indian ownership of certain lands, but Indians could not buy property in territory open to white settlement. The government encouraged colonization in both Texas and California by giving "pueblo grants," a type of community land grant similar to those in New Mexico.

The most common form of private land grant in California and Texas was the rancho, which consisted of a piece of land large enough to support livestock. As population increased, such private grants eventually extended into lands once controlled by the missions. As was true elsewhere in North America, the goal of most people in the Spanish Borderlands was private ownership of land. (*See also* **Agriculture; Labor.**)

Languages

North America was home to many different languages during the colonial period. In addition to English, Dutch, French, Spanish, and other European languages, there were many Native American languages and dialects. African slaves brought still other languages to North America.

Languages change over time as a result of contact with different cultures and other experiences of the people who speak them. The languages that European colonists brought with them to North America have gradually changed into the forms used today.

European colonization had a significant impact on Indian languages, causing many of them to disappear or decline in importance. African languages also died out. Native American and African languages affected European languages as well, mostly by providing new words.

Native American Languages

The Native Americans who lived in North America when Europeans arrived spoke several hundred distinct languages and dialects. These languages differed greatly, reflecting the long history of their development and the far-flung territory that these peoples inhabited. Experts have identified about 50 Native American language families—languages descended from a common language. These language families can be combined into a handful of larger groupings of related languages. There are also several language isolates—languages with no known relatives.

The Indian languages of North America contain a rich variety of sounds. Some include only a few consonant sounds, while others have many. The vowel sounds tend to be quite simple, similar to those in European languages. Native American languages also include a number of tone languages. In these, changes in the tone, or pitch, of a syllable affect the meaning of a word. Many Indian languages contain an unusual feature called polysynthesis, which involves uniting ideas in one long word that expresses the meaning of an entire sentence. The Nootka people of the Pacific Northwest, for example, have a word that means "You're all going to get some whale."

See second map in Native Americans (vol. 3).

Major Language Families. In colonial times, five major language groups existed in what is now the United States: the Algonquian, Iroquoian,

A Few Words Borrowed From the Indians

avocado	moose
barbecue	muskrat
bayou	potato
cannibal	raccoon
canoe	skunk
chipmunk	squash
hickory	tapioca
moccasin	toboggan

Muskogean, Siouan-Caddoan, and Uto-Aztecan. Each grouping consisted of several language families. Other important language groupings included the Athabaskan, spoken by the Navajo and Apache Indians; the Eskimo-Aleut languages of the continent's northern regions; and the Western languages used by Indians living along the Gulf of Mexico and in California.

Algonquian is a family of about 25 languages divided into three groups: Eastern, Central, and Western Algonquian. During the colonial period, the Algonquian languages were spoken in the northern parts of eastern and central North America. Algonquian speakers included the Abenaki Indians of New England, the Cree and Ojibwa of Canada, and the Cheyenne of the northern Great Plains. Algonquian languages have a fairly simple range of sounds and complex systems of grammar.

The spread of European settlement in the colonial period forced many Algonquian-speaking groups to move farther north and west. At the same time, contact with Europeans led to the development of new Algonquian dialects. These served as a common means of communication between Europeans and Native Americans and among different groups of Indians. Contact also led to the development of "pidgin" languages—simplified versions of a language that combine words and grammatical features of two or more languages.

Another major language family, the Iroquoian, was centered in northeastern North America, primarily in New York, the St. Lawrence River valley, and the eastern Great Lakes region. Among the Iroquoian-speaking peoples in these areas were the Huron Indians and the tribes of the Iroquois Confederacy. A southern branch of the language family included the Cherokee and Tuscarora Indians of the Southeast.

The sound systems of Iroquoian languages are relatively simple, generally containing from 9 to 11 consonants and from 5 to 7 vowels. Unlike European languages, the order in which words appear in a sentence depends on their importance to the topic of discussion rather than on their roles as nouns, verbs, or adjectives.

The Muskogean language family was limited to the southeastern part of the continent and included the languages of the Creek, Choctaw, and Chickasaw Indians. This region contained many languages besides Muskogean. Before the colonial period, a pidgin language called Mobilian developed as a means of communication for trade among Indian tribes.

The Muskogean languages have a simple sound system, with only three or four vowels and a relatively small number of consonants. They use changes in tone to distinguish words. In addition, a grammatical feature called "switch reference" marks every sentence or part of a sentence in a way that indicates whether the subject has changed. For example, speakers of Muskogean languages would use a switch reference between the sentence, "I found a stream," and the sentence, "It's over there," which has a new subject.

When the Europeans first arrived in North America, the Siouan and Caddoan language families extended from the eastern forests across the Great Plains. The languages of many Plains Indians, such as the Sioux, Crow, and Pawnee, were part of these families.

Siouan-Caddoan languages contain a large number of consonant sounds, including some that are very different from those of European languages, and from three to eight vowels. Among the most striking feature of these languages is the use of various prefixes—syllables added before a word—to indicate different ways in which an action is performed. For example, prefixes to the verb meaning "break" may indicate such actions as "break with the teeth" or "break with the hands."

Uto-Aztecan languages were spoken in the western region of the continent, from the southern part of present-day Idaho through Mexico and from the Pacific coast to the Great Plains. Though related, the languages in this family are very diverse. They include the languages of the Paiute, Shoshone, and Comanche Indians as well as the Hopi and several groups of California Indians.

Uto-Aztecan speakers often had close contact with other language groups, particularly in the Southwest. As a result, they often knew several other languages besides their own and borrowed words from those languages. Many Uto-Aztecan speakers in the Southwest learned Spanish and adopted Spanish words for their own languages.

Impact of Colonization. Only a small percentage of the many Indian languages spoken at the beginning of the colonial period have survived. Many disappeared over the years as Native American populations decreased and as Indians adopted the languages of Europeans.

Remember: *Consult the index at the end of Volume 4 to find more information on many topics.*

Indian languages had only a minor impact on the European languages that replaced them. Europeans borrowed some Indian words for use in their own languages. Many of these were names of North American animals, Indian objects, and place-names.

Few Europeans learned Native American languages, relying instead on translators to communicate with Indians. In some cases, Europeans and Native Americans developed pidgin languages as a way to exchange basic information. A single pidgin language might be adopted by many language groups. The Plains Indians used sign language. Consisting of various hand signals, it enabled speakers of different Indian languages to communicate among themselves and also with Europeans.

European Languages

A variety of European languages and dialects flourished in the North American colonies. In addition to the major languages of English, Dutch, French, and Spanish, some colonists spoke German, Swedish, Portuguese, and Russian. Over the years, these languages began to develop in new ways because of the separation from Europe, contact with other languages, and the needs and demands of colonial society.

Colonial English. The language spoken by the colonists who landed in Jamestown in 1607 was not the same as the English of today. Two differences were pronunciation and spelling. The word *sea* might be pronounced as *say,* for example, and the word *get* could be spelled *gett.* The colonists also used words, such as *thee* and *thou,* that are no longer part of everyday English.

The language spoken by the colonists began to change as soon as they left England. While on ships bound for America, they began to adopt some of

As different cultures met and interacted in the North American colonies, their languages influenced and enriched each other. African and Native American words sometimes came to English through French or Spanish. The American English spoken today has roots in the many languages that were spoken in colonial North America.

the speech used by sailors. The colonists came from various regions of England and spoke different dialects. When these people came into contact with each other, their language began to change as they adopted words, phrases, pronunciations, and speech patterns of others.

The greatest changes occurred in America. There the colonists encountered a strange environment with unfamiliar animals and plants. They borrowed many of the Indian names for objects and places, often changing them slightly to make them easier to pronounce. Hundreds of Indian words eventually became part of the English language, including *chipmunk, squash, tomato, hickory,* and *toboggan.*

Origins of American English Words

Native American	African	Spanish	French	Dutch	English
Choctaw *bayuk* (creek)			*bayou*		bayou
				baas (master)	boss
Micmac *khalibu* (large deer)			*caribou*		caribou
Nahuatl/ Aztec *cacahuatl*		*cacao*			cocoa
				doop (sauce)	dope
	ngombo (a thick soup)		*gombo*		gumbo
	hep (with it)				hip
Taino *hurakán* (wind)		*huracán*			hurricane
Inuit *qayaq* (small canoe)					kayak
Algonquian *ärähkun*					raccoon
Taino *zabana* (grassland)		*sabana*			savannah
				snoepen (sneak)	snoop
Nahuatl *tomatl*		*tomate*			tomato
	tot				tote
Cree *otchek*					woodchuck
	nyami (eat)	*ñame*			yam

Over time American English developed in its own way. It kept words—such as *molasses* and *trash*—that disappeared in Britain. It continued to use pronunciations common in the 1600s—for words such as *bath* and *fast*—which changed in Britain. Some words took on new meanings in the colonies. For example, the word *lumber* originally meant "unused goods," not wood.

As American English developed in the colonies, differences began to emerge as a result of regional variations in geography, economy, and population. In New England, where seaports played an important role in trade and communication, the language included many terms connected to water and the sea. Words relating to tobacco and plantation life appeared in the language of the South. English speakers in New York borrowed many words from the Dutch, who originally controlled that region. As newcomers arrived in the colonies, they adopted the language of the area where they settled. This helped reinforce the development and continuation of regional dialects.

By the end of the colonial period, American English—a language quite distinct from the one spoken in Britain—had firmly taken root. It continued to develop separately and to vary from region to region.

Colonial Dutch. Dutch colonists brought their language to North America when they settled New Netherland in the early 1600s. After England took control of New Netherland in 1664, Dutch colonists became increasingly isolated from the Netherlands. Their survival depended on communication with the English.

Contact with English-speaking people gradually changed the Dutch language in America. Dutch colonists borrowed English words and phrases, and a language known as "Low Dutch" began to emerge with different grammar and vocabulary and a number of different dialects. By the 1700s, visitors from the Netherlands had great difficulty understanding the speech of Dutch colonists.

Over time colonial "Low Dutch" began to decline in importance as younger generations of colonists adopted the English language for use outside the home. Strongholds of the Dutch language remained in certain places—such as the area around Albany, New York—until the late 1700s. Reminders of the Dutch language survive today in place-names throughout the Hudson and Mohawk river valleys of New York and in a few common words, such as *cookie, cruller,* and *sleigh.*

Colonial French. Most of the colonists of New France spoke a variety of dialects from the provinces of France rather than the standard French of the region around Paris. In the 1600s, New France included the St. Lawrence Valley and Acadia, as well as some outposts* in the Great Lakes region.

* ***outpost*** frontier settlement or military base

Most of the colonists of the St. Lawrence Valley—an area known as Canada—came from northern France, while those in Acadia came from southern France. The languages of northern and southern France, though very similar, differed in their use of words and certain forms of grammar. The French dialects used in Canada and Acadia reflected these differences. Though both dialects changed during the colonial period, the French spoken in Acadia experienced less change because of the region's isolation.

The language that developed in the French colony of LOUISIANA reflected a history involving a number of different groups. Many of the early

settlers came from the region around Paris and spoke the dialect used there. However, the colony also attracted immigrants from Canada and Acadia, who brought their own dialects. Other groups, including German immigrants, arrived later and added their languages to the colony. The language of Louisiana became further complicated by the gradual development of a creole* dialect, which combined elements of French and the languages of African slaves.

* ***creole*** language made up of a combination of languages

French speakers throughout North America borrowed some words from the Indians, primarily place-names and the names of animals, plants, or objects. In Louisiana the word *bayou,* meaning "creek," came from the Indians. Aside from such borrowed words, the influence of Native American languages on colonial French was quite limited.

Colonial Spanish. In 1492, the year that Christopher Columbus made his first voyage to America, Spain was united under one crown. Before that time, Spain consisted of separate kingdoms with different dialects of the Spanish language. After 1492 the language of Spain began to grow more unified and standardized.

Colonial Spanish did not develop in the same way as the language of Spain. Because of their isolation, the colonists of Spanish America continued to use pronunciation and forms of grammar that gradually changed or died out in Spain. At the same time, the colonists adopted many Indian words for unfamiliar animals, plants, and objects. These borrowed words—such as *hamaca, huracán, chocolate, and tomate*—became part of colonial Spanish. Much later these words were taken over by English-speaking people in America as *hammock, hurricane, chocolate,* and *tomato.*

African American Languages

Africans brought to the Americas as slaves in the colonial period spoke a variety of languages and dialects. These languages quickly died out for a number of reasons—most importantly, the total separation of slaves from their native cultures in Africa. African slaves in the colonies sometimes developed new forms of speech that were a unique mixture of African and European languages. Most of them gradually learned English, French, or Spanish, the languages of the colonial slaveholders.

Bits of African languages survived in colorful ways, primarily as borrowed words and phrases that were used by European colonists. In the English-speaking southern colonies, many words of African origin entered the vocabulary. Some—such as *gumbo* and *okra*—were mainly used in the southern regional dialect. Others—such as *banjo, jazz, mumbo jumbo,* and *phoney*—spread throughout English-speaking America.

In French Louisiana, the languages of black slaves gradually combined with French and developed into a creole dialect, which provided a basic form of communication between slaves and other people. The colonists of New Spain borrowed many words from African slaves, including the word *banana,* which eventually became part of the English language as well. (*See also* **African American Culture; Literacy; Schools and Schooling.**)

La Salle, René-Robert Cavelier de

1643–1687
French explorer

René-Robert Cavelier, Sieur de La Salle, was the first European to explore the MISSISSIPPI RIVER all the way to the Gulf of Mexico. As a result of his voyage, La Salle claimed the entire Mississippi valley for France, naming this vast territory LOUISIANA in honor of the French king, Louis XIV.

Born in Rouen, France, La Salle was educated by the JESUITS and became a member of their order* in 1660. He left the order in 1667 and moved to NEW FRANCE, where he began a career as a fur trader. La Salle's business thrived, and he began dreaming of building a great fur-trading empire south of the Great Lakes.

* ***order*** religious organization whose members live according to certain rules

Back in France in 1677, La Salle received permission from the king to explore and establish forts in regions to the west and south of New France. The French explorers Jacques Marquette and Louis JOLLIET had already traveled the Mississippi River as far south as present-day Arkansas. La Salle wanted to explore this great river to its mouth.

See third map in Exploration, Age of (vol. 2).

La Salle began raising funds and preparing for an expedition. He began the trip down the Mississippi River in 1682 with a small group of men. They reached the river's mouth on April 9 and held a ceremony in which La Salle formally claimed the river and its valley for France.

Returning to France the next year, the explorer received permission from the king to establish a colony on the Gulf of Mexico. In 1684 La Salle set sail for North America with four ships and a group of colonists. But the expedition was a disaster. After reaching the gulf in early 1685, La Salle failed to find the mouth of the Mississippi and landed on the coast of Texas near present-day Galveston. He established a temporary colony there, but most of the colonists were killed by disease or Indian attacks.

After other attempts to locate the Mississippi failed, La Salle set out in 1687 with about 20 men to try to reach New France over land. Tired and frightened, the men mutinied and murdered La Salle on March 19. Most of the other members of this expedition eventually died in the wilderness. (*See also* **Exploration, Age of; New France.**)

Las Casas, Bartolomé de

ca. 1474–1566
Spanish missionary and writer

Bartolomé de Las Casas spent most of his life fighting for the rights of Native Americans in the Spanish colonies. As part of his campaign to gain better treatment for the Indians, he wrote several books that provide valuable information on the people and history of the Americas.

Born in Seville, Spain, Las Casas was the son of a Spanish merchant. His father, Pedro de Las Casas, accompanied Christopher COLUMBUS on his second voyage to the Americas in 1493. When his father returned to Spain, he brought along a Taino Indian boy named Juanico, who became Bartolomé's close friend. In 1502 Las Casas went with his father to the island of Hispaniola in the West Indies. He spent his first years there helping organize military expeditions and learning native languages. He returned to Europe to study and then became a priest in the Dominican order*.

* ***order*** religious organization whose members live according to certain rules

In 1513 Las Casas joined an expedition to Cuba. He successfully converted many Native Americans to Christianity and received an *ENCOMIENDA*—a grant of land and Indian slaves—as a reward for his efforts. While in Cuba,

Bartolomé de Las Casas, a Spanish missionary, spent more than half his life struggling to protect the rights of Native Americans in the Spanish colonies. In 1542 he helped persuade the Spanish king to prohibit Indian slavery.

the missionary witnessed the harsh treatment that Indians received under the *encomienda* system. Convinced that this type of treatment was wrong, he began trying to help the Indians. In 1514 he freed his own Indians and started speaking out against the *encomienda* system.

Unable to convince colonial slaveholders to change their ways, Las Casas traveled to Spain to seek support from the king. The king sided with Las Casas and ruled that the Indians should be governed without the use of force. However, colonial officials did little to enforce this ruling.

For the next two decades, Las Casas continued his efforts to abolish *encomiendas* and defend the rights of the Indians. Meanwhile, his work as a missionary took him to what is now Venezuela, Peru, Guatemala, and Mexico, where he became a bishop. During this time, Las Casas wrote several important works, including *In Defense of the Indians* and *History of the Indies.* Because of his efforts to end Indian slavery, he was called the "Apostle to the Indies."

Another of his books, *The Devastation of the Indies,* was a powerful account of Spanish mistreatment of the Indians. Read at the royal court in Spain, it helped bring about passage of the so-called New Laws in 1542. The laws banned Indian slavery and began to phase out the *encomienda* system. But attempts to enforce the laws met great resistance and led to revolts in some parts of Spanish America. The government modified the laws, which made them less effective in protecting the Indians.

Las Casas continued to speak out on behalf of the Indians for the rest of his life. One of his greatest successes came in 1555, when he helped prevent the establishment of permanent *encomiendas* in Peru. Following his death in Mexico in 1566, Las Casas was buried in Spain. (*See also* **Missions and Missionaries; Slavery.**)

Laws and Legal Systems

Colonists from Great Britain, the Netherlands, France, and Spain based their laws and legal systems on the practices of their homelands. However, they also created new statutes* and adapted old ones to fit the circumstances of their North American environment. Law and legal institutions developed and changed throughout the colonial period.

* *statute* law made by a legislative body
* *common law* unwritten law based on custom and court decisions

British Colonies

The English system of courts and common law* had emerged over the course of centuries. The colonists brought this legal heritage with them to North America. From the start, however, they fashioned a body of laws distinctly their own.

Colonial Courts.

Colonial courts differed from British courts in a number of ways. In the colonies, proceedings were often informal and took place in English rather than in Latin. In Britain judges were well trained in law, and professional attorneys played an important role in the courts. In the colonies, by contrast, justices might have some knowledge of legal matters but little or no schooling in the law. However, in the 1700s, the situation began to change, and trained lawyers and judges became common in most colonies.

Perhaps the most famous trial in the British colonies was that of John Peter Zenger in 1735. The New York newspaperman was arrested for publishing articles that criticized the government, but a sympathetic jury set him free.

The colonial legal system included local courts and central courts. The local courts generally handled minor offenses, while the central courts had jurisdiction* over more serious crimes, such as murder and treason. Justices of the peace served as the main officials in the local courts. When crimes were committed, the justices heard cases and presided over the trials. Any accused person could request a jury trial, but he or she had to pay for the expense. Most defendants therefore "put themselves upon the court" and allowed the justice of the peace to decide their case. The justices relied primarily on a system of fines to keep order.

* ***jurisdiction*** area of authority

In some colonies, central courts moved around regularly to meet in different communities, while in others, they remained in the capital city. Jury trials were more common in the central courts, and judges were usually better trained than in the local courts. Even so, defendants often avoided trials by plea-bargaining—accepting conviction on a lesser offense in return for admission of guilt.

Colonial Law. English laws arrived in North America in several ways. Some laws came from royal charters, documents that granted permission for establishing a colony and included laws for governing it. Law books, brought by colonists or purchased by colonial assemblies, also contained English statutes. Finally, knowledge of English legal customs arrived with the colonists themselves. Though few early settlers practiced law, the number of trained English attorneys and judges immigrating to the colonies increased over time.

English laws usually changed in North America. Many colonists had been dissatisfied with the judicial system in England and wanted to modify it. The needs and goals of each colony also played a role in the changes.

In 1619 the VIRGINIA HOUSE OF BURGESSES began passing new criminal laws, including one on firearms and hunting. In England few people could carry guns except during military training, and it was illegal to hunt game in public forests. Such laws made little sense in the colonies, where game was plentiful and people needed to use weapons to hunt for food. Despite efforts by English authorities to control colonial lawmaking, the Carolinas and Georgia followed Virginia's lead and also modified their laws.

Religion played a role in the revision of laws as well. The PURITANS of New England based many of their laws on teachings in the Bible. In 1641 they created a system of laws in Massachusetts called the Body of Liberties. Other New England colonies adopted similar laws, though Rhode Island's legal code was much less strict than that of Massachusetts.

Law Libraries

Only a few colonial law libraries existed before the 1700s. Most were privately owned and included fewer than 100 books. By the mid-1700s, however, legal professionals were collecting law books. Two of the largest and most important collections belonged to Thomas Jefferson and John Adams. Jefferson's private library of more than 6,000 volumes included about 600 related to law. Adams considered his own collection in Massachusetts the "Best Library of Law in the State."

The middle colonies also shaped their own distinct justice systems. The QUAKERS of Pennsylvania and New Jersey lived under some of the least restrictive laws in the colonies. The laws of New York reflected both English and Dutch legal traditions. When the English took control of the colony of New Netherland in 1664, they allowed the Dutch residents to keep many of their courts and laws. Over time, however, English legal traditions became dominant.

Colonial law did not apply equally to all people. Women, for example, had fewer legal rights than men. A married woman could not sell property or sign a contract without her husband's consent. A man, on the other hand, could dispose of property without consulting his wife, even if the property

belonged to her. Colonial law also discriminated against Indians and African Americans. The settlers did not respect the Indians' customs and laws, nor did they extend the protection of European laws to them. Many colonies, especially those in the South, had special "black codes" or "slave codes" that strictly regulated the lives of slaves. Any violation of the rules was severely punished. By law, slaves were considered property—not people. They were forbidden to leave the plantation without permission or to carry a weapon.

Legal Procedure. Although legal procedures varied from colony to colony, they all included certain general features. The first stage in criminal cases involved a meeting of the grand jury—a group of free, white men from the community—to hear the charges against an accused person. If the grand jury found the charges reasonable, it issued an indictment—a formal accusation. At this point, the defendant could plea-bargain or request a jury trial or a bench trial—one heard by a judge without a jury. Many defendants chose plea-bargaining to avoid the expense of a trial. Sentences varied according to the nature of the offense and the rules of the colony or community.

Civil cases—those involving lawsuits against individuals—began with the filing of an official court document called a writ. A writ described in specific terms the nature of the lawsuit. After the writ was filed, the defendant was summoned to appear in court to hear the complaint and enter a plea. The defendant could confess, deny the charges, or challenge the facts of the case. Civil lawsuits rarely went to trial. In most cases, defendants and plaintiffs—those who started the lawsuit—settled through negotiation.

Legal Profession. Very few trained lawyers settled in North America in the early colonial period. Some colonies actually banned the practice of law. The Puritans disapproved of representing others for money, and the tight control Puritan officials of New England had over their communities limited the need for lawyers. This began to change in the late 1600s, however, as people of other faiths settled in the region. Rejecting the authority of the Puritan church, these newcomers used trained lawyers to help them protect their rights.

Few attorneys practiced at first in the middle colonies. Quakers also tried to eliminate lawyers from courts because they, like the Puritans, did not approve of defending others for money. Most colonists preferred to settle disputes through negotiation rather than trial, thus reducing the need for lawyers.

There was less opposition to lawyers in the southern colonies, which had the strongest English legal traditions. In the early years, most attorneys were wealthy planters who practiced law part-time. As the southern colonies grew, however, the need for full-time legal professionals increased, and members of the middle class began training for the law as a way to acquire both wealth and higher status*.

* ***status*** social position

The number of legal experts in the colonies expanded greatly in the late 1600s. During this period, the English crown tried to gain greater control over the colonies by uniting several of the northern colonies into the DOMINION OF NEW ENGLAND. The colonists saw the union as a threat to the rights and freedoms granted in their colonial charters. To counter the threat, they needed people with legal training and experience. Some colonies began recruiting legal professionals from England. At the same time, political problems

abroad led many English attorneys to seek opportunity and fortune in America. As more lawyers arrived, colonial capitals became centers of legal education and practice.

After 1700 the legal profession in the British colonies expanded steadily. Some Americans received legal training in Britain and returned to the colonies to practice. A growing number of lawyers also received their education by serving as apprentices* to other lawyers. Meanwhile, the colonies began requiring lawyers to pass qualifying tests and to be licensed by the governor. In addition, courts started disciplining lawyers to ensure high moral standards.

* ***apprentice*** person placed in the care of a merchant or crafts worker to learn a profession

By the mid-1700s, lawyers held prominent positions in most of the colonies, and they made up a large proportion of the representatives in the colonial assemblies. When conflict between Britain and the colonies broke out in the 1760s, the colonists looked increasingly to lawyers for leadership in resisting British policies. Several, including Patrick HENRY, Thomas JEFFERSON, and John ADAMS, played major roles in the movement for independence.

The Dutch Colony

The Dutch colony of NEW NETHERLAND based its system of law on that of the Netherlands. Even after the English took over in 1664, Dutch settlers were allowed to retain various elements of their legal tradition. Over time, however, the Dutch practices faded, and the colony adopted laws and legal procedures that more closely resembled those of the British colonies.

Colonial Law.

Dutch law consisted of statutes, privileges established by custom, church law, and civil law* based on ancient Roman traditions. In addition, every town in the Netherlands had its own laws, charters, freedoms, and privileges. Citizens carefully guarded these rights, which were recorded in local law books.

* ***civil law*** body of law that regulates and protects the rights of individuals

The DUTCH WEST INDIA COMPANY brought Dutch law to North America when it founded New Netherland in 1624. It would not allow colonists to pass new ordinances* unless they were approved by the company. Dutch laws, however, did not cover every situation that arose in the colony. The director general and his council, which had authority for administering the justice system, began to write new laws. They made them as close as possible to the laws of the Netherlands and sent them to the West India Company for approval.

* ***ordinance*** law or regulation usually made by the government of a city or town

The colony's ordinances dealt with a broad range of problems, from trespassing to prohibiting the sale of alcohol to Indians. Those involving fencing and the control of Indians, taverns, and livestock were usually approved. But the company could veto or rewrite any law that did not follow customary Dutch practices.

Colonial Courts.

Courts played a central role in New Netherland, administering both government and justice. Everyone in the colony had equal access to the courts and looked to them to protect their rights.

By 1664 New Netherland had 17 courts. Each included a *schout,* an official appointed by the director general and his council, and several magistrates* called *schepenen.* The *schout* acted as sheriff, prosecuting attorney, and head of the court. He could file criminal charges, arrest suspects, oversee

* ***magistrate*** official with administrative and often judicial functions

prosecutions and lawsuits, and issue sentences. The *schout* and magistrates made all court judgments. New Netherland did not have a tradition of trial by jury.

Legal Profession. Very few legal professionals lived in New Netherland. Instead, the administration of justice depended on public officials who had some knowledge of Dutch law. The director general of the colony and his council served as the highest judicial officials.

Despite the lack of attorneys, the colonists of New Netherland filed many lawsuits against each other. In an attempt to reduce the number of lawsuits, the director general established a special advisory group that had authority to negotiate disputes and make decisions without the need for a court case. All involved parties had to abide by the decisions or pay a fine.

French Colonies

Remember: *Words in small capital letters have separate entries, and the index at the end of Volume 4 will guide you to more information on many topics.*

In 1627 the French government granted the COMPANY OF ONE HUNDRED ASSOCIATES a charter to establish the colony of NEW FRANCE. The charter gave responsibility for the administration of justice to the company's investors. In the 1640s, large landowners—seigneurs—also gained legal authority. They had the power to establish local courts with jurisdiction over many criminal and civil matters. Supreme judicial authority, however, remained in the hands of the governor-general of New France. When the French crown took control of the colony in 1663, royal officials and institutions assumed responsibility for its legal system.

Law in New France. The Custom of Paris, a group of laws that had developed over centuries, served as the basis of civil law in New France. It dealt with issues of property, inheritance, and commercial matters. Influenced by Roman law, French criminal law operated under a system that emphasized secrecy and allowed royal judges to control all stages of the judicial process.

Only royal judges could start criminal proceedings. They were responsible for determining the exact nature of the crime, identifying suspects, and gathering evidence. The judges had to follow strict guidelines when evaluating evidence. Eyewitness testimony had to meet certain conditions, and two eyewitnesses were required for conviction. In determining sentences, judges could take into account the circumstances of a crime and the defendant's character and social position.

The secrecy of the French criminal system enabled witnesses to testify freely without fear of revenge from the accused. It put defendants at a disadvantage, however, because they did not know the exact charges or evidence against them. Moreover, defendants had no right to legal counsel or to cross-examine their accusers. Consequently, the fairness of the system depended largely on the quality of the evidence and the neutrality of the judges.

Legal Profession. It was important that the judges be well schooled in law because they controlled all aspects of criminal proceedings. In France all judges had university degrees in legal studies. However, the colonies

possessed no law schools, and fully qualified judges were rare. French lawyers were not allowed to practice in the colonies, so various people in New France performed the functions of legal professionals.

Heading the colonial judicial system was the intendant, the official concerned with day-to-day affairs in the colony. Court officers called bailiffs sometimes acted as lawyers for individuals bringing lawsuits to court. Notaries—clerks who drafted and kept records of legal documents—also served as lawyers.

When the British took control of Canada in 1763, they changed the criminal laws of the French colony but left the civil laws largely intact. Further changes were not made until Canadian independence in 1867. Even today, the legal systems of the province of Quebec—and the state of Louisiana—contain elements of French colonial law.

Spanish Colonies

Spain brought a strong and well-developed legal tradition to its American colonies. Although local circumstances forced some changes in laws and legal practices, for the most part, the colonial legal system remained remarkably similar to that of Spain. The Spanish legal system grew out of royal law and church law and custom.

Magistrates and Colonial Courts.

Key features of the Spanish legal system included the absence of a jury and the involvement of magistrates in all phases of the legal process. In the Spanish Borderlands*, magistrates played a role in criminal, civil, church, and military courts.

* ***Spanish Borderlands*** northern part of New Spain, area now occupied by Florida, Texas, New Mexico, Arizona, and California

Provincial governors, appointed by the Spanish crown, and town officials called *alcaldes* served as magistrates. Despite their responsibility for maintaining law and order, these officials had no formal legal training.

The Spanish colonies used a system for criminal proceedings that was similar to that of the French colonies. The magistrates took an active role in prosecuting cases and managing the judicial process, as well as judging the cases.

The initial phase of a criminal case, *sumaria,* resembled the English legal procedure of indictment—formal accusation of a crime. However, in the Spanish Borderlands, the charges could be brought by the victim, an uninvolved individual, or a magistrate. Following the *sumaria* came investigation of the crime, testimony from witnesses, arguments from the legal counsels of both sides, a ruling by the magistrate, and sentencing. Magistrates had considerable liberty in determining punishments and frequently modified them to suit specific cases. They based their decisions on written laws, custom, and the values of the community.

In civil cases, local magistrates tended to follow rules of procedure very closely, especially in matters involving property. Most civil cases in the Borderlands dealt with minor lawsuits and claims, which were generally settled rather quickly. When a case involved large sums, however, it might be appealed to higher courts, eventually reaching the provincial governor or regional authorities.

Few Indians in the Spanish Borderlands participated in the legal system. The PUEBLO INDIANS of New Mexico, however, were an exception. They took an active role in protecting their rights and used the colonial courts to help maintain their lands and cultural traditions.

Legal Profession. The Borderlands had few trained legal professionals. Spanish colonists who wanted to study law had to go to the university in Mexico City. Once they became lawyers, they preferred to remain in the government and business centers of the Spanish colonies, where there were plenty of clients. Earning a living as a lawyer in the Borderlands was difficult because of the region's widespread poverty. Only the wealthy could afford to pay for legal advice.

An important source of legal expertise throughout the Spanish colonies was the *escribano,* or notary. Although notaries did not have university training, they gained experience in legal matters through their work in drawing up wills, contracts, bills of sale, and other official papers crucial to the colonial legal system.

Despite the lack of legal professionals, Spanish colonists in the Borderlands had a great respect for the legal system. This respect helped Spain maintain control of its colonies. (*See also* **Colonial Administration; Crime and Punishment; Government, Provincial; Seigneurial System.**)

Lawyers

See *Laws and Legal Systems: British Colonies.*

Lee, Richard Henry

1732–1794

American statesman and patriot

*** *ratification*** formal approval

A political leader in the American Revolution, Richard Henry Lee served in both Continental Congresses. During the Second Continental Congress, he introduced a resolution calling for American independence, which led to the Declaration of Independence. Lee was one of the signers of this historic document.

Born in Virginia and educated in England, Lee served as a justice of the peace and a member of Virginia's assembly. A talented speaker and fierce opponent of British colonial policies, he became a leader of the independence movement. Lee joined his friends Thomas Jefferson and Patrick Henry in calling for the formation of committees of correspondence to spread news and ideas throughout the colonies and plan actions against the British.

While serving in the Continental Congresses from 1774 to 1779, Lee urged strong measures against Great Britain. His resolution for independence was adopted by members of the Second Continental Congress on July 2, 1776. Lee also supported a plan for a confederation of states.

A member of both Continental Congresses, Richard Henry Lee spoke out vigorously against British colonial policies.

After the Revolution, Lee left the congress, but he returned in 1784. He opposed ratification* of the Constitution because it lacked a bill of rights and gave too much power to the federal government. When a new United States government was formed under the Constitution in 1789, Lee was elected U.S. senator from Virginia. In the Senate, he played an important role in the adoption of the Bill of Rights. Lee retired from Congress in 1792 because of poor health and died two years later at his home in Virginia. (*See also* **American Revolution; Independence Movements.**)

Leisler's Rebellion

** militia* army of citizens who may be called into action in a time of emergency

** exhume* to take a body out of a grave or tomb

In the late 1600s, Jacob Leisler, a German-born merchant and a captain in the local militia*, led a revolt against the government of the colony of New York. Leisler's Rebellion was one of several colonial uprisings sparked by the Glorious Revolution in England.

In 1688 Parliament replaced King James II, a Roman Catholic, with the Protestant rulers William and Mary. News of this Glorious Revolution reached New York in May of 1689. Acting on a rumor that Catholics were going to invade the colony, the militia seized New York City's fort. Leisler, a fierce opponent of Catholicism and James II, led the attack. Shortly afterward, he declared himself lieutenant governor of New York. Leisler insisted that he was merely securing the colony on a short-term basis for the new Protestant monarchs.

William and Mary, however, took a different view of Leisler's actions. They appointed a new governor for New York and sent troops to establish order. Leisler and his followers resisted the new governor but surrendered to the English forces that arrived in March of 1691. Two months later, Leisler was tried for treason and hanged.

During the rebellion, Leisler had enjoyed the support of the lower classes, but the Dutch clergy and traders had generally opposed him. His followers—known as Leislerians—protested his execution. Their activities forced Parliament to review Leisler's trial and sentence. In 1695 the British government reversed the finding of treason, passed a bill legalizing his governorship, and ordered the return of Leisler's property to his family. Leislerians obtained permission to have their former leader's body exhumed*. In 1698, after a parade and much celebration of their victory over the upper classes, they reburied Leisler in the Dutch Reformed Church in New York City.

Lenni Lenape Indians

See *Delaware Indians*.

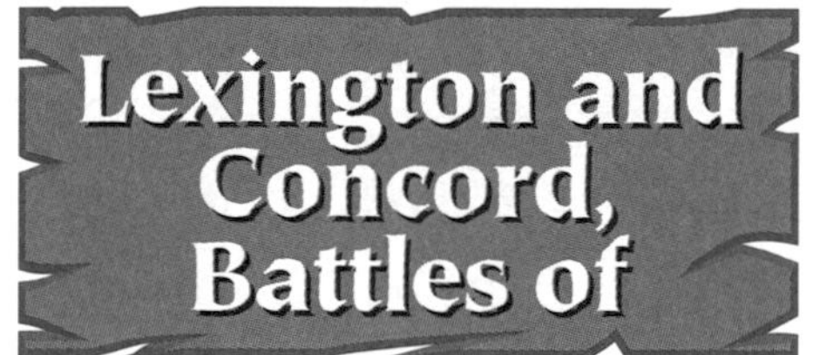

Lexington and Concord, Battles of

** boycott* refusal to buy goods as a means of protest

** militia* army of citizens who may be called into action in times of emergency

On April 19, 1775, British soldiers and American colonists fired the first shots of the American Revolution at Lexington and Concord in Massachusetts. Many people on both sides had believed that the conflict between Great Britain and the colonies could be settled without bloodshed, but the Battles of Lexington and Concord put an end to their hopes.

Prelude to the Fighting. Since the mid-1760s, British policies had faced increasing opposition in the colonies. American colonists resented the Proclamation of 1763, which restricted settlement on the western frontier. Parliament angered them further by passing a series of taxes, including the Sugar Act and the Stamp Act. Colonists argued that the British government had no right to tax them because they had no representatives in Parliament. They protested the acts by boycotting* British goods, writing pamphlets, and organizing demonstrations.

The British government responded to the colonists' defiance with a set of harsh laws known in North America as the Intolerable Acts. Expecting conflict in the near future, militia* groups such as the minutemen of Massachusetts

began training and stockpiling weapons. By April of 1775, the situation in Boston—the center of colonial resistance to British rule—was ready to explode.

The Battles. On the evening of April 18, General Thomas Gage, the British army commander at Boston, ordered 700 troops to march to the community of Concord and seize colonial stores of guns and ammunition. Their mission also included arresting John HANCOCK and Samuel ADAMS, two well-known patriots* who were staying nearby in the town of Lexington. Patriots in Boston learned of the plan and sent two riders, Paul REVERE and William Dawes, to warn Hancock and Adams and the colonists in the area. The patriot leaders escaped, and the next morning the British found 70 armed minutemen waiting on the green in Lexington. Shooting broke out, and when the smoke cleared, eight colonists lay dead.

* ***patriot*** American colonist who supported independence from Britain

The British Redcoats—named for the red jackets of their uniforms—continued their advance to Concord and occupied the town. They searched for weapons and burned the few military supplies they found. The smoke from the fires, as well as fast-spreading news of the shooting at Lexington, drew volunteers from the surrounding towns to join Concord's minutemen. Soon the American force numbered about 450 men. They fired on the British

The Battle of Lexington marked the beginning of the Revolutionary War. British soldiers, marching toward the town of Concord, exchanged shots with Massachusetts minutemen. Eight colonists were killed, and the news of the battle brought colonists rallying to the patriot cause.

troops, killing several men. The Redcoats turned to head back to the safety of Boston.

The 20-mile retreat was devastating to the British forces. Patriots fired on them from barns and trees along the route, picking soldiers off one by one. The militia followed the troops almost all the way to Boston. The British army was only saved from complete destruction by the arrival of reinforcements. The patriots suffered 93 dead and wounded, compared to 273 British casualties*. The clashes resulted in far fewer deaths than would occur in battles in the Revolution to come, but the importance of Lexington and Concord had little to do with the number of dead. As poet Ralph Waldo Emerson wrote some years later, the patriots who took up arms against the British that April day "fired the shot heard 'round the world."

* ***casualty*** person who is killed or injured

Effects of Lexington and Concord.

News of the fighting at Lexington and Concord stunned government officials in London. They had never expected the colonists to offer any serious resistance, and the fact that a small group of militiamen had outfought the larger British forces alarmed them. The battles convinced British authorities that a civil war with the colonists was unavoidable, and they began preparing for the fight.

In the colonies, the news of events at Lexington and Concord met with mixed reactions. Colonists who had hoped for a peaceful settlement and LOYALISTS who supported British rule realized with sadness that the two sides were moving toward war. Patriots, on the other hand, rejoiced at the success of their strategy against the larger and better-equipped British army. The battles gave the Americans much-needed confidence at the beginning of the long and difficult fight to come.

In his widely read 1776 pamphlet *Common Sense,* Thomas PAINE wrote that the Battles of Lexington and Concord marked the point of no return in the conflict between Great Britain and America. He asked the colonists how they could possibly continue to "love, honour, and faithfully serve the power that hath [has] carried fire and sword into your land?"

Until Lexington and Concord, only patriots in Massachusetts openly opposed the British. During the FIRST CONTINENTAL CONGRESS of 1774, however, the other American colonies had promised to defend Massachusetts if the British attacked. After the events at Lexington and Concord, they honored their promise. In May 1775, representatives at the SECOND CONTINENTAL CONGRESS created an American army, taking another big step toward war—and independence. (*See also* **Independence Movements.**)

Libraries and Learned Societies

The earliest colonial libraries were private collections of books held by individuals and Spanish missions. As the colonies developed, colleges and churches established libraries in many areas. Other types of libraries, and eventually learned societies*, appeared in the British colonies in the 1700s, providing a storehouse of knowledge and information and a source of ideas.

* ***learned society*** organization formed to promote scientific and practical knowledge

Personal Libraries.

Many of the early Spanish, French, English, and Dutch colonists brought books with them from Europe. Because books were expensive, important collections usually belonged to large landowners, rich merchants, and other wealthy individuals. Professionals such as ministers, doctors, and lawyers also had personal libraries. Most people could not afford many books, but even the humblest colonist generally owned a few volumes.

Colonial Americans had to do many things for themselves. Consequently, a good number of the books in personal libraries dealt with practical matters. Medical manuals were common because colonists often had to act as their own doctors. Books on law, farming, and livestock also provided useful information. Personal libraries also contained books about improving manners and moral character, as well as religious works such as Bibles, prayer books, and books of sermons. The collections of educated individuals frequently included Greek and Latin classics*, considered essential to a good education.

* ***classics*** works of outstanding quality, often from ancient Greece and Rome, that have served as models for later works

Most colonists in the 1600s disapproved of reading simply for enjoyment, but they did not object to getting pleasure from reading if it also served a practical purpose. Thus colonists might have books of plays and poetry in their libraries because these works helped teach language. Individual libraries were usually shared with neighbors, friends, and relatives. They were encouraged to borrow books freely, but it was a grave social error not to return a book within a reasonable period of time.

Many individual colonial libraries were quite extensive, numbering in the thousands of books. Among the most notable collections were those of New England minister Cotton MATHER, Virginia planter William BYRD, and statesmen Benjamin FRANKLIN and Thomas JEFFERSON. Jefferson's collection became the foundation for the United States Library of Congress.

College Libraries. The Jesuit College in Quebec, founded in 1635, possessed the greatest library in New France, with about 5,000 books by the mid-1700s. Harvard College in Massachusetts opened the first college library in the English colonies in 1638. It contained the personal collection of John Harvard, whose donation of money and books resulted in the naming of the college in his honor. The College of William and Mary in Virginia established a library in the 1690s, and Yale College, the College of New Jersey (now Princeton), and King's College (now Columbia University) followed in the 1700s.

Only students and faculty could use college libraries, not the general public. At first these collections were small and consisted primarily of works of theology*, along with some books on law, history, philosophy*, mathematics, and medicine. Over the years, as the collections grew in size, more books on various topics were added. To expand their libraries, colleges depended on gifts of books and money from wealthy patrons*, as well as interested scholars.

* ***theology*** study of the nature of God and of religious truth

* ***philosophy*** study related to ideas, the laws of nature, and the pursuit of truth

* ***patron*** person of wealth and influence who supports an artist, writer, or scholar; protector

Church and Community Libraries. Thomas Bray, a minister who worked to establish the Anglican Church in the English colonies, led the way in organizing parochial, or church-related, libraries in the late 1600s and early 1700s. These libraries were created to help improve the education of the clergy*. Although made up mainly of religious works, they also included Latin classics and books on history, geography, and gardening—to provide the clergy with a well-rounded education.

* ***clergy*** ministers, priests, and other church officials

Believing that libraries were essential in "civilizing" the colonies, Bray also played an important role in establishing libraries in cities and towns. The largest and best known of Bray's community collections was the Annapolitan Library in Annapolis, Maryland. It served as a model for similar, though smaller, libraries in Boston, New York, Philadelphia, and Charleston.

Winthrop's Books

One of the most extraordinary personal libraries in colonial America belonged to John Winthrop, the governor of Connecticut. A student of science, Winthrop collected books on astronomy, chemistry, mathematics, and other subjects. His home became a center for people interested in scientific research. Winthrop continued to add to the collection throughout his life. When he died in 1676 at age 70, his library included more than 1,000 volumes, rivaling the best libraries in Europe in size and in breadth and depth of scientific content.

Social Libraries. Two types of group, or "social," libraries met the needs of colonists who could not afford large personal collections of books. In proprietary libraries, members pooled their money to buy books and then shared ownership and use of the library. Subscription libraries charged members a small fee to borrow books.

In 1731 Benjamin Franklin founded the first social library in America, the Library Company of Philadelphia. It contained mostly books on history, medicine, agriculture, and government rather than religious works. Modeled on the Philadelphia library, the Redwood Library in Newport, Rhode Island, was established in 1750 and now ranks as the oldest library in the United States. The New York Society library, founded in 1754, is also still in existence.

Franklin believed that social libraries made good economic sense and played an important role in educating the public. By the mid-1700s, social libraries began to promote the idea of reading for enjoyment, not just for knowledge. They acquired more novels, plays, and poetry and made their collections available to new reading audiences.

Social libraries began to decline in importance after the colonial period because of changing membership and uncertain financial support. In the mid-1800s, free public libraries—financed by taxes—began to replace them as the most important type of community library.

Learned Societies. The members of learned societies were educated individuals who met to discuss the latest inventions and scientific discoveries. They also conducted research and published scholarly works. The oldest and best-known learned society in the colonies was the AMERICAN PHILOSOPHICAL SOCIETY, founded by Benjamin Franklin in Philadelphia in 1743. Other leading groups included the Society for the Promotion of Arts, Agriculture and Economy in New York, the Virginian Society for Promotion of Useful Knowledge, and the American Academy of Arts and Sciences in Boston.

Learned societies had close ties with social libraries. Their members often helped establish the libraries and obtain books for them, and the libraries frequently became research centers for the members of learned societies. (*See also* **Books; Education; Literacy; Literature.**)

Life Expectancy

Life expectancy refers to the average number of years that people can be expected to live past a certain age. It depends primarily on hereditary* and environmental factors. The inhabitants of North America during the colonial period did not live as long as do the people of today, and life expectancy varied from region to region.

* ***hereditary*** passed on from parent to child

As late as 1790, the average life expectancy of European colonists born in America was only about 40 years of age. Less than 2 percent of the population lived to be age 65 or older. Many individuals died in infancy or during childhood.

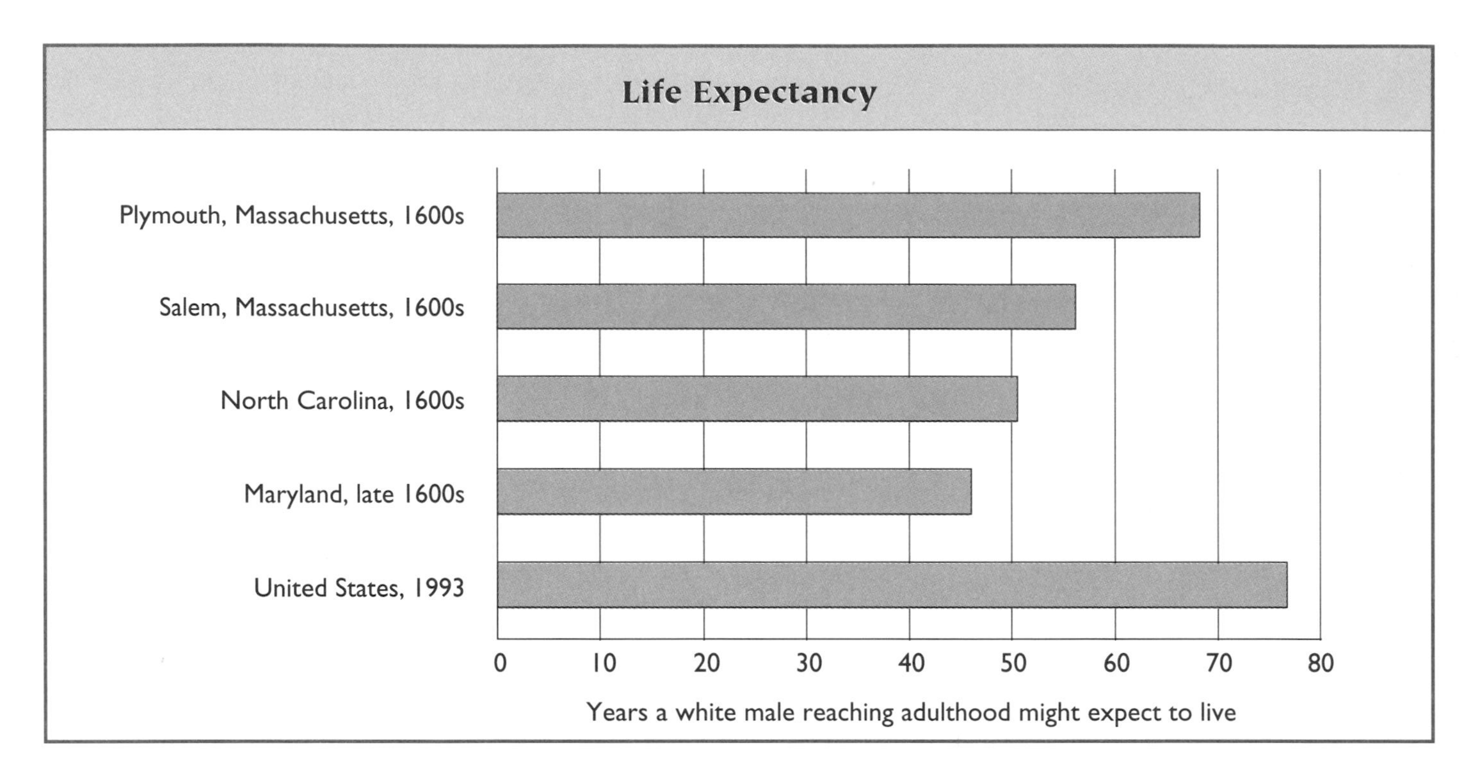

Life expectancy in the British colonies varied greatly from region to region. In the 1600s, an adult white male in Maryland would probably live to be about 46. In Plymouth, an adult white male could expect to reach the age of 68—nearly as high as the average life expectancy in the United States today.

New England enjoyed the highest life expectancy rates: a person who reached adulthood in Massachusetts could expect to live to be between about 55 and 69 years. In the South, by contrast, life expectancy for adults ranged from 40 to 50 years.

The shorter life expectancy in the colonial period was due primarily to difficult living conditions. Life was hard and people died frequently from various causes, including accidents and disease. The hot and humid climate of the South, in particular, was a breeding ground for disease and contributed significantly to lower life expectancy in that region. Poor nutrition, poor sanitation, and diseases contributed to high death rates among infants and children throughout the colonies. As many as 50 percent of all children in colonial America died before age 10.

A person who survived to adulthood was more likely to survive to an older age. Someone who reached age 20, for example, could expect to live at least another 10 years, while an individual who celebrated a fortieth birthday had a good chance of living to age 50, 60, or perhaps older. Even among adults, however, the death rate was still high. Women often died during childbirth, and diseases such as smallpox, malaria, and tuberculosis killed many adults.

The short life expectancies of colonial Americans had a significant impact on society. Parents wanted to have many children to ensure that a few would reach adulthood. Marriages were often brief because of the death of a spouse at a young age. Those who survived might marry several times. The early deaths of adults also left many children without one or both parents. Colonists who lived to old age generally were treated with great respect, and younger people often looked to them for knowledge and advice. During the

1700s, life expectancies began to rise slightly in some parts of the colonies because of improved standards of living and increased resistance to disease. (*See also* **Childhood and Adolescence; Death and Burial; Diseases and Disorders; Family; Health and Safety; Old Age.**)

Literacy

Literacy—the ability to read and write—was important to the settlers who came to North America. Colonists taught these skills to their children and, in some areas, also offered instruction to Native Americans and African Americans.

By the late 1600s, many English colonies had laws requiring that children receive some form of education. If there was no school nearby, parents were responsible for teaching their children to read and could be fined if they failed to do so. In some communities, colonists were supposed to educate their servants and apprentices* as well.

* ***apprentice*** person placed in the care of a merchant or crafts worker to learn a profession

Laws promoting literacy often had a religious goal. In Protestant regions, the primary reason for learning to read was to study the Scriptures. Colonial governments also looked on literacy as a way of ensuring social order. They believed that people who could read were likely to obey the laws and behave properly.

Colonial officials did not keep records on the number of people who were literate. Today scholars have come up with rough estimates of literacy in colonial times by checking signatures on documents. They assume that a person who could sign his or her name could read. Those who could not write often drew an *X* in place of a name. In New France and New Mexico, legal contracts and military records contain specific mention of individuals who could not write. At the end of the 1700s, only about a third of the men in New Mexico could sign their names.

In general, literacy was higher among men than women, probably because colonists considered reading and writing important to a man's ability to earn a living. In New England in the late 1600s, for example, nearly all men could read, but only about half the women were literate. Literacy was more common among city dwellers than among people living in rural areas because many cities had schools. In the 1760s, about 65 percent of the women in Boston could read, compared to a literacy rate of 30 to 40 percent among the women of rural New England. Occupation and social class influenced the rate of literacy as well. Ministers and merchants, for example, needed to know how to read and write, and wealthy people could afford to hire tutors for their children and to purchase books.

More colonists learned to read than to write. Reading was taught first, so children who left school at an early age to work on the farm or to help at home often missed the writing lessons. Furthermore, writing supplies—goose quill pens, ink, and paper—were expensive, and colonists did not consider writing a necessary skill for everyday life.

Literacy training for African Americans and Native Americans took different forms. Although slaveholders in New England sometimes taught their slaves to read the Bible, few free African Americans had the opportunity to attend school. Nevertheless, literacy gradually spread within the free black community.

Native Americans in the Spanish Borderlands* learned to read and write at missions established to convert them to Christianity. In Massachusetts, colonists

* ***Spanish Borderlands*** northern part of New Spain, area now occupied by Florida, Texas, New Mexico, Arizona, and California

published a translation of the Bible in the language of the local Indians in the 1660s. A written version of the Cherokee language came into use by the 1820s. The tribe published a newspaper, and many Cherokee learned to read.

Even for people who could not read or write, the written word played an important part in colonial life. Reading aloud was a favorite entertainment, and those who were literate read books, newspapers, and letters to family members and friends. Important public announcements and laws were read aloud in town squares. Letter writing was often a group project—everyone contributed ideas as one person wrote them down. Colonists could also hire professional writers, or scriveners, to write letters for them or to help them with legal documents.

As life got easier in the colonies and there was more time for education, literacy rates tended to rise. By 1776 an increasing number of schools and wider availability of printed materials helped spread literacy further throughout the colonies. (*See also* **Books; Education; Libraries and Learned Societies.**)